Three Works on Distributism

G. K. Chesterton

What's Wrong with the World

The Outline of Sanity

Utopia of Userers and Other Essays

What's Wrong With The World

What's Wrong with the World

Dedication

To C. F G. Masterman, M. P.

My Dear Charles,

I originally called this book "What is Wrong," and it would have satisfied your sardonic temper to note the number of social misunderstandings that arose from the use of the title. Many a mild lady visitor opened her eyes when I remarked casually, "I have been doing 'What is Wrong' all this morning." And one minister of religion moved quite sharply in his chair when I told him (as he understood it) that I had to run upstairs and do what was wrong, but should be down again in a minute. Exactly of what occult vice they silently accused me I cannot conjecture, but I know of what I accuse myself; and that is, of having written a very shapeless and inadequate book, and one quite unworthy to be dedicated to you. As far as literature goes, this book is what is wrong and no mistake.

It may seem a refinement of insolence to present so wild a composition to one who has recorded two or three of the really impressive visions of the moving millions of England. You are the only man alive who can make the map of England crawl with life; a most creepy and enviable accomplishment. Why then should I trouble you with a book which, even if it achieves its object (which is monstrously unlikely) can only be a thundering gallop of theory?

Well, I do it partly because I think you politicians are none the worse for a few inconvenient ideals; but more because you will recognise the many arguments we have had, those arguments which the most wonderful ladies in the world can never endure for very long. And, perhaps, you will agree with me that the thread of comradeship and conversation must be protected because it is so frivolous. It must be held sacred, it must not be snapped, because it is not worth tying together again. It is exactly because argument is idle that men (I mean males) must take it seriously; for when (we feel), until the crack of doom, shall we have so delightful a difference again? But most of all I offer it to you because there exists not only comradeship, but a very different thing, called friendship; an agreement under all the arguments and a thread which, please God, will never break.

Yours always,

G. K. Chesterton.

Part One. The Homelessness Of Man

I. The Medical Mistake

A book of modern social inquiry has a shape that is somewhat sharply defined. It begins as a rule with an analysis, with statistics, tables of population, decrease of crime among Congregationalists, growth of hysteria among policemen, and similar ascertained facts; it ends with a chapter that is generally called "The Remedy." It is almost wholly due to this careful, solid, and scientific method that "The Remedy" is never found. For this scheme of medical question and answer is a blunder; the first great blunder of sociology. It is always called stating the disease before we find the cure. But it is the whole definition and dignity of man that in social matters we must actually find the cure before we find the disease.

The fallacy is one of the fifty fallacies that come from the modern madness for biological or bodily metaphors. It is convenient to speak of the Social Organism, just as it is convenient to speak of the British Lion. But Britain is no more an organism than Britain is a lion. The moment we begin to give a nation the unity and simplicity of an animal, we begin to think wildly. Because every man is a biped, fifty men are not a centipede. This has produced, for instance, the gaping absurdity of perpetually talking about "young nations" and "dying nations," as if a nation had a fixed and physical span of life. Thus people will say that Spain has entered a final senility; they might as well say that Spain is losing all her teeth. Or people will say that Canada should soon produce a literature; which is like saying that Canada must soon grow a new moustache. Nations consist of people; the first generation may be decrepit, or the ten thousandth may be vigorous. Similar applications of the fallacy are made by those who see in the increasing size of national possessions, a simple increase in wisdom and stature, and in favor with God and man. These people, indeed, even fall short in subtlety of the parallel of a human body. They do not even ask whether an empire is growing taller in its youth, or only growing fatter in its old age. But of all the instances of error arising from this physical fancy, the worst is that we have

11

before us: the habit of exhaustively describing a social sickness, and then propounding a social drug.

Now we do talk first about the disease in cases of bodily breakdown; and that for an excellent reason. Because, though there may be doubt about the way in which the body broke down, there is no doubt at all about the shape in which it should be built up again. No doctor proposes to produce a new kind of man, with a new arrangement of eyes or limbs. The hospital, by necessity, may send a man home with one leg less: but it will not (in a creative rapture) send him home with one leg extra. Medical science is content with the normal human body, and only seeks to restore it.

But social science is by no means always content with the normal human soul; it has all sorts of fancy souls for sale. Man as a social idealist will say "I am tired of being a Puritan; I want to be a Pagan," or "Beyond this dark probation of Individualism I see the shining paradise of Collectivism." Now in bodily ills there is none of this difference about the ultimate ideal. The patient may or may not want quinine; but he certainly wants health. No one says "I am tired of this headache; I want some toothache," or "The only thing for this Russian influenza is a few German measles," or "Through this dark probation of catarrh I see the shining paradise of rheumatism." But exactly the whole difficulty in our public problems is that some men are aiming at cures which other men would regard as worse maladies; are offering ultimate conditions as states of health which others would uncompromisingly call states of disease. Mr. Belloc once said that he would no more part with the idea of property than with his teeth; yet to Mr. Bernard Shaw property is not a tooth, but a toothache. Lord Milner has sincerely attempted to introduce German efficiency; and many of us would as soon welcome German measles. Dr. Saleeby would honestly like to have Eugenics; but I would rather have rheumatics.

This is the arresting and dominant fact about modern social discussion; that the quarrel is not merely about the difficulties, but about the aim. We agree about the evil; it is about the good that we should tear each other's eyes out. We all admit that a lazy aristocracy is a bad thing. We should not by any means all admit that an active aristocracy would be a good thing. We all feel angry with an irreligious priesthood; but some of us would go mad with disgust at a really religious one. Everyone is indignant if our army is weak, including the people who would be even more indignant if it were strong. The social case is exactly the opposite of the medical case. We do not disagree, like doctors, about the precise nature of the illness, while agreeing about the nature of health. On the contrary, we all agree that England is unhealthy, but half of us would not look at her in what the other half would call blooming health. Public abuses are so prominent and pestilent that they sweep all generous people into a sort of fictitious unanimity. We forget that, while we agree about the abuses of things, we should differ very much about the uses of them. Mr. Cadbury and I would agree about the bad public house. It would be precisely in front of the good public-house that our painful personal fracas would occur.

I maintain, therefore, that the common sociological method is quite useless: that of first dissecting abject poverty or cataloguing prostitution. We all dislike abject poverty; but it might be another business if we began to discuss independent and dignified poverty. We all disapprove of prostitution; but we do not all approve of purity. The only way to discuss the social evil is to get at once to the social ideal. We can all see the national madness; but what is national sanity? I have called this book "What Is Wrong with the World?" and the upshot of the title can be easily and clearly stated. What is wrong is that we do not ask what is right.

II. Wanted, An Unpractical Man

There is a popular philosophical joke intended to typify the endless and useless arguments of philosophers; I mean the joke about which came first, the chicken or the egg? I am not sure that properly understood, it is so futile an inquiry after all. I am not concerned here to enter on those deep metaphysical and theological differences of which the chicken and egg debate is a frivolous, but a very felicitous, type. The evolutionary materialists are appropriately enough represented in the vision of all things coming from an egg, a dim and monstrous oval germ that had laid itself by accident. That other supernatural school of thought (to which I personally adhere) would be not unworthily typified in the fancy that this round world of ours is but an egg brooded upon by a sacred unbegotten bird; the mystic dove of the prophets. But it is to much humbler functions that I here call the awful power of such a distinction. Whether or no the living bird is at the beginning of our mental chain, it is absolutely necessary that it should be at the end of our mental chain. The bird is the thing to be aimed at--not with a gun, but a life-bestowing wand. What is essential to our right thinking is this: that the egg and the bird must not be thought of as equal cosmic occurrences recurring alternatively forever. They must not become a mere egg and bird pattern, like the egg and dart pattern. One is a means and the other an end; they are in different mental worlds. Leaving the complications of the human breakfast-table out of account, in an elemental sense, the egg only exists to produce the chicken. But the chicken does not exist only in order to produce another egg. He may also exist to amuse himself, to praise God, and even to suggest ideas to a French dramatist. Being a conscious life, he is, or may be, valuable in himself. Now our modern politics are full of a noisy forgetfulness; forgetfulness that the production of this happy and conscious life is after all the aim of all complexities and compromises. We talk of nothing but useful men and working institutions; that is, we only think of the chickens as things that will lay more eggs. Instead of seeking to breed our ideal bird, the eagle of Zeus or the Swan of Avon, or whatever we happen to want, we talk entirely in terms of the process and the embryo. The process itself, divorced from its divine object, becomes doubtful and even morbid; poison enters the embryo of everything; and our politics are rotten eggs.

Idealism is only considering everything in its practical essence. Idealism only means that we should consider a poker in reference to poking before we discuss its suitability for wife-beating; that we should ask if an egg is good enough for practical poultry-rearing before we decide that the egg is bad enough for practical politics. But I know that this primary pursuit of the theory (which is but pursuit of the aim) exposes one to the cheap charge of fiddling while Rome is burning. A school, of which Lord Rosebery is representative, has endeavored to substitute for the moral or social ideals which have hitherto been the motive of politics a general coherency or completeness in the social system which has gained the nick-name of "efficiency." I am not very certain of the secret doctrine of this sect in the matter. But, as far as I can make out, "efficiency" means that we ought to discover everything about a machine except what it is for. There has arisen in our time a most singular fancy: the fancy that when things go very wrong we need a practical man. It would be far truer to say, that when things go very wrong we need an unpractical man. Certainly, at least, we need a theorist. A practical man means a man accustomed to mere daily practice, to the way things commonly work. When things will not work, you must have the thinker, the man who has some doctrine about why they work at all. It is wrong to fiddle while Rome is burning; but it is quite right to study the theory of hydraulics while Rome is burning.

It is then necessary to drop one's daily agnosticism and attempt rerum cognoscere causas. If your aeroplane has a slight indisposition, a handy man may mend it. But, if it is seriously ill, it is all the more likely that some absent-minded old professor with wild white hair will have to be dragged out of a college or laboratory to analyze the evil. The more complicated the smash, the whiter-haired and more absent-minded will be the theorist who is needed to deal with it; and in some extreme cases, no one but the man (probably insane) who invented your flying-ship could possibly say what was the matter with it.

"Efficiency," of course, is futile for the same reason that strong men, will-power and the superman are futile. That is, it is futile because it only deals with actions after they have been performed. It has no philosophy for incidents before they happen; therefore it has no power of choice. An act can only be successful or unsuccessful when it is over; if it is to begin, it must be, in the abstract, right or wrong. There is no such thing as backing a winner; for he cannot be a winner when he is backed. There is no such thing as fighting on the winning side; one fights to find out which is the winning side. If any operation has occurred, that operation was efficient. If a man is murdered, the murder was efficient. A tropical sun is as efficient in making people lazy as a Lancashire foreman bully in making them energetic. Maeterlinck is as efficient in filling a man with strange spiritual tremors as Messrs. Crosse and Blackwell are in filling a man with jam. But it all depends on what you want to be filled with. Lord Rosebery, being a modern skeptic, probably prefers the spiritual tremors. I, being an orthodox Christian, prefer the jam. But both are efficient when they have been effected; and inefficient until they are effected. A man who thinks much about success must be the drowsiest sentimentalist; for he must be always looking back. If he only likes victory he must always come late for the battle. For the man of action there is nothing but idealism.

This definite ideal is a far more urgent and practical matter in our existing English trouble than any immediate plans or proposals. For the present chaos is due to a sort of general oblivion of all that men were originally aiming at. No man demands what he desires; each man demands what he fancies he can get. Soon people forget what the man really wanted first; and after a successful and vigorous political life, he forgets it himself. The whole is an extravagant riot of second bests, a pandemonium of pis-aller. Now this sort of pliability does not merely prevent any heroic consistency, it also prevents any really practical compromise. One can only find the middle distance between two points if the two points will stand still. We may make an arrangement between two litigants who cannot both get what they want; but not if they will not even tell us what they want. The keeper of a restaurant would much prefer that each customer should give his order smartly, though it were for stewed ibis or boiled elephant, rather than that each customer should sit holding his head in his hands, plunged in arithmetical calculations about how much food there can be on the premises. Most of us have suffered from a certain sort of ladies who, by their perverse unselfishness, give more trouble than the selfish; who almost clamor for the unpopular dish and scramble for the worst seat. Most of us have known parties or expeditions full of this seething fuss of self-effacement. From much meaner motives than those of such admirable women, our practical politicians keep things in the same confusion through the same doubt about their real demands. There is nothing that so much prevents a settlement as a tangle of small surrenders. We are bewildered on every side by politicians who are in favor of secular education, but think it hopeless to work for it; who desire total prohibition, but are certain they should not demand it; who regret compulsory education, but resignedly continue it; or who want peasant proprietorship and therefore vote for something else. It is this dazed and floundering opportunism that gets in the way of everything. If our statesmen were visionaries something practical might be done. If we ask for something in the abstract we might get something in the concrete. As it is, it is not only impossible to get what one wants, but it is impossible to get any part of it, because nobody can mark it out plainly like a map. That clear and even hard quality that there was in the old bargaining has wholly vanished. We forget that the word "compromise" contains, among other things, the rigid and ringing word "promise." Moderation is not vague; it is as definite as perfection. The middle point is as fixed as the extreme point.

If I am made to walk the plank by a pirate, it is vain for me to offer, as a common-sense compromise, to walk along the plank for a reasonable distance. It is exactly about the reasonable distance that the pirate and I differ. There is an exquisite mathematical split second at which the plank tips up. My common-sense ends just before that instant; the pirate's common-sense begins just beyond it. But the point itself is as hard as any geometrical diagram; as abstract as any theological dogma.

III. The New Hypocrite

But this new cloudy political cowardice has rendered useless the old English compromise. People have begun to be terrified of an improvement merely because it is complete. They call it utopian and revolutionary that anyone should really have his own way, or anything be really done, and done with. Compromise used to mean that half a loaf was better than no bread. Among modern statesmen it really seems to mean that half a loaf is better than a whole loaf.

As an instance to sharpen the argument, I take the one case of our everlasting education bills. We have actually contrived to invent a new kind of hypocrite. The old hypocrite, Tartuffe or Pecksniff, was a man whose aims were really worldly and practical, while he pretended that they were religious. The new hypocrite is one whose aims are really religious, while he pretends that they are worldly and practical. The Rev. Brown, the Wesleyan minister, sturdily declares that he cares nothing for creeds, but only for education; meanwhile, in truth, the wildest Wesleyanism is tearing his soul. The Rev. Smith, of the Church of England, explains gracefully, with the Oxford manner, that the only question for him is the prosperity and efficiency of the schools; while in truth all the evil passions of a curate are roaring within him. It is a fight of creeds masquerading as policies. I think these reverend gentlemen do themselves wrong; I think they are more pious than they will admit. Theology is not (as some suppose) expunged as an error. It is merely concealed, like a sin. Dr. Clifford really wants a theological atmosphere as much as Lord Halifax; only it is a different one. If Dr. Clifford would ask plainly for Puritanism and Lord Halifax ask plainly for Catholicism, something might be done for them. We are all, one hopes, imaginative enough to recognize the dignity and distinctness of another religion, like Islam or the cult of Apollo. I am quite ready to respect another man's faith; but it is too much to ask that I should respect his doubt, his worldly hesitations and fictions, his political bargain and make-believe. Most Nonconformists with an instinct for English history could see something poetic and national about the Archbishop of Canterbury as an Archbishop of Canterbury. It is when he does the rational British statesman that they very justifiably get annoyed. Most Anglicans with an eye for pluck and simplicity could admire Dr. Clifford as a Baptist minister. It is when he says that he is simply a citizen that nobody can possibly believe him.

But indeed the case is yet more curious than this. The one argument that used to be urged for our creedless vagueness was that at least it saved us from fanaticism. But it does not even do that. On the contrary, it creates and renews fanaticism with a force quite peculiar to itself. This is at once so strange and so true that I will ask the reader's attention to it with a little more precision.

Some people do not like the word "dogma." Fortunately they are free, and there is an alternative for them. There are two things, and two things only, for the human mind, a dogma and a prejudice. The Middle Ages were a rational epoch, an age of doctrine. Our age is, at its best, a poetical epoch, an age of prejudice. A doctrine is a definite point; a prejudice is a direction.

That an ox may be eaten, while a man should not be eaten, is a doctrine. That as little as possible of anything should be eaten is a prejudice; which is also sometimes called an ideal. Now a direction is always far more fantastic than a plan. I would rather have the most archaic map of the road to Brighton than a general recommendation to turn to the left. Straight lines that are not parallel must meet at last; but curves may recoil forever. A pair of lovers might walk along the frontier of France and Germany, one on the one side and one on the other, so long as they were not vaguely told to keep away from each other. And this is a strictly true parable of the effect of our modern vagueness in losing and separating men as in a mist.

It is not merely true that a creed unites men. Nay, a difference of creed unites men--so long as it is a clear difference. A boundary unites. Many a magnanimous Moslem and chivalrous Crusader must have been nearer to each other, because they were both dogmatists, than any two homeless agnostics in a pew of Mr. Campbell's chapel. "I say God is One," and "I say God is One but also Three," that is the beginning of a good quarrelsome, manly friendship. But our age would turn these creeds into tendencies. It would tell the Trinitarian to follow multiplicity as such (because it was his "temperament"), and he would turn up later with three hundred and thirty-three persons in the Trinity. Meanwhile, it would turn the Moslem into a Monist: a frightful intellectual fall. It would force that previously healthy person not only to admit that there was one God, but to admit that there was nobody else. When each had, for a long enough period, followed the gleam of his own nose (like the Dong) they would appear again; the Christian a Polytheist, and the Moslem a Panegoist, both quite mad, and far more unfit to understand each other than before.

It is exactly the same with politics. Our political vagueness divides men, it does not fuse them. Men will walk along the edge of a chasm in clear weather, but they will edge miles away from it in a fog. So a Tory can walk up to the very edge of Socialism, if he knows what is Socialism. But if he is told that Socialism is a spirit, a sublime atmosphere, a noble, indefinable tendency, why, then he keeps out of its way; and quite right too. One can meet an assertion with argument; but healthy bigotry is the only way in which one can meet a tendency. I am told that the Japanese method of wrestling consists not of suddenly pressing, but of suddenly giving way. This is one of my many reasons for disliking the Japanese civilization. To use surrender as a weapon is the very worst spirit of the East. But certainly there is no force so hard to fight as the force which it is easy to conquer; the force that always yields and then returns. Such is the force of a great impersonal prejudice, such as possesses the modern world on so many points. Against this there is no weapon at all except a rigid and steely sanity, a resolution not to listen to fads, and not to be infected by diseases.

In short, the rational human faith must armor itself with prejudice in an age of prejudices, just as it armoured itself with logic in an age of logic. But the difference between the two mental methods is marked and unmistakable. The essential of the difference is this: that prejudices are divergent, whereas creeds are always in collision. Believers bump into each other; whereas bigots keep out of each other's way. A creed is a collective thing, and even its sins are sociable. A prejudice is a private thing, and even its tolerance is misanthropic. So it is with our existing divisions. They keep out of each other's way; the Tory paper and the Radical paper do not answer each other; they ignore each other. Genuine controversy, fair cut and thrust before a common audience, has become in our special epoch very rare. For the sincere controversialist is above all things a good listener. The really burning enthusiast never interrupts; he listens to the enemy's arguments as eagerly as a spy would listen to the enemy's arrangements. But if you attempt an actual argument with a modern paper of opposite politics, you will find that no medium is admitted between violence and evasion. You will have no answer except slanging or silence. A modern editor must not have that eager ear that goes with the honest tongue. He may be deaf and silent; and that is called dignity. Or he may be deaf and noisy; and that is called slashing journalism. In neither case is there any controversy; for the whole object of modern party combatants is to charge out of earshot.

The only logical cure for all this is the assertion of a human ideal. In dealing with this, I will try to be as little transcendental as is consistent with reason; it is enough to say that unless we have some doctrine of a divine man, all abuses may be excused, since evolution may turn them into uses. It will be easy for the scientific plutocrat to maintain that humanity will adapt itself to any conditions which we now consider evil. The old tyrants invoked the past; the new tyrants will invoke the future evolution has produced the snail and the owl; evolution can produce a workman who wants no more space than a snail, and no more light than an owl. The employer need not mind sending a Kaffir to work underground; he will soon become an underground animal, like a mole. He need not mind sending a diver to hold his breath in the deep seas; he will soon be a deep-sea animal. Men need not trouble to alter conditions, conditions will so soon alter men. The head can be beaten small enough to fit the hat. Do not knock the fetters off the slave; knock the slave until he forgets the fetters. To all this plausible modern argument for oppression, the only adequate answer is, that there is a permanent human ideal that must not be either confused or destroyed. The most important man on earth is the perfect man who is not there. The Christian religion has specially uttered the ultimate sanity of Man, says Scripture, who shall judge the incarnate and human truth. Our lives and laws are not judged by divine superiority, but simply by human perfection. It is man, says Aristotle, who is the measure. It is the Son of Man, says Scripture, who shall judge the quick and the dead.

Doctrine, therefore, does not cause dissensions; rather a doctrine alone can cure our dissensions. It is necessary to ask, however, roughly, what abstract and ideal shape in state or family would fulfil the human hunger; and this apart from whether we can completely obtain it or not. But when we come to ask what is the need of normal men, what is the desire of all nations, what is the ideal house, or road, or rule, or republic, or king, or priesthood, then we are confronted with a strange and irritating difficulty peculiar to the present time; and we must call a temporary halt and examine that obstacle.

IV. The Fear Of The Past

The last few decades have been marked by a special cultivation of the romance of the future. We seem to have made up our minds to misunderstand what has happened; and we turn, with a sort of relief, to stating what will happen--which is (apparently) much easier. The modern man no longer presents the memoirs of his great grandfather; but is engaged in writing a detailed and authoritative biography of his great-grandson. Instead of trembling before the specters of the dead, we shudder abjectly under the shadow of the babe unborn. This spirit is apparent everywhere, even to the creation of a form of futurist romance. Sir Walter Scott stands at the dawn of the nineteenth century for the novel of the past; Mr. H. G. Wells stands at the dawn of the twentieth century for the novel of the future. The old story, we know, was supposed to begin: "Late on a winter's evening two horsemen might have been seen--." The new story has to begin: "Late on a winter's evening two aviators will be seen--." The movement is not without its elements of charm; there is something spirited, if eccentric, in the sight of so many people fighting over again the fights that have not yet happened; of people still glowing with the memory of tomorrow morning. A man in advance of the age is a familiar phrase enough. An age in advance of the age is really rather odd.

But when full allowance has been made for this harmless element of poetry and pretty human perversity in the thing, I shall not hesitate to maintain here that this cult of the future is not only a weakness but a cowardice of the age. It is the peculiar evil of this epoch that even its pugnacity is fundamentally frightened; and the Jingo is contemptible not because he is impudent, but because he is timid. The reason why modern armaments do not inflame the imagination like the arms and emblazonments of the Crusades is a reason quite apart from optical ugliness or beauty. Some battleships are as beautiful as the sea; and many Norman nosepieces were as ugly as Norman noses. The atmospheric ugliness that surrounds our scientific war is an emanation from that evil panic which is at the heart of it. The charge of the Crusades was a charge; it was charging towards God, the wild consolation of the braver. The charge of the modern armaments is not a charge at all. It is a rout, a retreat, a flight from the devil, who will catch the hindmost. It is impossible to imagine a mediaeval knight talking of longer and longer French lances, with precisely the quivering employed about larger and larger German ships The man who called the Blue Water School the "Blue Funk School" uttered a psychological truth which that school itself would scarcely essentially deny. Even the two-power standard, if it be a necessity, is in a sense a degrading necessity. Nothing has more alienated many magnanimous minds from Imperial enterprises than the fact that they are always exhibited as stealthy or sudden defenses against a world of cold rapacity and fear. The Boer War, for instance, was colored not so much by the creed that we were doing something right, as by the creed that Boers and Germans were probably doing something wrong; driving us (as it was said) to the sea. Mr. Chamberlain, I think, said that the war was a feather in his cap and so it was: a white feather.

Now this same primary panic that I feel in our rush towards patriotic armaments I feel also in our rush towards future visions of society. The modern mind is forced towards the future by a certain sense of fatigue, not unmixed with terror, with which it regards the past. It is propelled towards the coming time; it is, in the exact words of the popular phrase, knocked into the middle of next week. And the goad which drives it on thus eagerly is not an affectation for futurity Futurity does not exist, because it is still future. Rather it is a fear of the past; a fear not merely of the evil in the past, but of the good in the past also. The brain breaks down under the unbearable virtue of mankind. There have been so many flaming faiths that we cannot hold; so many harsh heroisms that we cannot imitate; so many great efforts of monumental building or of military glory which seem to us at once sublime and pathetic. The future is a refuge from the fierce competition of our forefathers. The older generation, not the younger, is knocking at our door. It is agreeable to escape, as Henley said, into the Street of By-and-Bye, where stands the Hostelry of Never. It is pleasant to play with children, especially unborn children. The future is a blank wall on which every man can write his own name as large as he likes; the past I find already covered with illegible scribbles, such as Plato, Isaiah, Shakespeare, Michael Angelo, Napoleon. I can make the future as narrow as myself; the past is obliged to be as broad and turbulent as humanity. And the upshot of this modern attitude is really this: that men invent new ideals because they dare not attempt old ideals. They look forward with enthusiasm, because they are afraid to look back.

Now in history there is no Revolution that is not a Restoration. Among the many things that leave me doubtful about the modern habit of fixing eyes on the future, none is stronger than this: that all the men in history who have really done anything with the future have had their eyes fixed upon the past. I need not mention the Renaissance, the very word proves my case. The originality of Michael Angelo and Shakespeare began with the digging up of old vases and manuscripts. The mildness of poets absolutely arose out of the mildness of antiquaries. So the great mediaeval revival was a memory of the Roman Empire. So the Reformation looked back to the Bible and Bible times. So the modern Catholic movement has looked back to patristic times. But that modern movement which many would count the most anarchic of all is in this sense the most conservative of all. Never was the past more venerated by men than it was by the French Revolutionists. They invoked the little republics of antiquity with the complete confidence of one who invokes the gods. The Sans-culottes believed (as their name might imply) in a return to simplicity. They believed most piously in a remote past; some might call it a mythical past. For some strange reason man must always thus plant his fruit trees in a graveyard. Man can only find life among the dead. Man is a misshapen monster, with his feet set forward and his face turned back. He can make the future luxuriant and gigantic, so long as he is thinking about the past. When he tries to think about the future itself, his mind diminishes to a pin point with imbecility, which some call Nirvana. To-morrow is the Gorgon; a man must only see it mirrored in the shining shield of yesterday. If he sees it directly he is turned to stone. This has been the fate of all those who have really seen fate and futurity as clear and inevitable. The Calvinists, with their perfect creed of predestination, were turned to stone. The modern sociological scientists (with their excruciating Eugenics) are turned to stone. The only difference is that the Puritans make dignified, and the Eugenists somewhat amusing, statues.

But there is one feature in the past which more than all the rest defies and depresses the moderns and drives them towards this featureless future. I mean the presence in the past of huge ideals, unfulfilled and sometimes abandoned. The sight of these splendid failures is melancholy to a restless and rather morbid generation;

and they maintain a strange silence about them--sometimes amounting to an unscrupulous silence. They keep them entirely out of their newspapers and almost entirely out of their history books. For example, they will often tell you (in their praises of the coming age) that we are moving on towards a United States of Europe. But they carefully omit to tell you that we are moving away from a United States of Europe, that such a thing existed literally in Roman and essentially in mediaeval times. They never admit that the international hatreds (which they call barbaric) are really very recent, the mere breakdown of the ideal of the Holy Roman Empire. Or again, they will tell you that there is going to be a social revolution, a great rising of the poor against the rich; but they never rub it in that France made that magnificent attempt, unaided, and that we and all the world allowed it to be trampled out and forgotten. I say decisively that nothing is so marked in modern writing as the prediction of such ideals in the future combined with the ignoring of them in the past. Anyone can test this for himself. Read any thirty or forty pages of pamphlets advocating peace in Europe and see how many of them praise the old Popes or Emperors for keeping the peace in Europe. Read any armful of essays and poems in praise of social democracy, and see how many of them praise the old Jacobins who created democracy and died for it. These colossal ruins are to the modern only enormous eyesores. He looks back along the valley of the past and sees a perspective of splendid but unfinished cities. They are unfinished, not always through enmity or accident, but often through fickleness, mental fatigue, and the lust for alien philosophies. We have not only left undone those things that we ought to have done, but we have even left undone those things that we wanted to do

It is very currently suggested that the modern man is the heir of all the ages, that he has got the good out of these successive human experiments. I know not what to say in answer to this, except to ask the reader to look at the modern man, as I have just looked at the modern man--in the looking-glass. Is it really true that you and I are two starry towers built up of all the most towering visions of the past? Have we really fulfilled all the great historic ideals one after the other, from our naked ancestor who was brave enough to kill a mammoth with a stone knife, through the Greek citizen and the Christian saint to our own grandfather or great-grandfather, who may have been sabred by the Manchester Yeomanry or shot in the '48? Are we still strong enough to spear mammoths, but now tender enough to spare them? Does the cosmos contain any mammoth that we have either speared or spared? When we decline (in a marked manner) to fly the red flag and fire across a barricade like our grandfathers, are we really declining in deference to sociologists--or to soldiers? Have we indeed outstripped the warrior and passed the ascetical saint? I fear we only outstrip the warrior in the sense that we should probably run away from him. And if we have passed the saint, I fear we have passed him without bowing.

This is, first and foremost, what I mean by the narrowness of the new ideas, the limiting effect of the future. Our modern prophetic idealism is narrow because it has undergone a persistent process of elimination. We must ask for new things because we are not allowed to ask for old things. The whole position is based on this idea that we have got all the good that can be got out of the ideas of the past. But we have not got all the good out of them, perhaps at this moment not any of the good out of them. And the need here is a need of complete freedom for restoration as well as revolution.

We often read nowadays of the valor or audacity with which some rebel attacks a hoary tyranny or an antiquated superstition. There is not really any courage at all in attacking hoary or antiquated things, any more than in offering to fight one's grandmother. The really courageous man is he who defies tyrannies young as the morning and superstitions fresh as the first flowers. The only true free-thinker is he whose intellect is as much free from the future as from the past. He cares as little for what will be as for what has been; he cares only for what ought to be. And for my present purpose I specially insist on this abstract independence. If I am to discuss what is wrong, one of the first things that are wrong is this: the deep and silent modern assumption that past things have become impossible. There is one metaphor of which the moderns are very fond; they are always saying, "You can't put the clock back." The simple and obvious answer is "You can." A clock, being a piece of human construction, can be restored by the human finger to any figure or hour. In the same way society, being a piece of human construction, can be reconstructed upon any plan that has ever existed.

There is another proverb, "As you have made your bed, so you must lie on it"; which again is simply a lie. If I have made my bed uncomfortable, please God I will make it again. We could restore the Heptarchy or the stage coaches if we chose. It might take some time to do, and it might be very inadvisable to do it; but certainly it is not impossible as bringing back last Friday is impossible. This is, as I say, the first freedom that I claim: the freedom to restore. I claim a right to propose as a solution the old patriarchal system of a Highland clan, if that should seem to eliminate the largest number of evils. It certainly would eliminate some evils; for instance, the unnatural sense of obeying cold and harsh strangers, mere bureaucrats and policemen. I claim the right to propose the complete independence of the small Greek or Italian towns, a sovereign city of Brixton or Brompton, if that seems the best way out of our troubles. It would be a way out of some of our troubles; we could not have in a small state, for instance, those enormous illusions about men or measures which are nourished by the great national or international newspapers. You could not persuade a city state that Mr. Beit was an Englishman, or Mr. Dillon a desperado, any more than you could persuade a Hampshire Village that the village drunkard was a teetotaller or the village idiot a statesman. Nevertheless, I do not as a fact propose that the Browns and the Smiths should be collected under separate tartans. Nor do I even propose that Clapham should declare its independence. I merely declare my independence. I merely claim my choice of all the tools in the universe; and I shall not admit that any of them are blunted merely because they have been used.

V. The Unfinished Temple

The task of modern idealists indeed is made much too easy for them by the fact that they are always taught that if a thing has been defeated it has been disproved. Logically, the case is quite clearly the other way. The lost causes are exactly those which might have saved the world. If a man says that the Young Pretender would have made England happy, it is hard to answer him. If anyone says that the Georges made England happy, I hope we all know what to answer. That which was prevented is always impregnable; and the only perfect King of England was he who was smothered. Exactly be cause Jacobitism failed we cannot call it a failure. Precisely because the Commune collapsed as a rebellion we cannot say that it collapsed as a system. But such outbursts were brief or incidental. Few people realize how many of the largest efforts, the facts that will fill history, were frustrated in their full design and come down to us as gigantic cripples. I have only space to allude to the two largest facts of modern history: the Catholic Church and that modern growth rooted in the French Revolution.

When four knights scattered the blood and brains of St. Thomas of Canterbury, it was not only a sign of anger but of a sort of black admiration. They wished for his blood, but they wished even more for his brains. Such a blow will remain forever unintelligible unless we realise what the brains of St. Thomas were thinking about just before they were distributed over the floor. They were thinking about the great mediaeval conception that the church is the judge of the world. Becket objected to a priest being tried even by the Lord Chief Justice. And his reason was simple: because the Lord Chief Justice was being tried by the priest. The judiciary was itself sub judice. The kings were themselves in the dock. The idea was to create an invisible kingdom, without armies or prisons, but with complete freedom to condemn publicly all the kingdoms of the earth. Whether such a supreme church would have cured society we cannot affirm definitely; because the church never was a supreme church. We only know that in England at any rate the princes conquered the saints. What the world wanted we see before us; and some of us call it a failure. But we cannot call what the church wanted a failure, simply because the church failed. Tracy struck a little too soon. England had not yet made the great Protestant discovery that the king can do no wrong. The king was whipped in the cathedral; a performance which I recommend to those who regret the unpopularity of church-going. But the discovery was made; and Henry VIII scattered Becket's bones as easily as Tracy had scattered his brains.

Of course, I mean that Catholicism was not tried; plenty of Catholics were tried, and found guilty. My point is that the world did not tire of the church's ideal, but of its reality. Monasteries were impugned not for the chastity of monks, but for the unchastity of monks. Christianity was unpopular not because of the humility, but of the arrogance of Christians. Certainly, if the church failed it was largely through the churchmen. But at the same time hostile elements had certainly begun to end it long before it could have done its work. In the nature of things it needed a common scheme of life and thought in Europe. Yet the mediaeval system began to be broken to pieces intellectually, long before it showed the slightest hint of falling to pieces morally. The huge early heresies, like the Albigenses, had not the faintest excuse in moral superiority. And it is actually true that the Reformation began to tear Europe apart before the Catholic Church had had time to pull it together. The Prussians, for instance, were not converted to Christianity at all until quite close to the Reformation. The poor creatures hardly had time to become Catholics before they were told to become Protestants. This explains a great deal of their subsequent conduct. But I have only taken this as the first and most evident case of the general truth: that the great ideals of the past failed not by being outlived (which must mean over-lived), but by not being lived enough. Mankind has not passed through the Middle Ages. Rather mankind has retreated from the Middle Ages in reaction and rout. The Christian ideal has not been tried and found wanting. It has been found difficult; and left untried.

It is, of course, the same in the case of the French Revolution. A great part of our present perplexity arises from the fact that the French Revolution has half succeeded and half failed. In one sense, Valmy was the decisive battle of the West, and in another Trafalgar. We have, indeed, destroyed the largest territorial tyrannies, and created a free peasantry in almost all Christian countries except England; of which we shall say more anon. But representative government, the one universal relic, is a very poor fragment of the full republican idea. The theory of the French Revolution presupposed two things in government, things which it achieved at the time, but which it has certainly not bequeathed to

29

its imitators in England, Germany, and America. The first of these was the idea of honorable poverty; that a statesman must be something of a stoic; the second was the idea of extreme publicity. Many imaginative English writers, including Carlyle, seem quite unable to imagine how it was that men like Robespierre and Marat were ardently admired. The best answer is that they were admired for being poor--poor when they might have been rich.

No one will pretend that this ideal exists at all in the haute politique of this country. Our national claim to political incorruptibility is actually based on exactly the opposite argument; it is based on the theory that wealthy men in assured positions will have no temptation to financial trickery. Whether the history of the English aristocracy, from the spoliation of the monasteries to the annexation of the mines, entirely supports this theory I am not now inquiring; but certainly it is our theory, that wealth will be a protection against political corruption. The English statesman is bribed not to be bribed. He is born with a silver spoon in his mouth, so that he may never afterwards be found with the silver spoons in his pocket. So strong is our faith in this protection by plutocracy, that we are more and more trusting our empire in the hands of families which inherit wealth without either blood or manners. Some of our political houses are parvenue by pedigree; they hand on vulgarity like a coat of-arms. In the case of many a modern statesman to say that he is born with a silver spoon in his mouth, is at once inadequate and excessive. He is born with a silver knife in his mouth. But all this only illustrates the English theory that poverty is perilous for a politician.

It will be the same if we compare the conditions that have come about with the Revolution legend touching publicity. The old democratic doctrine was that the more light that was let in to all departments of State, the easier it was for a righteous indignation to move promptly against wrong. In other words, monarchs were to live in glass houses, that mobs might throw stones. Again, no admirer of existing English politics (if there is any admirer of existing English politics) will really pretend that this ideal of publicity is exhausted, or even attempted. Obviously public life grows more private every day. The French have, indeed, continued the tradition of revealing secrets and making scandals; hence they are more flagrant and palpable than we, not in sin but in the confession of sin. The first trial of Dreyfus might have happened in England; it is exactly the second trial that would have been legally impossible. But, indeed, if we wish to realise how far we fall short of the original republican outline, the sharpest way to test it is to note how far we fall short even of the republican element in the older regime. Not only are we less democratic than Danton and Condorcet, but we are in many ways less democratic than Choiseul and Marie Antoinette. The richest nobles before the revolt were needy middle-class people compared with our Rothschilds and Roseberys. And in the matter of publicity the old French monarchy was infinitely more democratic than any of the monarchies of today. Practically anybody who chose could walk into the palace and see the king playing with his children, or paring his nails. The people possessed the monarch, as the people possess Primrose Hill; that is, they cannot move it, but they can sprawl all over it. The old French monarchy was founded on the excellent principle that a cat may look at a king. But nowadays a cat may not look at a king; unless it is a very tame cat. Even where the press is free for criticism it is only used for adulation. The substantial difference comes to something uncommonly like this: Eighteenth century tyranny meant that you could say "The K__ of Br__rd is a profligate." Twentieth century liberty really means that you are allowed to say "The King of Brentford is a model family man."

But we have delayed the main argument too long for the parenthetical purpose of showing that the great democratic dream, like the great mediaeval dream, has in a strict and practical sense been a dream unfulfilled. Whatever is the matter with modern England it is not that we have carried out too literally, or achieved with disappointing completeness, either the Catholicism of Becket or the equality of Marat. Now I have taken these two cases merely because they are typical of ten thousand other cases; the world is full of these unfulfilled ideas, these uncompleted temples. History does not consist of completed and crumbling ruins; rather it consists of half-built villas abandoned by a bankrupt-builder. This world is more like an unfinished suburb than a deserted cemetery.

VI. The Enemies Of Property

But it is for this especial reason that such an explanation is necessary on the very threshold of the definition of ideals. For owing to that historic fallacy with which I have just dealt, numbers of readers will expect me, when I propound an ideal, to propound a new ideal. Now I have no notion at all of propounding a new ideal. There is no new ideal imaginable by the madness of modern sophists, which will be anything like so startling as fulfilling any one of the old ones. On the day that any copybook maxim is carried out there will be something like an earthquake on the earth. There is only one thing new that can be done under the sun; and that is to look at the sun. If you attempt it on a blue day in June, you will know why men do not look straight at their ideals. There is only one really startling thing to be done with the ideal, and that is to do it. It is to face the flaming logical fact, and its frightful consequences. Christ knew that it would be a more stunning thunderbolt to fulfil the law than to destroy it. It is true of both the cases I have quoted, and of every case. The pagans had always adored purity: Athena, Artemis, Vesta. It was when the virgin martyrs began defiantly to practice purity that they rent them with wild beasts, and rolled them on red-hot coals. The world had always loved the notion of the poor man uppermost; it can be proved by every legend from Cinderella to Whittington, by every poem from the Magnificat to the Marseillaise. The kings went mad against France not because she idealized this ideal, but because she realized it. Joseph of Austria and Catherine of Russia quite agreed that the people should rule; what horrified them was that the people did. The French Revolution, therefore, is the type of all true revolutions, because its ideal is as old as the Old Adam, but its fulfilment almost as fresh, as miraculous, and as new as the New Jerusalem.

But in the modern world we are primarily confronted with the extraordinary spectacle of people turning to new ideals because they have not tried the old. Men have not got tired of Christianity; they have never found enough Christianity to get tired of. Men have never wearied of political justice; they have wearied of waiting for it.

Now, for the purpose of this book, I propose to take only one of these old ideals; but one that is perhaps the oldest. I take the principle of domesticity: the ideal house; the happy family, the holy family of history. For the moment it is only necessary to remark that it is like the church and like the republic, now chiefly assailed by those who have never known it, or by those who have failed to fulfil it. Numberless modern women have rebelled against domesticity in theory because they have never known it in practice. Hosts of the poor are driven to the workhouse without ever having known the house. Generally speaking, the cultured class is shrieking to be let out of the decent home, just as the working class is shouting to be let into it.

Now if we take this house or home as a test, we may very generally lay the simple spiritual foundations of the idea. God is that which can make something out of nothing. Man (it may truly be said) is that which can make something out of anything. In other words, while the joy of God be unlimited creation, the special joy of man is limited creation, the combination of creation with limits. Man's pleasure, therefore, is to possess conditions, but also to be partly possessed by them; to be half-controlled by the flute he plays or by the field he digs. The excitement is to get the utmost out of given conditions; the conditions will stretch, but not indefinitely. A man can write an immortal sonnet on an old envelope, or hack a hero out of a lump of rock. But hacking a sonnet out of a rock would be a laborious business, and making a hero out of an envelope is almost out of the sphere of practical politics. This fruitful strife with limitations, when it concerns some airy entertainment of an educated class, goes by the name of Art. But the mass of men have neither time nor aptitude for the invention of invisible or abstract beauty. For the mass of men the idea of artistic creation can only be expressed by an idea unpopular in present discussions--the idea of property. The average man cannot cut clay into the shape of a man; but he can cut earth into the shape of a garden; and though he arranges it with red geraniums and blue potatoes in alternate straight lines, he is still an artist; because he has chosen. The average man cannot paint the sunset whose colors be admires; but he can paint his own house with what color he chooses, and though he paints it pea green with pink spots, he is still an artist; because that is his choice. Property is merely the art of the democracy. It means that every man should have something that he can shape in his own image, as he is shaped in the image of heaven. But because he is not God, but only a graven image of God, his self-expression must deal with limits; properly with limits that are strict and even small.

I am well aware that the word "property" has been defied in our time by the corruption of the great capitalists. One would think, to hear people talk, that the Rothchilds and the Rockefellers were on the side of property. But obviously they are the enemies of property; because they are enemies of their own limitations. They do not want their own land; but other people's. When they remove their neighbor's landmark, they also remove their own. A man who loves a little triangular field ought to love it because it is triangular; anyone who destroys the shape, by giving him more land, is a thief who has stolen a triangle. A man with the true poetry of possession wishes to see the wall where his garden meets Smith's garden; the hedge where his farm touches Brown's. He cannot see the shape of his own land unless he sees the edges of his neighbor's. It is the negation of property that the Duke of Sutherland should have all the farms in one estate; just as it would be the negation of marriage if he had all our wives in one harem.

VII. The Free Family

As I have said, I propose to take only one central instance; I will take the institution called the private house or home; the shell and organ of the family. We will consider cosmic and political tendencies simply as they strike that ancient and unique roof. Very few words will suffice for all I have to say about the family itself. I leave alone the speculations about its animal origin and the details of its social reconstruction; I am concerned only with its palpable omnipresence. It is a necessity far mankind; it is (if you like to put it so) a trap for mankind. Only by the hypocritical ignoring of a huge fact can any one contrive to talk of "free love"; as if love were an episode like lighting a cigarette, or whistling a tune. Suppose whenever a man lit a cigarette, a towering genie arose from the rings of smoke and followed him everywhere as a huge slave. Suppose whenever a man whistled a tune he "drew an angel down" and had to walk about forever with a seraph on a string. These catastrophic images are but faint parallels to the earthquake consequences that Nature has attached to sex; and it is perfectly plain at the beginning that a man cannot be a free lover; he is either a traitor or a tied man. The second element that creates the family is that its consequences, though colossal, are gradual; the cigarette produces a baby giant, the song only an infant seraph. Thence arises the necessity for some prolonged system of co-operation; and thence arises the family in its full educational sense.

It may be said that this institution of the home is the one anarchist institution. That is to say, it is older than law, and stands outside the State. By its nature it is refreshed or corrupted by indefinable forces of custom or kinship. This is not to be understood as meaning that the State has no authority over families; that State authority is invoked and ought to be invoked in many abnormal cases. But in most normal cases of family joys and sorrows, the State has no mode of entry. It is not so much that the law should not interfere, as that the law cannot. Just as there are fields too far off for law, so there are fields too near; as a man may see the North Pole before he sees his own backbone. Small and near matters escape control at least as much as vast and remote ones; and the real pains and pleasures of the family form a strong instance of this. If a baby cries for the moon, the policeman cannot procure the moon--but neither can he stop the baby. Creatures so close to each other as husband and wife, or a mother and children, have powers of making each other happy or miserable with which no public coercion can deal. If a marriage could be dissolved every morning it would not give back his night's rest to a man kept awake by a curtain lecture; and what is the good of giving a man a lot of power where he only wants a little peace? The child must depend on the most imperfect mother; the mother may be devoted to the most unworthy children; in such relations legal revenges are vain. Even in the abnormal cases where the law may operate, this difficulty is constantly found; as many a bewildered magistrate knows. He has to save children from starvation by taking away their breadwinner. And he often has to break a wife's heart because her husband has already broken her head. The State has no tool delicate enough to deracinate the rooted habits and tangled affections of the family; the two sexes, whether happy or unhappy, are glued together too tightly for us to get the blade of a legal penknife in between them. The man and the woman are one flesh-- yes, even when they are not one spirit. Man is a quadruped. Upon this ancient and anarchic intimacy, types of government have little or no effect; it is happy or unhappy, by its own sexual wholesomeness and genial habit, under the republic of Switzerland or the despotism of Siam. Even a republic in Siam would not have done much towards freeing the Siamese Twins.

The problem is not in marriage, but in sex; and would be felt under the freest concubinage. Nevertheless, the overwhelming mass of mankind has not believed in freedom in this matter, but rather in a more or less lasting tie. Tribes and civilizations differ about the occasions on which we may loosen the bond, but they all agree that there is a bond to be loosened, not a mere universal detachment. For the purposes of this book I am not concerned to discuss that mystical view of marriage in which I myself believe: the great European tradition which has made marriage a sacrament. It is enough to say here that heathen and Christian alike have regarded marriage as a tie; a thing not normally to be sundered. Briefly, this human belief in a sexual bond rests on a principle of which the modern mind has made a very inadequate study. It is, perhaps, most nearly paralleled by the principle of the second wind in walking.

The principle is this: that in everything worth having, even in every pleasure, there is a point of pain or tedium that must be survived, so that the pleasure may revive and endure. The joy of battle comes after the first fear of death; the joy of reading Virgil comes after the bore of learning him; the glow of the sea-bather comes after the icy shock of the sea bath; and the success of the marriage comes after the failure of the honeymoon. All human vows, laws, and contracts are so many ways of surviving with success this breaking point, this instant of potential surrender.

In everything on this earth that is worth doing, there is a stage when no one would do it, except for necessity or honor. It is then that the Institution upholds a man and helps him on to the firmer ground ahead. Whether this solid fact of human nature is sufficient to justify the sublime dedication of Christian marriage is quite an other matter, it is amply sufficient to justify the general human feeling of marriage as a fixed thing, dissolution of which is a fault or, at least, an ignominy. The essential element is not so much duration as security. Two people must be tied together in order to do themselves justice; for twenty minutes at a dance, or for twenty years in a marriage In both cases the point is, that if a man is bored in the first five minutes he must go on and force himself to be happy. Coercion is a kind of encouragement; and anarchy (or what some call liberty) is essentially oppressive, because it is essentially discouraging. If we all floated in the air like bubbles, free to drift anywhere at any instant, the practical result would be that no one would have the courage to begin a conversation. It would be so embarrassing to start a sentence in a friendly whisper, and then have to shout the last half of it because the other party was floating away into the free and formless ether. The two must hold each other to do justice to each other. If Americans can be divorced for "incompatibility of temper" I cannot conceive why they are not all divorced. I have known many happy marriages, but never a compatible one. The whole aim of marriage is to fight through and survive the instant when incompatibility becomes unquestionable. For a man and a woman, as such, are incompatible.

VIII. The Wildness Of Domesticity

In the course of this crude study we shall have to touch on what is called the problem of poverty, especially the dehumanized poverty of modern industrialism. But in this primary matter of the ideal the difficulty is not the problem of poverty, but the problem of wealth. It is the special psychology of leisure and luxury that falsifies life. Some experience of modern movements of the sort called "advanced" has led me to the conviction that they generally repose upon some experience peculiar to the rich. It is so with that fallacy of free love of which I have already spoken; the idea of sexuality as a string of episodes. That implies a long holiday in which to get tired of one woman, and a motor car in which to wander looking for others; it also implies money for maintenances. An omnibus conductor has hardly time to love his own wife, let alone other people's. And the success with which nuptial estrangements are depicted in modern "problem plays" is due to the fact that there is only one thing that a drama cannot depict--that is a hard day's work. I could give many other instances of this plutocratic assumption behind progressive fads. For instance, there is a plutocratic assumption behind the phrase "Why should woman be economically dependent upon man?" The answer is that among poor and practical people she isn't; except in the sense in which he is dependent upon her. A hunter has to tear his clothes; there must be somebody to mend them. A fisher has to catch fish; there must be somebody to cook them. It is surely quite clear that this modern notion that woman is a mere "pretty clinging parasite," "a plaything," etc., arose through the somber contemplation of some rich banking family, in which the banker, at least, went to the city and pretended to do something, while the banker's wife went to the Park and did not pretend to do anything at all. A poor man and his wife are a business partnership. If one partner in a firm of publishers interviews the authors while the other interviews the clerks, is one of them economically dependent? Was Hodder a pretty parasite clinging to Stoughton? Was Marshall a mere plaything for Snelgrove?

But of all the modern notions generated by mere wealth the worst is this: the notion that domesticity is dull and tame. Inside the home (they say) is dead decorum and routine; outside is adventure and variety. This is indeed a rich man's opinion. The rich man knows that his own house moves on vast and soundless wheels of wealth, is run by regiments of servants, by a swift and silent ritual. On the other hand, every sort of vagabondage of romance is open to him in the streets outside. He has plenty of money and can afford to be a tramp. His wildest adventure will end in a restaurant, while the yokel's tamest adventure may end in a police-court. If he smashes a window he can pay for it; if he smashes a man he can pension him. He can (like the millionaire in the story) buy an hotel to get a glass of gin. And because he, the luxurious man, dictates the tone of nearly all "advanced" and "progressive" thought, we have almost forgotten what a home really means to the overwhelming millions of mankind.

For the truth is, that to the moderately poor the home is the only place of liberty. Nay, it is the only place of anarchy. It is the only spot on the earth where a man can alter arrangements suddenly, make an experiment or indulge in a whim. Everywhere else he goes he must accept the strict rules of the shop, inn, club, or museum that he happens to enter. He can eat his meals on the floor in his own house if he likes. I often do it myself; it gives a curious, childish, poetic, picnic feeling. There would be considerable trouble if I tried to do it in an A.B.C. tea-shop. A man can wear a dressing gown and slippers in his house; while I am sure that this would not be permitted at the Savoy, though I never actually tested the point. If you go to a restaurant you must drink some of the wines on the wine list, all of them if you insist, but certainly some of them. But if you have a house and garden you can try to make hollyhock tea or convolvulus wine if you like. For a plain, hard-working man the home is not the one tame place in the world of adventure. It is the one wild place in the world of rules and set tasks. The home is the one place where he can put the carpet on the ceiling or the slates on the floor if he wants to. When a man spends every night staggering from bar to bar or from music-hall to music-hall, we say that he is living an irregular life. But he is not; he is living a highly regular life, under the dull, and often oppressive, laws of such places. Some times he is not allowed even to sit down in the bars; and frequently he is not allowed to sing in the music-halls. Hotels may be defined as places where you are forced to dress; and theaters may be defined as places where you are forbidden to smoke. A man can only picnic at home.

Now I take, as I have said, this small human omnipotence, this possession of a definite cell or chamber of liberty, as the working model for the present inquiry. Whether we can give every English man a free home of his own or not, at least we should desire it; and he desires it. For the moment we speak of what he wants, not of what he expects to get. He wants, for instance, a separate house; he does not want a semi-detached house. He may be forced in the commercial race to share one wall with another man. Similarly he might be forced in a three-legged race to share one leg with another man; but it is not so that he pictures himself in his dreams of elegance and liberty. Again, he does not desire a flat. He can eat and sleep and praise God in a flat; he can eat and sleep and praise God in a railway train. But a railway train is not a house, because it is a house on wheels. And a flat is not a house, because it is a house on stilts. An idea of earthy contact and foundation, as well as an idea of separation and independence, is a part of this instructive human picture.

I take, then, this one institution as a test. As every normal man desires a woman, and children born of a woman, every normal man desires a house of his own to put them into. He does not merely want a roof above him and a chair below him; he wants an objective and visible kingdom; a fire at which he can cook what food he likes, a door he can open to what friends he chooses. This is the normal appetite of men; I do not say there are not exceptions. There may be saints above the need and philanthropists below it. Opalstein, now he is a duke, may have got used to more than this; and when he was a convict may have got used to less. But the normality of the thing is enormous. To give nearly everybody ordinary houses would please nearly everybody; that is what I assert without apology. Now in modern England (as you eagerly point out) it is very difficult to give nearly everybody houses. Quite so; I merely set up the desideratum; and ask the reader to leave it standing there while he turns with me to a consideration of what really happens in the social wars of our time.

IX. History Of Hudge And Gudge

There is, let us say, a certain filthy rookery in Hoxton, dripping with disease and honeycombed with crime and promiscuity. There are, let us say, two noble and courageous young men, of pure intentions and (if you prefer it) noble birth; let us call them Hudge and Gudge. Hudge, let us say, is of a bustling sort; he points out that the people must at all costs be got out of this den; he subscribes and collects money, but he finds (despite the large financial interests of the Hudges) that the thing will have to be done on the cheap if it is to be done on the spot. He therefore, runs up a row of tall bare tenements like beehives; and soon has all the poor people bundled into their little brick cells, which are

certainly better than their old quarters, in so far as they are weather
proof, well ventilated and supplied with clean water. But Gudge
has a more delicate nature. He feels a nameless something lacking
in the little brick boxes; he raises numberless objections; he even
assails the celebrated Hudge Report, with the Gudge Minority
Report; and by the end of a year or so has come to telling Hudge
heatedly that the people were much happier where they were
before. As the people preserve in both places precisely the same air
of dazed amiability, it is very difficult to find out which is right.
But at least one might safely say that no people ever liked stench
or starvation as such, but only some peculiar pleasures en tangled
with them. Not so feels the sensitive Gudge. Long before the final
quarrel (Hudge v. Gudge and Another), Gudge has succeeded in
persuading himself that slums and stinks are really very nice
things; that the habit of sleeping fourteen in a room is what has
made our England great; and that the smell of open drains is
absolutely essential to the rearing of a viking breed.

But, meanwhile, has there been no degeneration in Hudge?
Alas, I fear there has. Those maniacally ugly buildings which he
originally put up as unpretentious sheds barely to shelter human
life, grow every day more and more lovely to his deluded eye.
Things he would never have dreamed of defending, except as
crude necessities, things like common kitchens or infamous
asbestos stoves, begin to shine quite sacredly before him, merely
because they reflect the wrath of Gudge. He maintains, with the aid
of eager little books by Socialists, that man is really happier in a
hive than in a house. The practical difficulty of keeping total
strangers out of your bedroom he describes as Brotherhood; and
the necessity for climbing twenty-three flights of cold stone stairs,
I dare say he calls Effort. The net result of their philanthropic
adventure is this: that one has come to defending indefensible
slums and still more indefensible slum-landlords, while the other
has come to treating as divine the sheds and pipes which he only
meant as desperate. Gudge is now a corrupt and apoplectic old
Tory in the Carlton Club; if you mention poverty to him he roars at
you in a thick, hoarse voice something that is conjectured to be
"Do 'em good!" Nor is Hudge more happy; for he is a lean
vegetarian with a gray, pointed beard and an unnaturally easy
smile, who goes about telling everybody that at last we shall all

sleep in one universal bedroom; and he lives in a Garden City, like one forgotten of God.

Such is the lamentable history of Hudge and Gudge; which I merely introduce as a type of an endless and exasperating misunderstanding which is always occurring in modern England. To get men out of a rookery men are put into a tenement; and at the beginning the healthy human soul loathes them both. A man's first desire is to get away as far as possible from the rookery, even should his mad course lead him to a model dwelling. The second desire is, naturally, to get away from the model dwelling, even if it should lead a man back to the rookery. But I am neither a Hudgian nor a Gudgian; and I think the mistakes of these two famous and fascinating persons arose from one simple fact. They arose from the fact that neither Hudge nor Gudge had ever thought for an instant what sort of house a man might probably like for himself. In short, they did not begin with the ideal; and, therefore, were not practical politicians.

We may now return to the purpose of our awkward parenthesis about the praise of the future and the failures of the past. A house of his own being the obvious ideal for every man, we may now ask (taking this need as typical of all such needs) why he hasn't got it; and whether it is in any philosophical sense his own fault. Now, I think that in some philosophical sense it is his own fault, I think in a yet more philosophical sense it is the fault of his philosophy. And this is what I have now to attempt to explain.

Burke, a fine rhetorician, who rarely faced realities, said, I think, that an Englishman's house is his castle. This is honestly entertaining; for as it happens the Englishman is almost the only man in Europe whose house is not his castle. Nearly everywhere else exists the assumption of peasant proprietorship; that a poor man may be a landlord, though he is only lord of his own land. Making the landlord and the tenant the same person has certain trivial advantages, as that the tenant pays no rent, while the landlord does a little work. But I am not concerned with the defense of small proprietorship, but merely with the fact that it exists almost everywhere except in England. It is also true, however, that this estate of small possession is attacked everywhere today; it has never existed among ourselves, and it may be destroyed among our neighbors. We have, therefore, to ask ourselves what it is in human affairs generally, and in this domestic ideal in particular, that has really ruined the natural human creation, especially in this country.

Man has always lost his way. He has been a tramp ever since Eden; but he always knew, or thought he knew, what he was looking for. Every man has a house somewhere in the elaborate cosmos; his house waits for him waist deep in slow Norfolk rivers or sunning itself upon Sussex downs. Man has always been looking for that home which is the subject matter of this book. But in the bleak and blinding hail of skepticism to which he has been now so long subjected, he has begun for the first time to be chilled, not merely in his hopes, but in his desires. For the first time in history he begins really to doubt the object of his wanderings on the earth. He has always lost his way; but now he has lost his address.

Under the pressure of certain upper-class philosophies (or in other words, under the pressure of Hudge and Gudge) the average man has really become bewildered about the goal of his efforts; and his efforts, therefore, grow feebler and feebler. His simple notion of having a home of his own is derided as bourgeois, as sentimental, or as despicably Christian. Under various verbal forms he is recommended to go on to the streets--which is called Individualism; or to the work-house--which is called Collectivism. We shall consider this process somewhat more carefully in a moment. But it may be said here that Hudge and Gudge, or the governing class generally, will never fail for lack of some modern phrase to cover their ancient predominance. The great lords will refuse the English peasant his three acres and a cow on advanced grounds, if they cannot refuse it longer on reactionary grounds. They will deny him the three acres on grounds of State Ownership. They will forbid him the cow on grounds of humanitarianism.

And this brings us to the ultimate analysis of this singular influence that has prevented doctrinal demands by the English people. There are, I believe, some who still deny that England is governed by an oligarchy. It is quite enough for me to know that a man might have gone to sleep some thirty years ago over the day's newspaper and woke up last week over the later newspaper, and fancied he was reading about the same people. In one paper he would have found a Lord Robert Cecil, a Mr. Gladstone, a Mr.

Lyttleton, a Churchill, a Chamberlain, a Trevelyan, an Acland. In the other paper he would find a Lord Robert Cecil, a Mr. Gladstone, a Mr. Lyttleton, a Churchill, a Chamberlain, a Trevelyan, an Acland. If this is not being governed by families I cannot imagine what it is. I suppose it is being governed by extraordinary democratic coincidences.

X. Oppression By Optimism

But we are not here concerned with the nature and existence of the aristocracy, but with the origin of its peculiar power, why is it the last of the true oligarchies of Europe; and why does there seem no very immediate prospect of our seeing the end of it? The explanation is simple though it remains strangely unnoticed. The friends of aristocracy often praise it for preserving ancient and gracious traditions. The enemies of aristocracy often blame it for clinging to cruel or antiquated customs. Both its enemies and its friends are wrong. Generally speaking the aristocracy does not preserve either good or bad traditions; it does not preserve anything except game. Who would dream of looking among aristocrats anywhere for an old custom? One might as well look for an old costume! The god of the aristocrats is not tradition, but fashion, which is the opposite of tradition. If you wanted to find an old-world Norwegian head-dress, would you look for it in the Scandinavian Smart Set? No; the aristocrats never have customs; at the best they have habits, like the animals. Only the mob has customs.

The real power of the English aristocrats has lain in exactly the opposite of tradition. The simple key to the power of our upper classes is this: that they have always kept carefully on the side of what is called Progress. They have always been up to date, and this comes quite easy to an aristocracy. For the aristocracy are the supreme instances of that frame of mind of which we spoke just now. Novelty is to them a luxury verging on a necessity. They, above all, are so bored with the past and with the present, that they gape, with a horrible hunger, for the future.

But whatever else the great lords forgot they never forgot that it was their business to stand for the new things, for whatever was being most talked about among university dons or fussy financiers. Thus they were on the side of the Reformation against the Church, of the Whigs against the Stuarts, of the Baconian science against the old philosophy, of the manufacturing system against the operatives, and (to-day) of the increased power of the State against the old-fashioned individualists. In short, the rich are always modern; it is their business. But the immediate effect of this fact upon the question we are studying is somewhat singular.

In each of the separate holes or quandaries in which the ordinary Englishman has been placed, he has been told that his situation is, for some particular reason, all for the best. He woke up one fine morning and discovered that the public things, which for eight hundred years he had used at once as inns and sanctuaries, had all been suddenly and savagely abolished, to increase the private wealth of about six or seven men. One would think he might have been annoyed at that; in many places he was, and was put down by the soldiery. But it was not merely the army that kept him quiet. He was kept quiet by the sages as well as the soldiers; the six or seven men who took away the inns of the poor told him that they were not doing it for themselves, but for the religion of the future, the great dawn of Protestantism and truth. So whenever a seventeenth century noble was caught pulling down a peasant's fence and stealing his field, the noble pointed excitedly at the face of Charles I or James II (which at that moment, perhaps, wore a cross expression) and thus diverted the simple peasant's attention. The great Puritan lords created the Commonwealth, and destroyed the common land. They saved their poorer countrymen from the disgrace of paying Ship Money, by taking from them the plow money and spade money which they were doubtless too weak to guard. A fine old English rhyme has immortalized this easy aristocratic habit--

You prosecute the man or woman Who steals the goose from off the common, But leave the larger felon loose Who steals the common from the goose.

But here, as in the case of the monasteries, we confront the strange problem of submission. If they stole the common from the goose, one can only say that he was a great goose to stand it. The truth is that they reasoned with the goose; they explained to him that all this was needed to get the Stuart fox over seas. So in the nineteenth century the great nobles who became mine-owners and railway directors earnestly assured everybody that they did not do this from preference, but owing to a newly discovered Economic Law. So the prosperous politicians of our own generation introduce bills to prevent poor mothers from going about with their own babies; or they calmly forbid their tenants to drink beer in public inns. But this insolence is not (as you would suppose) howled at by everybody as outrageous feudalism. It is gently rebuked as Socialism. For an aristocracy is always progressive; it is a form of going the pace. Their parties grow later and later at night; for they are trying to live to-morrow.

XI. The Homelessness Of Jones

Thus the Future of which we spoke at the beginning has (in England at least) always been the ally of tyranny. The ordinary Englishman has been duped out of his old possessions, such as they were, and always in the name of progress. The destroyers of the abbeys took away his bread and gave him a stone, assuring him that it was a precious stone, the white pebble of the Lord's elect. They took away his maypole and his original rural life and promised him instead the Golden Age of Peace and Commerce inaugurated at the Crystal Palace. And now they are taking away the little that remains of his dignity as a householder and the head of a family, promising him instead Utopias which are called (appropriately enough) "Anticipations" or "News from Nowhere." We come back, in fact, to the main feature which has already been mentioned. The past is communal: the future must be individualist. In the past are all the evils of democracy, variety and violence and doubt, but the future is pure despotism, for the future is pure caprice. Yesterday, I know I was a human fool, but to-morrow I can easily be the Superman.

The modern Englishman, however, is like a man who should be perpetually kept out, for one reason after another, from the house in which he had meant his married life to begin. This man (Jones let us call him) has always desired the divinely ordinary things; he has married for love, he has chosen or built a small house that fits like a coat; he is ready to be a great grandfather and a local god. And just as he is moving in, something goes wrong. Some tyranny, personal or political, suddenly debars him from the home; and he has to take his meals in the front garden. A passing philosopher (who is also, by a mere coincidence, the man who turned him out) pauses, and leaning elegantly on the railings, explains to him that he is now living that bold life upon the bounty of nature which will be the life of the sublime future. He finds life in the front garden more bold than bountiful, and has to move into mean lodgings in the next spring. The philosopher (who turned him out), happening to call at these lodgings, with the probable intention of raising the rent, stops to explain to him that he is now in the real life of mercantile endeavor; the economic struggle between him and the landlady is the only thing out of which, in the sublime future, the wealth of nations can come. He is defeated in the economic struggle, and goes to the workhouse. The philosopher who turned him out (happening at that very moment to be inspecting the workhouse) assures him that he is now at last in that golden republic which is the goal of mankind; he is in an equal, scientific, Socialistic commonwealth, owned by the State and ruled by public officers; in fact, the commonwealth of the sublime future.

Nevertheless, there are signs that the irrational Jones still dreams at night of this old idea of having an ordinary home. He asked for so little, and he has been offered so much. He has been offered bribes of worlds and systems; he has been offered Eden and Utopia and the New Jerusalem, and he only wanted a house; and that has been refused him.

Such an apologue is literally no exaggeration of the facts of English history. The rich did literally turn the poor out of the old guest house on to the road, briefly telling them that it was the road of progress. They did literally force them into factories and the modern wage-slavery, assuring them all the time that this was the only way to wealth and civilization. Just as they had dragged the rustic from the convent food and ale by saying that the streets of heaven were paved with gold, so now they dragged him from the village food and ale by telling him that the streets of London were paved with gold. As he entered the gloomy porch of Puritanism, so he entered the gloomy porch of Industrialism, being told that each of them was the gate of the future. Hitherto he has only gone from prison to prison, nay, into darkening prisons, for Calvinism opened one small window upon heaven. And now he is asked, in the same educated and authoritative tones, to enter another dark porch, at which he has to surrender, into unseen hands, his children, his small possessions and all the habits of his fathers.

Whether this last opening be in truth any more inviting than the old openings of Puritanism and Industrialism can be discussed later. But there can be little doubt, I think, that if some form of Collectivism is imposed upon England it will be imposed, as everything else has been, by an instructed political class upon a people partly apathetic and partly hypnotized. The aristocracy will be as ready to "administer" Collectivism as they were to administer Puritanism or Manchesterism; in some ways such a centralized political power is necessarily attractive to them. It will not be so hard as some innocent Socialists seem to suppose to induce the Honorable Tomnoddy to take over the milk supply as well as the stamp supply--at an increased salary. Mr. Bernard Shaw has remarked that rich men are better than poor men on parish councils because they are free from "financial timidity." Now, the English ruling class is quite free from financial timidity. The Duke of Sussex will be quite ready to be Administrator of Sussex at the same screw. Sir William Harcourt, that typical aristocrat, put it quite correctly. "We" (that is, the aristocracy) "are all Socialists now."

But this is not the essential note on which I desire to end. My main contention is that, whether necessary or not, both Industrialism and Collectivism have been accepted as necessities-- not as naked ideals or desires. Nobody liked the Manchester School; it was endured as the only way of producing wealth. Nobody likes the Marxian school; it is endured as the only way of preventing poverty. Nobody's real heart is in the idea of preventing a free man from owning his own farm, or an old woman from cultivating her own garden, any more than anybody's real heart was in the heartless battle of the machines. The purpose of this chapter is sufficiently served in indicating that this proposal also is a pis aller, a desperate second best--like teetotalism. I do not propose to prove here that Socialism is a poison; it is enough if I maintain that it is a medicine and not a wine.

The idea of private property universal but private, the idea of families free but still families, of domesticity democratic but still domestic, of one man one house--this remains the real vision and magnet of mankind. The world may accept something more official and general, less human and intimate. But the world will be like a broken-hearted woman who makes a humdrum marriage because she may not make a happy one; Socialism may be the world's deliverance, but it is not the world's desire.

What's Wrong with the World

Part Two. Imperialism, Or The Mistake About Man

I. The Charm Of Jingoism

I have cast about widely to find a title for this section; and I confess that the word "Imperialism" is a clumsy version of my meaning. But no other word came nearer; "Militarism" would have been even more misleading, and "The Superman" makes nonsense of any discussion that he enters. Perhaps, upon the whole, the word "Caesarism" would have been better; but I desire a popular word; and Imperialism (as the reader will perceive) does cover for the most part the men and theories that I mean to discuss.

This small confusion is increased, however, by the fact that I do also disbelieve in Imperialism in its popular sense, as a mode or theory of the patriotic sentiment of this country. But popular Imperialism in England has very little to do with the sort of Caesarean Imperialism I wish to sketch. I differ from the Colonial idealism of Rhodes' and Kipling; but I do not think, as some of its opponents do, that it is an insolent creation of English harshness and rapacity. Imperialism, I think, is a fiction created, not by English hardness, but by English softness; nay, in a sense, even by English kindness.

The reasons for believing in Australia are mostly as sentimental as the most sentimental reasons for believing in heaven. New South Wales is quite literally regarded as a place where the wicked cease from troubling and the weary are at rest; that is, a paradise for uncles who have turned dishonest and for nephews who are born tired. British Columbia is in strict sense a fairyland, it is a world where a magic and irrational luck is supposed to attend the youngest sons. This strange optimism about the ends of the earth is an English weakness; but to show that it is not a coldness or a harshness it is quite sufficient to say that no one shared it more than that gigantic English sentimentalist--the great Charles Dickens. The end of "David Copperfield" is unreal not merely because it is an optimistic ending, but because it is an Imperialistic ending. The decorous British happiness planned out for David Copperfield and Agnes would be embarrassed by the perpetual presence of the hopeless tragedy of Emily, or the more hopeless farce of Micawber. Therefore, both Emily and Micawber are shipped off to a vague colony where changes come over them with no conceivable cause, except the climate. The tragic woman becomes contented and the comic man becomes responsible, solely as the result of a sea voyage and the first sight of a kangaroo.

To Imperialism in the light political sense, therefore, my only objection is that it is an illusion of comfort; that an Empire whose heart is failing should be specially proud of the extremities, is to me no more sublime a fact than that an old dandy whose brain is gone should still be proud of his legs. It consoles men for the evident ugliness and apathy of England with legends of fair youth and heroic strenuousness in distant continents and islands. A man can sit amid the squalor of Seven Dials and feel that life is innocent and godlike in the bush or on the veldt. Just so a man might sit in the squalor of Seven Dials and feel that life was innocent and godlike in Brixton and Surbiton. Brixton and Surbiton are "new"; they are expanding; they are "nearer to nature," in the sense that they have eaten up nature mile by mile. The only objection is the objection of fact. The young men of Brixton are not young giants. The lovers of Surbiton are not all pagan poets, singing with the sweet energy of the spring. Nor are the people of the Colonies when you meet them young giants or pagan poets. They are mostly Cockneys who have lost their last music of real things by getting out of the sound of Bow Bells. Mr. Rudyard Kipling, a man of real though decadent genius, threw a theoretic glamour over them which is already fading. Mr. Kipling is, in a precise and rather startling sense, the exception that proves the rule. For he has imagination, of an oriental and cruel kind, but he has it, not because he grew up in a new country, but precisely because he grew up in the oldest country upon earth. He is rooted in a past--an Asiatic past. He might never have written "Kabul River" if he had been born in Melbourne.

I say frankly, therefore (lest there should be any air of evasion), that Imperialism in its common patriotic pretensions appears to me both weak and perilous. It is the attempt of a European country to create a kind of sham Europe which it can dominate, instead of the real Europe, which it can only share. It is a love of living with one's inferiors. The notion of restoring the

Roman Empire by oneself and for oneself is a dream that has haunted every Christian nation in a different shape and in almost every shape as a snare. The Spanish are a consistent and conservative people; therefore they embodied that attempt at Empire in long and lingering dynasties. The French are a violent people, and therefore they twice conquered that Empire by violence of arms. The English are above all a poetical and optimistic people; and therefore their Empire is something vague and yet sympathetic, something distant and yet dear. But this dream of theirs of being powerful in the uttermost places, though a native weakness, is still a weakness in them; much more of a weakness than gold was to Spain or glory to Napoleon. If ever we were in collision with our real brothers and rivals we should leave all this fancy out of account. We should no more dream of pitting Australian armies against German than of pitting Tasmanian sculpture against French. I have thus explained, lest anyone should accuse me of concealing an unpopular attitude, why I do not believe in Imperialism as commonly understood. I think it not merely an occasional wrong to other peoples, but a continuous feebleness, a running sore, in my own. But it is also true that I have dwelt on this Imperialism that is an amiable delusion partly in order to show how different it is from the deeper, more sinister and yet more persuasive thing that I have been forced to call Imperialism for the convenience of this chapter. In order to get to the root of this evil and quite un-English Imperialism we must cast back and begin anew with a more general discussion of the first needs of human intercourse.

II. Wisdom And The Weather

It is admitted, one may hope, that common things are never commonplace. Birth is covered with curtains precisely because it is a staggering and monstrous prodigy. Death and first love, though they happen to everybody, can stop one's heart with the very thought of them. But while this is granted, something further may be claimed. It is not merely true that these universal things are strange; it is moreover true that they are subtle. In the last analysis most common things will be found to be highly complicated. Some men of science do indeed get over the difficulty by dealing only with the easy part of it: thus, they will call first love the instinct of sex, and the awe of death the instinct of self-preservation. But this is only getting over the difficulty of describing peacock green by calling it blue. There is blue in it. That there is a strong physical element in both romance and the Memento Mori makes them if possible more baffling than if they had been wholly intellectual. No man could say exactly how much his sexuality was colored by a clean love of beauty, or by the mere boyish itch for irrevocable adventures, like running away to sea. No man could say how far his animal dread of the end was mixed up with mystical traditions touching morals and religion. It is exactly because these things are animal, but not quite animal, that the dance of all the difficulties begins. The materialists analyze the easy part, deny the hard part and go home to their tea.

It is complete error to suppose that because a thing is vulgar therefore it is not refined; that is, subtle and hard to define. A drawing-room song of my youth which began "In the gloaming, O, my darling," was vulgar enough as a song; but the connection between human passion and the twilight is none the less an exquisite and even inscrutable thing. Or to take another obvious instance: the jokes about a mother-in-law are scarcely delicate, but the problem of a mother-in-law is extremely delicate. A mother-in-law is subtle because she is a thing like the twilight. She is a mystical blend of two inconsistent things--law and a mother. The caricatures misrepresent her; but they arise out of a real human enigma. "Comic Cuts" deals with the difficulty wrongly, but it would need George Meredith at his best to deal with the difficulty rightly. The nearest statement of the problem perhaps is this: it is not that a mother-in-law must be nasty, but that she must be very nice.

But it is best perhaps to take in illustration some daily custom we have all heard despised as vulgar or trite. Take, for the sake of argument, the custom of talking about the weather. Stevenson calls it "the very nadir and scoff of good conversationalists." Now there are very deep reasons for talking about the weather, reasons that are delicate as well as deep; they lie in layer upon layer of stratified sagacity. First of all it is a gesture of primeval worship. The sky must be invoked; and to begin everything with the weather is a sort of pagan way of beginning everything with prayer. Jones and Brown talk about the weather: but so do Milton and Shelley. Then it is an expression of that elementary idea in politeness--equality. For the very word politeness is only the Greek for citizenship. The word politeness is akin to the word policeman: a charming thought. Properly understood, the citizen should be more polite than the gentleman; perhaps the policeman should be the most courtly and elegant of the three. But all good manners must obviously begin with the sharing of something in a simple style. Two men should share an umbrella; if they have not got an umbrella, they should at least share the rain, with all its rich potentialities of wit and philosophy. "For He maketh His sun to shine...." This is the second element in the weather; its recognition of human equality in that we all have our hats under the dark blue spangled umbrella of the universe. Arising out of this is the third wholesome strain in the custom; I mean that it begins with the body and with our inevitable bodily brotherhood. All true friendliness begins with fire and food and drink and the recognition of rain or frost. Those who will not begin at the bodily end of things are already prigs and may soon be Christian Scientists. Each human soul has in a sense to enact for itself the gigantic humility of the Incarnation. Every man must descend into the flesh to meet mankind.

Briefly, in the mere observation "a fine day" there is the whole great human idea of comradeship. Now, pure comradeship is another of those broad and yet bewildering things. We all enjoy it; yet when we come to talk about it we almost always talk nonsense, chiefly because we suppose it to be a simpler affair than it is. It is simple to conduct; but it is by no means simple to analyze. Comradeship is at the most only one half of human life; the other half is Love, a thing so different that one might fancy it had been made for another universe. And I do not mean mere sex love; any kind of concentrated passion, maternal love, or even the fiercer kinds of friendship are in their nature alien to pure comradeship. Both sides are essential to life; and both are known in differing degrees to everybody of every age or sex. But very broadly speaking it may still be said that women stand for the dignity of love and men for the dignity of comradeship. I mean that the institution would hardly be expected if the males of the tribe did not mount guard over it. The affections in which women excel have so much more authority and intensity that pure comradeship would be washed away if it were not rallied and guarded in clubs, corps, colleges, banquets and regiments. Most of us have heard the voice in which the hostess tells her husband not to sit too long over the cigars. It is the dreadful voice of Love, seeking to destroy Comradeship.

All true comradeship has in it those three elements which I have remarked in the ordinary exclamation about the weather. First, it has a sort of broad philosophy like the common sky, emphasizing that we are all under the same cosmic conditions. We are all in the same boat, the "winged rock" of Mr. Herbert Trench. Secondly, it recognizes this bond as the essential one; for comradeship is simply humanity seen in that one aspect in which men are really equal. The old writers were entirely wise when they talked of the equality of men; but they were also very wise in not mentioning women. Women are always authoritarian; they are always above or below; that is why marriage is a sort of poetical see-saw. There are only three things in the world that women do not understand; and they are Liberty, Equality, and Fraternity. But men (a class little understood in the modern world) find these things the breath of their nostrils; and our most learned ladies will not even begin to understand them until they make allowance for this kind of cool camaraderie. Lastly, it contains the third quality of the weather, the insistence upon the body and its indispensable satisfaction. No one has even begun to understand comradeship who does not accept with it a certain hearty eagerness in eating, drinking, or smoking, an uproarious materialism which to many women appears only hoggish. You may call the thing an orgy or a sacrament; it is certainly an essential. It is at root a resistance to the superciliousness of the individual. Nay, its very swaggering and howling are humble. In the heart of its rowdiness there is a sort of mad modesty; a desire to melt the separate soul into the mass of unpretentious masculinity. It is a clamorous confession of the weakness of all flesh. No man must be superior to the things that are common to men. This sort of equality must be bodily and gross and comic. Not only are we all in the same boat, but we are all seasick.

The word comradeship just now promises to become as fatuous as the word "affinity." There are clubs of a Socialist sort where all the members, men and women, call each other "Comrade." I have no serious emotions, hostile or otherwise, about this particular habit: at the worst it is conventionality, and at the best flirtation. I am convinced here only to point out a rational principle. If you choose to lump all flowers together, lilies and dahlias and tulips and chrysanthemums and call them all daisies, you will find that you have spoiled the very fine word daisy. If you choose to call every human attachment comradeship, if you include under that name the respect of a youth for a venerable prophetess, the interest of a man in a beautiful woman who baffles him, the pleasure of a philosophical old fogy in a girl who is impudent and innocent, the end of the meanest quarrel or the beginning of the most mountainous love; if you are going to call all these comradeship, you will gain nothing, you will only lose a word. Daisies are obvious and universal and open; but they are only one kind of flower. Comradeship is obvious and universal and open; but it is only one kind of affection; it has characteristics that would destroy any other kind. Anyone who has known true comradeship in a club or in a regiment, knows that it is impersonal. There is a pedantic phrase used in debating clubs which is strictly true to the masculine emotion; they call it "speaking to the question." Women speak to each other; men speak to the subject they are speaking about. Many an honest man has sat in a ring of his five best friends under heaven and forgotten who was in the room while he explained some system. This is not peculiar to intellectual men; men are all theoretical, whether they are talking about God or about golf. Men are all impersonal; that is to say, republican. No one remembers after a really good talk who has said the good things. Every man speaks to a visionary multitude; a mystical cloud, that is called the club.

It is obvious that this cool and careless quality which is essential to the collective affection of males involves disadvantages and dangers. It leads to spitting; it leads to coarse speech; it must lead to these things so long as it is honorable; comradeship must be in some degree ugly. The moment beauty is mentioned in male friendship, the nostrils are stopped with the smell of abominable things. Friendship must be physically dirty if it is to be morally clean. It must be in its shirt sleeves. The chaos of habits that always goes with males when left entirely to themselves has only one honorable cure; and that is the strict discipline of a monastery. Anyone who has seen our unhappy young idealists in East End Settlements losing their collars in the wash and living on tinned salmon will fully understand why it was decided by the wisdom of St. Bernard or St. Benedict, that if men were to live without women, they must not live without rules. Something of the same sort of artificial exactitude, of course, is obtained in an army; and an army also has to be in many ways monastic; only that it has celibacy without chastity. But these things do not apply to normal married men. These have a quite sufficient restraint on their instinctive anarchy in the savage common-sense of the other sex. There is only one very timid sort of man that is not afraid of women.

III. The Common Vision

Now this masculine love of an open and level camaraderie is the life within all democracies and attempts to govern by debate; without it the republic would be a dead formula. Even as it is, of course, the spirit of democracy frequently differs widely from the letter, and a pothouse is often a better test than a Parliament. Democracy in its human sense is not arbitrament by the majority; it is not even arbitrament by everybody. It can be more nearly defined as arbitrament by anybody. I mean that it rests on that club habit of taking a total stranger for granted, of assuming certain things to be inevitably common to yourself and him. Only the things that anybody may be presumed to hold have the full authority of democracy. Look out of the window and notice the first man who walks by. The Liberals may have swept England with an over-whelming majority; but you would not stake a button that the man is a Liberal. The Bible may be read in all schools and respected in all law courts; but you would not bet a straw that he believes in the Bible. But you would bet your week's wages, let us say, that he believes in wearing clothes. You would bet that he believes that physical courage is a fine thing, or that parents have authority over children. Of course, he might be the millionth man who does not believe these things; if it comes to that, he might be the Bearded Lady dressed up as a man. But these prodigies are quite a different thing from any mere calculation of numbers. People who hold these views are not a minority, but a monstrosity. But of these universal dogmas that have full democratic authority the only test is this test of anybody. What you would observe before any newcomer in a tavern--that is the real English law. The first man you see from the window, he is the King of England.

The decay of taverns, which is but a part of the general decay of democracy, has undoubtedly weakened this masculine spirit of equality. I remember that a roomful of Socialists literally laughed when I told them that there were no two nobler words in all poetry than Public House. They thought it was a joke. Why they should think it a joke, since they want to make all houses public houses, I cannot imagine. But if anyone wishes to see the real rowdy egalitarianism which is necessary (to males, at least) he can find it as well as anywhere in the great old tavern disputes which come down to us in such books as Boswell's Johnson. It is worth while to mention that one name especially because the modern world in its morbidity has done it a strange injustice. The demeanor of Johnson, it is said, was "harsh and despotic." It was occasionally harsh, but it was never despotic. Johnson was not in the least a despot; Johnson was a demagogue, he shouted against a shouting crowd. The very fact that he wrangled with other people is proof that other people were allowed to wrangle with him. His very brutality was based on the idea of an equal scrimmage, like that of football. It is strictly true that he bawled and banged the table because he was a modest man. He was honestly afraid of being overwhelmed or even overlooked. Addison had exquisite manners and was the king of his company; he was polite to everybody; but superior to everybody; therefore he has been handed down forever in the immortal insult of Pope--

"Like Cato, give his little Senate laws And sit attentive to his own applause."

Johnson, so far from being king of his company, was a sort of Irish Member in his own Parliament. Addison was a courteous superior and was hated. Johnson was an insolent equal and therefore was loved by all who knew him, and handed down in a marvellous book, which is one of the mere miracles of love.

This doctrine of equality is essential to conversation; so much may be admitted by anyone who knows what conversation is. Once arguing at a table in a tavern the most famous man on earth would wish to be obscure, so that his brilliant remarks might blaze like the stars on the background of his obscurity. To anything worth calling a man nothing can be conceived more cold or cheerless than to be king of your company. But it may be said that in masculine sports and games, other than the great game of debate, there is definite emulation and eclipse. There is indeed emulation, but this is only an ardent sort of equality. Games are competitive, because that is the only way of making them exciting. But if anyone doubts that men must forever return to the ideal of equality, it is only necessary to answer that there is such a thing as a handicap. If men exulted in mere superiority, they would seek to see how far such superiority could go; they would be glad when one strong runner came in miles ahead of all the rest. But what men like is not the triumph of superiors, but the struggle of equals; and, therefore, they introduce even into their competitive sports an artificial equality. It is sad to think how few of those who arrange our sporting handicaps can be supposed with any probability to realize that they are abstract and even severe republicans.

No; the real objection to equality and self-rule has nothing to do with any of these free and festive aspects of mankind; all men are democrats when they are happy. The philosophic opponent of democracy would substantially sum up his position by saying that it "will not work." Before going further, I will register in passing a protest against the assumption that working is the one test of humanity. Heaven does not work; it plays. Men are most themselves when they are free; and if I find that men are snobs in their work but democrats on their holidays, I shall take the liberty to believe their holidays. But it is this question of work which really perplexes the question of equality; and it is with that that we must now deal. Perhaps the truth can be put most pointedly thus: that democracy has one real enemy, and that is civilization. Those utilitarian miracles which science has made are anti-democratic, not so much in their perversion, or even in their practical result, as in their primary shape and purpose. The Frame-Breaking Rioters were right; not perhaps in thinking that machines would make fewer men workmen; but certainly in thinking that machines would make fewer men masters. More wheels do mean fewer handles; fewer handles do mean fewer hands. The machinery of science must be individualistic and isolated. A mob can shout round a palace; but a mob cannot shout down a telephone. The specialist appears and democracy is half spoiled at a stroke.

IV. The Insane Necessity

The common conception among the dregs of Darwinian culture is that men have slowly worked their way out of inequality into a state of comparative equality. The truth is, I fancy, almost exactly the opposite. All men have normally and naturally begun with the idea of equality; they have only abandoned it late and reluctantly, and always for some material reason of detail. They have never naturally felt that one class of men was superior to another; they have always been driven to assume it through certain practical limitations of space and time.

For example, there is one element which must always tend to oligarchy--or rather to despotism; I mean the element of hurry. If the house has caught fire a man must ring up the fire engines; a committee cannot ring them up. If a camp is surprised by night somebody must give the order to fire; there is no time to vote it. It is solely a question of the physical limitations of time and space; not at all of any mental limitations in the mass of men commanded. If all the people in the house were men of destiny it would still be better that they should not all talk into the telephone at once; nay, it would be better that the silliest man of all should speak uninterrupted. If an army actually consisted of nothing but Hanibals and Napoleons, it would still be better in the case of a surprise that they should not all give orders together. Nay, it would be better if the stupidest of them all gave the orders. Thus, we see that merely military subordination, so far from resting on the inequality of men, actually rests on the equality of men. Discipline does not involve the Carlylean notion that somebody is always right when everybody is wrong, and that we must discover and crown that somebody. On the contrary, discipline means that in certain frightfully rapid circumstances, one can trust anybody so long as he is not everybody. The military spirit does not mean (as Carlyle fancied) obeying the strongest and wisest man. On the contrary, the military spirit means, if anything, obeying the weakest and stupidest man, obeying him merely because he is a man, and not a thousand men. Submission to a weak man is discipline. Submission to a strong man is only servility.

Now it can be easily shown that the thing we call aristocracy in Europe is not in its origin and spirit an aristocracy at all. It is not a system of spiritual degrees and distinctions like, for example, the caste system of India, or even like the old Greek distinction between free men and slaves. It is simply the remains of a military organization, framed partly to sustain the sinking Roman Empire, partly to break and avenge the awful onslaught of Islam. The word Duke simply means Colonel, just as the word Emperor simply means Commander-in-Chief. The whole story is told in the single title of Counts of the Holy Roman Empire, which merely means officers in the European army against the contemporary Yellow Peril. Now in an army nobody ever dreams of supposing that difference of rank represents a difference of moral reality. Nobody ever says about a regiment, "Your Major is very humorous and energetic; your Colonel, of course, must be even more humorous and yet more energetic." No one ever says, in reporting a mess-room conversation, "Lieutenant Jones was very witty, but was naturally inferior to Captain Smith." The essence of an army is the idea of official inequality, founded on unofficial equality. The Colonel is not obeyed because he is the best man, but because he is the Colonel. Such was probably the spirit of the system of dukes and counts when it first arose out of the military spirit and military necessities of Rome. With the decline of those necessities it has gradually ceased to have meaning as a military organization, and become honeycombed with unclean plutocracy. Even now it is not a spiritual aristocracy--it is not so bad as all that. It is simply an army without an enemy--billeted upon the people.

Man, therefore, has a specialist as well as comrade-like aspect; and the case of militarism is not the only case of such specialist submission. The tinker and tailor, as well as the soldier and sailor, require a certain rigidity of rapidity of action: at least, if the tinker is not organized that is largely why he does not tink on any large scale. The tinker and tailor often represent the two nomadic races in Europe: the Gipsy and the Jew; but the Jew alone has influence because he alone accepts some sort of discipline. Man, we say, has two sides, the specialist side where he must have subordination, and the social side where he must have equality. There is a truth in the saying that ten tailors go to make a man; but we must remember also that ten Poets Laureate or ten Astronomers Royal go to make a man, too. Ten million tradesmen go to make Man himself; but humanity consists of tradesmen when they are not talking shop. Now the peculiar peril of our time, which I call for argument's sake Imperialism or Caesarism, is the complete eclipse of comradeship and equality by specialism and domination.

There are only two kinds of social structure conceivable--personal government and impersonal government. If my anarchic friends will not have rules--they will have rulers. Preferring personal government, with its tact and flexibility, is called Royalism. Preferring impersonal government, with its dogmas and definitions, is called Republicanism. Objecting broadmindedly both to kings and creeds is called Bosh; at least, I know no more philosophic word for it. You can be guided by the shrewdness or presence of mind of one ruler, or by the equality and ascertained justice of one rule; but you must have one or the other, or you are not a nation, but a nasty mess. Now men in their aspect of equality and debate adore the idea of rules; they develop and complicate them greatly to excess. A man finds far more regulations and definitions in his club, where there are rules, than in his home, where there is a ruler. A deliberate assembly, the House of Commons, for instance, carries this mummery to the point of a methodical madness. The whole system is stiff with rigid unreason; like the Royal Court in Lewis Carroll. You would think the Speaker would speak; therefore he is mostly silent. You would think a man would take off his hat to stop and put it on to go away; therefore he takes off his hat to walk out and puts it on to stop in. Names are forbidden, and a man must call his own father "my right honorable friend the member for West Birmingham." These are, perhaps, fantasies of decay: but fundamentally they answer a masculine appetite. Men feel that rules, even if irrational, are universal; men feel that law is equal, even when it is not equitable. There is a wild fairness in the thing--as there is in tossing up.

Again, it is gravely unfortunate that when critics do attack such cases as the Commons it is always on the points (perhaps the few points) where the Commons are right. They denounce the House as the Talking-Shop, and complain that it wastes time in wordy mazes. Now this is just one respect in which the Commons are actually like the Common People. If they love leisure and long debate, it is because all men love it; that they really represent England. There the Parliament does approach to the virile virtues of the pothouse.

The real truth is that adumbrated in the introductory section when we spoke of the sense of home and property, as now we speak of the sense of counsel and community. All men do naturally love the idea of leisure, laughter, loud and equal argument; but there stands a specter in our hall. We are conscious of the towering modern challenge that is called specialism or cut-throat competition--Business. Business will have nothing to do with leisure; business will have no truck with comradeship; business will pretend to no patience with all the legal fictions and fantastic handicaps by which comradeship protects its egalitarian ideal. The modern millionaire, when engaged in the agreeable and typical task of sacking his own father, will certainly not refer to him as the right honorable clerk from the Laburnum Road, Brixton. Therefore there has arisen in modern life a literary fashion devoting itself to the romance of business, to great demigods of greed and to fairyland of finance. This popular philosophy is utterly despotic and anti-democratic; this fashion is the flower of that Caesarism against which I am concerned to protest. The ideal millionaire is strong in the possession of a brain of steel. The fact that the real millionaire is rather more often strong in the possession of a head of wood, does not alter the spirit and trend of the idolatry. The essential argument is "Specialists must be despots; men must be specialists. You cannot have equality in a soap factory; so you cannot have it anywhere. You cannot have comradeship in a wheat corner; so you cannot have it at all. We must have commercial civilization; therefore we must destroy democracy." I know that plutocrats have seldom sufficient fancy to soar to such examples as soap or wheat. They generally confine themselves, with fine freshness of mind, to a comparison between the state and a ship. One anti-democratic writer remarked that he would not like to sail in a vessel in which the cabin-boy had an equal vote with the captain. It might easily be urged in answer that many a ship (the Victoria, for instance) was sunk because an admiral gave an order which a cabin-boy could see was wrong. But this is a debating reply; the essential fallacy is both deeper and simpler. The elementary fact is that we were all born in a state; we were not all born on a ship; like some of our great British bankers. A ship still remains a specialist experiment, like a diving-bell or a flying ship: in such peculiar perils the need for promptitude constitutes the need for autocracy. But we live and die in the vessel of the state; and if we cannot find freedom camaraderie and the popular element in the state, we cannot find it at all. And the modern doctrine of commercial despotism means that we shall not find it at all. Our specialist trades in their highly civilized state cannot (it says) be run without the whole brutal business of bossing and sacking, "too old at forty" and all the rest of the filth. And they must be run, and therefore we call on Caesar. Nobody but the Superman could descend to do such dirty work.

Now (to reiterate my title) this is what is wrong. This is the huge modern heresy of altering the human soul to fit its conditions, instead of altering human conditions to fit the human soul. If soap boiling is really inconsistent with brotherhood, so much the worst for soap-boiling, not for brotherhood. If civilization really cannot get on with democracy, so much the worse for civilization, not for democracy. Certainly, it would be far better to go back to village communes, if they really are communes. Certainly, it would be better to do without soap rather than to do without society. Certainly, we would sacrifice all our wires, wheels, systems, specialties, physical science and frenzied finance for one half-hour of happiness such as has often come to us with comrades in a common tavern. I do not say the sacrifice will be necessary; I only say it will be easy.

What's Wrong with the World

Part Three. Feminism, Or The Mistake About Woman

I. The Unmilitary Suffragette

It will be better to adopt in this chapter the same process that appeared a piece of mental justice in the last. My general opinions on the feminine question are such as many suffragists would warmly approve; and it would be easy to state them without any open reference to the current controversy. But just as it seemed more decent to say first that I was not in favor of Imperialism even in its practical and popular sense, so it seems more decent to say the same of Female Suffrage, in its practical and popular sense. In other words, it is only fair to state, however hurriedly, the superficial objection to the Suffragettes before we go on to the really subtle questions behind the Suffrage.

Well, to get this honest but unpleasant business over, the objection to the Suffragettes is not that they are Militant Suffragettes. On the contrary, it is that they are not militant enough. A revolution is a military thing; it has all the military virtues; one of which is that it comes to an end. Two parties fight with deadly weapons, but under certain rules of arbitrary honor; the party that wins becomes the government and proceeds to govern. The aim of civil war, like the aim of all war, is peace. Now the Suffragettes cannot raise civil war in this soldierly and decisive sense; first, because they are women; and, secondly, because they are very few women. But they can raise something else; which is altogether another pair of shoes. They do not create revolution; what they do create is anarchy; and the difference between these is not a question of violence, but a question of fruitfulness and finality. Revolution of its nature produces government; anarchy only produces more anarchy. Men may have what opinions they please about the beheading of King Charles or King Louis, but they cannot deny that Bradshaw and Cromwell ruled, that Carnot and Napoleon governed. Someone conquered; something occurred. You can only knock off the King's head once. But you can knock off the King's hat any number of times. Destruction is finite, obstruction is infinite: so long as rebellion takes the form of mere disorder (instead of an attempt to enforce a new order) there is no logical end to it; it can feed on itself and renew itself forever. If Napoleon had not wanted to be a Consul, but only wanted to be a nuisance, he could, possibly, have prevented any government arising successfully out of the Revolution. But such a proceeding would not have deserved the dignified name of rebellion.

It is exactly this unmilitant quality in the Suffragettes that makes their superficial problem. The problem is that their action has none of the advantages of ultimate violence; it does not afford a test. War is a dreadful thing; but it does prove two points sharply and unanswerably--numbers, and an unnatural valor. One does discover the two urgent matters; how many rebels there are alive, and how many are ready to be dead. But a tiny minority, even an interested minority, may maintain mere disorder forever. There is also, of course, in the case of these women, the further falsity that is introduced by their sex. It is false to state the matter as a mere brutal question of strength. If his muscles give a man a vote, then his horse ought to have two votes and his elephant five votes. The truth is more subtle than that; it is that bodily outbreak is a man's instinctive weapon, like the hoofs to the horse or the tusks to the elephant. All riot is a threat of war; but the woman is brandishing a weapon she can never use. There are many weapons that she could and does use. If (for example) all the women nagged for a vote they would get it in a month. But there again, one must remember, it would be necessary to get all the women to nag. And that brings us to the end of the political surface of the matter. The working objection to the Suffragette philosophy is simply that overmastering millions of women do not agree with it. I am aware that some maintain that women ought to have votes whether the majority wants them or not; but this is surely a strange and childish case of setting up formal democracy to the destruction of actual democracy. What should the mass of women decide if they do not decide their general place in the State? These people practically say that females may vote about everything except about Female Suffrage.

But having again cleared my conscience of my merely political and possibly unpopular opinion, I will again cast back and try to treat the matter in a slower and more sympathetic style; attempt to trace the real roots of woman's position in the western state, and the causes of our existing traditions or perhaps prejudices upon the point. And for this purpose it is again necessary to travel far from the modern topic, the mere Suffragette of today, and to go back to subjects which, though much more old, are, I think, considerably more fresh.

II. The Universal Stick

Cast your eye round the room in which you sit, and select some three or four things that have been with man almost since his beginning; which at least we hear of early in the centuries and often among the tribes. Let me suppose that you see a knife on the table, a stick in the corner, or a fire on the hearth. About each of these you will notice one speciality; that not one of them is special. Each of these ancestral things is a universal thing; made to supply many different needs; and while tottering pedants nose about to find the cause and origin of some old custom, the truth is that it had fifty causes or a hundred origins. The knife is meant to cut wood, to cut cheese, to cut pencils, to cut throats; for a myriad ingenious or innocent human objects. The stick is meant partly to hold a man up, partly to knock a man down; partly to point with like a finger-post, partly to balance with like a balancing pole, partly to trifle with like a cigarette, partly to kill with like a club of a giant; it is a crutch and a cudgel; an elongated finger and an extra leg. The case is the same, of course, with the fire; about which the strangest modern views have arisen. A queer fancy seems to be current that a fire exists to warm people. It exists to warm people, to light their darkness, to raise their spirits, to toast their muffins, to air their rooms, to cook their chestnuts, to tell stories to their children, to make checkered shadows on their walls, to boil their hurried kettles, and to be the red heart of a man's house and that hearth for which, as the great heathens said, a man should die.

Now it is the great mark of our modernity that people are always proposing substitutes for these old things; and these substitutes always answer one purpose where the old thing answered ten. The modern man will wave a cigarette instead of a stick; he will cut his pencil with a little screwing pencil-sharpener instead of a knife; and he will even boldly offer to be warmed by hot water pipes instead of a fire. I have my doubts about pencil-sharpeners even for sharpening pencils; and about hot water pipes even for heat. But when we think of all those other requirements that these institutions answered, there opens before us the whole horrible harlequinade of our civilization. We see as in a vision a world where a man tries to cut his throat with a pencil-sharpener; where a man must learn single-stick with a cigarette; where a man must try to toast muffins at electric lamps, and see red and golden castles in the surface of hot water pipes.

The principle of which I speak can be seen everywhere in a comparison between the ancient and universal things and the modern and specialist things. The object of a theodolite is to lie level; the object of a stick is to swing loose at any angle; to whirl like the very wheel of liberty. The object of a lancet is to lance; when used for slashing, gashing, ripping, lopping off heads and limbs, it is a disappointing instrument. The object of an electric light is merely to light (a despicable modesty); and the object of an asbestos stove... I wonder what is the object of an asbestos stove? If a man found a coil of rope in a desert he could at least think of all the things that can be done with a coil of rope; and some of them might even be practical. He could tow a boat or lasso a horse. He could play cat's-cradle, or pick oakum. He could construct a rope-ladder for an eloping heiress, or cord her boxes for a travelling maiden aunt. He could learn to tie a bow, or he could hang himself. Far otherwise with the unfortunate traveller who should find a telephone in the desert. You can telephone with a telephone; you cannot do anything else with it. And though this is one of the wildest joys of life, it falls by one degree from its full delirium when there is nobody to answer you. The contention is, in brief, that you must pull up a hundred roots, and not one, before you uproot any of these hoary and simple expedients. It is only with great difficulty that a modern scientific sociologist can be got to see that any old method has a leg to stand on. But almost every old method has four or five legs to stand on. Almost all the old institutions are quadrupeds; and some of them are centipedes.

Consider these cases, old and new, and you will observe the operation of a general tendency. Everywhere there was one big thing that served six purposes; everywhere now there are six small things; or, rather (and there is the trouble), there are just five and a half. Nevertheless, we will not say that this separation and specialism is entirely useless or inexcusable. I have often thanked God for the telephone; I may any day thank God for the lancet; and there is none of these brilliant and narrow inventions (except, of course, the asbestos stove) which might not be at some moment necessary and lovely. But I do not think the most austere upholder of specialism will deny that there is in these old, many-sided institutions an element of unity and universality which may well be preserved in its due proportion and place. Spiritually, at least, it will be admitted that some all-round balance is needed to equalize the extravagance of experts. It would not be difficult to carry the parable of the knife and stick into higher regions. Religion, the immortal maiden, has been a maid-of-all-work as well as a servant of mankind. She provided men at once with the theoretic laws of an unalterable cosmos and also with the practical rules of the rapid and thrilling game of morality. She taught logic to the student and told fairy tales to the children; it was her business to confront the nameless gods whose fears are on all flesh, and also to see the streets were spotted with silver and scarlet, that there was a day for wearing ribbons or an hour for ringing bells. The large uses of religion have been broken up into lesser specialities, just as the uses of the hearth have been broken up into hot water pipes and electric bulbs. The romance of ritual and colored emblem has been taken over by that narrowest of all trades, modern art (the sort called art for art's sake), and men are in modern practice informed that they may use all symbols so long as they mean nothing by them. The romance of conscience has been dried up into the science of ethics; which may well be called decency for decency's sake, decency unborn of cosmic energies and barren of artistic flower. The cry to the dim gods, cut off from ethics and cosmology, has become mere Psychical Research. Everything has been sundered from everything else, and everything has grown cold. Soon we shall hear of specialists dividing the tune from the words of a song, on the ground that they spoil each other; and I did once meet a man who openly advocated the separation of almonds and raisins. This world is all one wild divorce court; nevertheless, there are many who still hear in their souls the thunder of authority of human habit; those whom Man hath joined let no man sunder.

This book must avoid religion, but there must (I say) be many, religious and irreligious, who will concede that this power of answering many purposes was a sort of strength which should not wholly die out of our lives. As a part of personal character, even the moderns will agree that many-sidedness is a merit and a merit that may easily be overlooked. This balance and universality has been the vision of many groups of men in many ages. It was the Liberal Education of Aristotle; the jack-of-all-trades artistry of Leonardo da Vinci and his friends; the august amateurishness of the Cavalier Person of Quality like Sir William Temple or the great Earl of Dorset. It has appeared in literature in our time in the most erratic and opposite shapes, set to almost inaudible music by Walter Pater and enunciated through a foghorn by Walt Whitman. But the great mass of men have always been unable to achieve this literal universality, because of the nature of their work in the world. Not, let it be noted, because of the existence of their work. Leonardo da Vinci must have worked pretty hard; on the other hand, many a government office clerk, village constable or elusive plumber may do (to all human appearance) no work at all, and yet show no signs of the Aristotelian universalism. What makes it difficult for the average man to be a universalist is that the average man has to be a specialist; he has not only to learn one trade, but to learn it so well as to uphold him in a more or less ruthless society. This is generally true of males from the first hunter to the last electrical engineer; each has not merely to act, but to excel. Nimrod has not only to be a mighty hunter before the Lord, but also a mighty hunter before the other hunters. The electrical engineer has to be a very electrical engineer, or he is outstripped by engineers yet more electrical. Those very miracles of the human mind on which the modern world prides itself, and rightly in the main, would be impossible without a certain concentration which disturbs the pure balance of reason more than does religious bigotry. No creed can be so limiting as that awful adjuration that the cobbler must not go beyond his last. So the largest and wildest shots of our world are but in one direction and with a defined trajectory: the gunner cannot go beyond his shot, and his shot so often falls short; the astronomer cannot go beyond his telescope and his telescope goes such a little way. All these are like men who have stood on the high peak of a mountain and seen the horizon like a single ring and who then descend down different paths towards different towns, traveling slow or fast. It is right; there must be people traveling to different towns; there must be specialists; but shall no one behold the horizon? Shall all mankind be specialist surgeons or peculiar plumbers; shall all humanity be monomaniac? Tradition has decided that only half of humanity shall be monomaniac. It has decided that in every home there shall be a tradesman and a Jack-of-all-trades. But it has also decided, among other things, that the Jack-of-all-trades shall be a Jill-of-all-trades. It has decided, rightly or wrongly, that this specialism and this universalism shall be divided between the sexes. Cleverness shall be left for men and wisdom for women. For cleverness kills wisdom; that is one of the few sad and certain things.

But for women this ideal of comprehensive capacity (or common-sense) must long ago have been washed away. It must have melted in the frightful furnaces of ambition and eager technicality. A man must be partly a one-idead man, because he is a one-weaponed man--and he is flung naked into the fight. The world's demand comes to him direct; to his wife indirectly. In short, he must (as the books on Success say) give "his best"; and what a small part of a man "his best" is! His second and third best are often much better. If he is the first violin he must fiddle for life; he must not remember that he is a fine fourth bagpipe, a fair fifteenth billiard-cue, a foil, a fountain pen, a hand at whist, a gun, and an image of God.

III. The Emancipation Of Domesticity

And it should be remarked in passing that this force upon a man to develop one feature has nothing to do with what is commonly called our competitive system, but would equally exist under any rationally conceivable kind of Collectivism. Unless the Socialists are frankly ready for a fall in the standard of violins, telescopes and electric lights, they must somehow create a moral demand on the individual that he shall keep up his present concentration on these things. It was only by men being in some degree specialist that there ever were any telescopes; they must certainly be in some degree specialist in order to keep them going. It is not by making a man a State wage-earner that you can prevent him thinking principally about the very difficult way he earns his wages. There is only one way to preserve in the world that high levity and that more leisurely outlook which fulfils the old vision of universalism. That is, to permit the existence of a partly protected half of humanity; a half which the harassing industrial demand troubles indeed, but only troubles indirectly. In other words, there must be in every center of humanity one human being upon a larger plan; one who does not "give her best," but gives her all.

Our old analogy of the fire remains the most workable one. The fire need not blaze like electricity nor boil like boiling water; its point is that it blazes more than water and warms more than light. The wife is like the fire, or to put things in their proper proportion, the fire is like the wife. Like the fire, the woman is expected to cook: not to excel in cooking, but to cook; to cook better than her husband who is earning the coke by lecturing on botany or breaking stones. Like the fire, the woman is expected to tell tales to the children, not original and artistic tales, but tales-- better tales than would probably be told by a first-class cook. Like the fire, the woman is expected to illuminate and ventilate, not by the most startling revelations or the wildest winds of thought, but better than a man can do it after breaking stones or lecturing. But she cannot be expected to endure anything like this universal duty if she is also to endure the direct cruelty of competitive or bureaucratic toil. Woman must be a cook, but not a competitive cook; a school mistress, but not a competitive schoolmistress; a house-decorator but not a competitive house-decorator; a dressmaker, but not a competitive dressmaker. She should have not one trade but twenty hobbies; she, unlike the man, may develop all her second bests. This is what has been really aimed at from the first in what is called the seclusion, or even the oppression, of women. Women were not kept at home in order to keep them narrow; on the contrary, they were kept at home in order to keep them broad. The world outside the home was one mass of narrowness, a maze of cramped paths, a madhouse of monomaniacs. It was only by partly limiting and protecting the woman that she was enabled to play at five or six professions and so come almost as near to God as the child when he plays at a hundred trades. But the woman's professions, unlike the child's, were all truly and almost terribly fruitful; so tragically real that nothing but her universality and balance prevented them being merely morbid. This is the substance of the contention I offer about the historic female position. I do not deny that women have been wronged and even tortured; but I doubt if they were ever tortured so much as they are tortured now by the absurd modern attempt to make them domestic empresses and competitive clerks at the same time. I do not deny that even under the old tradition women had a harder time than men; that is why we take off our hats. I do not deny that all these various female functions were exasperating; but I say that there was some aim and meaning in keeping them various. I do not pause even to deny that woman was a servant; but at least she was a general servant.

The shortest way of summarizing the position is to say that woman stands for the idea of Sanity; that intellectual home to which the mind must return after every excursion on extravagance. The mind that finds its way to wild places is the poet's; but the mind that never finds its way back is the lunatic's. There must in every machine be a part that moves and a part that stands still; there must be in everything that changes a part that is unchangeable. And many of the phenomena which moderns hastily condemn are really parts of this position of the woman as the center and pillar of health. Much of what is called her subservience, and even her pliability, is merely the subservience and pliability of a universal remedy; she varies as medicines vary, with the disease. She has to be an optimist to the morbid husband, a salutary pessimist to the happy-go-lucky husband. She has to prevent the Quixote from being put upon, and the bully from putting upon others. The French King wrote--

"Toujours femme varie Bien fol qui s'y fie,"

but the truth is that woman always varies, and that is exactly why we always trust her. To correct every adventure and extravagance with its antidote in common-sense is not (as the moderns seem to think) to be in the position of a spy or a slave. It is to be in the position of Aristotle or (at the lowest) Herbert Spencer, to be a universal morality, a complete system of thought. The slave flatters; the complete moralist rebukes. It is, in short, to be a Trimmer in the true sense of that honorable term; which for some reason or other is always used in a sense exactly opposite to its own. It seems really to be supposed that a Trimmer means a cowardly person who always goes over to the stronger side. It really means a highly chivalrous person who always goes over to the weaker side; like one who trims a boat by sitting where there are few people seated. Woman is a trimmer; and it is a generous, dangerous and romantic trade.

The final fact which fixes this is a sufficiently plain one. Supposing it to be conceded that humanity has acted at least not unnaturally in dividing itself into two halves, respectively typifying the ideals of special talent and of general sanity (since they are genuinely difficult to combine completely in one mind), it is not difficult to see why the line of cleavage has followed the line of sex, or why the female became the emblem of the universal and the male of the special and superior. Two gigantic facts of nature fixed it thus: first, that the woman who frequently fulfilled her functions literally could not be specially prominent in experiment and adventure; and second, that the same natural operation surrounded her with very young children, who require to be taught not so much anything as everything. Babies need not to be taught a trade, but to be introduced to a world. To put the matter shortly, woman is generally shut up in a house with a human being at the time when he asks all the questions that there are, and some that there aren't. It would be odd if she retained any of the narrowness of a specialist. Now if anyone says that this duty of general enlightenment (even when freed from modern rules and hours, and exercised more spontaneously by a more protected person) is in itself too exacting and oppressive, I can understand the view. I can only answer that our race has thought it worth while to cast this burden on women in order to keep common-sense in the world. But when people begin to talk about this domestic duty as not merely difficult but trivial and dreary, I simply give up the question. For I cannot with the utmost energy of imagination conceive what they mean. When domesticity, for instance, is called drudgery, all the difficulty arises from a double meaning in the word. If drudgery only means dreadfully hard work, I admit the woman drudges in the home, as a man might drudge at the Cathedral of Amiens or drudge behind a gun at Trafalgar. But if it means that the hard work is more heavy because it is trifling, colorless and of small import to the soul, then as I say, I give it up; I do not know what the words mean. To be Queen Elizabeth within a definite area, deciding sales, banquets, labors and holidays; to be Whiteley within a certain area, providing toys, boots, sheets, cakes and books, to be Aristotle within a certain area, teaching morals, manners, theology, and hygiene; I can understand how this might exhaust the mind, but I cannot imagine how it could narrow it. How can it be a large career to tell other people's children about the Rule of Three, and a small career to tell one's own children about the universe? How can it be broad to be the same thing to everyone, and narrow to be everything to someone? No; a woman's function is laborious, but because it is gigantic, not because it is minute. I will pity Mrs. Jones for the hugeness of her task; I will never pity her for its smallness.

But though the essential of the woman's task is universality, this does not, of course, prevent her from having one or two severe though largely wholesome prejudices. She has, on the whole, been more conscious than man that she is only one half of humanity; but she has expressed it (if one may say so of a lady) by getting her teeth into the two or three things which she thinks she stands for. I would observe here in parenthesis that much of the recent official trouble about women has arisen from the fact that they transfer to things of doubt and reason that sacred stubbornness only proper to the primary things which a woman was set to guard. One's own children, one's own altar, ought to be a matter of principle--or if you like, a matter of prejudice. On the other hand, who wrote Junius's Letters ought not to be a principle or a prejudice, it ought to be a matter of free and almost indifferent inquiry. But take an energetic modern girl secretary to a league to show that George III wrote Junius, and in three months she will believe it, too, out of mere loyalty to her employers. Modern women defend their office with all the fierceness of domesticity. They fight for desk and typewriter as for hearth and home, and develop a sort of wolfish wifehood on behalf of the invisible head of the firm. That is why they do office work so well; and that is why they ought not to do it.

IV. The Romance Of Thrift

The larger part of womankind, however, have had to fight for things slightly more intoxicating to the eye than the desk or the typewriter; and it cannot be denied that in defending these, women have developed the quality called prejudice to a powerful and even menacing degree. But these prejudices will always be found to fortify the main position of the woman, that she is to remain a general overseer, an autocrat within small compass but on all sides. On the one or two points on which she really misunderstands the man's position, it is almost entirely in order to preserve her own. The two points on which woman, actually and of herself, is most tenacious may be roughly summarized as the ideal of thrift and the ideal of dignity.

Unfortunately for this book it is written by a male, and these two qualities, if not hateful to a man, are at least hateful in a man. But if we are to settle the sex question at all fairly, all males must make an imaginative attempt to enter into the attitude of all good women toward these two things. The difficulty exists especially, perhaps, in the thing called thrift; we men have so much encouraged each other in throwing money right and left, that there has come at last to be a sort of chivalrous and poetical air about losing sixpence. But on a broader and more candid consideration the case scarcely stands so.

Thrift is the really romantic thing; economy is more romantic than extravagance. Heaven knows I for one speak disinterestedly in the matter; for I cannot clearly remember saving a half-penny ever since I was born. But the thing is true; economy, properly understood, is the more poetic. Thrift is poetic because it is creative; waste is unpoetic because it is waste. It is prosaic to throw money away, because it is prosaic to throw anything away; it is negative; it is a confession of indifference, that is, it is a confession of failure. The most prosaic thing about the house is the dustbin, and the one great objection to the new fastidious and aesthetic homestead is simply that in such a moral menage the dustbin must be bigger than the house. If a man could undertake to make use of all things in his dustbin he would be a broader genius than Shakespeare. When science began to use by-products; when science found that colors could be made out of coaltar, she made her greatest and perhaps her only claim on the real respect of the human soul. Now the aim of the good woman is to use the by-products, or, in other words, to rummage in the dustbin.

A man can only fully comprehend it if he thinks of some sudden joke or expedient got up with such materials as may be found in a private house on a rainy day. A man's definite daily work is generally run with such rigid convenience of modern science that thrift, the picking up of potential helps here and there, has almost become unmeaning to him. He comes across it most (as I say) when he is playing some game within four walls; when in charades, a hearthrug will just do for a fur coat, or a tea-cozy just do for a cocked hat; when a toy theater needs timber and cardboard, and the house has just enough firewood and just enough bandboxes. This is the man's occasional glimpse and pleasing parody of thrift. But many a good housekeeper plays the same game every day with ends of cheese and scraps of silk, not because she is mean, but on the contrary, because she is magnanimous; because she wishes her creative mercy to be over all her works, that not one sardine should be destroyed, or cast as rubbish to the void, when she has made the pile complete.

The modern world must somehow be made to understand (in theology and other things) that a view may be vast, broad, universal, liberal and yet come into conflict with another view that is vast, broad, universal and liberal also. There is never a war between two sects, but only between two universal Catholic Churches. The only possible collision is the collision of one cosmos with another. So in a smaller way it must be first made clear that this female economic ideal is a part of that female variety of outlook and all-round art of life which we have already attributed to the sex: thrift is not a small or timid or provincial thing; it is part of that great idea of the woman watching on all sides out of all the windows of the soul and being answerable for everything. For in the average human house there is one hole by which money comes in and a hundred by which it goes out; man has to do with the one hole, woman with the hundred. But though the very stinginess of a woman is a part of her spiritual breadth, it is none the less true that it brings her into conflict with the special kind of spiritual breadth that belongs to the males of the tribe. It brings her into conflict with that shapeless cataract of Comradeship, of chaotic feasting and deafening debate, which we noted in the last section. The very touch of the eternal in the two sexual tastes brings them the more into antagonism; for one stands for a universal vigilance and the other for an almost infinite output. Partly through the nature of his moral weakness, and partly through the nature of his physical strength, the male is normally prone to expand things into a sort of eternity; he always thinks of a dinner party as lasting all night; and he always thinks of a night as lasting forever. When the working women in the poor districts come to the doors of the public houses and try to get their husbands home, simple minded "social workers" always imagine that every husband is a tragic drunkard and every wife a broken-hearted saint. It never occurs to them that the poor woman is only doing under coarser conventions exactly what every fashionable hostess does when she tries to get the men from arguing over the cigars to come and gossip over the teacups. These women are not exasperated merely at the amount of money that is wasted in beer; they are exasperated also at the amount of time that is wasted in talk. It is not merely what goeth into the mouth but what cometh out the mouth that, in their opinion, defileth a man. They will raise against an argument (like their sisters of all ranks) the ridiculous objection that nobody is convinced by it; as if a man wanted to make a body-slave of anybody with whom he had played single-stick. But the real female prejudice on this point is not without a basis; the real feeling is this, that the most masculine pleasures have a quality of the ephemeral. A duchess may ruin a duke for a diamond necklace; but there is the necklace. A coster may ruin his wife for a pot of beer; and where is the beer? The duchess quarrels with another duchess in order to crush her, to produce a result; the coster does not argue with another coster in order to convince him, but in order to enjoy at once the sound of his own voice, the clearness of his own opinions and the sense of masculine society. There is this element of a fine fruitlessness about the male enjoyments; wine is poured into a bottomless bucket; thought plunges into a bottomless abyss. All this has set woman against the

Public House--that is, against the Parliament House. She is there to prevent waste; and the "pub" and the parliament are the very palaces of waste. In the upper classes the "pub" is called the club, but that makes no more difference to the reason than it does to the rhyme. High and low, the woman's objection to the Public House is perfectly definite and rational, it is that the Public House wastes the energies that could be used on the private house.

As it is about feminine thrift against masculine waste, so it is about feminine dignity against masculine rowdiness. The woman has a fixed and very well-founded idea that if she does not insist on good manners nobody else will. Babies are not always strong on the point of dignity, and grown-up men are quite unpresentable. It is true that there are many very polite men, but none that I ever heard of who were not either fascinating women or obeying them. But indeed the female ideal of dignity, like the female ideal of thrift, lies deeper and may easily be misunderstood. It rests ultimately on a strong idea of spiritual isolation; the same that makes women religious. They do not like being melted down; they dislike and avoid the mob. That anonymous quality we have remarked in the club conversation would be common impertinence in a case of ladies. I remember an artistic and eager lady asking me in her grand green drawing-room whether I believed in comradeship between the sexes, and why not. I was driven back on offering the obvious and sincere answer "Because if I were to treat you for two minutes like a comrade you would turn me out of the house." The only certain rule on this subject is always to deal with woman and never with women. "Women" is a profligate word; I have used it repeatedly in this chapter; but it always has a blackguard sound. It smells of oriental cynicism and hedonism. Every woman is a captive queen. But every crowd of women is only a harem broken loose.

I am not expressing my own views here, but those of nearly all the women I have known. It is quite unfair to say that a woman hates other women individually; but I think it would be quite true to say that she detests them in a confused heap. And this is not because she despises her own sex, but because she respects it; and respects especially that sanctity and separation of each item which is represented in manners by the idea of dignity and in morals by the idea of chastity.

V. The Coldness Of Chloe

We hear much of the human error which accepts what is sham and what is real. But it is worth while to remember that with unfamiliar things we often mistake what is real for what is sham. It is true that a very young man may think the wig of an actress is her hair. But it is equally true that a child yet younger may call the hair of a negro his wig. Just because the woolly savage is remote and barbaric he seems to be unnaturally neat and tidy. Everyone must have noticed the same thing in the fixed and almost offensive color of all unfamiliar things, tropic birds and tropic blossoms. Tropic birds look like staring toys out of a toy-shop. Tropic flowers simply look like artificial flowers, like things cut out of wax. This is a deep matter, and, I think, not unconnected with divinity; but anyhow it is the truth that when we see things for the first time we feel instantly that they are fictive creations; we feel the finger of God. It is only when we are thoroughly used to them and our five wits are wearied, that we see them as wild and objectless; like the shapeless tree-tops or the shifting cloud. It is the design in Nature that strikes us first; the sense of the crosses and confusions in that design only comes afterwards through experience and an almost eerie monotony. If a man saw the stars abruptly by accident he would think them as festive and as artificial as a firework. We talk of the folly of painting the lily; but if we saw the lily without warning we should think that it was painted. We talk of the devil not being so black as he is painted; but that very phrase is a testimony to the kinship between what is called vivid and what is called artificial. If the modern sage had only one glimpse of grass and sky, he would say that grass was not as green as it was painted; that sky was not as blue as it was painted. If one could see the whole universe suddenly, it would look like a bright-colored toy, just as the South American hornbill looks like a bright-colored toy. And so they are--both of them, I mean.

But it was not with this aspect of the startling air of artifice about all strange objects that I meant to deal. I mean merely, as a guide to history, that we should not be surprised if things wrought in fashions remote from ours seem artificial; we should convince ourselves that nine times out of ten these things are nakedly and almost indecently honest. You will hear men talk of the frosted classicism of Corneille or of the powdered pomposities of the eighteenth century, but all these phrases are very superficial. There never was an artificial epoch. There never was an age of reason. Men were always men and women women: and their two generous appetites always were the expression of passion and the telling of truth. We can see something stiff and quaint in their mode of expression, just as our descendants will see something stiff and quaint in our coarsest slum sketch or our most naked pathological play. But men have never talked about anything but important things; and the next force in femininity which we have to consider can be considered best perhaps in some dusty old volume of verses by a person of quality.

The eighteenth century is spoken of as the period of artificiality, in externals at least; but, indeed, there may be two words about that. In modern speech one uses artificiality as meaning indefinitely a sort of deceit; and the eighteenth century was far too artificial to deceive. It cultivated that completest art that does not conceal the art. Its fashions and costumes positively revealed nature by allowing artifice; as in that obvious instance of a barbering that frosted every head with the same silver. It would be fantastic to call this a quaint humility that concealed youth; but, at least, it was not one with the evil pride that conceals old age. Under the eighteenth century fashion people did not so much all pretend to be young, as all agree to be old. The same applies to the most odd and unnatural of their fashions; they were freakish, but they were not false. A lady may or may not be as red as she is painted, but plainly she was not so black as she was patched.

But I only introduce the reader into this atmosphere of the older and franker fictions that he may be induced to have patience for a moment with a certain element which is very common in the decoration and literature of that age and of the two centuries preceding it. It is necessary to mention it in such a connection because it is exactly one of those things that look as superficial as powder, and are really as rooted as hair.

In all the old flowery and pastoral love-songs, those of the seventeenth and eighteenth centuries especially, you will find a perpetual reproach against woman in the matter of her coldness; ceaseless and stale similes that compare her eyes to northern stars, her heart to ice, or her bosom to snow. Now most of us have always supposed these old and iterant phrases to be a mere pattern of dead words, a thing like a cold wall-paper. Yet I think those old cavalier poets who wrote about the coldness of Chloe had hold of a psychological truth missed in nearly all the realistic novels of today. Our psychological romancers perpetually represent wives as striking terror into their husbands by rolling on the floor, gnashing their teeth, throwing about the furniture or poisoning the coffee; all this upon some strange fixed theory that women are what they call emotional. But in truth the old and frigid form is much nearer to the vital fact. Most men if they spoke with any sincerity would agree that the most terrible quality in women, whether in friendship, courtship or marriage, was not so much being emotional as being unemotional.

There is an awful armor of ice which may be the legitimate protection of a more delicate organism; but whatever be the psychological explanation there can surely be no question of the fact. The instinctive cry of the female in anger is noli me tangere. I take this as the most obvious and at the same time the least hackneyed instance of a fundamental quality in the female tradition, which has tended in our time to be almost immeasurably misunderstood, both by the cant of moralists and the cant of immoralists. The proper name for the thing is modesty; but as we live in an age of prejudice and must not call things by their right names, we will yield to a more modern nomenclature and call it dignity. Whatever else it is, it is the thing which a thousand poets and a million lovers have called the coldness of Chloe. It is akin to the classical, and is at least the opposite of the grotesque. And since we are talking here chiefly in types and symbols, perhaps as good an embodiment as any of the idea may be found in the mere fact of a woman wearing a skirt. It is highly typical of the rabid plagiarism which now passes everywhere for emancipation, that a little while ago it was common for an "advanced" woman to claim the right to wear trousers; a right about as grotesque as the right to wear a false nose. Whether female liberty is much advanced by the act of wearing a skirt on each leg I do not know; perhaps Turkish women might offer some information on the point. But if the western woman walks about (as it were) trailing the curtains of the harem with her, it is quite certain that the woven mansion is meant for a perambulating palace, not for a perambulating prison. It is quite certain that the skirt means female dignity, not female submission; it can be proved by the simplest of all tests. No ruler would deliberately dress up in the recognized fetters of a slave; no judge would appear covered with broad arrows. But when men wish to be safely impressive, as judges, priests or kings, they do wear skirts, the long, trailing robes of female dignity The whole world is under petticoat government; for even men wear petticoats when they wish to govern.

VI. The Pedant And The Savage

We say then that the female holds up with two strong arms these two pillars of civilization; we say also that she could do neither, but for her position; her curious position of private omnipotence, universality on a small scale. The first element is thrift; not the destructive thrift of the miser, but the creative thrift of the peasant; the second element is dignity, which is but the expression of sacred personality and privacy. Now I know the question that will be abruptly and automatically asked by all that know the dull tricks and turns of the modern sexual quarrel. The advanced person will at once begin to argue about whether these instincts are inherent and inevitable in woman or whether they are merely prejudices produced by her history and education. Now I do not propose to discuss whether woman could now be educated out of her habits touching thrift and dignity; and that for two excellent reasons. First it is a question which cannot conceivably ever find any answer: that is why modern people are so fond of it. From the nature of the case it is obviously impossible to decide whether any of the peculiarities of civilized man have been strictly necessary to his civilization. It is not self-evident (for instance), that even the habit of standing upright was the only path of human progress. There might have been a quadrupedal civilization, in which a city gentleman put on four boots to go to the city every morning. Or there might have been a reptilian civilization, in which he rolled up to the office on his stomach; it is impossible to say that intelligence might not have developed in such creatures. All we can say is that man as he is walks upright; and that woman is something almost more upright than uprightness.

And the second point is this: that upon the whole we rather prefer women (nay, even men) to walk upright; so we do not waste much of our noble lives in inventing any other way for them to walk. In short, my second reason for not speculating upon whether woman might get rid of these peculiarities, is that I do not want her to get rid of them; nor does she. I will not exhaust my intelligence by inventing ways in which mankind might unlearn the violin or forget how to ride horses; and the art of domesticity seems to me as special and as valuable as all the ancient arts of our race. Nor do I propose to enter at all into those formless and floundering speculations about how woman was or is regarded in the primitive times that we cannot remember, or in the savage countries which we cannot understand. Even if these people segregated their women for low or barbaric reasons it would not make our reasons barbaric; and I am haunted with a tenacious suspicion that these people's feelings were really, under other forms, very much the same as ours. Some impatient trader, some superficial missionary, walks across an island and sees the squaw digging in the fields while the man is playing a flute; and immediately says that the man is a mere lord of creation and the woman a mere serf. He does not remember that he might see the same thing in half the back gardens in Brixton, merely because women are at once more conscientious and more impatient, while men are at once more quiescent and more greedy for pleasure. It may often be in Hawaii simply as it is in Hoxton. That is, the woman does not work because the man tells her to work and she obeys. On the contrary, the woman works because she has told the man to work and he hasn't obeyed. I do not affirm that this is the whole truth, but I do affirm that we have too little comprehension of the souls of savages to know how far it is untrue. It is the same with the relations of our hasty and surface science, with the problem of sexual dignity and modesty. Professors find all over the world fragmentary ceremonies in which the bride affects some sort of reluctance, hides from her husband, or runs away from him. The professor then pompously proclaims that this is a survival of Marriage by Capture. I wonder he never says that the veil thrown over the bride is really a net. I gravely doubt whether women ever were married by capture I think they pretended to be; as they do still.

It is equally obvious that these two necessary sanctities of thrift and dignity are bound to come into collision with the wordiness, the wastefulness, and the perpetual pleasure-seeking of masculine companionship. Wise women allow for the thing; foolish women try to crush it; but all women try to counteract it, and they do well. In many a home all round us at this moment, we know that the nursery rhyme is reversed. The queen is in the counting-house, counting out the money. The king is in the parlor, eating bread and honey. But it must be strictly understood that the king has captured the honey in some heroic wars. The quarrel can be found in moldering Gothic carvings and in crabbed Greek manuscripts. In every age, in every land, in every tribe and village, has been waged the great sexual war between the Private House and the Public House. I have seen a collection of mediaeval English poems, divided into sections such as "Religious Carols," "Drinking Songs," and so on; and the section headed, "Poems of Domestic Life" consisted entirely (literally, entirely) of the complaints of husbands who were bullied by their wives. Though the English was archaic, the words were in many cases precisely the same as those which I have heard in the streets and public houses of Battersea, protests on behalf of an extension of time and talk, protests against the nervous impatience and the devouring utilitarianism of the female. Such, I say, is the quarrel; it can never be anything but a quarrel; but the aim of all morals and all society is to keep it a lovers' quarrel.

VII. The Modern Surrender Of Woman

But in this corner called England, at this end of the century, there has happened a strange and startling thing. Openly and to all appearance, this ancestral conflict has silently and abruptly ended; one of the two sexes has suddenly surrendered to the other. By the beginning of the twentieth century, within the last few years, the woman has in public surrendered to the man. She has seriously and officially owned that the man has been right all along; that the public house (or Parliament) is really more important than the private house; that politics are not (as woman had always maintained) an excuse for pots of beer, but are a sacred solemnity to which new female worshipers may kneel; that the talkative patriots in the tavern are not only admirable but enviable; that talk is not a waste of time, and therefore (as a consequence, surely) that taverns are not a waste of money. All we men had grown used to our wives and mothers, and grandmothers, and great aunts all pouring a chorus of contempt upon our hobbies of sport, drink and party politics. And now comes Miss Pankhurst with tears in her eyes, owning that all the women were wrong and all the men were right; humbly imploring to be admitted into so much as an outer court, from which she may catch a glimpse of those masculine merits which her erring sisters had so thoughtlessly scorned.

Now this development naturally perturbs and even paralyzes us. Males, like females, in the course of that old fight between the public and private house, had indulged in overstatement and extravagance, feeling that they must keep up their end of the see-saw. We told our wives that Parliament had sat late on most essential business; but it never crossed our minds that our wives would believe it. We said that everyone must have a vote in the country; similarly our wives said that no one must have a pipe in the drawing room. In both cases the idea was the same. "It does not matter much, but if you let those things slide there is chaos." We said that Lord Huggins or Mr. Buggins was absolutely necessary to the country. We knew quite well that nothing is necessary to the country except that the men should be men and the women women. We knew this; we thought the women knew it even more clearly; and we thought the women would say it. Suddenly, without warning, the women have begun to say all the nonsense that we ourselves hardly believed when we said it. The solemnity of politics; the necessity of votes; the necessity of Huggins; the necessity of Buggins; all these flow in a pellucid stream from the lips of all the suffragette speakers. I suppose in every fight, however old, one has a vague aspiration to conquer; but we never wanted to conquer women so completely as this. We only expected that they might leave us a little more margin for our nonsense; we never expected that they would accept it seriously as sense. Therefore I am all at sea about the existing situation; I scarcely know whether to be relieved or enraged by this substitution of the feeble platform lecture for the forcible curtain-lecture. I am lost without the trenchant and candid Mrs. Caudle. I really do not know what to do with the prostrate and penitent Miss Pankhurst. This surrender of the modern woman has taken us all so much by surprise that it is desirable to pause a moment, and collect our wits about what she is really saying.

As I have already remarked, there is one very simple answer to all this; these are not the modern women, but about one in two thousand of the modern women. This fact is important to a democrat; but it is of very little importance to the typically modern mind. Both the characteristic modern parties believed in a government by the few; the only difference is whether it is the Conservative few or Progressive few. It might be put, somewhat coarsely perhaps, by saying that one believes in any minority that is rich and the other in any minority that is mad. But in this state of things the democratic argument obviously falls out for the moment; and we are bound to take the prominent minority, merely because it is prominent. Let us eliminate altogether from our minds the thousands of women who detest this cause, and the millions of women who have hardly heard of it. Let us concede that the English people itself is not and will not be for a very long time within the sphere of practical politics. Let us confine ourselves to saying that these particular women want a vote and to asking themselves what a vote is. If we ask these ladies ourselves what a vote is, we shall get a very vague reply. It is the only question, as a rule, for which they are not prepared. For the truth is that they go mainly by precedent; by the mere fact that men have votes already. So far from being a mutinous movement, it is really a very Conservative one; it is in the narrowest rut of the British Constitution. Let us take a little wider and freer sweep of thought and ask ourselves what is the ultimate point and meaning of this odd business called voting.

VIII. The Brand Of The Fleur-De-Lis

Seemingly from the dawn of man all nations have had governments; and all nations have been ashamed of them. Nothing is more openly fallacious than to fancy that in ruder or simpler ages ruling, judging and punishing appeared perfectly innocent and dignified. These things were always regarded as the penalties of the Fall; as part of the humiliation of mankind, as bad in themselves. That the king can do no wrong was never anything but a legal fiction; and it is a legal fiction still. The doctrine of Divine Right was not a piece of idealism, but rather a piece of realism, a practical way of ruling amid the ruin of humanity; a very pragmatist piece of faith. The religious basis of government was not so much that people put their trust in princes, as that they did not put their trust in any child of man. It was so with all the ugly institutions which disfigure human history. Torture and slavery were never talked of as good things; they were always talked of as necessary evils. A pagan spoke of one man owning ten slaves just as a modern business man speaks of one merchant sacking ten clerks: "It's very horrible; but how else can society be conducted?" A mediaeval scholastic regarded the possibility of a man being burned to death just as a modern business man regards the possibility of a man being starved to death: "It is a shocking torture; but can you organize a painless world?" It is possible that a future society may find a way of doing without the question by hunger as we have done without the question by fire. It is equally possible, for the matter of that, that a future society may reestablish legal torture with the whole apparatus of rack and fagot. The most modern of countries, America, has introduced with a vague savor of science, a method which it calls "the third degree." This is simply the extortion of secrets by nervous fatigue; which is surely uncommonly close to their extortion by bodily pain. And this is legal and scientific in America. Amateur ordinary America, of course, simply burns people alive in broad daylight, as they did in the Reformation Wars. But though some punishments are more inhuman than others there is no such thing as humane punishment.

As long as nineteen men claim the right in any sense or shape to take hold of the twentieth man and make him even mildly uncomfortable, so long the whole proceeding must be a humiliating one for all concerned. And the proof of how poignantly men have always felt this lies in the fact that the headsman and the hangman, the jailors and the torturers, were always regarded not merely with fear but with contempt; while all kinds of careless smiters, bankrupt knights and swashbucklers and outlaws, were regarded with indulgence or even admiration. To kill a man lawlessly was pardoned. To kill a man lawfully was unpardonable. The most bare-faced duelist might almost brandish his weapon. But the executioner was always masked.

This is the first essential element in government, coercion; a necessary but not a noble element. I may remark in passing that when people say that government rests on force they give an admirable instance of the foggy and muddled cynicism of modernity. Government does not rest on force. Government is force; it rests on consent or a conception of justice. A king or a community holding a certain thing to be abnormal, evil, uses the general strength to crush it out; the strength is his tool, but the belief is his only sanction. You might as well say that glass is the real reason for telescopes. But arising from whatever reason the act of government is coercive and is burdened with all the coarse and painful qualities of coercion. And if anyone asks what is the use of insisting on the ugliness of this task of state violence since all mankind is condemned to employ it, I have a simple answer to that. It would be useless to insist on it if all humanity were condemned to it. But it is not irrelevant to insist on its ugliness so long as half of humanity is kept out of it.

All government then is coercive; we happen to have created a government which is not only coercive; but collective. There are only two kinds of government, as I have already said, the despotic and the democratic. Aristocracy is not a government, it is a riot; that most effective kind of riot, a riot of the rich. The most intelligent apologists of aristocracy, sophists like Burke and Nietzsche, have never claimed for aristocracy any virtues but the virtues of a riot, the accidental virtues, courage, variety and adventure. There is no case anywhere of aristocracy having established a universal and applicable order, as despots and democracies have often done; as the last Caesars created the Roman law, as the last Jacobins created the Code Napoleon. With the first of these elementary forms of government, that of the king or chieftain, we are not in this matter of the sexes immediately concerned. We shall return to it later when we remark how differently mankind has dealt with female claims in the despotic as against the democratic field. But for the moment the essential point is that in self-governing countries this coercion of criminals is a collective coercion. The abnormal person is theoretically thumped by a million fists and kicked by a million feet. If a man is flogged we all flogged him; if a man is hanged, we all hanged him. That is the only possible meaning of democracy, which can give any meaning to the first two syllables and also to the last two. In this sense each citizen has the high responsibility of a rioter. Every statute is a declaration of war, to be backed by arms. Every tribunal is a revolutionary tribunal. In a republic all punishment is as sacred and solemn as lynching.

IX. Sincerity And The Gallows

When, therefore, it is said that the tradition against Female Suffrage keeps women out of activity, social influence and citizenship, let us a little more soberly and strictly ask ourselves what it actually does keep her out of. It does definitely keep her out of the collective act of coercion; the act of punishment by a mob. The human tradition does say that, if twenty men hang a man from a tree or lamp-post, they shall be twenty men and not women. Now I do not think any reasonable Suffragist will deny that exclusion from this function, to say the least of it, might be maintained to be a protection as well as a veto. No candid person will wholly dismiss the proposition that the idea of having a Lord Chancellor but not a Lady Chancellor may at least be connected with the idea of having a headsman but not a headswoman, a hangman but not a hangwoman. Nor will it be adequate to answer (as is so often answered to this contention) that in modern civilization women would not really be required to capture, to sentence, or to slay; that all this is done indirectly, that specialists kill our criminals as they kill our cattle. To urge this is not to urge the reality of the vote, but to urge its unreality. Democracy was meant to be a more direct way of ruling, not a more indirect way; and if we do not feel that we are all jailers, so much the worse for us, and for the prisoners. If it is really an unwomanly thing to lock up a robber or a tyrant, it ought to be no softening of the situation that the woman does not feel as if she were doing the thing that she certainly is doing. It is bad enough that men can only associate on paper who could once associate in the street; it is bad enough that men have made a vote very much of a fiction. It is much worse that a great class should claim the vote be cause it is a fiction, who would be sickened by it if it were a fact. If votes for women do not mean mobs for women they do not mean what they were meant to mean. A woman can make a cross on a paper as well as a man; a child could do it as well as a woman; and a chimpanzee after a few lessons could do it as well as a child. But nobody ought to regard it merely as making a cross on paper; everyone ought to regard it as what it ultimately is, branding the fleur-de-lis, marking the broad arrow, signing the death warrant. Both men and women ought to face more fully the things they do or cause to be done; face them or leave off doing them.

On that disastrous day when public executions were abolished, private executions were renewed and ratified, perhaps forever. Things grossly unsuited to the moral sentiment of a society cannot be safely done in broad daylight; but I see no reason why we should not still be roasting heretics alive, in a private room. It is very likely (to speak in the manner foolishly called Irish) that if there were public executions there would be no executions. The old open-air punishments, the pillory and the gibbet, at least fixed responsibility upon the law; and in actual practice they gave the mob an opportunity of throwing roses as well as rotten eggs; of crying "Hosannah" as well as "Crucify." But I do not like the public executioner being turned into the private executioner. I think it is a crooked oriental, sinister sort of business, and smells of the harem and the divan rather than of the forum and the market place. In modern times the official has lost all the social honor and dignity of the common hangman. He is only the bearer of the bowstring.

Here, however, I suggest a plea for a brutal publicity only in order to emphasize the fact that it is this brutal publicity and nothing else from which women have been excluded. I also say it to emphasize the fact that the mere modern veiling of the brutality does not make the situation different, unless we openly say that we are giving the suffrage, not only because it is power but because it is not, or in other words, that women are not so much to vote as to play voting. No suffragist, I suppose, will take up that position; and a few suffragists will wholly deny that this human necessity of pains and penalties is an ugly, humiliating business, and that good motives as well as bad may have helped to keep women out of it. More than once I have remarked in these pages that female limitations may be the limits of a temple as well as of a prison, the disabilities of a priest and not of a pariah. I noted it, I think, in the case of the pontifical feminine dress. In the same way it is not evidently irrational, if men decided that a woman, like a priest, must not be a shedder of blood.

X. The Higher Anarchy

But there is a further fact; forgotten also because we moderns forget that there is a female point of view. The woman's wisdom stands partly, not only for a wholesome hesitation about punishment, but even for a wholesome hesitation about absolute rules. There was something feminine and perversely true in that phrase of Wilde's, that people should not be treated as the rule, but all of them as exceptions. Made by a man the remark was a little effeminate; for Wilde did lack the masculine power of dogma and of democratic cooperation. But if a woman had said it it would have been simply true; a woman does treat each person as a peculiar person. In other words, she stands for Anarchy; a very ancient and arguable philosophy; not anarchy in the sense of having no customs in one's life (which is inconceivable), but anarchy in the sense of having no rules for one's mind. To her, almost certainly, are due all those working traditions that cannot be found in books, especially those of education; it was she who first gave a child a stuffed stocking for being good or stood him in the corner for being naughty. This unclassified knowledge is sometimes called rule of thumb and sometimes motherwit. The last phrase suggests the whole truth, for none ever called it fatherwit.

Now anarchy is only tact when it works badly. Tact is only anarchy when it works well. And we ought to realize that in one half of the world--the private house--it does work well. We modern men are perpetually forgetting that the case for clear rules and crude penalties is not self-evident, that there is a great deal to be said for the benevolent lawlessness of the autocrat, especially on a small scale; in short, that government is only one side of life. The other half is called Society, in which women are admittedly dominant. And they have always been ready to maintain that their kingdom is better governed than ours, because (in the logical and legal sense) it is not governed at all. "Whenever you have a real difficulty," they say, "when a boy is bumptious or an aunt is stingy, when a silly girl will marry somebody, or a wicked man won't marry somebody, all your lumbering Roman Law and British Constitution come to a standstill. A snub from a duchess or a slanging from a fish-wife are much more likely to put things straight." So, at least, rang the ancient female challenge down the ages until the recent female capitulation. So streamed the red standard of the higher anarchy until Miss Pankhurst hoisted the white flag.

It must be remembered that the modern world has done deep treason to the eternal intellect by believing in the swing of the pendulum. A man must be dead before he swings. It has substituted an idea of fatalistic alternation for the mediaeval freedom of the soul seeking truth. All modern thinkers are reactionaries; for their thought is always a reaction from what went before. When you meet a modern man he is always coming from a place, not going to it. Thus, mankind has in nearly all places and periods seen that there is a soul and a body as plainly as that there is a sun and moon. But because a narrow Protestant sect called Materialists declared for a short time that there was no soul, another narrow Protestant sect called Christian Science is now maintaining that there is no body. Now just in the same way the unreasonable neglect of government by the Manchester School has produced, not a reasonable regard for government, but an unreasonable neglect of everything else. So that to hear people talk to-day one would fancy that every important human function must be organized and avenged by law; that all education must be state education, and all employment state employment; that everybody and everything must be brought to the foot of the august and prehistoric gibbet. But a somewhat more liberal and sympathetic examination of mankind will convince us that the cross is even older than the gibbet, that voluntary suffering was before and independent of compulsory; and in short that in most important matters a man has always been free to ruin himself if he chose. The huge fundamental function upon which all anthropology turns, that of sex and childbirth, has never been inside the political state, but always outside of it. The state concerned itself with the trivial question of killing people, but wisely left alone the whole business of getting them born. A Eugenist might indeed plausibly say that the government is an absent-minded and inconsistent person who occupies himself with providing for the old age of people who have never been infants. I will not deal here in any detail with the fact that some Eugenists have in our time made the maniacal answer that the police ought to control marriage and birth as they control labor and death. Except for this inhuman handful (with whom I regret to say I shall have to deal with later) all the Eugenists I know divide themselves into two sections: ingenious people who once meant this, and rather bewildered people who swear they never meant it--nor anything else. But if it be conceded (by a breezier estimate of men) that they do mostly desire marriage to remain free from government, it does not follow that they desire it to remain free from everything. If man does not control the marriage market by law, is it controlled at all? Surely the answer is broadly that man does not control the marriage market by law, but the woman does control it by sympathy and prejudice. There was until lately a law forbidding a man to marry his deceased wife's sister; yet the thing happened constantly. There was no law forbidding a man to marry his deceased wife's scullery-maid; yet it did not happen nearly so often. It did not happen because the marriage market is managed in the spirit and by the authority of women; and women are generally conservative where classes are concerned. It is the same with that system of exclusiveness by which ladies have so often contrived (as by a process of elimination) to prevent marriages that they did not want and even sometimes procure those they did. There is no need of the broad arrow and the fleur-de lis, the turnkey's chains or the hangman's halter. You need not strangle a man if you can silence him. The branded shoulder is less effective and final than the cold shoulder; and you need not trouble to lock a man in when you can lock him out.

The same, of course, is true of the colossal architecture which we call infant education: an architecture reared wholly by women. Nothing can ever overcome that one enormous sex superiority, that even the male child is born closer to his mother than to his father. No one, staring at that frightful female privilege, can quite believe in the equality of the sexes. Here and there we read of a girl brought up like a tom-boy; but every boy is brought up like a tame girl. The flesh and spirit of femininity surround him from the first like the four walls of a house; and even the vaguest or most brutal man has been womanized by being born. Man that is born of a woman has short days and full of misery; but nobody can picture the obscenity and bestial tragedy that would belong to such a monster as man that was born of a man.

XI. The Queen And The Suffragettes

But, indeed, with this educational matter I must of necessity embroil myself later. The fourth section of discussion is supposed to be about the child, but I think it will be mostly about the mother. In this place I have systematically insisted on the large part of life that is governed, not by man with his vote, but by woman with her voice, or more often, with her horrible silence. Only one thing remains to be added. In a sprawling and explanatory style has been traced out the idea that government is ultimately coercion, that coercion must mean cold definitions as well as cruel consequences, and that therefore there is something to be said for the old human habit of keeping one-half of humanity out of so harsh and dirty a business. But the case is stronger still.

Voting is not only coercion, but collective coercion. I think Queen Victoria would have been yet more popular and satisfying if she had never signed a death warrant. I think Queen Elizabeth would have stood out as more solid and splendid in history if she had not earned (among those who happen to know her history) the nickname of Bloody Bess. I think, in short, that the great historic woman is more herself when she is persuasive rather than coercive. But I feel all mankind behind me when I say that if a woman has this power it should be despotic power--not democratic power. There is a much stronger historic argument for giving Miss Pankhurst a throne than for giving her a vote. She might have a crown, or at least a coronet, like so many of her supporters; for these old powers are purely personal and therefore female. Miss Pankhurst as a despot might be as virtuous as Queen Victoria, and she certainly would find it difficult to be as wicked as Queen Bess, but the point is that, good or bad, she would be irresponsible--she would not be governed by a rule and by a ruler. There are only two ways of governing: by a rule and by a ruler. And it is seriously true to say of a woman, in education and domesticity, that the freedom of the autocrat appears to be necessary to her. She is never responsible until she is irresponsible. In case this sounds like an idle contradiction, I confidently appeal to the cold facts of history. Almost every despotic or oligarchic state has admitted women to its privileges. Scarcely one democratic state has ever admitted them to its rights The reason is very simple: that something female is endangered much more by the violence of the crowd. In short, one Pankhurst is an exception, but a thousand Pankhursts are a nightmare, a Bacchic orgie, a Witches Sabbath. For in all legends men have thought of women as sublime separately but horrible in a herd.

XII. The Modern Slave

Now I have only taken the test case of Female Suffrage because it is topical and concrete; it is not of great moment for me as a political proposal. I can quite imagine anyone substantially agreeing with my view of woman as universalist and autocrat in a limited area; and still thinking that she would be none the worse for a ballot paper. The real question is whether this old ideal of woman as the great amateur is admitted or not. There are many modern things which threaten it much more than suffragism; notably the increase of self-supporting women, even in the most severe or the most squalid employments. If there be something against nature in the idea of a horde of wild women governing, there is something truly intolerable in the idea of a herd of tame women being governed. And there are elements in human psychology that make this situation particularly poignant or ignominious. The ugly exactitudes of business, the bells and clocks the fixed hours and rigid departments, were all meant for the male: who, as a rule, can only do one thing and can only with the greatest difficulty be induced to do that. If clerks do not try to shirk their work, our whole great commercial system breaks down. It is breaking down, under the inroad of women who are adopting the unprecedented and impossible course of taking the system seriously and doing it well. Their very efficiency is the definition of their slavery. It is generally a very bad sign when one is trusted very much by one's employers. And if the evasive clerks have a look of being blackguards, the earnest ladies are often something very like blacklegs. But the more immediate point is that the modern working woman bears a double burden, for she endures both the grinding officialism of the new office and the distracting scrupulosity of the old home. Few men understand what conscientiousness is. They understand duty, which generally means one duty; but conscientiousness is the duty of the universalist. It is limited by no work days or holidays; it is a lawless, limitless, devouring decorum. If women are to be subjected to the dull rule of commerce, we must find some way of emancipating them from the wild rule of conscience. But I rather fancy you will find it easier to leave the conscience and knock off the commerce. As it is, the modern clerk or secretary exhausts herself to put one thing straight in the ledger and then goes home to put everything straight in the house.

This condition (described by some as emancipated) is at least the reverse of my ideal. I would give woman, not more rights, but more privileges. Instead of sending her to seek such freedom as notoriously prevails in banks and factories, I would design specially a house in which she can be free. And with that we come to the last point of all; the point at which we can perceive the needs of women, like the rights of men, stopped and falsified by something which it is the object of this book to expose.

The Feminist (which means, I think, one who dislikes the chief feminine characteristics) has heard my loose monologue, bursting all the time with one pent-up protest. At this point he will break out and say, "But what are we to do? There is modern commerce and its clerks; there is the modern family with its unmarried daughters; specialism is expected everywhere; female thrift and conscientiousness are demanded and supplied. What does it matter whether we should in the abstract prefer the old human and housekeeping woman; we might prefer the Garden of Eden. But since women have trades they ought to have trades unions. Since women work in factories, they ought to vote on factory-acts. If they are unmarried they must be commercial; if they are commercial they must be political. We must have new rules for a new world--even if it be not a better one." I said to a Feminist once: "The question is not whether women are good enough for votes: it is whether votes are good enough for women." He only answered: "Ah, you go and say that to the women chain-makers on Cradley Heath."

Now this is the attitude which I attack. It is the huge heresy of Precedent. It is the view that because we have got into a mess we must grow messier to suit it; that because we have taken a wrong turn some time ago we must go forward and not backwards; that because we have lost our way we must lose our map also; and because we have missed our ideal, we must forget it. "There are numbers of excellent people who do not think votes unfeminine; and there may be enthusiasts for our beautiful modern industry who do not think factories unfeminine." But if these things are unfeminine it is no answer to say that they fit into each other. I am not satisfied with the statement that my daughter must have unwomanly powers because she has unwomanly wrongs. Industrial soot and political printer's ink are two blacks which do not make a white. Most of the Feminists would probably agree with me that womanhood is under shameful tyranny in the shops and mills. But

I want to destroy the tyranny. They want to destroy womanhood. That is the only difference.

Whether we can recover the clear vision of woman as a tower with many windows, the fixed eternal feminine from which her sons, the specialists, go forth; whether we can preserve the tradition of a central thing which is even more human than democracy and even more practical than politics; whether, in word, it is possible to re-establish the family, freed from the filthy cynicism and cruelty of the commercial epoch, I shall discuss in the last section of this book. But meanwhile do not talk to me about the poor chain-makers on Cradley Heath. I know all about them and what they are doing. They are engaged in a very wide-spread and flourishing industry of the present age. They are making chains.

What's Wrong with the World

Part Four. Education: Or The Mistake About The Child

I. The Calvinism Of To-Day

When I wrote a little volume on my friend Mr. Bernard Shaw, it is needless to say that he reviewed it. I naturally felt tempted to answer and to criticise the book from the same disinterested and impartial standpoint from which Mr. Shaw had criticised the subject of it. I was not withheld by any feeling that the joke was getting a little obvious; for an obvious joke is only a successful joke; it is only the unsuccessful clowns who comfort themselves with being subtle. The real reason why I did not answer Mr. Shaw's amusing attack was this: that one simple phrase in it surrendered to me all that I have ever wanted, or could want from him to all eternity. I told Mr. Shaw (in substance) that he was a charming and clever fellow, but a common Calvinist. He admitted that this was true, and there (so far as I am concerned) is an end of the matter. He said that, of course, Calvin was quite right in holding that "if once a man is born it is too late to damn or save him." That is the fundamental and subterranean secret; that is the last lie in hell.

The difference between Puritanism and Catholicism is not about whether some priestly word or gesture is significant and sacred. It is about whether any word or gesture is significant and sacred. To the Catholic every other daily act is dramatic dedication to the service of good or of evil. To the Calvinist no act can have that sort of solemnity, because the person doing it has been dedicated from eternity, and is merely filling up his time until the crack of doom. The difference is something subtler than plum-puddings or private theatricals; the difference is that to a Christian of my kind this short earthly life is intensely thrilling and precious; to a Calvinist like Mr. Shaw it is confessedly automatic and uninteresting. To me these threescore years and ten are the battle. To the Fabian Calvinist (by his own confession) they are only a long procession of the victors in laurels and the vanquished in chains. To me earthly life is the drama; to him it is the epilogue.

Shavians think about the embryo; Spiritualists about the ghost; Christians about the man. It is as well to have these things clear.

Now all our sociology and eugenics and the rest of it are not so much materialist as confusedly Calvinist, they are chiefly occupied in educating the child before he exists. The whole movement is full of a singular depression about what one can do with the populace, combined with a strange disembodied gayety about what may be done with posterity. These essential Calvinists have, indeed, abolished some of the more liberal and universal parts of Calvinism, such as the belief in an intellectual design or an everlasting happiness. But though Mr. Shaw and his friends admit it is a superstition that a man is judged after death, they stick to their central doctrine, that he is judged before he is born.

In consequence of this atmosphere of Calvinism in the cultured world of to-day, it is apparently necessary to begin all arguments on education with some mention of obstetrics and the unknown world of the prenatal. All I shall have to say, however, on heredity will be very brief, because I shall confine myself to what is known about it, and that is very nearly nothing. It is by no means self-evident, but it is a current modern dogma, that nothing actually enters the body at birth except a life derived and compounded from the parents. There is at least quite as much to be said for the Christian theory that an element comes from God, or the Buddhist theory that such an element comes from previous existences. But this is not a religious work, and I must submit to those very narrow intellectual limits which the absence of theology always imposes. Leaving the soul on one side, let us suppose for the sake of argument that the human character in the first case comes wholly from parents; and then let us curtly state our knowledge rather than our ignorance.

II. The Tribal Terror

Popular science, like that of Mr. Blatchford, is in this matter as mild as old wives' tales. Mr. Blatchford, with colossal simplicity, explained to millions of clerks and workingmen that the mother is like a bottle of blue beads and the father is like a bottle of yellow beads; and so the child is like a bottle of mixed blue beads and yellow. He might just as well have said that if the father has two legs and the mother has two legs, the child will have four legs. Obviously it is not a question of simple addition or simple division of a number of hard detached "qualities," like beads. It is an organic crisis and transformation of the most mysterious sort; so that even if the result is unavoidable, it will still be unexpected. It is not like blue beads mixed with yellow beads; it is like blue mixed with yellow; the result of which is green, a totally novel and unique experience, a new emotion. A man might live in a complete cosmos of blue and yellow, like the "Edinburgh Review"; a man might never have seen anything but a golden cornfield and a sapphire sky; and still he might never have had so wild a fancy as green. If you paid a sovereign for a bluebell; if you spilled the mustard on the blue-books; if you married a canary to a blue baboon; there is nothing in any of these wild weddings that contains even a hint of green. Green is not a mental combination, like addition; it is a physical result like birth. So, apart from the fact that nobody ever really understands parents or children either, yet even if we could understand the parents, we could not make any conjecture about the children. Each time the force works in a different way; each time the constituent colors combine into a different spectacle. A girl may actually inherit her ugliness from her mother's good looks. A boy may actually get his weakness from his father's strength. Even if we admit it is really a fate, for us it must remain a fairy tale. Considered in regard to its causes, the Calvinists and materialists may be right or wrong; we leave them their dreary debate. But considered in regard to its results there is no doubt about it. The thing is always a new color; a strange star. Every birth is as lonely as a miracle. Every child is as uninvited as a monstrosity.

On all such subjects there is no science, but only a sort of ardent ignorance; and nobody has ever been able to offer any theories of moral heredity which justified themselves in the only scientific sense; that is that one could calculate on them beforehand. There are six cases, say, of a grandson having the same twitch of mouth or vice of character as his grandfather; or perhaps there are sixteen cases, or perhaps sixty. But there are not two cases, there is not one case, there are no cases at all, of anybody betting half a crown that the grandfather will have a grandson with the twitch or the vice. In short, we deal with heredity as we deal with omens, affinities and the fulfillment of dreams. The things do happen, and when they happen we record them; but not even a lunatic ever reckons on them. Indeed, heredity, like dreams and omens, is a barbaric notion; that is, not necessarily an untrue, but a dim, groping and unsystematized notion. A civilized man feels himself a little more free from his family. Before Christianity these tales of tribal doom occupied the savage north; and since the Reformation and the revolt against Christianity (which is the religion of a civilized freedom) savagery is slowly creeping back in the form of realistic novels and problem plays. The curse of Rougon-Macquart is as heathen and superstitious as the curse of Ravenswood; only not so well written. But in this twilight barbaric sense the feeling of a racial fate is not irrational, and may be allowed like a hundred other half emotions that make life whole. The only essential of tragedy is that one should take it lightly. But even when the barbarian deluge rose to its highest in the madder novels of Zola (such as that called "The Human Beast", a gross libel on beasts as well as humanity), even then the application of the hereditary idea to practice is avowedly timid and fumbling. The students of heredity are savages in this vital sense; that they stare back at marvels, but they dare not stare forward to schemes. In practice no one is mad enough to legislate or educate upon dogmas of physical inheritance; and even the language of the thing is rarely used except for special modern purposes, such as the endowment of research or the oppression of the poor.

III. The Tricks Of Environment

After all the modern clatter of Calvinism, therefore, it is only with the born child that anybody dares to deal; and the question is not eugenics but education. Or again, to adopt that rather tiresome terminology of popular science, it is not a question of heredity but of environment. I will not needlessly complicate this question by urging at length that environment also is open to some of the objections and hesitations which paralyze the employment of heredity. I will merely suggest in passing that even about the effect of environment modern people talk much too cheerfully and cheaply. The idea that surroundings will mold a man is always mixed up with the totally different idea that they will mold him in one particular way. To take the broadest case, landscape no doubt affects the soul; but how it affects it is quite another matter. To be born among pine-trees might mean loving pine-trees. It might mean loathing pine-trees. It might quite seriously mean never having seen a pine-tree. Or it might mean any mixture of these or any degree of any of them. So that the scientific method here lacks a little in precision. I am not speaking without the book; on the contrary, I am speaking with the blue book, with the guide-book and the atlas. It may be that the Highlanders are poetical because they inhabit mountains; but are the Swiss prosaic because they inhabit mountains? It may be the Swiss have fought for freedom because they had hills; did the Dutch fight for freedom because they hadn't? Personally I should think it quite likely. Environment might work negatively as well as positively. The Swiss may be sensible, not in spite of their wild skyline, but be cause of their wild skyline. The Flemings may be fantastic artists, not in spite of their dull skyline, but because of it.

I only pause on this parenthesis to show that, even in matters admittedly within its range, popular science goes a great deal too fast, and drops enormous links of logic. Nevertheless, it remains the working reality that what we have to deal with in the case of children is, for all practical purposes, environment; or, to use the older word, education. When all such deductions are made, education is at least a form of will-worship; not of cowardly fact-worship; it deals with a department that we can control; it does not merely darken us with the barbarian pessimism of Zola and the heredity-hunt. We shall certainly make fools of ourselves; that is what is meant by philosophy. But we shall not merely make beasts of ourselves; which is the nearest popular definition for merely following the laws of Nature and cowering under the vengeance of the flesh. Education contains much moonshine; but not of the sort that makes mere mooncalves and idiots the slaves of a silver magnet, the one eye of the world. In this decent arena there are fads, but not frenzies. Doubtless we shall often find a mare's nest; but it will not always be the nightmare's.

IV. The Truth About Education

When a man is asked to write down what he really thinks on education, a certain gravity grips and stiffens his soul, which might be mistaken by the superficial for disgust. If it be really true that men sickened of sacred words and wearied of theology, if this largely unreasoning irritation against "dogma" did arise out of some ridiculous excess of such things among priests in the past, then I fancy we must be laying up a fine crop of cant for our descendants to grow tired of. Probably the word "education" will some day seem honestly as old and objectless as the word "justification" now seems in a Puritan folio. Gibbon thought it frightfully funny that people should have fought about the difference between the "Homoousion" and the "Homoiousion." The time will come when somebody will laugh louder to think that men thundered against Sectarian Education and also against Secular Education; that men of prominence and position actually denounced the schools for teaching a creed and also for not teaching a faith. The two Greek words in Gibbon look rather alike; but they really mean quite different things. Faith and creed do not look alike, but they mean exactly the same thing. Creed happens to be the Latin for faith.

Now having read numberless newspaper articles on education, and even written a good many of them, and having heard deafening and indeterminate discussion going on all around me almost ever since I was born, about whether religion was part of education, about whether hygiene was an essential of education, about whether militarism was inconsistent with true education, I naturally pondered much on this recurring substantive, and I am ashamed to say that it was comparatively late in life that I saw the main fact about it.

Of course, the main fact about education is that there is no such thing. It does not exist, as theology or soldiering exist. Theology is a word like geology, soldiering is a word like soldering; these sciences may be healthy or no as hobbies; but they deal with stone and kettles, with definite things. But education is not a word like geology or kettles. Education is a word like "transmission" or "inheritance"; it is not an object, but a method. It must mean the conveying of certain facts, views or qualities, to the last baby born. They might be the most trivial facts or the most preposterous views or the most offensive qualities; but if they are handed on from one generation to another they are education. Education is not a thing like theology, it is not an inferior or superior thing; it is not a thing in the same category of terms. Theology and education are to each other like a love-letter to the General Post Office. Mr. Fagin was quite as educational as Dr. Strong; in practice probably more educational. It is giving something--perhaps poison. Education is tradition, and tradition (as its name implies) can be treason.

This first truth is frankly banal; but it is so perpetually ignored in our political prosing that it must be made plain. A little boy in a little house, son of a little tradesman, is taught to eat his breakfast, to take his medicine, to love his country, to say his prayers, and to wear his Sunday clothes. Obviously Fagin, if he found such a boy, would teach him to drink gin, to lie, to betray his country, to blaspheme and to wear false whiskers. But so also Mr. Salt the vegetarian would abolish the boy's breakfast; Mrs. Eddy would throw away his medicine; Count Tolstoi would rebuke him for loving his country; Mr. Blatchford would stop his prayers, and Mr. Edward Carpenter would theoretically denounce Sunday clothes, and perhaps all clothes. I do not defend any of these advanced views, not even Fagin's. But I do ask what, between the lot of them, has become of the abstract entity called education. It is not (as commonly supposed) that the tradesman teaches education plus Christianity; Mr. Salt, education plus vegetarianism; Fagin, education plus crime. The truth is, that there is nothing in common at all between these teachers, except that they teach. In short, the only thing they share is the one thing they profess to dislike: the general idea of authority. It is quaint that people talk of separating dogma from education. Dogma is actually the only thing that cannot be separated from education. It is education. A teacher who is not dogmatic is simply a teacher who is not teaching.

V. An Evil Cry

The fashionable fallacy is that by education we can give people something that we have not got. To hear people talk one would think it was some sort of magic chemistry, by which, out of a laborious hotchpotch of hygienic meals, baths, breathing exercises, fresh air and freehand drawing, we can produce something splendid by accident; we can create what we cannot conceive. These pages have, of course, no other general purpose than to point out that we cannot create anything good until we have conceived it. It is odd that these people, who in the matter of heredity are so sullenly attached to law, in the matter of environment seem almost to believe in miracle. They insist that nothing but what was in the bodies of the parents can go to make the bodies of the children. But they seem somehow to think that things can get into the heads of the children which were not in the heads of the parents, or, indeed, anywhere else.

There has arisen in this connection a foolish and wicked cry typical of the confusion. I mean the cry, "Save the children." It is, of course, part of that modern morbidity that insists on treating the State (which is the home of man) as a sort of desperate expedient in time of panic. This terrified opportunism is also the origin of the Socialist and other schemes. Just as they would collect and share all the food as men do in a famine, so they would divide the children from their fathers, as men do in a shipwreck. That a human community might conceivably not be in a condition of famine or shipwreck never seems to cross their minds. This cry of "Save the children" has in it the hateful implication that it is impossible to save the fathers; in other words, that many millions of grown-up, sane, responsible and self-supporting Europeans are to be treated as dirt or debris and swept away out of the discussion; called dipsomaniacs because they drink in public houses instead of private houses; called unemployables because nobody knows how to get them work; called dullards if they still adhere to conventions, and called loafers if they still love liberty. Now I am concerned, first and last, to maintain that unless you can save the fathers, you cannot save the children; that at present we cannot save others, for we cannot save ourselves. We cannot teach citizenship if we are not citizens; we cannot free others if we have forgotten the appetite of freedom. Education is only truth in a state of transmission; and how can we pass on truth if it has never come into our hand? Thus we find that education is of all the cases the clearest for our general purpose. It is vain to save children; for they cannot remain children. By hypothesis we are teaching them to be men; and how can it be so simple to teach an ideal manhood to others if it is so vain and hopeless to find one for ourselves?

I know that certain crazy pedants have attempted to counter this difficulty by maintaining that education is not instruction at all, does not teach by authority at all. They present the process as coming, not from the outside, from the teacher, but entirely from inside the boy. Education, they say, is the Latin for leading out or drawing out the dormant faculties of each person. Somewhere far down in the dim boyish soul is a primordial yearning to learn Greek accents or to wear clean collars; and the schoolmaster only gently and tenderly liberates this imprisoned purpose. Sealed up in the newborn babe are the intrinsic secrets of how to eat asparagus and what was the date of Bannockburn. The educator only draws out the child's own unapparent love of long division; only leads out the child's slightly veiled preference for milk pudding to tarts. I am not sure that I believe in the derivation; I have heard the disgraceful suggestion that "educator," if applied to a Roman schoolmaster, did not mean leading our young functions into freedom; but only meant taking out little boys for a walk. But I am much more certain that I do not agree with the doctrine; I think it would be about as sane to say that the baby's milk comes from the baby as to say that the baby's educational merits do. There is, indeed, in each living creature a collection of forces and functions; but education means producing these in particular shapes and training them to particular purposes, or it means nothing at all. Speaking is the most practical instance of the whole situation. You may indeed "draw out" squeals and grunts from the child by simply poking him and pulling him about, a pleasant but cruel pastime to which many psychologists are addicted. But you will wait and watch very patiently indeed before you draw the English language out of him. That you have got to put into him; and there is an end of the matter.

VI. Authority The Unavoidable

But the important point here is only that you cannot anyhow get rid of authority in education; it is not so much (as poor Conservatives say) that parental authority ought to be preserved, as that it cannot be destroyed. Mr. Bernard Shaw once said that he hated the idea of forming a child's mind. In that case Mr. Bernard Shaw had better hang himself; for he hates something inseparable from human life. I only mentioned educere and the drawing out of the faculties in order to point out that even this mental trick does not avoid the inevitable idea of parental or scholastic authority. The educator drawing out is just as arbitrary and coercive as the instructor pouring in; for he draws out what he chooses. He decides what in the child shall be developed and what shall not be developed. He does not (I suppose) draw out the neglected faculty of forgery. He does not (so far at least) lead out, with timid steps, a shy talent for torture. The only result of all this pompous and precise distinction between the educator and the instructor is that the instructor pokes where he likes and the educator pulls where he likes. Exactly the same intellectual violence is done to the creature who is poked and pulled. Now we must all accept the responsibility of this intellectual violence. Education is violent; because it is creative. It is creative because it is human. It is as reckless as playing on the fiddle; as dogmatic as drawing a picture; as brutal as building a house. In short, it is what all human action is; it is an interference with life and growth. After that it is a trifling and even a jocular question whether we say of this tremendous tormentor, the artist Man, that he puts things into us like an apothecary, or draws things out of us, like a dentist.

The point is that Man does what he likes. He claims the right to take his mother Nature under his control; he claims the right to make his child the Superman, in his image. Once flinch from this creative authority of man, and the whole courageous raid which we call civilization wavers and falls to pieces. Now most modern freedom is at root fear. It is not so much that we are too bold to endure rules; it is rather that we are too timid to endure responsibilities. And Mr. Shaw and such people are especially shrinking from that awful and ancestral responsibility to which our fathers committed us when they took the wild step of becoming men. I mean the responsibility of affirming the truth of our human tradition and handing it on with a voice of authority, an unshaken voice. That is the one eternal education; to be sure enough that something is true that you dare to tell it to a child. From this high audacious duty the moderns are fleeing on every side; and the only excuse for them is, (of course,) that their modern philosophies are so half-baked and hypothetical that they cannot convince themselves enough to convince even a newborn babe. This, of course, is connected with the decay of democracy; and is somewhat of a separate subject. Suffice it to say here that when I say that we should instruct our children, I mean that we should do it, not that Mr. Sully or Professor Earl Barnes should do it. The trouble in too many of our modern schools is that the State, being controlled so specially by the few, allows cranks and experiments to go straight to the schoolroom when they have never passed through the Parliament, the public house, the private house, the church, or the marketplace. Obviously, it ought to be the oldest things that are taught to the youngest people; the assured and experienced truths that are put first to the baby. But in a school to-day the baby has to submit to a system that is younger than himself. The flopping infant of four actually has more experience, and has weathered the world longer, than the dogma to which he is made to submit. Many a school boasts of having the last ideas in education, when it has not even the first idea; for the first idea is that even innocence, divine as it is, may learn something from experience. But this, as I say, is all due to the mere fact that we are managed by a little oligarchy; my system presupposes that men who govern themselves will govern their children. To-day we all use Popular Education as meaning education of the people. I wish I could use it as meaning education by the people.

The urgent point at present is that these expansive educators do not avoid the violence of authority an inch more than the old school masters. Nay, it might be maintained that they avoid it less. The old village schoolmaster beat a boy for not learning grammar and sent him out into the playground to play anything he liked; or at nothing, if he liked that better. The modern scientific schoolmaster pursues him into the playground and makes him play at cricket, because exercise is so good for the health. The modern Dr. Busby is a doctor of medicine as well as a doctor of divinity. He may say that the good of exercise is self-evident; but he must say it, and say it with authority. It cannot really be self-evident or it never could have been compulsory. But this is in modern practice a very mild case. In modern practice the free educationists forbid far more things than the old-fashioned educationists. A person with a taste for paradox (if any such shameless creature could exist) might with some plausibility maintain concerning all our expansion since the failure of Luther's frank paganism and its replacement by Calvin's Puritanism, that all this expansion has not been an expansion, but the closing in of a prison, so that less and less beautiful and humane things have been permitted. The Puritans destroyed images; the Rationalists forbade fairy tales. Count Tostoi practically issued one of his papal encyclicals against music; and I have heard of modern educationists who forbid children to play with tin soldiers. I remember a meek little madman who came up to me at some Socialist soiree or other, and asked me to use my influence (have I any influence?) against adventure stories for boys. It seems they breed an appetite for blood. But never mind that; one must keep one's temper in this madhouse. I need only insist here that these things, even if a just deprivation, are a deprivation. I do not deny that the old vetoes and punishments were often idiotic and cruel; though they are much more so in a country like England (where in practice only a rich man decrees the punishment and only a poor man receives it) than in countries with a clearer popular tradition--such as Russia. In Russia flogging is often inflicted by peasants on a peasant. In modern England flogging can only in practice be inflicted by a gentleman on a very poor man. Thus only a few days ago as I write a small boy (a son of the poor, of course) was sentenced to flogging and imprisonment for five years for having picked up a small piece of coal which the experts value at 5d. I am entirely on the side of such liberals and humanitarians as have protested against this almost bestial ignorance about boys. But I do think it a little unfair that these humanitarians, who excuse boys for being robbers, should denounce them for playing at robbers. I do think that those who understand a guttersnipe playing with a piece of coal might, by a sudden spurt of imagination, understand him playing with a tin soldier. To sum it up in one sentence: I think my meek little madman might have understood that there is many a boy who would rather be flogged, and unjustly flogged, than have his adventure story taken away.

VII. The Humility Of Mrs. Grundy

In short, the new education is as harsh as the old, whether or no it is as high. The freest fad, as much as the strictest formula, is stiff with authority. It is because the humane father thinks soldiers wrong that they are forbidden; there is no pretense, there can be no pretense, that the boy would think so. The average boy's impression certainly would be simply this: "If your father is a Methodist you must not play with soldiers on Sunday. If your father is a Socialist you must not play with them even on week days." All educationists are utterly dogmatic and authoritarian. You cannot have free education; for if you left a child free you would not educate him at all. Is there, then, no distinction or difference between the most hide-bound conventionalists and the most brilliant and bizarre innovators? Is there no difference between the heaviest heavy father and the most reckless and speculative maiden aunt? Yes; there is. The difference is that the heavy father, in his heavy way, is a democrat. He does not urge a thing merely because to his fancy it should be done; but, because (in his own admirable republican formula) "Everybody does it." The conventional authority does claim some popular mandate; the unconventional authority does not. The Puritan who forbids soldiers on Sunday is at least expressing Puritan opinion; not merely his own opinion. He is not a despot; he is a democracy, a tyrannical democracy, a dingy and local democracy perhaps; but one that could do and has done the two ultimate virile things--fight and appeal to God. But the veto of the new educationist is like the veto of the House of Lords; it does not pretend to be representative. These innovators are always talking about the blushing modesty of Mrs. Grundy. I do not know whether Mrs. Grundy is more modest than they are; but I am sure she is more humble.

But there is a further complication. The more anarchic modern may again attempt to escape the dilemma by saying that education should only be an enlargement of the mind, an opening of all the organs of receptivity. Light (he says) should be brought into darkness; blinded and thwarted existences in all our ugly corners should merely be permitted to perceive and expand; in short, enlightenment should be shed over darkest London. Now here is just the trouble; that, in so far as this is involved, there is no darkest London. London is not dark at all; not even at night. We have said that if education is a solid substance, then there is none of it. We may now say that if education is an abstract expansion there is no lack of it. There is far too much of it. In fact, there is nothing else.

There are no uneducated people. Everybody in England is educated; only most people are educated wrong. The state schools were not the first schools, but among the last schools to be established; and London had been educating Londoners long before the London School Board. The error is a highly practical one. It is persistently assumed that unless a child is civilized by the established schools, he must remain a barbarian. I wish he did. Every child in London becomes a highly civilized person. But here are so many different civilizations, most of them born tired. Anyone will tell you that the trouble with the poor is not so much that the old are still foolish, but rather that the young are already wise. Without going to school at all, the gutter-boy would be educated. Without going to school at all, he would be over-educated. The real object of our schools should be not so much to suggest complexity as solely to restore simplicity. You will hear venerable idealists declare we must make war on the ignorance of the poor; but, indeed, we have rather to make war on their knowledge. Real educationists have to resist a kind of roaring cataract of culture. The truant is being taught all day. If the children do not look at the large letters in the spelling-book, they need only walk outside and look at the large letters on the poster. If they do not care for the colored maps provided by the school, they can gape at the colored maps provided by the Daily Mail. If they tire of electricity, they can take to electric trams. If they are unmoved by music, they can take to drink. If they will not work so as to get a prize from their school, they may work to get a prize from Prizy Bits. If they cannot learn enough about law and citizenship to please the teacher, they learn enough about them to avoid the policeman. If they will not learn history forwards from the right end in the history books, they will learn it backwards from the wrong end in the party newspapers. And this is the tragedy of the whole affair: that the London poor, a particularly quick-witted and civilized class, learn everything tail foremost, learn even what is right in the way of what is wrong. They do not see the first principles of law in a law book; they only see its last results in the police news. They do not see the truths of politics in a general survey. They only see the lies of politics, at a General Election.

But whatever be the pathos of the London poor, it has nothing to do with being uneducated. So far from being without guidance, they are guided constantly, earnestly, excitedly; only guided wrong. The poor are not at all neglected, they are merely oppressed; nay, rather they are persecuted. There are no people in London who are not appealed to by the rich; the appeals of the rich shriek from every hoarding and shout from every hustings. For it should always be remembered that the queer, abrupt ugliness of our streets and costumes are not the creation of democracy, but of aristocracy. The House of Lords objected to the Embankment being disfigured by trams. But most of the rich men who disfigure the street-walls with their wares are actually in the House of Lords. The peers make the country seats beautiful by making the town streets hideous. This, however, is parenthetical. The point is, that the poor in London are not left alone, but rather deafened and bewildered with raucous and despotic advice. They are not like sheep without a shepherd. They are more like one sheep whom twenty-seven shepherds are shouting at. All the newspapers, all the new advertisements, all the new medicines and new theologies, all the glare and blare of the gas and brass of modern times--it is against these that the national school must bear up if it can. I will not question that our elementary education is better than barbaric ignorance. But there is no barbaric ignorance. I do not doubt that our schools would be good for uninstructed boys. But there are no uninstructed boys. A modern London school ought not merely to be clearer, kindlier, more clever and more rapid than ignorance and darkness. It must also be clearer than a picture postcard, cleverer than a Limerick competition, quicker than the tram, and kindlier than the tavern. The school, in fact, has the responsibility of universal rivalry. We need not deny that everywhere there is a light that must conquer darkness. But here we demand a light that can conquer light.

VIII. The Broken Rainbow

I will take one case that will serve both as symbol and example: the case of color. We hear the realists (those sentimental fellows) talking about the gray streets and the gray lives of the poor. But whatever the poor streets are they are not gray; but motley, striped, spotted, piebald and patched like a quilt. Hoxton is not aesthetic enough to be monochrome; and there is nothing of the Celtic twilight about it. As a matter of fact, a London gutter-boy walks unscathed among furnaces of color. Watch him walk along a line of hoardings, and you will see him now against glowing green, like a traveler in a tropic forest; now black like a bird against the burning blue of the Midi; now passant across a field gules, like the golden leopards of England. He ought to understand the irrational rapture of that cry of Mr. Stephen Phillips about "that bluer blue, that greener green." There is no blue much bluer than Reckitt's Blue and no blacking blacker than Day and Martin's; no more emphatic yellow than that of Colman's Mustard. If, despite this chaos of color, like a shattered rainbow, the spirit of the small boy is not exactly intoxicated with art and culture, the cause certainly does not lie in universal grayness or the mere starving of his senses. It lies in the fact that the colors are presented in the wrong connection, on the wrong scale, and, above all, from the wrong motive. It is not colors he lacks, but a philosophy of colors. In short, there is nothing wrong with Reckitt's Blue except that it is not Reckitt's. Blue does not belong to Reckitt, but to the sky; black does not belong to Day and Martin, but to the abyss. Even the finest posters are only very little things on a very large scale. There is something specially irritant in this way about the iteration of advertisements of mustard: a condiment, a small luxury; a thing in its nature not to be taken in quantity. There is a special irony in these starving streets to see such a great deal of mustard to such very little meat. Yellow is a bright pigment; mustard is a pungent pleasure. But to look at these seas of yellow is to be like a man who should swallow gallons of mustard. He would either die, or lose the taste of mustard altogether.

Now suppose we compare these gigantic trivialities on the hoardings with those tiny and tremendous pictures in which the mediaevals recorded their dreams; little pictures where the blue sky is hardly longer than a single sapphire, and the fires of judgment only a pigmy patch of gold. The difference here is not merely that poster art is in its nature more hasty than illumination art; it is not even merely that the ancient artist was serving the Lord while the modern artist is serving the lords. It is that the old artist contrived to convey an impression that colors really were significant and precious things, like jewels and talismanic stones. The color was often arbitrary; but it was always authoritative. If a bird was blue, if a tree was golden, if a fish was silver, if a cloud was scarlet, the artist managed to convey that these colors were important and almost painfully intense; all the red red-hot and all the gold tried in the fire. Now that is the spirit touching color which the schools must recover and protect if they are really to give the children any imaginative appetite or pleasure in the thing. It is not so much an indulgence in color; it is rather, if anything, a sort of fiery thrift. It fenced in a green field in heraldry as straitly as a green field in peasant proprietorship. It would not fling away gold leaf any more than gold coin; it would not heedlessly pour out purple or crimson, any more than it would spill good wine or shed blameless blood. That is the hard task before educationists in this special matter; they have to teach people to relish colors like liquors. They have the heavy business of turning drunkards into wine tasters. If even the twentieth century succeeds in doing these things, it will almost catch up with the twelfth.

The principle covers, however, the whole of modern life. Morris and the merely aesthetic mediaevalists always indicated that a crowd in the time of Chaucer would have been brightly clad and glittering, compared with a crowd in the time of Queen Victoria. I am not so sure that the real distinction is here. There would be brown frocks of friars in the first scene as well as brown bowlers of clerks in the second. There would be purple plumes of factory girls in the second scene as well as purple lenten vestments in the first. There would be white waistcoats against white ermine; gold watch chains against gold lions. The real difference is this: that the brown earth-color of the monk's coat was instinctively chosen to express labor and humility, whereas the brown color of the clerk's hat was not chosen to express anything. The monk did mean to say that he robed himself in dust. I am sure the clerk does not mean to say that he crowns himself with clay. He is not putting dust on his head, as the only diadem of man. Purple, at once rich and somber, does suggest a triumph temporarily eclipsed by a tragedy. But the factory girl does not intend her hat to express a triumph temporarily eclipsed by a tragedy; far from it. White ermine was meant to express moral purity; white waistcoats were not. Gold lions do suggest a flaming magnanimity; gold watch chains do not. The point is not that we have lost the material hues, but that we have lost the trick of turning them to the best advantage. We are not like children who have lost their paint box and are left alone with a gray lead-pencil. We are like children who have mixed all the colors in the paint-box together and lost the paper of instructions. Even then (I do not deny) one has some fun.

Now this abundance of colors and loss of a color scheme is a pretty perfect parable of all that is wrong with our modern ideals and especially with our modern education. It is the same with ethical education, economic education, every sort of education. The growing London child will find no lack of highly controversial teachers who will teach him that geography means painting the map red; that economics means taxing the foreigner, that patriotism means the peculiarly un-English habit of flying a flag on Empire Day. In mentioning these examples specially I do not mean to imply that there are no similar crudities and popular fallacies upon the other political side. I mention them because they constitute a very special and arresting feature of the situation. I mean this, that there were always Radical revolutionists; but now there are Tory revolutionists also. The modern Conservative no longer conserves. He is avowedly an innovator. Thus all the current defenses of the House of Lords which describe it as a bulwark against the mob, are intellectually done for; the bottom has fallen out of them; because on five or six of the most turbulent topics of the day, the House of Lords is a mob itself; and exceedingly likely to behave like one.

IX. The Need For Narrowness

Through all this chaos, then we come back once more to our main conclusion. The true task of culture to-day is not a task of expansion, but very decidedly of selection--and rejection. The educationist must find a creed and teach it. Even if it be not a theological creed, it must still be as fastidious and as firm as theology. In short, it must be orthodox. The teacher may think it antiquated to have to decide precisely between the faith of Calvin and of Laud, the faith of Aquinas and of Swedenborg; but he still has to choose between the faith of Kipling and of Shaw, between the world of Blatchford and of General Booth. Call it, if you will, a narrow question whether your child shall be brought up by the vicar or the minister or the popish priest. You have still to face that larger, more liberal, more highly civilized question, of whether he shall be brought up by Harmsworth or by Pearson, by Mr. Eustace Miles with his Simple Life or Mr. Peter Keary with his Strenuous Life; whether he shall most eagerly read Miss Annie S. Swan or Mr. Bart Kennedy; in short, whether he shall end up in the mere violence of the S. D. F., or in the mere vulgarity of the Primrose League. They say that nowadays the creeds are crumbling; I doubt it, but at least the sects are increasing; and education must now be sectarian education, merely for practical purposes. Out of all this throng of theories it must somehow select a theory; out of all these thundering voices it must manage to hear a voice; out of all this awful and aching battle of blinding lights, without one shadow to give shape to them, it must manage somehow to trace and to track a star.

I have spoken so far of popular education, which began too vague and vast and which therefore has accomplished little. But as it happens there is in England something to compare it with. There is an institution, or class of institutions, which began with the same popular object, which has since followed a much narrower object, but which had the great advantage that it did follow some object, unlike our modern elementary schools.

In all these problems I should urge the solution which is positive, or, as silly people say, "optimistic." I should set my face, that is, against most of the solutions that are solely negative and abolitionist. Most educators of the poor seem to think that they have to teach the poor man not to drink. I should be quite content if they teach him to drink; for it is mere ignorance about how to drink and when to drink that is accountable for most of his tragedies. I do not propose (like some of my revolutionary friends) that we should abolish the public schools. I propose the much more lurid and desperate experiment that we should make them public. I do not wish to make Parliament stop working, but rather to make it work; not to shut up churches, but rather to open them; not to put out the lamp of learning or destroy the hedge of property, but only to make some rude effort to make universities fairly universal and property decently proper.

In many cases, let it be remembered, such action is not merely going back to the old ideal, but is even going back to the old reality. It would be a great step forward for the gin shop to go back to the inn. It is incontrovertibly true that to mediaevalize the public schools would be to democratize the public schools. Parliament did once really mean (as its name seems to imply) a place where people were allowed to talk. It is only lately that the general increase of efficiency, that is, of the Speaker, has made it mostly a place where people are prevented from talking. The poor do not go to the modern church, but they went to the ancient church all right; and if the common man in the past had a grave respect for property, it may conceivably have been because he sometimes had some of his own. I therefore can claim that I have no vulgar itch of innovation in anything I say about any of these institutions. Certainly I have none in that particular one which I am now obliged to pick out of the list; a type of institution to which I have genuine and personal reasons for being friendly and grateful: I mean the great Tudor foundations, the public schools of England. They have been praised for a great many things, mostly, I am sorry to say, praised by themselves and their children. And yet for some reason no one has ever praised them the one really convincing reason.

X. The Case For The Public Schools

The word success can of course be used in two senses. It may be used with reference to a thing serving its immediate and peculiar purpose, as of a wheel going around; or it can be used with reference to a thing adding to the general welfare, as of a wheel being a useful discovery. It is one thing to say that Smith's flying machine is a failure, and quite another to say that Smith has failed to make a flying machine. Now this is very broadly the difference between the old English public schools and the new democratic schools. Perhaps the old public schools are (as I personally think they are) ultimately weakening the country rather than strengthening it, and are therefore, in that ultimate sense, inefficient. But there is such a thing as being efficiently inefficient. You can make your flying ship so that it flies, even if you also make it so that it kills you. Now the public school system may not work satisfactorily, but it works; the public schools may not achieve what we want, but they achieve what they want. The popular elementary schools do not in that sense achieve anything at all. It is very difficult to point to any guttersnipe in the street and say that he embodies the ideal for which popular education has been working, in the sense that the fresh-faced, foolish boy in "Etons" does embody the ideal for which the headmasters of Harrow and Winchester have been working. The aristocratic educationists have the positive purpose of turning out gentlemen, and they do turn out gentlemen, even when they expel them. The popular educationists would say that they had the far nobler idea of turning out citizens. I concede that it is a much nobler idea, but where are the citizens? I know that the boy in "Etons" is stiff with a rather silly and sentimental stoicism, called being a man of the world. I do not fancy that the errand-boy is rigid with that republican stoicism that is called being a citizen. The schoolboy will really say with fresh and innocent hauteur, "I am an English gentleman." I cannot so easily picture the errand-boy drawing up his head to the stars and answering, "Romanus civis sum." Let it be granted that our elementary teachers are teaching the very broadest code of morals, while our great headmasters are teaching only the narrowest code of manners. Let it be granted that both these things are being taught. But only one of them is being learned.

It is always said that great reformers or masters of events can manage to bring about some specific and practical reforms, but that they never fulfill their visions or satisfy their souls. I believe there is a real sense in which this apparent platitude is quite untrue. By a strange inversion the political idealist often does not get what he asks for, but does get what he wants. The silent pressure of his ideal lasts much longer and reshapes the world much more than the actualities by which he attempted to suggest it. What perishes is the letter, which he thought so practical. What endures is the spirit, which he felt to be unattainable and even unutterable. It is exactly his schemes that are not fulfilled; it is exactly his vision that is fulfilled. Thus the ten or twelve paper constitutions of the French Revolution, which seemed so business-like to the framers of them, seem to us to have flown away on the wind as the wildest fancies. What has not flown away, what is a fixed fact in Europe, is the ideal and vision. The Republic, the idea of a land full of mere citizens all with some minimum of manners and minimum of wealth, the vision of the eighteenth century, the reality of the twentieth. So I think it will generally be with the creator of social things, desirable or undesirable. All his schemes will fail, all his tools break in his hands. His compromises will collapse, his concessions will be useless. He must brace himself to bear his fate; he shall have nothing but his heart's desire.

Now if one may compare very small things with very great, one may say that the English aristocratic schools can claim something of the same sort of success and solid splendor as the French democratic politics. At least they can claim the same sort of superiority over the distracted and fumbling attempts of modern England to establish democratic education. Such success as has attended the public schoolboy throughout the Empire, a success exaggerated indeed by himself, but still positive and a fact of a certain indisputable shape and size, has been due to the central and supreme circumstance that the managers of our public schools did know what sort of boy they liked. They wanted something and they got something; instead of going to work in the broad-minded manner and wanting everything and getting nothing.

The only thing in question is the quality of the thing they got. There is something highly maddening in the circumstance that when modern people attack an institution that really does demand reform, they always attack it for the wrong reasons. Thus many opponents of our public schools, imagining themselves to be very democratic, have exhausted themselves in an unmeaning attack upon the study of Greek. I can understand how Greek may be regarded as useless, especially by those thirsting to throw themselves into the cut throat commerce which is the negation of citizenship; but I do not understand how it can be considered undemocratic. I quite understand why Mr. Carnegie has a hatred of Greek. It is obscurely founded on the firm and sound impression that in any self-governing Greek city he would have been killed. But I cannot comprehend why any chance democrat, say Mr. Quelch, or Mr. Will Crooks, I or Mr. John M. Robertson, should be opposed to people learning the Greek alphabet, which was the alphabet of liberty. Why should Radicals dislike Greek? In that language is written all the earliest and, Heaven knows, the most heroic history of the Radical party. Why should Greek disgust a democrat, when the very word democrat is Greek?

A similar mistake, though a less serious one, is merely attacking the athletics of public schools as something promoting animalism and brutality. Now brutality, in the only immoral sense, is not a vice of the English public schools. There is much moral bullying, owing to the general lack of moral courage in the public-school atmosphere. These schools do, upon the whole, encourage physical courage; but they do not merely discourage moral courage, they forbid it. The ultimate result of the thing is seen in the egregious English officer who cannot even endure to wear a bright uniform except when it is blurred and hidden in the smoke of battle. This, like all the affectations of our present plutocracy, is an entirely modern thing. It was unknown to the old aristocrats. The Black Prince would certainly have asked that any knight who had the courage to lift his crest among his enemies, should also have the courage to lift it among his friends. As regards moral courage, then it is not so much that the public schools support it feebly, as that they suppress it firmly. But physical courage they do, on the whole, support; and physical courage is a magnificent fundamental. The one great, wise Englishman of the eighteenth century said truly that if a man lost that virtue he could never be sure of keeping any other. Now it is one of the mean and morbid modern lies that physical courage is connected with cruelty. The Tolstoian and Kiplingite are nowhere more at one than in maintaining this. They have, I believe, some small sectarian quarrel with each other, the one saying that courage must be abandoned because it is connected with cruelty, and the other maintaining that cruelty is charming because it is a part of courage. But it is all, thank God, a lie. An energy and boldness of body may make a man stupid or reckless or dull or drunk or hungry, but it does not make him spiteful. And we may admit heartily (without joining in that perpetual praise which public-school men are always pouring upon themselves) that this does operate to the removal of mere evil cruelty in the public schools. English public school life is extremely like English public life, for which it is the preparatory school. It is like it specially in this, that things are either very open, common and conventional, or else are very secret indeed. Now there is cruelty in public schools, just as there is kleptomania and secret drinking and vices without a name. But these things do not flourish in the full daylight and common consciousness of the school, and no more does cruelty. A tiny trio of sullen-looking boys gather in corners and seem to have some ugly business always; it may be indecent literature, it may be the beginning of drink, it may occasionally be cruelty to little boys. But on this stage the bully is not a braggart. The proverb says that bullies are always cowardly, but these bullies are more than cowardly; they are shy.

As a third instance of the wrong form of revolt against the public schools, I may mention the habit of using the word aristocracy with a double implication. To put the plain truth as briefly as possible, if aristocracy means rule by a rich ring, England has aristocracy and the English public schools support it. If it means rule by ancient families or flawless blood, England has not got aristocracy, and the public schools systematically destroy it. In these circles real aristocracy, like real democracy, has become bad form. A modern fashionable host dare not praise his ancestry; it would so often be an insult to half the other oligarchs at table, who have no ancestry. We have said he has not the moral courage to wear his uniform; still less has he the moral courage to wear his coat-of-arms. The whole thing now is only a vague hotchpotch of nice and nasty gentlemen. The nice gentleman never refers to anyone else's father, the nasty gentleman never refers to his own. That is the only difference, the rest is the public-school manner. But Eton and Harrow have to be aristocratic because they consist so largely of parvenues. The public school is not a sort of refuge for aristocrats, like an asylum, a place where they go in and never come out. It is a factory for aristocrats; they come out without ever having perceptibly gone in. The poor little private schools, in their old-world, sentimental, feudal style, used to stick up a notice, "For the Sons of Gentlemen only." If the public schools stuck up a notice it ought to be inscribed, "For the Fathers of Gentlemen only." In two generations they can do the trick.

XI. The School For Hypocrites

These are the false accusations; the accusation of classicism, the accusation of cruelty, and the accusation of an exclusiveness based on perfection of pedigree. English public-school boys are not pedants, they are not torturers; and they are not, in the vast majority of cases, people fiercely proud of their ancestry, or even people with any ancestry to be proud of. They are taught to be courteous, to be good tempered, to be brave in a bodily sense, to be clean in a bodily sense; they are generally kind to animals, generally civil to servants, and to anyone in any sense their equal, the jolliest companions on earth. Is there then anything wrong in the public-school ideal? I think we all feel there is something very wrong in it, but a blinding network of newspaper phraseology obscures and entangles us; so that it is hard to trace to its beginning, beyond all words and phrases, the faults in this great English achievement.

Surely, when all is said, the ultimate objection to the English public school is its utterly blatant and indecent disregard of the duty of telling the truth. I know there does still linger among maiden ladies in remote country houses a notion that English schoolboys are taught to tell the truth, but it cannot be maintained seriously for a moment. Very occasionally, very vaguely, English schoolboys are told not to tell lies, which is a totally different thing. I may silently support all the obscene fictions and forgeries in the universe, without once telling a lie. I may wear another man's coat, steal another man's wit, apostatize to another man's creed, or poison another man's coffee, all without ever telling a lie. But no English school-boy is ever taught to tell the truth, for the very simple reason that he is never taught to desire the truth. From the very first he is taught to be totally careless about whether a fact is a fact; he is taught to care only whether the fact can be used on his "side" when he is engaged in "playing the game." He takes sides in his Union debating society to settle whether Charles I ought to have been killed, with the same solemn and pompous frivolity with which he takes sides in the cricket field to decide whether Rugby or Westminster shall win. He is never allowed to admit the abstract notion of the truth, that the match is a matter of what may happen, but that Charles I is a matter of what did happen--or did not. He is Liberal or Tory at the general election exactly as he is Oxford or Cambridge at the boat race. He knows that sport deals with the unknown; he has not even a notion that politics should deal with the known. If anyone really doubts this self-evident proposition, that the public schools definitely discourage the love of truth, there is one fact which I should think would settle him. England is the country of the Party System, and it has always been chiefly run by public-school men. Is there anyone out of Hanwell who will maintain that the Party System, whatever its conveniences or inconveniences, could have been created by people particularly fond of truth?

The very English happiness on this point is itself a hypocrisy. When a man really tells the truth, the first truth he tells is that he himself is a liar. David said in his haste, that is, in his honesty, that all men are liars. It was afterwards, in some leisurely official explanation, that he said the Kings of Israel at least told the truth. When Lord Curzon was Viceroy he delivered a moral lecture to the Indians on their reputed indifference to veracity, to actuality and intellectual honor. A great many people indignantly discussed whether orientals deserved to receive this rebuke; whether Indians were indeed in a position to receive such severe admonition. No one seemed to ask, as I should venture to ask, whether Lord Curzon was in a position to give it. He is an ordinary party politician; a party politician means a politician who might have belonged to either party. Being such a person, he must again and again, at every twist and turn of party strategy, either have deceived others or grossly deceived himself. I do not know the East; nor do I like what I know. I am quite ready to believe that when Lord Curzon went out he found a very false atmosphere. I only say it must have been something startlingly and chokingly false if it was falser than that English atmosphere from which he came. The English Parliament actually cares for everything except veracity. The public-school man is kind, courageous, polite, clean, companionable; but, in the most awful sense of the words, the truth is not in him.

This weakness of untruthfulness in the English public schools, in the English political system, and to some extent in the English character, is a weakness which necessarily produces a curious crop of superstitions, of lying legends, of evident delusions clung to through low spiritual self-indulgence. There are so many of these public-school superstitions that I have here only space for one of them, which may be called the superstition of soap. It appears to have been shared by the ablutionary Pharisees, who resembled the English public-school aristocrats in so many respects: in their care about club rules and traditions, in their offensive optimism at the expense of other people, and above all in their unimaginative plodding patriotism in the worst interests of their country. Now the old human common sense about washing is that it is a great pleasure. Water (applied externally) is a splendid thing, like wine. Sybarites bathe in wine, and Nonconformists drink water; but we are not concerned with these frantic exceptions. Washing being a pleasure, it stands to reason that rich people can afford it more than poor people, and as long as this was recognized all was well; and it was very right that rich people should offer baths to poor people, as they might offer any other agreeable thing--a drink or a donkey ride. But one dreadful day, somewhere about the middle of the nineteenth century, somebody discovered (somebody pretty well off) the two great modern truths, that washing is a virtue in the rich and therefore a duty in the poor. For a duty is a virtue that one can't do. And a virtue is generally a duty that one can do quite easily; like the bodily cleanliness of the upper classes. But in the public-school tradition of public life, soap has become creditable simply because it is pleasant. Baths are represented as a part of the decay of the Roman Empire; but the same baths are represented as part of the energy and rejuvenation of the British Empire. There are distinguished public school men, bishops, dons, headmasters, and high politicians, who, in the course of the eulogies which from time to time they pass upon themselves, have actually identified physical cleanliness with moral purity. They say (if I remember rightly) that a public-school man is clean inside and out. As if everyone did not know that while saints can afford to be dirty, seducers have to be clean. As if everyone did not know that the harlot must be clean, because it is her business to captivate, while the good wife may be dirty, because it is her business to clean. As if we did not all know that whenever God's thunder cracks above us, it is very likely indeed to find the simplest man in a muck cart and the most complex blackguard in a bath.

There are other instances, of course, of this oily trick of turning the pleasures of a gentleman into the virtues of an Anglo-Saxon. Sport, like soap, is an admirable thing, but, like soap, it is an agreeable thing. And it does not sum up all mortal merits to be a sportsman playing the game in a world where it is so often necessary to be a workman doing the work. By all means let a gentleman congratulate himself that he has not lost his natural love of pleasure, as against the blase, and unchildlike. But when one has the childlike joy it is best to have also the childlike unconsciousness; and I do not think we should have special affection for the little boy who ever lastingly explained that it was his duty to play Hide and Seek and one of his family virtues to be prominent in Puss in the Corner.

Another such irritating hypocrisy is the oligarchic attitude towards mendicity as against organized charity. Here again, as in the case of cleanliness and of athletics, the attitude would be perfectly human and intelligible if it were not maintained as a merit. Just as the obvious thing about soap is that it is a convenience, so the obvious thing about beggars is that they are an inconvenience. The rich would deserve very little blame if they simply said that they never dealt directly with beggars, because in modern urban civilization it is impossible to deal directly with beggars; or if not impossible, at least very difficult. But these people do not refuse money to beggars on the ground that such charity is difficult. They refuse it on the grossly hypocritical ground that such charity is easy. They say, with the most grotesque gravity, "Anyone can put his hand in his pocket and give a poor man a penny; but we, philanthropists, go home and brood and travail over the poor man's troubles until we have discovered exactly what jail, reformatory, workhouse, or lunatic asylum it will really be best for him to go to." This is all sheer lying. They do not brood about the man when they get home, and if they did it would not alter the original fact that their motive for discouraging beggars is the perfectly rational one that beggars are a bother. A man may easily be forgiven for not doing this or that incidental act of charity, especially when the question is as genuinely difficult as is the case of mendicity. But there is something quite pestilently Pecksniffian about shrinking from a hard task on the plea that it is not hard enough. If any man will really try talking to the ten beggars who come to his door he will soon find out whether it is really so much easier than the labor of writing a check for a hospital.

XII. The Staleness Of The New Schools

For this deep and disabling reason therefore, its cynical and abandoned indifference to the truth, the English public school does not provide us with the ideal that we require. We can only ask its modern critics to remember that right or wrong the thing can be done; the factory is working, the wheels are going around, the gentlemen are being produced, with their soap, cricket and organized charity all complete. And in this, as we have said before, the public school really has an advantage over all the other educational schemes of our time. You can pick out a public-school man in any of the many companies into which they stray, from a Chinese opium den to a German Jewish dinner-party. But I doubt if you could tell which little match girl had been brought up by undenominational religion and which by secular education. The great English aristocracy which has ruled us since the Reformation is really, in this sense, a model to the moderns. It did have an ideal, and therefore it has produced a reality.

We may repeat here that these pages propose mainly to show one thing: that progress ought to be based on principle, while our modern progress is mostly based on precedent. We go, not by what may be affirmed in theory, but by what has been already admitted in practice. That is why the Jacobites are the last Tories in history with whom a high-spirited person can have much sympathy. They wanted a specific thing; they were ready to go forward for it, and so they were also ready to go back for it. But modern Tories have only the dullness of defending situations that they had not the excitement of creating. Revolutionists make a reform, Conservatives only conserve the reform. They never reform the reform, which is often very much wanted. Just as the rivalry of armaments is only a sort of sulky plagiarism, so the rivalry of parties is only a sort of sulky inheritance. Men have votes, so women must soon have votes; poor children are taught by force, so they must soon be fed by force; the police shut public houses by twelve o'clock, so soon they must shut them by eleven o'clock; children stop at school till they are fourteen, so soon they will stop till they are forty. No gleam of reason, no momentary return to first principles, no abstract asking of any obvious question, can interrupt this mad and monotonous gallop of mere progress by precedent. It is a good way to prevent real revolution. By this logic of events, the Radical gets as much into a rut as the Conservative. We meet one hoary old lunatic who says his grandfather told him to stand by one stile. We meet another hoary old lunatic who says his grandfather told him only to walk along one lane.

I say we may repeat here this primary part of the argument, because we have just now come to the place where it is most startlingly and strongly shown. The final proof that our elementary schools have no definite ideal of their own is the fact that they so openly imitate the ideals of the public schools. In the elementary schools we have all the ethical prejudices and exaggerations of Eton and Harrow carefully copied for people to whom they do not even roughly apply. We have the same wildly disproportionate doctrine of the effect of physical cleanliness on moral character. Educators and educational politicians declare, amid warm cheers, that cleanliness is far more important than all the squabbles about moral and religious training. It would really seem that so long as a little boy washes his hands it does not matter whether he is washing off his mother's jam or his brother's gore. We have the same grossly insincere pretense that sport always encourages a sense of honor, when we know that it often ruins it. Above all, we have the same great upperclass assumption that things are done best by large institutions handling large sums of money and ordering everybody about; and that trivial and impulsive charity is in some way contemptible. As Mr. Blatchford says, "The world does not want piety, but soap--and Socialism." Piety is one of the popular virtues, whereas soap and Socialism are two hobbies of the upper middle class.

These "healthy" ideals, as they are called, which our politicians and schoolmasters have borrowed from the aristocratic schools and applied to the democratic, are by no means particularly appropriate to an impoverished democracy. A vague admiration for organized government and a vague distrust of individual aid cannot be made to fit in at all into the lives of people among whom kindness means lending a saucepan and honor means keeping out of the workhouse. It resolves itself either into discouraging that system of prompt and patchwork generosity which is a daily glory of the poor, or else into hazy advice to people who have no money not to give it recklessly away. Nor is the exaggerated glory of athletics, defensible enough in dealing with the rich who, if they did not romp and race, would eat and drink unwholesomely, by any means so much to the point when applied to people, most of whom will take a great deal of exercise anyhow, with spade or hammer, pickax or saw. And for the third case, of washing, it is obvious that the same sort of rhetoric about corporeal daintiness which is proper to an ornamental class cannot, merely as it stands, be applicable to a dustman. A gentleman is expected to be substantially spotless all the time. But it is no more discreditable for a scavenger to be dirty than for a deep-sea diver to be wet. A sweep is no more disgraced when he is covered with soot than Michael Angelo when he is covered with clay, or Bayard when he is covered with blood. Nor have these extenders of the public-school tradition done or suggested anything by way of a substitute for the present snobbish system which makes cleanliness almost impossible to the poor; I mean the general ritual of linen and the wearing of the cast-off clothes of the rich. One man moves into another man's clothes as he moves into another man's house. No wonder that our educationists are not horrified at a man picking up the aristocrat's second-hand trousers, when they themselves have only taken up the aristocrat's second-hand ideas.

XIII. The Outlawed Parent

There is one thing at least of which there is never so much as a whisper inside the popular schools; and that is the opinion of the people. The only persons who seem to have nothing to do with the education of the children are the parents. Yet the English poor have very definite traditions in many ways. They are hidden under embarrassment and irony; and those psychologists who have disentangled them talk of them as very strange, barbaric and secretive things. But, as a matter of fact, the traditions of the poor are mostly simply the traditions of humanity, a thing which many of us have not seen for some time. For instance, workingmen have a tradition that if one is talking about a vile thing it is better to talk of it in coarse language; one is the less likely to be seduced into excusing it. But mankind had this tradition also, until the Puritans and their children, the Ibsenites, started the opposite idea, that it does not matter what you say so long as you say it with long words and a long face. Or again, the educated classes have tabooed most jesting about personal appearance; but in doing this they taboo not only the humor of the slums, but more than half the healthy literature of the world; they put polite nose-bags on the noses of Punch and Bardolph, Stiggins and Cyrano de Bergerac. Again, the educated classes have adopted a hideous and heathen custom of considering death as too dreadful to talk about, and letting it remain a secret for each person, like some private malformation. The poor, on the contrary, make a great gossip and display about bereavement; and they are right. They have hold of a truth of psychology which is at the back of all the funeral customs of the children of men. The way to lessen sorrow is to make a lot of it. The way to endure a painful crisis is to insist very much that it is a crisis; to permit people who must feel sad at least to feel important. In this the poor are simply the priests of the universal civilization; and in their stuffy feasts and solemn chattering there is the smell of the baked meats of Hamlet and the dust and echo of the funeral games of Patroclus.

The things philanthropists barely excuse (or do not excuse) in the life of the laboring classes are simply the things we have to excuse in all the greatest monuments of man. It may be that the laborer is as gross as Shakespeare or as garrulous as Homer; that if he is religious he talks nearly as much about hell as Dante; that if he is worldly he talks nearly as much about drink as Dickens. Nor is the poor man without historic support if he thinks less of that ceremonial washing which Christ dismissed, and rather more of that ceremonial drinking which Christ specially sanctified. The only difference between the poor man of to-day and the saints and heroes of history is that which in all classes separates the common man who can feel things from the great man who can express them. What he feels is merely the heritage of man. Now nobody expects of course that the cabmen and coal-heavers can be complete instructors of their children any more than the squires and colonels and tea merchants are complete instructors of their children. There must be an educational specialist in loco parentis. But the master at Harrow is in loco parentis; the master in Hoxton is rather contra parentem. The vague politics of the squire, the vaguer virtues of the colonel, the soul and spiritual yearnings of a tea merchant, are, in veritable practice, conveyed to the children of these people at the English public schools. But I wish here to ask a very plain and emphatic question. Can anyone alive even pretend to point out any way in which these special virtues and traditions of the poor are reproduced in the education of the poor? I do not wish the coster's irony to appeal as coarsely in the school as it does in the tap room; but does it appear at all? Is the child taught to sympathize at all with his father's admirable cheerfulness and slang? I do not expect the pathetic, eager pietas of the mother, with her funeral clothes and funeral baked meats, to be exactly imitated in the educational system; but has it any influence at all on the educational system? Does any elementary schoolmaster accord it even an instant's consideration or respect? I do not expect the schoolmaster to hate hospitals and C.O.S. centers so much as the schoolboy's father; but does he hate them at all? Does he sympathize in the least with the poor man's point of honor against official institutions? Is it not quite certain that the ordinary elementary schoolmaster will think it not merely natural but simply conscientious to eradicate all these rugged legends of a laborious people, and on principle to preach soap and Socialism against beer and liberty? In the lower classes the school master does not work for the parent, but against the parent. Modern education means handing down the customs of the minority, and rooting out the customs of the majority. Instead of their Christlike charity, their Shakespearean laughter and their high Homeric reverence for the dead, the poor have imposed on them mere pedantic copies of the prejudices of the remote rich. They must think a bathroom a necessity because to the lucky it is a luxury; they must swing Swedish clubs because their masters are afraid of English cudgels; and they must get over their prejudice against being fed by the parish, because aristocrats feel no shame about being fed by the nation.

XIV. Folly And Female Education

It is the same in the case of girls. I am often solemnly asked what I think of the new ideas about female education. But there are no new ideas about female education. There is not, there never has been, even the vestige of a new idea. All the educational reformers did was to ask what was being done to boys and then go and do it to girls; just as they asked what was being taught to young squires and then taught it to young chimney sweeps. What they call new ideas are very old ideas in the wrong place. Boys play football, why shouldn't girls play football; boys have school colors, why shouldn't girls have school-colors; boys go in hundreds to day-schools, why shouldn't girls go in hundreds to day-schools; boys go to Oxford, why shouldn't girls go to Oxford--in short, boys grow mustaches, why shouldn't girls grow mustaches--that is about their notion of a new idea. There is no brain-work in the thing at all; no root query of what sex is, of whether it alters this or that, and why, anymore than there is any imaginative grip of the humor and heart of the populace in the popular education. There is nothing but plodding, elaborate, elephantine imitation. And just as in the case of elementary teaching, the cases are of a cold and reckless inappropriateness. Even a savage could see that bodily things, at least, which are good for a man are very likely to be bad for a woman. Yet there is no boy's game, however brutal, which these mild lunatics have not promoted among girls. To take a stronger case, they give girls very heavy home-work; never reflecting that all girls have home-work already in their homes. It is all a part of the same silly subjugation; there must be a hard stick-up collar round the neck of a woman, because it is already a nuisance round the neck of a man. Though a Saxon serf, if he wore that collar of cardboard, would ask for his collar of brass.

It will then be answered, not without a sneer, "And what would you prefer? Would you go back to the elegant early Victorian female, with ringlets and smelling-bottle, doing a little in water colors, dabbling a little in Italian, playing a little on the harp, writing in vulgar albums and painting on senseless screens? Do you prefer that?" To which I answer, "Emphatically, yes." I solidly prefer it to the new female education, for this reason, that I can see in it an intellectual design, while there is none in the other. I am by no means sure that even in point of practical fact that elegant female would not have been more than a match for most of the inelegant females. I fancy Jane Austen was stronger, sharper and shrewder than Charlotte Bronte; I am quite certain she was stronger, sharper and shrewder than George Eliot. She could do one thing neither of them could do: she could coolly and sensibly describe a man. I am not sure that the old great lady who could only smatter Italian was not more vigorous than the new great lady who can only stammer American; nor am I certain that the bygone duchesses who were scarcely successful when they painted Melrose Abbey, were so much more weak-minded than the modern duchesses who paint only their own faces, and are bad at that. But that is not the point. What was the theory, what was the idea, in their old, weak water-colors and their shaky Italian? The idea was the same which in a ruder rank expressed itself in home-made wines and hereditary recipes; and which still, in a thousand unexpected ways, can be found clinging to the women of the poor. It was the idea I urged in the second part of this book: that the world must keep one great amateur, lest we all become artists and perish. Somebody must renounce all specialist conquests, that she may conquer all the conquerors. That she may be a queen of life, she must not be a private soldier in it. I do not think the elegant female with her bad Italian was a perfect product, any more than I think the slum woman talking gin and funerals is a perfect product; alas! there are few perfect products. But they come from a comprehensible idea; and the new woman comes from nothing and nowhere. It is right to have an ideal, it is right to have the right ideal, and these two have the right ideal. The slum mother with her funerals is the degenerate daughter of Antigone, the obstinate priestess of the household gods. The lady talking bad Italian was the decayed tenth cousin of Portia, the great and golden Italian lady, the Renascence amateur of life, who could be a barrister because she could be anything. Sunken and neglected in the sea of modern monotony and imitation, the types hold tightly to their original truths. Antigone, ugly, dirty and often drunken, will still bury her father. The elegant female, vapid and fading away to nothing, still feels faintly the fundamental difference between herself and her husband: that he must be Something in the City, that she may be everything in the country.

There was a time when you and I and all of us were all very close to God; so that even now the color of a pebble (or a paint), the smell of a flower (or a firework), comes to our hearts with a kind of authority and certainty; as if they were fragments of a muddled message, or features of a forgotten face. To pour that fiery simplicity upon the whole of life is the only real aim of education; and closest to the child comes the woman--she understands. To say what she understands is beyond me; save only this, that it is not a solemnity. Rather it is a towering levity, an uproarious amateurishness of the universe, such as we felt when we were little, and would as soon sing as garden, as soon paint as run. To smatter the tongues of men and angels, to dabble in the dreadful sciences, to juggle with pillars and pyramids and toss up the planets like balls, this is that inner audacity and indifference which the human soul, like a conjurer catching oranges, must keep up forever. This is that insanely frivolous thing we call sanity. And the elegant female, drooping her ringlets over her water-colors, knew it and acted on it. She was juggling with frantic and flaming suns. She was maintaining the bold equilibrium of inferiorities which is the most mysterious of superiorities and perhaps the most unattainable. She was maintaining the prime truth of woman, the universal mother: that if a thing is worth doing, it is worth doing badly.

Part Five. The Home Of Man

I. The Empire Of The Insect

A cultivated Conservative friend of mine once exhibited great distress because in a gay moment I once called Edmund Burke an atheist. I need scarcely say that the remark lacked something of biographical precision; it was meant to. Burke was certainly not an atheist in his conscious cosmic theory, though he had not a special and flaming faith in God, like Robespierre. Nevertheless, the remark had reference to a truth which it is here relevant to repeat. I mean that in the quarrel over the French Revolution, Burke did stand for the atheistic attitude and mode of argument, as Robespierre stood for the theistic. The Revolution appealed to the idea of an abstract and eternal justice, beyond all local custom or convenience. If there are commands of God, then there must be rights of man. Here Burke made his brilliant diversion; he did not attack the Robespierre doctrine with the old mediaeval doctrine of jus divinum (which, like the Robespierre doctrine, was theistic), he attacked it with the modern argument of scientific relativity; in short, the argument of evolution. He suggested that humanity was everywhere molded by or fitted to its environment and institutions; in fact, that each people practically got, not only the tyrant it deserved, but the tyrant it ought to have. "I know nothing of the rights of men," he said, "but I know something of the rights of Englishmen." There you have the essential atheist. His argument is that we have got some protection by natural accident and growth; and why should we profess to think beyond it, for all the world as if we were the images of God! We are born under a House of Lords, as birds under a house of leaves; we live under a monarchy as niggers live under a tropic sun; it is not their fault if they are slaves, and it is not ours if we are snobs. Thus, long before Darwin struck his great blow at democracy, the essential of the Darwinian argument had been already urged against the French Revolution. Man, said Burke in effect, must adapt himself to everything, like an animal; he must not try to alter everything, like an angel. The last weak cry of the pious, pretty, half-artificial optimism and deism of the eighteenth

141

century came in the voice of Sterne, saying, "God tempers the wind to the shorn lamb." And Burke, the iron evolutionist, essentially answered, "No; God tempers the shorn lamb to the wind." It is the lamb that has to adapt himself. That is, he either dies or becomes a particular kind of lamb who likes standing in a draught.

The subconscious popular instinct against Darwinism was not a mere offense at the grotesque notion of visiting one's grandfather in a cage in the Regent's Park. Men go in for drink, practical jokes and many other grotesque things; they do not much mind making beasts of themselves, and would not much mind having beasts made of their forefathers. The real instinct was much deeper and much more valuable. It was this: that when once one begins to think of man as a shifting and alterable thing, it is always easy for the strong and crafty to twist him into new shapes for all kinds of unnatural purposes. The popular instinct sees in such developments the possibility of backs bowed and hunch-backed for their burden, or limbs twisted for their task. It has a very well-grounded guess that whatever is done swiftly and systematically will mostly be done by a successful class and almost solely in their interests. It has therefore a vision of inhuman hybrids and half-human experiments much in the style of Mr. Wells's "Island of Dr. Moreau." The rich man may come to breeding a tribe of dwarfs to be his jockeys, and a tribe of giants to be his hall-porters. Grooms might be born bow-legged and tailors born cross-legged; perfumers might have long, large noses and a crouching attitude, like hounds of scent; and professional wine-tasters might have the horrible expression of one tasting wine stamped upon their faces as infants. Whatever wild image one employs it cannot keep pace with the panic of the human fancy, when once it supposes that the fixed type called man could be changed. If some millionaire wanted arms, some porter must grow ten arms like an octopus; if he wants legs, some messenger-boy must go with a hundred trotting legs like a centipede. In the distorted mirror of hypothesis, that is, of the unknown, men can dimly see such monstrous and evil shapes; men run all to eye, or all to fingers, with nothing left but one nostril or one ear. That is the nightmare with which the mere notion of adaptation threatens us. That is the nightmare that is not so very far from the reality.

142

It will be said that not the wildest evolutionist really asks that we should become in any way unhuman or copy any other animal. Pardon me, that is exactly what not merely the wildest evolutionists urge, but some of the tamest evolutionists too. There has risen high in recent history an important cultus which bids fair to be the religion of the future--which means the religion of those few weak-minded people who live in the future. It is typical of our time that it has to look for its god through a microscope; and our time has marked a definite adoration of the insect. Like most things we call new, of course, it is not at all new as an idea; it is only new as an idolatry. Virgil takes bees seriously but I doubt if he would have kept bees as carefully as he wrote about them. The wise king told the sluggard to watch the ant, a charming occupation--for a sluggard. But in our own time has appeared a very different tone, and more than one great man, as well as numberless intelligent men, have in our time seriously suggested that we should study the insect because we are his inferiors. The old moralists merely took the virtues of man and distributed them quite decoratively and arbitrarily among the animals. The ant was an almost heraldic symbol of industry, as the lion was of courage, or, for the matter of that, the pelican of charity. But if the mediaevals had been convinced that a lion was not courageous, they would have dropped the lion and kept the courage; if the pelican is not charitable, they would say, so much the worse for the pelican. The old moralists, I say, permitted the ant to enforce and typify man's morality; they never allowed the ant to upset it. They used the ant for industry as the lark for punctuality; they looked up at the flapping birds and down at the crawling insects for a homely lesson. But we have lived to see a sect that does not look down at the insects, but looks up at the insects, that asks us essentially to bow down and worship beetles, like ancient Egyptians.

Maurice Maeterlinck is a man of unmistakable genius, and genius always carries a magnifying glass. In the terrible crystal of his lens we have seen the bees not as a little yellow swarm, but rather in golden armies and hierarchies of warriors and queens. Imagination perpetually peers and creeps further down the avenues and vistas in the tubes of science, and one fancies every frantic reversal of proportions; the earwig striding across the echoing plain like an elephant, or the grasshopper coming roaring above our roofs like a vast aeroplane, as he leaps from Hertfordshire to Surrey. One seems to enter in a dream a temple of enormous entomology, whose architecture is based on something wilder than arms or backbones; in which the ribbed columns have the half-crawling look of dim and monstrous caterpillars; or the dome is a starry spider hung horribly in the void. There is one of the modern works of engineering that gives one something of this nameless fear of the exaggerations of an underworld; and that is the curious curved architecture of the under ground railway, commonly called the Twopenny Tube. Those squat archways, without any upright line or pillar, look as if they had been tunneled by huge worms who have never learned to lift their heads. It is the very underground palace of the Serpent, the spirit of changing shape and color, that is the enemy of man.

But it is not merely by such strange aesthetic suggestions that writers like Maeterlinck have influenced us in the matter; there is also an ethical side to the business. The upshot of M. Maeterlinck's book on bees is an admiration, one might also say an envy, of their collective spirituality; of the fact that they live only for something which he calls the Soul of the Hive. And this admiration for the communal morality of insects is expressed in many other modern writers in various quarters and shapes; in Mr. Benjamin Kidd's theory of living only for the evolutionary future of our race, and in the great interest of some Socialists in ants, which they generally prefer to bees, I suppose, because they are not so brightly colored. Not least among the hundred evidences of this vague insectolatry are the floods of flattery poured by modern people on that energetic nation of the Far East of which it has been said that "Patriotism is its only religion"; or, in other words, that it lives only for the Soul of the Hive. When at long intervals of the centuries Christendom grows weak, morbid or skeptical, and mysterious Asia begins to move against us her dim populations and to pour them westward like a dark movement of matter, in such cases it has been very common to compare the invasion to a plague of lice or incessant armies of locusts. The Eastern armies were indeed like insects; in their blind, busy destructiveness, in their black nihilism of personal outlook, in their hateful indifference to individual life and love, in their base belief in mere numbers, in their pessimistic courage and their atheistic patriotism, the riders and raiders of the East are indeed like all the creeping things of the earth. But never before, I think, have Christians called a Turk a locust and meant it as a compliment. Now for the first time we worship as well as fear; and trace with adoration that enormous form advancing vast and vague out of Asia, faintly discernible amid the mystic clouds of winged creatures hung over the wasted lands, thronging the skies like thunder and discoloring the skies like rain; Beelzebub, the Lord of Flies.

In resisting this horrible theory of the Soul of the Hive, we of Christendom stand not for ourselves, but for all humanity; for the essential and distinctive human idea that one good and happy man is an end in himself, that a soul is worth saving. Nay, for those who like such biological fancies it might well be said that we stand as chiefs and champions of a whole section of nature, princes of the house whose cognizance is the backbone, standing for the milk of the individual mother and the courage of the wandering cub, representing the pathetic chivalry of the dog, the humor and perversity of cats, the affection of the tranquil horse, the loneliness of the lion. It is more to the point, however, to urge that this mere glorification of society as it is in the social insects is a transformation and a dissolution in one of the outlines which have been specially the symbols of man. In the cloud and confusion of the flies and bees is growing fainter and fainter, as is finally disappearing, the idea of the human family. The hive has become larger than the house, the bees are destroying their captors; what the locust hath left, the caterpillar hath eaten; and the little house and garden of our friend Jones is in a bad way.

II. The Fallacy Of The Umbrella Stand

When Lord Morley said that the House of Lords must be either mended or ended, he used a phrase which has caused some confusion; because it might seem to suggest that mending and ending are somewhat similar things. I wish specially to insist on the fact that mending and ending are opposite things. You mend a thing because you like it; you end a thing because you don't. To mend is to strengthen. I, for instance, disbelieve in oligarchy; so I would no more mend the House of Lords than I would mend a thumbscrew. On the other hand, I do believe in the family; therefore I would mend the family as I would mend a chair; and I will never deny for a moment that the modern family is a chair that wants mending. But here comes in the essential point about the mass of modern advanced sociologists. Here are two institutions that have always been fundamental with mankind, the family and the state. Anarchists, I believe, disbelieve in both. It is quite unfair to say that Socialists believe in the state, but do not believe in the family; thousands of Socialists believe more in the family than any Tory. But it is true to say that while anarchists would end both, Socialists are specially engaged in mending (that is, strengthening and renewing) the state; and they are not specially engaged in strengthening and renewing the family. They are not doing anything to define the functions of father, mother, and child, as such; they are not tightening the machine up again; they are not blackening in again the fading lines of the old drawing. With the state they are doing this; they are sharpening its machinery, they are blackening in its black dogmatic lines, they are making mere government in every way stronger and in some ways harsher than before. While they leave the home in ruins, they restore the hive, especially the stings. Indeed, some schemes of labor and Poor Law reform recently advanced by distinguished Socialists, amount to little more than putting the largest number of people in the despotic power of Mr. Bumble. Apparently, progress means being moved on--by the police.

The point it is my purpose to urge might perhaps be suggested thus: that Socialists and most social reformers of their color are vividly conscious of the line between the kind of things that belong to the state and the kind of things that belong to mere chaos or uncoercible nature; they may force children to go to school before the sun rises, but they will not try to force the sun to rise; they will not, like Canute, banish the sea, but only the sea-bathers. But inside the outline of the state their lines are confused, and entities melt into each other. They have no firm instinctive sense of one thing being in its nature private and another public, of one thing being necessarily bond and another free. That is why piece by piece, and quite silently, personal liberty is being stolen from Englishmen, as personal land has been silently stolen ever since the sixteenth century.

I can only put it sufficiently curtly in a careless simile. A Socialist means a man who thinks a walking-stick like an umbrella because they both go into the umbrella-stand. Yet they are as different as a battle-ax and a bootjack. The essential idea of an umbrella is breadth and protection. The essential idea of a stick is slenderness and, partly, attack. The stick is the sword, the umbrella is the shield, but it is a shield against another and more nameless enemy--the hostile but anonymous universe. More properly, therefore, the umbrella is the roof; it is a kind of collapsible house. But the vital difference goes far deeper than this; it branches off into two kingdoms of man's mind, with a chasm between. For the point is this: that the umbrella is a shield against an enemy so actual as to be a mere nuisance; whereas the stick is a sword against enemies so entirely imaginary as to be a pure pleasure. The stick is not merely a sword, but a court sword; it is a thing of purely ceremonial swagger. One cannot express the emotion in any way except by saying that a man feels more like a man with a stick in his hand, just as he feels more like a man with a sword at his side. But nobody ever had any swelling sentiments about an umbrella; it is a convenience, like a door scraper. An umbrella is a necessary evil. A walking-stick is a quite unnecessary good. This, I fancy, is the real explanation of the perpetual losing of umbrellas; one does not hear of people losing walking sticks. For a walking-stick is a pleasure, a piece of real personal property; it is missed even when it is not needed. When my right hand forgets its stick may it forget its cunning. But anybody may forget an umbrella, as anybody might forget a shed that he has stood up in out of the rain. Anybody can forget a necessary thing.

If I might pursue the figure of speech, I might briefly say that the whole Collectivist error consists in saying that because two men can share an umbrella, therefore two men can share a walking-stick. Umbrellas might possibly be replaced by some kind of common awnings covering certain streets from particular showers. But there is nothing but nonsense in the notion of swinging a communal stick; it is as if one spoke of twirling a communal mustache. It will be said that this is a frank fantasia and that no sociologists suggest such follies. Pardon me if they do. I will give a precise parallel to the case of confusion of sticks and umbrellas, a parallel from a perpetually reiterated suggestion of reform. At least sixty Socialists out of a hundred, when they have spoken of common laundries, will go on at once to speak of common kitchens. This is just as mechanical and unintelligent as the fanciful case I have quoted. Sticks and umbrellas are both stiff rods that go into holes in a stand in the hall. Kitchens and washhouses are both large rooms full of heat and damp and steam. But the soul and function of the two things are utterly opposite. There is only one way of washing a shirt; that is, there is only one right way. There is no taste and fancy in tattered shirts. Nobody says, "Tompkins likes five holes in his shirt, but I must say, give me the good old four holes." Nobody says, "This washerwoman rips up the left leg of my pyjamas; now if there is one thing I insist on it is the right leg ripped up." The ideal washing is simply to send a thing back washed. But it is by no means true that the ideal cooking is simply to send a thing back cooked. Cooking is an art; it has in it personality, and even perversity, for the definition of an art is that which must be personal and may be perverse. I know a man, not otherwise dainty, who cannot touch common sausages unless they are almost burned to a coal. He wants his sausages fried to rags, yet he does not insist on his shirts being boiled to rags. I do not say that such points of culinary delicacy are of high importance. I do not say that the communal ideal must give way to them. What I say is that the communal ideal is not conscious of their existence, and therefore goes wrong from the very start, mixing a wholly public thing with a highly individual one. Perhaps we ought to accept communal kitchens in the social crisis, just as we should accept communal cat's-meat in a siege. But the cultured Socialist, quite at his ease, by no means in a siege, talks about communal kitchens as if they were the same kind of thing as communal laundries. This shows at the start that he misunderstands human nature. It is as different as three men singing the same chorus from three men playing three tunes on the same piano.

III. The Dreadful Duty Of Gudge

In the quarrel earlier alluded to between the energetic Progressive and the obstinate Conservative (or, to talk a tenderer language, between Hudge and Gudge), the state of cross-purposes is at the present moment acute. The Tory says he wants to preserve family life in Cindertown; the Socialist very reasonably points out to him that in Cindertown at present there isn't any family life to preserve. But Hudge, the Socialist, in his turn, is highly vague and mysterious about whether he would preserve the family life if there were any; or whether he will try to restore it where it has disappeared. It is all very confusing. The Tory sometimes talks as if he wanted to tighten the domestic bonds that do not exist; the Socialist as if he wanted to loosen the bonds that do not bind anybody. The question we all want to ask of both of them is the original ideal question, "Do you want to keep the family at all?" If Hudge, the Socialist, does want the family he must be prepared for the natural restraints, distinctions and divisions of labor in the family. He must brace himself up to bear the idea of the woman having a preference for the private house and a man for the public house. He must manage to endure somehow the idea of a woman being womanly, which does not mean soft and yielding, but handy, thrifty, rather hard, and very humorous. He must confront without a quiver the notion of a child who shall be childish, that is, full of energy, but without an idea of independence; fundamentally as eager for authority as for information and butter-scotch. If a man, a woman and a child live together any more in free and sovereign households, these ancient relations will recur; and Hudge must put up with it. He can only avoid it by destroying the family, driving both sexes into sexless hives and hordes, and bringing up all children as the children of the state--like Oliver Twist. But if these stern words must be addressed to Hudge, neither shall Gudge escape a somewhat severe admonition. For the plain truth to be told pretty sharply to the Tory is this, that if he wants the family to remain, if he wants to be strong enough to resist the rending forces of our essentially savage commerce, he must make some very big sacrifices and try to equalize property. The overwhelming mass of the English people at this particular instant are simply too poor to be domestic. They are as domestic as they can manage; they are much more domestic than the governing class; but they cannot get what good there was originally meant to be in this institution, simply because they have not got enough money. The man ought to stand for a certain magnanimity, quite lawfully expressed in throwing money away: but if under given circumstances he can only do it by throwing the week's food away, then he is not magnanimous, but mean. The woman ought to stand for a certain wisdom which is well expressed in valuing things rightly and guarding money sensibly; but how is she to guard money if there is no money to guard? The child ought to look on his mother as a fountain of natural fun and poetry; but how can he unless the fountain, like other fountains, is allowed to play? What chance have any of these ancient arts and functions in a house so hideously topsy-turvy; a house where the woman is out working and the man isn't; and the child is forced by law to think his schoolmaster's requirements more important than his mother's? No, Gudge and his friends in the House of Lords and the Carlton Club must make up their minds on this matter, and that very quickly. If they are content to have England turned into a beehive and an ant-hill, decorated here and there with a few faded butterflies playing at an old game called domesticity in the intervals of the divorce court, then let them have their empire of insects; they will find plenty of Socialists who will give it to them. But if they want a domestic England, they must "shell out," as the phrase goes, to a vastly greater extent than any Radical politician has yet dared to suggest; they must endure burdens much heavier than the Budget and strokes much deadlier than the death duties; for the thing to be done is nothing more nor less than the distribution of the great fortunes and the great estates. We can now only avoid Socialism by a change as vast as Socialism. If we are to save property, we must distribute property, almost as sternly and sweepingly as did the French Revolution. If we are to preserve the family we must revolutionize the nation.

IV. A Last Instance

And now, as this book is drawing to a close, I will whisper in the reader's ear a horrible suspicion that has sometimes haunted me: the suspicion that Hudge and Gudge are secretly in partnership. That the quarrel they keep up in public is very much of a put-up job, and that the way in which they perpetually play into each other's hands is not an everlasting coincidence. Gudge, the plutocrat, wants an anarchic industrialism; Hudge, the idealist, provides him with lyric praises of anarchy. Gudge wants women-workers because they are cheaper; Hudge calls the woman's work "freedom to live her own life." Gudge wants steady and obedient workmen, Hudge preaches teetotalism--to workmen, not to Gudge--Gudge wants a tame and timid population who will never take arms against tyranny; Hudge proves from Tolstoi that nobody must take arms against anything. Gudge is naturally a healthy and well-washed gentleman; Hudge earnestly preaches the perfection of Gudge's washing to people who can't practice it. Above all, Gudge rules by a coarse and cruel system of sacking and sweating and bi-sexual toil which is totally inconsistent with the free family and which is bound to destroy it; therefore Hudge, stretching out his arms to the universe with a prophetic smile, tells us that the family is something that we shall soon gloriously outgrow.

I do not know whether the partnership of Hudge and Gudge is conscious or unconscious. I only know that between them they still keep the common man homeless. I only know I still meet Jones walking the streets in the gray twilight, looking sadly at the poles and barriers and low red goblin lanterns which still guard the house which is none the less his because he has never been in it.

V. Conclusion

Here, it may be said, my book ends just where it ought to begin. I have said that the strong centers of modern English property must swiftly or slowly be broken up, if even the idea of property is to remain among Englishmen. There are two ways in which it could be done, a cold administration by quite detached officials, which is called Collectivism, or a personal distribution, so as to produce what is called Peasant Proprietorship. I think the latter solution the finer and more fully human, because it makes each man as somebody blamed somebody for saying of the Pope, a sort of small god. A man on his own turf tastes eternity or, in other words, will give ten minutes more work than is required. But I believe I am justified in shutting the door on this vista of argument, instead of opening it. For this book is not designed to prove the case for Peasant Proprietorship, but to prove the case against modern sages who turn reform to a routine. The whole of this book has been a rambling and elaborate urging of one purely ethical fact. And if by any chance it should happen that there are still some who do not quite see what that point is, I will end with one plain parable, which is none the worse for being also a fact.

A little while ago certain doctors and other persons permitted by modern law to dictate to their shabbier fellow-citizens, sent out an order that all little girls should have their hair cut short. I mean, of course, all little girls whose parents were poor. Many very unhealthy habits are common among rich little girls, but it will be long before any doctors interfere forcibly with them. Now, the case for this particular interference was this, that the poor are pressed down from above into such stinking and suffocating underworlds of squalor, that poor people must not be allowed to have hair, because in their case it must mean lice in the hair. Therefore, the doctors propose to abolish the hair. It never seems to have occurred to them to abolish the lice. Yet it could be done. As is common in most modern discussions the unmentionable thing is the pivot of the whole discussion. It is obvious to any Christian man (that is, to any man with a free soul) that any coercion applied to a cabman's daughter ought, if possible, to be applied to a Cabinet Minister's daughter. I will not ask why the doctors do not, as a matter of fact apply their rule to a Cabinet Minister's daughter. I will not ask, because I know. They do not because they dare not. But what is the excuse they would urge, what is the plausible argument they would use, for thus cutting and clipping poor children and not rich? Their argument would be that the disease is more likely to be in the hair of poor people than of rich. And why? Because the poor children are forced (against all the instincts of the highly domestic working classes) to crowd together in close rooms under a wildly inefficient system of public instruction; and because in one out of the forty children there may be offense. And why? Because the poor man is so ground down by the great rents of the great ground landlords that his wife often has to work as well as he. Therefore she has no time to look after the children, therefore one in forty of them is dirty. Because the workingman has these two persons on top of him, the landlord sitting (literally) on his stomach, and the schoolmaster sitting (literally) on his head, the workingman must allow his little girl's hair, first to be neglected from poverty, next to be poisoned by promiscuity, and, lastly, to be abolished by hygiene. He, perhaps, was proud of his little girl's hair. But he does not count.

Upon this simple principle (or rather precedent) the sociological doctor drives gayly ahead. When a crapulous tyranny crushes men down into the dirt, so that their very hair is dirty, the scientific course is clear. It would be long and laborious to cut off the heads of the tyrants; it is easier to cut off the hair of the slaves. In the same way, if it should ever happen that poor children, screaming with toothache, disturbed any schoolmaster or artistic gentleman, it would be easy to pull out all the teeth of the poor; if their nails were disgustingly dirty, their nails could be plucked out; if their noses were indecently blown, their noses could be cut off. The appearance of our humbler fellow-citizen could be quite strikingly simplified before we had done with him. But all this is not a bit wilder than the brute fact that a doctor can walk into the house of a free man, whose daughter's hair may be as clean as spring flowers, and order him to cut it off. It never seems to strike these people that the lesson of lice in the slums is the wrongness of slums, not the wrongness of hair. Hair is, to say the least of it, a rooted thing. Its enemy (like the other insects and oriental armies of whom we have spoken) sweep upon us but seldom. In truth, it is only by eternal institutions like hair that we can test passing institutions like empires. If a house is so built as to knock a man's head off when he enters it, it is built wrong.

The mob can never rebel unless it is conservative, at least enough to have conserved some reasons for rebelling. It is the most awful thought in all our anarchy, that most of the ancient blows struck for freedom would not be struck at all to-day, because of the obscuration of the clean, popular customs from which they came.

The insult that brought down the hammer of Wat Tyler might now be called a medical examination. That which Virginius loathed and avenged as foul slavery might now be praised as free love. The cruel taunt of Foulon, "Let them eat grass," might now be represented as the dying cry of an idealistic vegetarian. Those great scissors of science that would snip off the curls of the poor little school children are ceaselessly snapping closer and closer to cut off all the corners and fringes of the arts and honors of the poor. Soon they will be twisting necks to suit clean collars, and hacking feet to fit new boots. It never seems to strike them that the body is more than raiment; that the Sabbath was made for man; that all institutions shall be judged and damned by whether they have fitted the normal flesh and spirit. It is the test of political sanity to keep your head. It is the test of artistic sanity to keep your hair on.

Now the whole parable and purpose of these last pages, and indeed of all these pages, is this: to assert that we must instantly begin all over again, and begin at the other end. I begin with a little girl's hair. That I know is a good thing at any rate. Whatever else is evil, the pride of a good mother in the beauty of her daughter is good. It is one of those adamantine tendernesses which are the touchstones of every age and race. If other things are against it, other things must go down. If landlords and laws and sciences are against it, landlords and laws and sciences must go down. With the red hair of one she-urchin in the gutter I will set fire to all modern civilization. Because a girl should have long hair, she should have clean hair; because she should have clean hair, she should not have an unclean home: because she should not have an unclean home, she should have a free and leisured mother; because she should have a free mother, she should not have an usurious landlord; because there should not be an usurious landlord, there should be a redistribution of property; because there should be a redistribution of property, there shall be a revolution. That little urchin with the gold-red hair, whom I have just watched toddling past my house, she shall not be lopped and lamed and altered; her hair shall not be cut short like a convict's; no, all the kingdoms of the earth shall be hacked about and mutilated to suit her. She is the human and sacred image; all around her the social fabric shall sway and split and fall; the pillars of society shall be shaken, and the roofs of ages come rushing down, and not one hair of her head shall be harmed.

What's Wrong with the World

What's Wrong with the World

Three Notes

I. On Female Suffrage

Not wishing to overload this long essay with too many parentheses, apart from its thesis of progress and precedent, I append here three notes on points of detail that may possibly be misunderstood.

The first refers to the female controversy. It may seem to many that I dismiss too curtly the contention that all women should have votes, even if most women do not desire them. It is constantly said in this connection that males have received the vote (the agricultural laborers for instance) when only a minority of them were in favor of it. Mr. Galsworthy, one of the few fine fighting intellects of our time, has talked this language in the "Nation." Now, broadly, I have only to answer here, as everywhere in this book, that history is not a toboggan slide, but a road to be reconsidered and even retraced. If we really forced General Elections upon free laborers who definitely disliked General Elections, then it was a thoroughly undemocratic thing to do; if we are democrats we ought to undo it. We want the will of the people, not the votes of the people; and to give a man a vote against his will is to make voting more valuable than the democracy it declares.

But this analogy is false, for a plain and particular reason. Many voteless women regard a vote as unwomanly. Nobody says that most voteless men regarded a vote as unmanly. Nobody says that any voteless men regarded it as unmanly. Not in the stillest hamlet or the most stagnant fen could you find a yokel or a tramp who thought he lost his sexual dignity by being part of a political mob. If he did not care about a vote it was solely because he did not know about a vote; he did not understand the word any better than Bimetallism. His opposition, if it existed, was merely negative. His indifference to a vote was really indifference.

But the female sentiment against the franchise, whatever its size, is positive. It is not negative; it is by no means indifferent. Such women as are opposed to the change regard it (rightly or wrongly) as unfeminine. That is, as insulting certain affirmative traditions to which they are attached. You may think such a view prejudiced; but I violently deny that any democrat has a right to override such prejudices, if they are popular and positive. Thus he would not have a right to make millions of Moslems vote with a cross if they had a prejudice in favor of voting with a crescent. Unless this is admitted, democracy is a farce we need scarcely keep up. If it is admitted, the Suffragists have not merely to awaken an indifferent, but to convert a hostile majority.

II. On Cleanliness In Education

On re-reading my protest, which I honestly think much needed, against our heathen idolatry of mere ablution, I see that it may possibly be misread. I hasten to say that I think washing a most important thing to be taught both to rich and poor. I do not attack the positive but the relative position of soap. Let it be insisted on even as much as now; but let other things be insisted on much more. I am even ready to admit that cleanliness is next to godliness; but the moderns will not even admit godliness to be next to cleanliness. In their talk about Thomas Becket and such saints and heroes they make soap more important than soul; they reject godliness whenever it is not cleanliness. If we resent this about remote saints and heroes, we should resent it more about the many saints and heroes of the slums, whose unclean hands cleanse the world. Dirt is evil chiefly as evidence of sloth; but the fact remains that the classes that wash most are those that work least. Concerning these, the practical course is simple; soap should be urged on them and advertised as what it is--a luxury. With regard to the poor also the practical course is not hard to harmonize with our thesis. If we want to give poor people soap we must set out deliberately to give them luxuries. If we will not make them rich enough to be clean, then emphatically we must do what we did with the saints. We must reverence them for being dirty.

III. On Peasant Proprietorship

I have not dealt with any details touching distributed ownership, or its possibility in England, for the reason stated in the text. This book deals with what is wrong, wrong in our root of argument and effort. This wrong is, I say, that we will go forward because we dare not go back. Thus the Socialist says that property is already concentrated into Trusts and Stores: the only hope is to concentrate it further in the State. I say the only hope is to unconcentrate it; that is, to repent and return; the only step forward is the step backward.

But in connection with this distribution I have laid myself open to another potential mistake. In speaking of a sweeping redistribution, I speak of decision in the aim, not necessarily of abruptness in the means. It is not at all too late to restore an approximately rational state of English possessions without any mere confiscation. A policy of buying out landlordism, steadily adopted in England as it has already been adopted in Ireland (notably in Mr. Wyndham's wise and fruitful Act), would in a very short time release the lower end of the see-saw and make the whole plank swing more level. The objection to this course is not at all that it would not do, only that it will not be done. If we leave things as they are, there will almost certainly be a crash of confiscation. If we hesitate, we shall soon have to hurry. But if we start doing it quickly we have still time to do it slowly.

This point, however, is not essential to my book. All I have to urge between these two boards is that I dislike the big Whiteley shop, and that I dislike Socialism because it will (according to Socialists) be so like that shop. It is its fulfilment, not its reversal. I do not object to Socialism because it will revolutionize our commerce, but because it will leave it so horribly the same.

THE OUTLINE OF SANITY

The Outline of Sanity

CONTENTS

I. Some General Ideas

1. The Beginning Of The Quarrel

I have been asked to republish these notes — which appeared in a weekly paper — as a rough sketch of certain aspects of the institution of Private Property, now so completely forgotten amid the journalistic jubilations over Private Enterprise. The very fact that the publicists say so much of the latter and so little of the former is a measure of the moral tone of the times. A pickpocket is obviously a champion of private enterprise. But it would perhaps be an exaggeration to say that a pickpocket is a champion of private property. The point about Capitalism and Commercialism, as conducted of late, is that they have really preached the extension of business rather than the preservation of belongings; and have at best tried to disguise the pickpocket with some of the virtues of the pirate. The point about Communism is that it only reforms the pickpocket by forbidding pockets.

Pockets and possessions generally seem to me to have not only a more normal but a more dignified defence than the rather dirty individualism that talks about private enterprise. In the hope that it may possibly help others to understand it, I have decided to reproduce these studies as they stand, hasty and sometimes merely topical as they were. It is indeed very hard to reproduce them in this form, because they were editorial notes to a controversy largely conducted by others; but the general idea is at least present. In any case, "private enterprise" is no very noble way of stating the truth of one of the Ten Commandments. But there was at least a time when it was more or less true. The Manchester Radicals preached a rather crude and cruel sort of competition; but at least they practised what they preached. The newspapers now praising private enterprise are preaching the very opposite of anything that anybody dreams of practising. The practical tendency of all trade and business to-day is towards big commercial combinations, often more imperial, more impersonal, more international than many a communist commonwealth — things that are at least collective if not collectivist. It is all very well to repeat distractedly, "What are we coming to, with all this Bolshevism?" It is equally relevant to add, "What are we coming to, even without Bolshevism?" The obvious answer is — Monopoly. It is certainly not private enterprise. The American Trust is not private enterprise. It would be truer to call the Spanish Inquisition private judgment. Monopoly is neither private nor enterprising. It exists to prevent private enterprise. And that system of trust or monopoly, that complete destruction of property, would still be the present goal of all our progress, if there were not a Bolshevist in the world.

Now I am one of those who believe that the cure for centralization is decentralization. It has been described as a paradox. There is apparently something elvish and fantastic about saying that when capital has come to be too much in the hand of the few, the right thing is to restore it into the hands of the many. The Socialist would put it in the hands of even fewer people; but those people would be politicians, who (as we know) always administer it in the interests of the many. But before I put before the reader things written in the very thick of the current controversy, I foresee it will be necessary to preface them with these few paragraphs, explaining a few of the terms and amplifying a few of the assumptions. I was in the weekly paper arguing with people who knew the shorthand of this particular argument; but to be clearly understood, we must begin with a few definitions or, at least, descriptions. I assure the reader that I use words in quite a definite sense, but it is possible that he may use them in a different sense; and a muddle and misunderstanding of that sort does not even rise to the dignity of a difference of opinion.

For instance, Capitalism is really a very unpleasant word. It is also a very unpleasant thing. Yet the thing I have in mind, when I say so, is quite definite and definable; only the name is a very unworkable word for it. But obviously we must have some word for it. When I say "Capitalism," I commonly mean something that may be stated thus: "That economic condition in which there is a class of capitalists, roughly recognizable and relatively small, in whose possession so much of the capital is concentrated as to necessitate a very large majority of the citizens serving those capitalists for a wage." This particular state of things can and does exist, and we must have some word for it, and some way of discussing it. But this is undoubtedly a very bad word, because it is used by other people to mean quite other things. Some people seem to mean merely private property. Others suppose that capitalism must mean anything involving the use of capital. But if that use is too literal, it is also too loose and even too large. If the use of capital is capitalism, then everything is capitalism. Bolshevism is capitalism and anarchist communism is capitalism; and every revolutionary scheme, however wild, is still capitalism. Lenin and Trotsky believe as much as Lloyd George and Thomas that the economic operations of to-day must leave something over for the economic operations of to-morrow. And that is all that capital means in its economic sense. In that case, the word is useless. My use of it may be arbitrary, but it is not useless. If capitalism means private property, I am capitalist. If capitalism means capital, everybody is capitalist. But if capitalism means this particular condition of capital, only paid out to the mass in the form of wages, then it does mean something, even if it ought to mean something else.

The truth is that what we call Capitalism ought to be called Proletarianism. The point of it is not that some people have capital, but that most people only have wages because they do not have capital. I have made an heroic effort in my time to walk about the world always saying Proletarianism instead of Capitalism. But my path has been a thorny one of troubles and misunderstandings. I find that when I criticize the Duke of Northumberland for his Proletarianism, my meaning does not get home. When I say I should often agree with the Morning Post if it were not so deplorably Proletarian, there seems to be some strange momentary impediment to the complete communion of mind with mind. Yet that would be strictly accurate; for what I complain of, in the current defence of existing capitalism, is that it is a defence of keeping most men in wage dependence; that is, keeping most men without capital. I am not the sort of precision who prefers conveying correctly what he doesn't mean, rather than conveying incorrectly what he does. I am totally indifferent to the term as compared to the meaning. I do not care whether I call one thing or the other by this mere printed word beginning with a "C," so long as it is applied to one thing and not the other. I do not mind using a term as arbitrary as a mathematical sign, if it is accepted like a mathematical sign. I do not mind calling Property x and Capitalism y, so long as nobody thinks it necessary to say that x=y. I do not mind saying "cat" for capitalism and "dog" for distributism, so long as people understand that the things are different enough to fight like cat and dog. The proposal of the wider distribution of capital remains the same, whatever we call it, or whatever we call the present glaring contradiction of it. It is the same whether we state it by saying that there is too much capitalism in the one sense or too little capitalism in the other. And it is really quite pedantic to say that the use of capital must be capitalist. We might as fairly say that anything social must be Socialist; that Socialism can be identified with a social evening or a social glass. Which, I grieve to say, is not the case.

Nevertheless, there is enough verbal vagueness about Socialism to call for a word of definition. Socialism is a system which makes the corporate unity of society responsible for all its economic processes, or all those affecting life and essential living. If anything important is sold, the Government has sold it; if anything important is given, the Government has given it; if anything important is even tolerated, the Government is responsible for tolerating it. This is the very reverse of anarchy; it is an extreme enthusiasm for authority. It is in many ways worthy of the moral dignity of the mind; it is a collective acceptance of a very complete responsibility. But it is silly of Socialists to complain of our saying that it must be a destruction of liberty. It is almost equally silly of Anti-Socialists to complain of the unnatural and unbalanced brutality of the Bolshevist Government in crushing a political opposition. A Socialist Government is one which in its nature does not tolerate any true and real opposition. For there the Government provides everything; and it is absurd to ask a Government to provide an opposition.

You cannot go to the Sultan and say reproachfully, "You have made no arrangements for your brother dethroning you and seizing the Caliphate." You cannot go to a medieval king and say, "Kindly lend me two thousand spears and one thousand bowmen, as I wish to raise a rebellion against you." Still less can you reproach a Government which professes to set up everything, because it has not set up anything to pull down all it has set up. Opposition and rebellion depend on property and liberty. They can only be tolerated where other rights have been allowed to strike root, besides the central right of the ruler. Those rights must be protected by a morality which even the ruler will hesitate to defy. The critic of the State can only exist where a religious sense of right protects his claims to his own bow and spear; or at least, to his own pen or his own printing-press. It is absurd to suppose that he could borrow the royal pen to advocate regicide or use the Government printing-presses to expose the corruption of the Government. Yet it is the whole point of Socialism, the whole case for Socialism, that unless all printing-presses are Government printing-presses, printers may be oppressed. Everything is staked on the State's justice; it is putting all the eggs in one basket. Many of them will be rotten eggs; but even then you will not be allowed to use them at political elections.

About fifteen years ago a few of us began to preach, in the old New Age and New Witness, a policy of small distributed property (which has since assumed the awkward but accurate name of Distributism), as we should have said then, against the two extremes of Capitalism and Communism. The first criticism we received was from the most brilliant Fabians, especially Mr. Bernard Shaw. And the form which that first criticism took was simply to tell us that our ideal was impossible. It was only a case of Catholic credulity about fairy-tales. The Law of Rent, and other economic laws, made it inevitable that the little rivulets of property should run down into the pool of plutocracy. In truth, it was the Fabian wit, and not merely the Tory fool, who confronted our vision with that venerable verbal opening, "If it were all divided up to-morrow — "

Nevertheless, we had an answer even in those days, and though we have since found many others, it will clarify the question if I repeat this point of principle. It is true that I believe in fairy-tales — in the sense that I marvel so much at what does exist that I am the readier to admit what might. I understand the man who believes in the Sea Serpent on the ground that there are more fish in the sea than ever came out of it. But I do it the more because the other man, in his ardour for disproving the Sea Serpent, always argues that there are not only no snakes in Iceland, but none in the world. Suppose Mr. Bernard Shaw, commenting on this credulity, were to blame me for believing (on the word of some lying priest) that stones could be thrown up into the air and hang there suspended like a rainbow. Suppose he told me tenderly that I should not believe this Popish fable of the magic stones, if I had ever had the Law of Gravity scientifically explained to me. And suppose, after all this, I found he was only talking about the impossibility of building an arch. I think most of us would form two main conclusions about him and his school. First, we should think them very ill-informed about what is really meant by recognizing a law of nature. A law of nature can be recognized by resisting it, or out-manoeuvring it, or even using it against itself, as in the case of the arch. And second, and much more strongly, we should think them astonishingly ill-informed about what has already been done upon this earth.

Similarly, the first fact in the discussion of whether small properties can exist is the fact that they do exist. It is a fact almost equally unmistakable that they not only exist but endure. Mr. Shaw affirmed, in a sort of abstract fury, that "small properties will not stay small." Now it is interesting to note here that the opponents of anything like a several proprietary bring two highly inconsistent charges against it. They are perpetually telling us that the peasant life in Latin or other countries is monotonous, is unprogressive, is covered with weedy superstitions, and is a sort of survival of the Stone Age. Yet even while they taunt us with its survival, they argue that it can never survive. They point to the peasant as a perennial stick-in-the-mud; and then refuse to plant him anywhere, on the specific ground that he would not stick. Now, the first of the two types of denunciation is arguable enough; but in order to denounce peasantries, the critics must admit that there are peasantries to denounce. And if it were true that they always tended rapidly to disappear, it would not be true that they exhibited those primitive customs and conservative opinions which they not only do, in fact, exhibit, but which the critics reproach them with exhibiting. They cannot in common sense accuse a thing at once of being antiquated and of being ephemeral. It is, of course, the dry fact, to be seen in broad daylight, that small peasant properties are not ephemeral. But anyhow, Mr. Shaw and his school must not say that arches cannot be built, and then that they disfigure the landscape. The Distributive State is not a hypothesis for him to demolish; it is a phenomenon for him to explain.

The truth is that the conception that small property evolves into Capitalism is a precise picture of what practically never takes place. The truth is attested even by facts of geography, facts which, as it seems to me, have been strangely overlooked. Nine times out of ten, an industrial civilization of the modern capitalist type does not arise, wherever else it may arise, in places where there has hitherto been a distributive civilization like that of a peasantry. Capitalism is a monster that grows in deserts. Industrial servitude has almost everywhere arisen in those empty spaces where the older civilization was thin or absent. Thus it grew up easily in the North of England rather than the South; precisely because the North had been comparatively empty and barbarous through all the ages when the South had a civilization of guilds and peasantries. Thus it grew up easily in the American continent rather than the European; precisely because it had nothing to supplant in America but a few savages, while in Europe it had to supplant the culture of multitudinous farms. Everywhere it has been but one stride from the mudhut to the manufacturing town. Everywhere the mudhut which really turned into the free farm has never since moved an inch towards the manufacturing town. Wherever there was the mere lord and the mere serf, they could almost instantly be turned into the mere employer and the mere employee. Wherever there has been the free man, even when he was relatively less rich and powerful, his mere memory has made complete industrial capitalism impossible. It is an enemy that has sown these tares, but even as an enemy he is a coward. For he can only sow them in waste places, where no wheat can spring up and choke them.

To take up our parable again, we say first that arches exist; and not only exist but remain. A hundred Roman aqueducts and amphitheatres are there to show that they can remain as long or longer than anything else. And if a progressive person informs us that an arch always turns into a factory chimney, or even that an arch always falls down because it is weaker than a factory chimney, or even that wherever it does fall down people perceive that they must replace it by a factory chimney — why, we shall be so audacious as to cast doubts on all these three assertions. All we could possibly admit is that the principle supporting the chimney is simpler than the principle of the arch; and for that very reason the factory chimney, like the feudal tower, can rise the more easily in a howling wilderness.

But the image has yet a further application. If at this moment the Latin countries are largely made our model in the matter of the small property, it is only in the sense in which they would have been, through certain periods of history, the only exemplars of the arch. There was a time when all arches were Roman arches; and when a man living by the Liffey or the Thames would know as little about them as Mr. Shaw knows about peasant proprietors. But that does not mean that we fight for something merely foreign, or advance the arch as a sort of Italian ensign; any more than we want to make the Thames as yellow as the Tiber, or have any particular taste in macaroni or malaria. The principle of the arch is human, and applicable to and by all humanity. So is the principle of well-distributed private property. That a few Roman arches stood in ruins in Britain is not a proof that arches cannot be built, but on the contrary, a proof that they can.

And now, to complete the coincidence or analogy, what is the principle of the arch? You can call it, if you like, an affront to gravitation; you will be more correct if you call it an appeal to gravitation. The principle asserts that by combining separate stones of a particular shape in a particular way, we can ensure that their very tendency to fall shall prevent them from falling. And though my image is merely an illustration, it does to a great extent hold even as to the success of more equalized properties. What upholds an arch is an equality of pressure of the separate stones upon each other. The equality is at once mutual aid and mutual obstruction. It is not difficult to show that in a healthy society the moral pressure of different private properties acts in exactly the same way. But if the other school finds the key or comparison insufficient, it must find some other. It is clear that no natural forces can frustrate the fact. To say that any law, such as that of rent, makes against it is true only in the sense that many natural laws make against all morality and the very essentials of manhood. In that sense, scientific arguments are as irrelevant to our case for property as Mr. Shaw used to say they were to his case against vivisection.

Lastly, it is not only true that the arch of property remains, it is true that the building of such arches increases, both in quantity and quality. For instance, the French peasant before the French Revolution was already indefinitely a proprietor; it has made his property more private and more absolute, not less. The French are now less than ever likely to abandon the system, when it has proved for the second, if not the hundredth time, the most stable type of prosperity in the stress of war. A revolution as heroic, and even more unconquerable, has already in Ireland disregarded alike the Socialist dream and the Capitalist reality, with a driving energy of which no one has yet dared to foresee the limits. So, when the round arch of the Romans and the Normans had remained for ages as a sort of relic, the rebirth of Christendom found for it a further application and issue. It sprang in an instant to the titanic stature of the Gothic; where man seemed to be a god who had hanged his worlds upon nothing. Then was unsealed again something of that ancient secret which had so strangely described the priest as the builder of bridges. And when I look to-day at some of the bridges which he built above the air, I can understand a man still calling them impossible, as their only possible praise.

What do we mean by that "equality of pressure" as of the stones in an arch? More will be said of this in detail; but in general we mean that the modern passion for incessant and restless buying and selling goes along with the extreme inequality of men too rich or too poor. The explanation of the continuity of peasantries (which their opponents are simply forced to leave unexplained) is that, where that independence exists, it is valued exactly as any other dignity is valued when it is regarded as normal to a man; as no man goes naked or is beaten with a stick for hire.

The theory that those who start reasonably equal cannot remain reasonably equal is a fallacy founded entirely on a society in which they start extremely unequal. It is quite true that when capitalism has passed a certain point, the broken fragments of property are very easily devoured. In other words, it is true when there is a small amount of small property; but it is quite untrue when there is a large amount of small property. To argue from what happened in the rush of big business and the rout of scattered small businesses to what must always happen when the parties are more on a level, is quite illogical. It is proving from Niagara that there is no such thing as a lake. Once tip up the lake and the whole of the water will rush one way; as the whole economic tendency of capitalist inequality rushes one way. Leave the lake as a lake, or the level as a level, and there is nothing to prevent the lake remaining until the crack of doom — as many levels of peasantry

173

seem likely to remain until the crack of doom. This fact is proved by experience, even if it is not explained by experience; but, as a matter of fact, it is possible to suggest not only the experience but the explanation. The truth is that there is no economic tendency whatever towards the disappearance of small property, until that property becomes so very small as to cease to act as property at all. If one man has a hundred acres and another man has half an acre, it is likely enough that he will be unable to live on half an acre. Then there will be an economic tendency for him to sell his land and make the other man the proud possessor of a hundred and a half. But if one man has thirty acres and the other man has forty acres, there is no economic tendency of any kind whatever to make the first man sell to the second. It is simply false to say that the first man cannot be secure of thirty or the second man content with forty. It is sheer nonsense; like saying that any man who owns a bull terrier will be bound to sell it to somebody who owns a mastiff. It is like saying that I cannot own a horse because I have an eccentric neighbour who owns an elephant.

Needless to say, those who insist that roughly equalized ownership cannot exist, base their whole argument on the notion that it has existed. They have to suppose, in order to prove their point, that people in England, for instance, did begin as equals and rapidly reached inequality. And it only rounds off the humour of their whole position that they assume the existence of what they call an impossibility in the one case where it has really not occurred. They talk as if ten miners had run a race, and one of them became the Duke of Northumberland. They talk as if the first Rothschild was a peasant who patiently planted better cabbages than the other peasants. The truth is that England became a capitalist country because it had long been an oligarchical country. It would be much harder to point out in what way a country like Denmark need become oligarchical. But the case is even stronger when we add the ethical to the economic common sense. When there is once established a widely scattered ownership, there is a public opinion that is stronger than any law; and very often (what in modern times is even more remarkable) a law that is really an expression of public opinion. It may be very difficult for modern people to imagine a world in which men are not generally admired for covetousness and crushing their neighbours but I assure them that such strange patches of an earthly paradise do really remain on earth.

The truth is that this first objection of impossibility in the abstract flies flat in the face of all the facts of experience and human nature. It is not true that a moral custom cannot hold most men content with a reasonable status, and careful to preserve it. It is as if we were to say that because some men are more attractive to women than others, therefore the inhabitants of Balham under Queen Victoria could not possibly have been arranged on a monogamous model, with one man one wife. Sooner or later, it might be said, all females would be found clustering round the fascinating few, and nothing but bachelorhood be left for the unattractive many. Sooner or later the suburb must consist of a hundred hermitages and three harems. But this is not the case. It is not the case at present, whatever may happen if the moral tradition of marriage is really lost in Balham. So long as that moral tradition is alive, so long as stealing other people's wives is reprobated or being faithful to a spouse is admired, there are limits to the extent to which the wildest profligate in Balham can disturb the balance of the sexes. So any land-grabber would very rapidly find that there were limits to the extent to which he could buy up land in an Irish or Spanish or Serbian village. When it is really thought hateful to take Naboth's vineyard, as it is to take Uriah's wife, there is little difficulty in finding a local prophet to pronounce the judgment of the Lord. In an atmosphere of capitalism the man who lays field to field is flattered; but in an atmosphere of property he is promptly jeered at or possibly stoned. The result is that the village has not sunk into plutocracy or the suburb into polygamy.

Property is a point of honour. The true contrary of the word "property" is the word "prostitution." And it is not true that a human being will always sell what is sacred to that sense of self-ownership, whether it be the body or the boundary. A few do it in both cases; and by doing it they always become outcasts. But it is not true that a majority must do it; and anybody who says it is, is ignorant, not of our plans and proposals, not of anybody's visions and ideals, not of distributism or division of capital by this or that process, but of the facts of history and the substance of humanity. He is a barbarian who has never seen an arch.

In the notes I have here jotted down it will be obvious, of course, that the restoration of this pattern, simple as it is, is much more complicated in a complicated society. Here I have only traced it in the simplest form as it stood, and still stands, at the beginning of our discussion. I disregard the view that such "reaction" cannot be. I hold the old mystical dogma that what Man has done, Man can do. My critics seem to hold a still more mystical dogma: that Man cannot possibly do a thing because he has done it. That is what seems to be meant by saying that small property is "antiquated." It really means that all property is dead. There is nothing to be reached upon the present lines except the increasing loss of property by everybody, as something swallowed up into a system equally impersonal and inhuman, whether we call it Communism or Capitalism. If we cannot go back, it hardly seems worth while to go forward.

There is nothing in front but a flat wilderness of standardization either by Bolshevism or Big Business. But it is strange that some of us should have seen sanity, if only in a vision, while the rest go forward chained eternally to enlargement without liberty and progress without hope.

= = = = = = = = = = = = = = = = =

2. The Peril Of The Hour

When we are for a moment satisfied, or sated, with reading the latest news of the loftiest social circles, or the most exact records of the most responsible courts of justice, we naturally turn to the serial story in the newspaper, called "Poisoned by Her Mother" or "The Mystery of the Crimson Wedding Ring," in search of something calmer and more quietly convincing, more restful, more domestic, and more like real life. But as we turn over the pages, in passing from the incredible fact to the comparatively credible fiction, we are very likely to encounter a particular phrase on the general subject of social degeneracy. It is one of a number of phrases that seem to be kept in solid blocks in the printing-offices of newspapers. Like most of these solid statements, it is of a soothing character. It is like the headline of "Hopes of a Settlement," by which we learn that things are unsettled; or that topic of the "Revival of Trade," which it is part of the journalistic trade periodically to revive. The sentence to which I refer is to this effect: that the fears about social degeneracy need not disturb us, because such fears have been expressed in every age; and there are always romantic and retrospective persons, poets, and such riff-raff, who look back to imaginary "good old times."

It is the mark of such statements that they seem to satisfy the mind; in other words, it is the mark of such thoughts that they stop us from thinking. The man who has thus praised progress does not think it necessary to progress any further. The man who has dismissed a complaint, as being old, does not himself think it necessary to say anything new. He is content to repeat this apology for existing things; and seems unable to offer any more thoughts on the subject. Now, as a matter of fact, there are a number of further thoughts that might be suggested by the subject. Of course, it is quite true that this notion of the decline of a state has been suggested in many periods, by many persons, some of them, unfortunately, poets. Thus, for instance, Byron, notoriously so moody and melodramatic, had somehow or other got it into his head that the Isles of Greece were less glorious in arts and arms in the last days of Turkish rule than in the days of the battle of Salamis or the Republic of Plato. So again Wordsworth, in an equally sentimental fashion, seems to insinuate that the Republic of Venice was not quite so powerful when Napoleon trod it out like a dying ember as when its commerce and art filled the seas of the world with a conflagration of colour. So many writers in the eighteenth and nineteenth centuries have even gone so far as to suggest that modern Spain played a less predominant part than Spain in the days of the discovery of America or the victory of Lepanto. Some, even more lacking in that Optimism which is the soul of commerce, have made an equally perverse comparison between the earlier and the later conditions of the commercial aristocracy of Holland. Some have even maintained that Tyre and Sidon are not quite so fashionable as they used to be; and somebody once said something about "the ruins of Carthage."

In somewhat simpler language, we may say that all this argument has a very big and obvious hole in it. When a man says, "People were as pessimistic as you are in societies which were not declining, but were even advancing," it is permissible to reply, "Yes, and people were probably as optimistic as you are in

177

societies which really declined." For, after all, there were societies which really declined. It is true that Horace said that every generation seemed to be worse than the last, and implied that Rome was going to the dogs, at the very moment when all the external world was being brought under the eagles. But it is quite likely that the last forgotten court poet, praising the last forgotten Augustulus at the stiff court of Byzantium, contradicted all the seditious rumours of social decline, exactly as our newspapers do, by saying that, after all, Horace had said the same thing. And it is also possible that Horace was right; that it was in his time that the turn was taken which led from Horatius on the bridge to Heracleius in the palace; that if Rome was not immediately going to the dogs, the dogs were coming to Rome, and their distant howling could first be heard in that hour of the uplifted eagles; that there had begun a long advance that was also a long decline, but ended in the Dark Ages. Rome had gone back to the Wolf.

I say this view is at least tenable, though it does not really represent my own; but it is quite sufficiently reasonable to refuse to be dismissed with the cheap cheerfulness of the current maxim. There has been, there can be, such a thing as social decline; and the only question is, at any given moment, whether Byzantium had declined or whether Britain is declining. In other words, we must judge any such case of alleged degeneracy on its own merits. It is no answer to say, what is, of course, perfectly true, that some people are naturally prone to such pessimism. We are not judging them, but the situation which they judged or misjudged. We may say that schoolboys have always disliked having to go to school. But there is such a thing as a bad school. We may say the farmers always grumble at the weather. But there is such a thing as a bad harvest. And we have to consider as a question of the facts of the case, and not of the feelings of the farmer, whether the moral world of modern England is likely to have a bad harvest.

Now the reasons for regarding the present problem of Europe, and especially of England, as most menacing and tragic, are entirely objective reasons; and have nothing to do with this alleged mood of melancholy reaction. The present system, whether we call it capitalism or anything else, especially as it exists in industrial countries, has already become a danger; and is rapidly becoming a death-trap. The evil is evident in the plainest private experience and in the coldest economic science. To take the practical test first, it is not merely alleged by the enemies of the system, but avowed by the defenders of it. In the Labour disputes of our time, it is not the employees but the employers who declare that business is bad. The successful business man is not pleading success; he is pleading bankruptcy. The case for Capitalists is the case against Capitalism. What is even more extraordinary is that its exponent has to fall back on the rhetoric of Socialism. He merely says that miners or railwaymen must go on working "in the interests of the public." It will be noted that the capitalists now never use the argument of private property. They confine themselves entirely to this sort of sentimental version of general social responsibility. It is amusing to read the capitalist press on Socialists who sentimentally plead for people who are "failures." It is now the chief argument of almost every capitalist in every strike that he is himself on the brink of failure.

I have one simple objection to this simple argument in the papers about Strikes and the Socialist peril. My objection is that their argument leads straight to Socialism. In itself it cannot possibly lead to anything else. If workmen are to go on working because they are the servants of the public, there cannot be any deduction except that they ought to be the servants of the public authority. If the Government ought to act in the interests of the public, and there is no more to be said, then obviously the Government ought to take over the whole business, and there is nothing else to be done. I do not think the matter is so simple as this; but they do. I do not think this argument for Socialism is conclusive. But according to the Anti-Socialists the argument for Socialism is quite conclusive. The public alone is to be considered, and the Government can do anything it likes so long as it considers the public. Presumably it can disregard the liberty of the employees and force them to work, possibly in chains. Presumably also it can disregard the property of the employers, and pay the proletariat for them, if necessary out of their trouser-pockets. All these consequences follow from the highly Bolshevist doctrine bawled at us every morning in the capitalist press. That is all they have to say; and if it is the only thing to be said, then the other is the only thing to be done.

In the last paragraph it is noted that if we were left to the logic of the leader-writers on the Socialist peril, they could only lead us straight to Socialism. And as some of us most heartily and vigorously refuse to be led to Socialism, we have long adopted the harder alternative called trying to think things out. And we shall certainly land in Socialism or in something worse called Socialism, or else in mere chaos and ruin, if we make no effort to see the situation as a whole apart from our immediate irritations. Now the capitalist system, good or bad, right or wrong, rests upon two ideas: that the rich will always be rich enough to hire the poor; and the poor will always be poor enough to want to be hired. But it also presumes that each side is bargaining with the other, and that neither is thinking primarily of the public. The owner of an omnibus does not run it for the good of all mankind, despite the universal fraternity blazoned in the Latin name of the vehicle. He runs it to make a profit for himself, and the poorer man consents to drive it in order to get wages for himself. Similarly, the omnibus-conductor is not filled with an abstract altruistic desire for the nice conduct of a crowded omnibus instead of a clouded cane. He does not want to conduct omnibuses because conduct is three-fourths of life. He is bargaining for the biggest wage he can get. Now the case for capitalism was that through this private bargain the public did really get served. And so for some time it did. But the only original case for capitalism collapses entirely, if we have to ask either party to go on for the good of the public. If capitalism cannot pay what will tempt men to work, capitalism is on capitalist principles simply bankrupt. If a tea-merchant cannot pay clerks, and cannot import tea without clerks, then his business is bust and there is an end of it. Nobody in the old capitalist conditions said the clerks were bound to work for less, so that a poor old lady might get a cup of tea.

So it is really the capitalist press that proves on capitalist principles that capitalism has come to an end. If it had not, it would not be necessary for them to make the social and sentimental appeals they do make. It would not be necessary for them to appeal for the intervention of the Government like Socialists. It would not have been necessary for them to plead the discomfort of passengers like sentimentalists or altruists. The truth is that everybody has now abandoned the argument on which the whole of the old capitalism was based: the argument that if men were left to bargain individually the public would benefit automatically. We have to find a new basis of some kind; and the ordinary Conservatives are falling back on the Communist basis without knowing it. Now I respectfully decline to fall back on the Communist basis. But I am sure it is perfectly impossible to continue to fall back on the old Capitalist basis. Those who try to do so tie themselves in quite impossible knots. The most practical and pressing affairs of the hour exhibit the contradiction day after day. For instance, when some great strike or lock-out takes place in a big business like that of the mines, we are always assured that no great saving could be achieved by cutting out private profits, because those private profits are now negligible and the trade in question is not now greatly enriching the few. Whatever be the value of this particular argument, it obviously entirely destroys the general argument. The general argument for capitalism or individualism is that men will not adventure unless there are considerable prizes in the lottery. It is what is familiar in all Socialistic debates as the argument of "the incentive of gain." But if there is no gain, there is certainly no incentive. If royalty-owners and shareholders only get a little insecure or doubtful profit out of profiteering, it seems as if they might as well fall to the lowly estate of soldiers and servants of society. I have never understood, by the way, why Tory debaters are so very anxious to prove against Socialism that "State servants" must be incompetent and inert. Surely it might be left to others to point out the lethargy of Nelson or the dull routine of Gordon.

But this collapse of industrial individualism, which is not only a collapse but a contradiction (since it has to contradict all its own commonest maxims), is not only an accident of our condition, though it is most marked in our country. Anybody who can think in theories, those highly practical things, will see that sooner or later this paralysis in the system is inevitable. Capitalism is a contradiction; it is even a contradiction in terms. It takes a long time to box the compass, and a still longer time to see that it has done so; but the wheel has come full circle now. Capitalism is contradictory as soon as it is complete; because it is dealing with the mass of men in two opposite ways at once. When most men are wage-earners, it is more and more difficult for most men to be customers. For, the capitalist is always trying to cut down what his servant demands, and in doing so is cutting down what his customer can spend. As soon as his business is in any difficulties, as at present in the coal business, he tries to reduce what he has to spend on wages, and in doing so reduces what others have to spend on coal. He is wanting the same man to be rich and poor at the same time. This contradiction in capitalism does not appear in the earlier stages, because there are still populations not reduced to the common proletarian condition. But as soon as the wealthy as a whole are employing the wage-earners as a whole, this contradiction stares them in the face like an ironic doom and judgment. Employer and employee are simplified and solidified to the relation of Robinson Crusoe and Man Friday. Robinson Crusoe may say he has two problems: the supply of cheap labour and the prospect of trade with the natives. But as he is dealing in these two different ways with the same man, he will get into a muddle. Robinson Crusoe may possibly force Friday to work for nothing but his bare keep, the white man possessing all the weapons. As in the Geddes parallel, he may economize with an Axe. But he cannot cut down Friday's salary to nothing and then expect Friday to give him gold and silver and orient pearls in return for rum and rifles. Now in proportion as capitalism covers the whole earth, links up large populations, and is ruled by centralized systems, the nearer and nearer approaches this resemblance to the lonely figures on the remote island. If the trade with the natives is really going down, so as to necessitate the wages of the natives also going down, we can only say that the case is rather more tragic if the excuse is true than if it is false. We can only say that Crusoe is now indeed alone, and that Friday is unquestionably unlucky.

I think it very important that people should understand that there is a principle at work behind the industrial troubles of England in our time; and that, whoever be right or wrong in any particular quarrel, it is no particular person or party who is responsible for our commercial experiment being faced with failure. It is a vicious circle into which wage-earning society will finally sink when it begins to lose profits and lower wages; and though some industrial countries are still rich enough to remain ignorant of the strain, it is only because their progress is incomplete; when they reach the goal they will find the riddle. In our own country, which concerns most of us most, we are already falling into that vicious circle of sinking wages and decreasing demand. And as I am going to suggest here, in however sketchy a manner, the line of escape from this slowly closing snare, and because I know some of the things that are commonly said about any such suggestion, I have a reason for reminding the reader of all these things at this stage.

"Safe! Of course it's not safe! It's a beggarly chance to cheat the gallows." Such was the intemperate exclamation of Captain Wicks in the romance of Stevenson; and the same romancer has put a somewhat similar piece of candour into the mouth of Alan Breck Stewart. "But mind you, it's no small thing! ye maun lie bare and hard . . . and ye shall sleep with your hand upon your weapons. Aye, man, ye shall taigle many a weary foot or we get clear. I tell ye this at the start, for it's a life that I ken well. But if ye ask what other chance you have, I answer; Nane."

And I myself am sometimes tempted to talk in this abrupt manner, after listening to long and thoughtful disquisitions throwing doubt on the detailed perfection of a Distributist State, as compared with the rich happiness and final repose that crowns the present Capitalist and Industrial State. People ask us how we should deal with the unskilled labour at the docks, and what we have to offer to replace the radiant popularity of Lord Devonport and the permanent industrial peace of the Port of London. Those who ask us what we shall do with the docks seldom seem to ask themselves what the docks will do with themselves, if our commerce steadily declines like that of so many commercial cities in the past. Other people ask us how we should deal with workmen holding shares in a business that might possibly go bankrupt. It never occurs to them to answer their own question, in a capitalist state in which business after business is going bankrupt. We have got to deal with the smallest and most remote possibilities of our more simple and static society, while they do not deal with the biggest and most blatant facts about their own complex and collapsing one. They are inquisitive about the details of our scheme, and wish to arrange beforehand a science of casuistry for all the exceptions. But they dare not look their own systems in the face, where ruin has become the rule. Other people wish to know whether a machine would be permitted to exist in this or that position in our Utopia; as an exhibit in a museum, or a toy in the nursery, or a "torture implement of the twentieth century" shown in the Chamber of Horrors. But those who ask us so anxiously how men are to work without machines do not tell us how machines are to work if men do not work them, or how either machines or men are to work if there is no work to do. They are so eager to discover the weak points in our proposal that they have not yet discovered any strong points in their own practice. Strange that our vain and sentimental vision should be so vivid to these realists that they can see its every detail; and that their own reality should be so vague to them that they cannot see it at all; that they cannot see the most obvious and overwhelming fact about it: that it is no longer there.

For it is one of the grim and even grisly jokes of the situation that the very complaint they always make of us is specially and peculiarly true of them. They are always telling us that we think we can bring back the past, or the barbarous simplicity and superstition of the past; apparently under the impression that we want to bring back the ninth century. But they do really think they can bring back the nineteenth century. They are always telling us that this or that tradition has gone for ever, that this or that craft or creed has gone for ever; but they dare not face the fact that their own vulgar and huckstering commerce has gone for ever. They call us reactionaries if we talk of a Revival of Faith or a Revival of Catholicism. But they go on calmly plastering their papers with the headline of a Revival of Trade. What a cry out of the distant past! What a voice from the tomb! They have no reason whatever for believing that there will be a revival of trade, except that their great-grandfathers would have found it impossible to believe in a decline of trade. They have no conceivable ground for supposing that we shall grow richer, except that our ancestors never prepared us for the prospect of growing poorer. Yet it is they who are always blaming us for depending on a sentimental tradition of the wisdom of our ancestors. It is they who are always rejecting social ideals merely because they were the social ideals of some former age. They are always telling us that the mill will never grind again the water that is past; without noticing that their own mills are already idle and grinding nothing at all — like ruined mills in some watery Early Victorian landscape suitable to their watery Early Victorian quotation. They are always telling us that we are fighting against the tide of time, as Mrs. Partington with a mop fought against the tide of the sea. And they cannot even see that time itself has made Mrs. Partington as antiquated a figure as Mother Shipton. They are always telling us that in resisting capitalism and commercialism we are like Canute rebuking the waves; and they do not even know that the England of Cobden is already as dead as the England of Canute. They are always seeking to overwhelm us in the water-floods, to sweep us away upon these weary and washy metaphors of tide and time; for all the world as if they could call back the rivers that have left our cities so far behind, or summon back the seven seas to their allegiance to the trident; or bridle again, with gold for the few and iron for the many, the roaring river of the Clyde.

We may well be tempted to the exclamation of Captain Wicks. We are not choosing between a possible peasantry and a successful commerce. We are choosing between a peasantry that might succeed and a commerce that has already failed. We are not seeking to lure men away from a thriving business to a sort of holiday in Arcadia or the peasant type of Utopia. We are trying to make suggestions about starting anew after a bankrupt business has really gone bankrupt. We can see no possible reason for supposing that English trade will regain its nineteenth-century predominance, except mere Victorian sentimentalism and that particular sort of lying which the newspapers call "optimism." They taunt us for trying to bring back the conditions of the Middle Ages; as if we were trying to bring back the bows or the body-armour of the Middle Ages. Well, helmets have come back; and body-armour may come back; and bows and arrows will have to come back, a long time before there is any return of that fortunate moment on whose luck they live. It is quite as likely that the long bow will be found through some accident superior to the rifle as that the battleship will be able any longer to rule the waves without reference to the aeroplane. The commercial system implied the security of our commercial routes; and that implied the superiority of our national navy. Everybody who faces facts knows that aviation has altered the whole theory of that naval security. The whole huge horrible problem of a big population on a small island dependent on insecure imports is a problem quite as much for

Capitalists and Collectivists as for Distributists. We are not choosing between model villages as part of a serene system of town-planning. We are making a sortie from a besieged city, sword in hand; a sortie from the ruin of Carthage. "Safe! Of course it's not safe!" said Captain Wicks.

I think it is not unlikely that in any case a simpler social life will return; even if it return by the road of ruin. I think the soul will find simplicity again, if it be in the Dark Ages. But we are Christians and concerned with the body as well as the soul; we are Englishmen and we do not desire, if we can help it, that the English people should be merely the People of the Ruins. And we do most earnestly desire a serious consideration of whether the transition cannot be made in the light of reason and tradition; whether we cannot yet do deliberately and well what nemesis will do wastefully and without pity; whether we cannot build a bridge from these slippery downward slopes to freer and firmer land beyond, without consenting yet that our most noble nation must descend into that valley of humiliation in which nations disappear from history. For this purpose, with great conviction of our principles and with no shame of being open to argument about their application, we have called our companions to council.

=================

3. The Chance Of Recovery

Once upon a time, or conceivably even more than once, there was a man who went into a public-house and asked for a glass of beer. I will not mention his name, for various and obvious reasons; it may be libel nowadays to say this about a man; or it may lay him open to police prosecution under the more humane laws of our day. So far as this first recorded action is concerned, his name may have been anything: William Shakespeare or Geoffrey Chaucer or Charles Dickens or Henry Fielding, or any of those common names that crop up everywhere in the populace. The important thing about him is that he asked for a glass of beer. The still more important thing about him is that he drank it; and the most important thing of all is that he spat it out again (I regret to say) and threw the pewter mug at the publican. For the beer was abominably bad.

186

True, he had not yet submitted it to any chemical analysis; but, after he had drank a little of it, he felt an inward, a very inward, persuasion that there was something wrong about it. When he had been ill for a week, steadily getting worse all the time, he took some of the beer to the Public Analyst; and that learned man, after boiling it, freezing it, turning it green, blue, and yellow, and so on, told him that it did indeed contain a vast quantity of deadly poison. "To continue drinking it," said the man of science thoughtfully, "will undoubtedly be a course attended with risks, but life is inseparable from risk. And before you decide to abandon it, you must make up your mind what Substitute you propose to put into your inside, in place of the beverage which at present (more or less) reposes there. If you will bring me a list of your selections in this difficult matter, I will willingly point out the various scientific objections that can be raised to all of them."

The man went away, and became more and more ill; and indeed he noticed that nobody else seemed to be really well. As he passed the tavern, his eye chanced to fall upon various friends of his writhing in agony on the ground, and indeed not a few of them lying dead and stiff in heaps about the road. To his simple mind this seemed a matter of some concern to the community; so he hurried to a police court and laid before a magistrate a complaint against the inn. "It would indeed appear," said the Justice of the Peace, "that the house you mention is one in which people are systematically murdered by means of poison. But before you demand so drastic a course as that of pulling it down or even shutting it up, you have to consider a problem of no little difficulty. Have you considered precisely what building you would Put In Its Place, whether a — ." At this point I regret to say that the man gave a loud scream and was forcibly removed from the court announcing that he was going mad. Indeed, this conviction of his mental malady increased with his bodily malady; to such an extent that he consulted a distinguished Doctor of Psychology and Psycho-Analysis, who said to him confidentially, "As a matter of diagnosis, there can be no doubt that you are suffering from Bink's Aberration; but when we come to treatment I may say frankly that it is very difficult to find anything to take the place of that affliction. Have you considered what is the alternative to madness — ?" Whereupon the man sprang up waving his arms and cried,

187

"There is none. There is no alternative to madness. It is inevitable. It is universal. We must make the best of it."

So making the best of it, he killed the doctor and then went back and killed the magistrate and the public analyst, and is now in an asylum, as happy as the day is long.

In the fable appearing above the case is propounded which is primarily necessary to see at the start of a sketch of social renewal. It concerned a gentleman who was asked what he would substitute for the poison that had been put into his inside, or what constructive scheme he had to put in place of the den of assassins that had poisoned him. A similar demand is made of those of us who regard plutocracy as a poison or the present plutocratic state as something like a den of thieves. In the parable of the poison it is possible that the reader may share some of the impatience of the hero. He will say that nobody would be such a fool as not to get rid of prussic acid or professional criminals, merely because there were differences of opinion about the course of action that would follow getting rid of them. But I would ask the reader to be a little more patient, not only with me but with himself; and ask himself why it is that we act with this promptitude in the case of poison and crime. It is not, even here, really because we are indifferent to the substitute. We should not regard one poison as an antidote to the other poison, if it made the malady worse. We should not set a thief to catch a thief, if it really increased the amount of thieving. The principle upon which we are acting, even if we are acting too quickly to think, or thinking too quickly to define, is nevertheless a principle that we could define. If we merely give a man an emetic after he has taken a poison, it is not because we think he can live on emetics any more than he can live on poisons. It is because we think that after he has first recovered from the poison, and then recovered from the emetic, there will come a time when he himself will think he would like a little ordinary food. That is the starting-point of the whole speculation, so far as we are concerned. If certain impediments are removed, it is not so much a question of what we would do as of what he would do. So if we save the lives of a number of people from the den of poisoners, we do not at that moment ask what they will do with their lives. We assume that they will do something a little more sensible than taking poison. In other words, the very simple first principle upon which all such

188

reforms rest, is that there is some tendency to recovery in every living thing if we remove the pressure of an immediate peril or pain. Now at the beginning of all this rough outline of a social reform, which I propose to trace here, I wish to make clear this general principle of recovery, without which it will be unintelligible. We believe that if things were released they would recover; but we also believe (and this is very important in the practical question) that if things even begin to be released, they will begin to recover. If the man merely leaves off drinking the bad beer, his body will make some effort to recover its ordinary condition. If the man merely escapes from those who are slowly poisoning him, to some extent the very air he breathes will be an antidote to his poison.

As I hope to explain in the essays that follow, I think the question of the real social reform divides itself into two distinct stages and even ideas. One is arresting a race towards mad monopoly that is already going on, reversing that revolution and returning to something that is more or less normal, but by no means ideal; the other is trying to inspire that more normal society with something that is in a real sense ideal, though not necessarily merely Utopian. But the first thing to be understood is that any relief from the present pressure will probably have more moral effect than most of our critics imagine. Hitherto all the triumphs have been triumphs of plutocratic monopoly; all the defeats have been defeats of private property. I venture to guess that one real defeat of a monopoly would have an instant and incalculable effect, far beyond itself, like the first defeats in the field of a military empire like Prussia parading itself as invincible. As each group or family finds again the real experience of private property, it will become a centre of influence, a mission. What we are dealing with is not a question of a General Election to be counted by a calculating machine. It is a question of a popular movement, that never depends on mere numbers.

That is why we have so often taken, merely as a working model, the matter of a peasantry. The point about a peasantry is that it is not a machine, as practically every ideal social state is a machine; that is, a thing that will work only as it is set down to work in the pattern. You make laws for a Utopia; it is only by keeping those laws that it can be kept a Utopia. You do not make laws for a peasantry. You make a peasantry; and the peasants make the laws. I do not mean, as will be clear enough when I come to more detailed matters, that laws must not be used for the establishment of a peasantry or even for the protection of it. But I mean that the character of a peasantry does not depend on laws. The character of a peasantry depends on peasants. Men have remained side by side for centuries in their separate and fairly equal farms, without many of them losing their land, without any of them buying up the bulk of the land. Yet very often there was no law against their buying up the bulk of the land. Peasants could not buy because peasants would not sell. That is, this form of moderate equality, when once it exists, is not merely a legal formula; it is also a moral and psychological fact. People behave when they find themselves in that position as they do when they find themselves at home. That is, they stay there; or at least they behave normally there. There is nothing in abstract logic to prove that people cannot thus feel at home in a Socialist Utopia. But the Socialists who describe Utopias generally feel themselves in some dim way that people will not; and that is why they have to make their mere laws of economic control so elaborate and so clear. They use their army of officials to move men about like crowds of captives, from old quarters to new quarters, and doubtless to better quarters. But we believe that the slaves that we free will fight for us like soldiers.

In other words, all that I ask in this preliminary note is that the reader should understand that we are trying to make something that will run of itself. A machine will not run of itself. A man will run of himself; even if he runs into a good many things that he would have been wiser to avoid. When freed from certain disadvantages, he can to some extent take over the responsibility. All schemes of collective concentration have in them the character of controlling the man even when he is free; if you will, of controlling him to keep him free. They have the idea that the man will not be poisoned if he has a doctor standing behind his chair at dinner-time, to check the mouthfuls and measure the wine. We have the idea that the man may need a doctor when he is poisoned, but no longer needs him when he is unpoisoned. We do not say, as they possibly do say, that he will always be perfectly happy or perfectly good; because there are other elements in life besides the economic; and even the economic is affected by original sin. We do not say that because he does not need a doctor he does not need a priest or a wife or a friend or a God; or that his relations to these things can be ensured by any social scheme. But we do say that there is something which is much more real and much more reliable than any social scheme; and that is a society. There is such a thing as people finding a social life that suits them and enables them to get on reasonably well with each other. You do not have to wait till you have established that sort of society everywhere. It makes all the difference so soon as you have established it anywhere. So if I am told at the start: "You do not think Socialism or reformed Capitalism will save England; do you really think Distributism will save England?" I answer, "No; I think Englishmen will save England, if they begin to have half a chance."

I am therefore in this sense hopeful; I believe that the breakdown has been a breakdown of machinery and not of men. And I fully agree, as I have just explained, that leaving work for a man is very different from leaving a plan for a machine. I ask the reader to realize this distinction, at this stage of the description, before I go on to describe more definitely some of the possible directions of reform. I am not at all ashamed of being ready to listen to reason; I am not at all afraid of leaving matters open to adjustment; I am not at all annoyed at the prospect of those who carry out these principles varying in many ways in their programmes. I am much too much in earnest to treat my own programme as a party programme; or to pretend that my private bill must become an Act of Parliament without any amendments. But I have a particular cause, in this particular case, for insisting in this chapter that there is a reasonable chance of escape; and for asking that the reasonable chance should be considered with reasonable cheerfulness. I do not care very much for that sort of American virtue which is now sometimes called optimism. It has too much of the flavour of Christian Science to be a comfortable thing for Christians. But I do feel, in the facts of this particular case, that there is a reason for warning people against a too hasty exhibition of pessimism and the pride of impotence. I do ask everybody to consider, in a free and open fashion, whether something of the sort here indicated cannot be carried out, even if it be carried out differently in detail; for it is a matter of the understanding of men. The position is much too serious for men to be anything but cheerful. And in this connection I would venture to utter a warning.

A man has been led by a foolish guide or a self-confident fellow-traveller to the brink of a precipice, which he might well have fallen over in the dark. It may well be said that there is nothing to be done but to sit down and wait for the light. Still, it might be well to pass the hours of darkness in some discussion about how it will be best for them to make their way backwards to more secure ground; and the recollection of any facts and the formulation of any coherent plan of travel will not be waste of time, especially if there is nothing else to do. But there is one piece of advice which we should be inclined to give to the guide who has misguided the simple stranger — especially if he is a really simple stranger, a man perhaps of rude education and elementary emotions. We should strongly advise him not to beguile the time by proving conclusively that it is impossible to go back, that there is no really secure ground behind, that there is no chance of finding the homeward path again, that the steps recently taken are irrevocable, and that progress must go forward and can never return. If he is a tactful man, in spite of his previous error, he will avoid this tone in conversation. If he is not a tactful man, it is not altogether impossible that before the end of the conversation, somebody will go over the precipice after all; and it will not be the simple stranger.

An army has marched across a wilderness, its column, in the military phrase, in the air; under a confident commander who is certain he will pick up new communications which will be far better than the old ones. When the soldiers are almost worn out with marching, and the rank and file of them have suffered horrible privations from hunger and exposure, they find they have only advanced unsupported into a hostile country; and that the signs of military occupation to be seen on every side are only those of an enemy closing round. The march is suddenly halted and the commander addresses his men. There are a great many things that he may say. Some may hold that he had much better say nothing at all. Many may hold that the less he says the better. Others may urge, very truly, that courage is even more needed for a retreat than for an advance. He may be advised to rouse his disappointed men by threatening the enemy with a more dramatic disappointment; by declaring that they will best him yet; that they will dash out of the net even as it is thrown, and that their escape will be far more victorious than his victory. But anyhow there is one kind of speech which the commander will not make to his men, unless he is much more of a fool than his original blunder proves him. He will not say: "We have now taken up a position which may appear to you very depressing; but I assure you it is nothing to the depression which you will certainly suffer as you make a series of inevitably futile attempts to improve it, or to fall back on what you may foolishly regard as a stronger position. I am very much amused at your absurd suggestions for getting back to our old communications; for I never thought much of your mangy old communications anyhow." There have been mutinies in the desert before now; and it is possible that the general will not be killed in battle with the enemy.

A great nation and civilization has followed for a hundred years or more a form of progress which held itself independent of certain old communications, in the form of ancient traditions about the land, the hearth, or the altar. It has advanced under leaders who were confident, not to say cocksure. They were quite sure that their economic rules were rigid, that their political theory was right, that their commerce was beneficent, that their parliaments were popular, that their press was enlightened, that their science was humane. In this confidence they committed their people to certain new and enormous experiments; to making their own independent nation an eternal debtor to a few rich men; to piling up private property in heaps on the faith of financiers; to covering their land with iron and stone and stripping it of grass and grain; to driving food out of their own country in the hope of buying it back again from the ends of the earth; to loading up their little island with iron and gold till it was weighted like a sinking ship; to letting the rich grow richer and fewer and the poor poorer and more numerous; to letting the whole world be cloven in two with a war of mere masters and mere servants; to losing every type of moderate prosperity and candid patriotism, till there was no independence without luxury and no labour without ugliness; to leaving the millions of mankind dependent on indirect and distant discipline and indirect and distant sustenance, working themselves to death for they knew not whom and taking the means of life from they knew not where; and all hanging on a thread of alien trade which grew thinner and thinner. To the people who have been brought into this position many things may still be said. It will be right to remind them that mere wild revolt will make things worse and not better. It may be true to say that certain complexities must be tolerated for a time because they correspond to other complexities, and the two must be carefully simplified together. But if I may say one word to the princes and rulers of such a people, who have led them into such a pass, I would say to them as seriously as anything was ever said by man to men: "For God's sake, for our sake, but, above all, for your own sake, do not be in this blind haste to tell them there is no way out of the trap into which your folly has led them; that there is no road except the road by which you have brought them to ruin; that there is no progress except the progress that has ended here. Do not be so eager to prove to your hapless victims that what is hapless is also hopeless. Do not be so anxious to convince them, now that you are at the end of your experiment, that you are also at the end of your resources. Do not be so very eloquent, so very elaborate, so very rational and radiantly convincing in proving that your own error is even more irrevocable and irremediable than it is. Do not try to minimize the industrial disease by showing it is an incurable disease. Do not brighten the dark problem of the coal-pit by proving it is a bottomless pit. Do not tell the people there is no way but this; for many even now will not endure this. Do not say to men that this alone is possible; for many already think it impossible to bear. And at some later time, at some eleventh hour, when the fates have grown darker and the ends have grown clearer, the mass of men may suddenly understand into what a blind alley your progress has led them. Then they may turn on you in the trap. And if they bore all else, they might not bear the final taunt that you can do nothing; that you will not even try to do anything. 'What art thou, man, and why art thou despairing?' wrote the poet. 'God shall forgive thee all but thy despair.' Man also may forgive you for blundering and may not forgive you for despairing."

==================

4. On A Sense Of Proportion

Those of us who study the papers and the parliamentary speeches with proper attention must have by this time a fairly precise idea of the nature of the evil of Socialism. It is a remote Utopian dream impossible of fulfilment and also an overwhelming practical danger that threatens us at every moment. It is only a thing that is as distant as the end of the world and as near as the end of the street. All that is clear enough; but the aspect of it that arrests me at this moment is more especially the Utopian aspect. A person who used to write in the Daily Mail paid some attention to this aspect; and represented this social ideal, or indeed almost any other social ideal, as a sort of paradise of poltroons. He suggested that "weaklings" wished to be protected from the strain and stress of our vigorous individualism, and so cried out for this paternal government or grand-motherly legislation. And it was while I was reading his remarks, with a deep and never-failing enjoyment, that the image of the Individualist rose before me; of the sort of man who probably writes such remarks and certainly reads them.

The reader refolds the Daily Mail and rises from his intensely individualistic breakfast-table, where he has just dispatched his bold and adventurous breakfast; the bacon cut in rashers from the wild boar which but lately turned to bay in his back garden; the eggs perilously snatched from swaying nest and flapping bird at the top of those toppling trees which gave the house its appropriate name of Pine Crest. He puts on his curious and creative hat, built on some bold plan entirely made up out of his own curious and creative head. He walks outside his unique and unparalleled house, also built with his own well-won wealth according to his own well-conceived architectural design, and seeming by its very outline against the sky to express his own passionate personality. He strides down the street, making his own way over hill and dale towards the place of his own chosen and favourite labour, the workshop of his imaginative craft. He lingers on the way, now to pluck a flower, now to compose a poem, for his time is his own; he is an individual and a free man and not as these Communists. He can work at his own craft when he will, and labour far into the night to make up for an idle morning. Such is the life of the clerk in a world of private enterprise and practical individualism; such the manner of his free passage from his home. He continues to stride lightly along, until he sees afar off the picturesque and striking tower of that workshop in which he will, as with the creative strokes of a god . . .

He sees it, I say, afar off. The expression is not wholly accidental. For that is exactly the defect in all that sort of journalistic philosophy of individualism and enterprise; that those things are at present even more remote and improbable than communal visions. It is not the dreadful Bolshevist republic that is afar off. It is not the Socialistic State that is Utopian. In that sense, it is not even Utopia that is Utopian. The Socialist State may in one sense be very truly described as terribly and menacingly near. The Socialist State is exceedingly like the Capitalist State, in which the clerk reads and the journalist writes. Utopia is exactly like the present state of affairs, only worse.

It would make no difference to the clerk if his job became a part of a Government department to-morrow. He would be equally civilized and equally uncivic if the distant and shadowy person at the head of the department were a Government official. Indeed, it does make very little difference to him now, whether he or his sons and daughters are employed at the Post Office on bold and revolutionary Socialistic principles or employed at the Stores on wild and adventurous Individualist principles. I never heard of anything resembling civil war between the daughter at the Stores and the daughter in the Post Office. I doubt whether the young lady at the Post Office is so imbued with Bolshevist principles that she would think it a part of the Higher Morality to expropriate something without payment off the counter of the Stores. I doubt whether the young lady at the Stores shudders when she passes a red pillar box, seeing in it an outpost of the Red Peril.

What is really a long way off is this individuality and liberty the Daily Mail praised. It is the tower that a man has built for himself that is seen in the distance. It is Private Enterprise that is Utopian, in the sense of something as distant as Utopia. It is Private Property that is for us an ideal and for our critics an impossibility. It is that which can really be discussed almost exactly as the writer in the Daily Mail discusses Collectivism. It is that which some people consider a goal and some people a mirage. It is that which its friends maintain to be the final satisfaction of modern hopes and hungers, and its enemies maintain to be a contradiction to common sense and common human possibilities. All the controversialists who have become conscious of the real issue are already saying of our ideal exactly what used to be said of the Socialists' ideal. They are saying that private property is too ideal not to be impossible. They are saying that private enterprise is too good to be true. They are saying that the idea of ordinary men owning ordinary possessions is against the laws of political economy and requires an alteration in human nature. They are saying that all practical business men know that the thing would never work, exactly as the same obliging people are always prepared to know that State management would never work. For they hold the simple and touching faith that no management except their own could ever work. They call this the law of nature; and they call anybody who ventures to doubt it a weakling. But the point to see is that, although the normal solution of private property for all is even now not very widely realized, in so far as it is realized by the rulers of the modern market (and therefore of the modern world) it is to this normal notion of property that they apply the same criticism as they applied to the abnormal notion of Communism. They say it is Utopian; and they are right. They say it is idealistic; and they are right. They say it is quixotic; and they are right. It deserves every name that will indicate how completely they have driven justice out of the world; every name that will measure how remote from them and their sort is the standard of honourable living; every name that will emphasize and repeat the fact that property and liberty are sundered from them and theirs, by an abyss between heaven and hell.

That is the real issue to be fought out with our serious critics; and I have written here a series of articles dealing more directly with it. It is the question of whether this ideal can be anything but an ideal; not the question of whether it is to be confounded with the present contemptible reality. It is simply the question of whether this good thing is really too good to be true. For the present I will merely say that if the pessimists are convinced of their pessimism, if the sceptics really hold that our social ideal is now banished for ever by mechanical difficulties or materialistic fate, they have at least reached a remarkable and curious conclusion. It is hardly stranger to say that man will have henceforth to be separated from his arms and legs, owing to the improved pattern of wheels, than to say that he must for ever say farewell to two supports so natural as the sense of choosing for himself and of owning something of his own. These critics, whether they figure as critics of Socialism or Distributism, are very fond of talking about extravagant stretches of the imagination or impossible strains upon human nature. I confess I have to stretch and strain my own human imagination and human nature very far, to conceive anything so crooked and uncanny as the human race ending with a complete forgetfulness of the possessive pronoun.

Nevertheless, as we say, it is with these critics we are in controversy. Distribution may be a dream; three acres and a cow may be a joke; cows may be fabulous animals; liberty may be a name; private enterprise may be a wild goose chase on which the world can go no further. But as for the people who talk as if property and private enterprise were the principles now in operation — those people are so blind and deaf and dead to all the realities of their own daily existence, that they can be dismissed from the debate.

In this sense, therefore, we are indeed Utopian; in the sense that our task is possibly more distant and certainly more difficult. We are more revolutionary in the sense that a revolution means a reversal: a reversal of direction, even if it were accompanied with a restraint upon pace. The world we want is much more different from the existing world than the existing world is different from the world of Socialism. Indeed, as has been already noted, there is not much difference between the present world and Socialism; except that we have left out the less important and more ornamental notions of Socialism, such additional fancies as justice, citizenship, the abolition of hunger, and so on. We have already accepted anything that anybody of intelligence ever disliked in Socialism. We have everything that critics used to complain of in the desolate utility and unity of Looking Backward. In so far as the world of Wells or Webb was criticized as a centralized, impersonal, and monotonous civilization, that is an exact description of existing civilization. Nothing has been left out but some idle fancies about feeding the poor or giving rights to the populace. In every other way the unification and regimentation is already complete. Utopia has done its worst. Capitalism has done all that Socialism threatened to do. The clerk has exactly the sort of passive functions and permissive pleasures that he would have in the most monstrous model village. I do not sneer at him; he has many intelligent tastes and domestic virtues in spite of the civilization he enjoys. They are exactly the tastes and virtues he could have as a tenant and servant of the State. But from the moment he wakes up to the moment he goes to sleep again, his life is run in grooves made for him by other people, and often other people he will never even know. He lives in a house that he does not own, that he did not make, that he does not want. He moves everywhere in ruts; he always goes up to his work on rails. He has forgotten what his fathers, the hunters and the pilgrims and the wandering minstrels, meant by finding their way to a place. He thinks in terms of wages; that is, he has forgotten the real meaning of wealth. His highest ambition is concerned with getting this or that subordinate post in a business that is already a bureaucracy. There is a certain amount of competition for that post inside that business; but so there would be inside any bureaucracy. This is a point that the apologists of monopoly often miss. They sometimes plead that even in such a system there may still be a competition among servants; presumably a competition in servility. But so there might be after Nationalization, when they were all Government servants. The whole objection to State Socialism vanishes, if that is an answer to the objection. If every shop were as thoroughly nationalized as a police station, it would not prevent the pleasing virtues of jealousy, intrigue, and selfish ambition from blooming and blossoming among them, as they sometimes do even among policemen.

Anyhow, that world exists; and to challenge that world may be called Utopian; to change that world may be called insanely Utopian. In that sense the name may be applied to me and those who agree with me, and we shall not quarrel with it. But in another sense the name is highly misleading and particularly inappropriate. The word "Utopia" implies not only difficulty of attainment but also other qualities attached to it in such examples as the Utopia of Mr. Wells. And it is essential to explain at once why they do not attach to our Utopia — if it is a Utopia.

There is such a thing as what we should call ideal Distributism; though we should not, in this vale of tears, expect

Distributism to be ideal. In the same sense there certainly is such a thing as ideal Communism. But there is no such thing as ideal Capitalism; and there is no such thing as a Capitalist ideal. As we have already noticed (though it has not been noticed often enough), whenever the capitalist does become an idealist, and specially when he does become a sentimentalist, he always talks like a Socialist. He always talks about "social service" and our common interests in the whole community. From this it follows that in so far as such a man is likely to have such a thing as a Utopia, it will be more or less in the style of a Socialist Utopia. The successful financier can put up with an imperfect world, whether or no he has the Christian humility to recognize himself as one of its imperfections. But if he is called upon to conceive a perfect world, it will be something in the way of the pattern state of the Fabians or the I.L.P. He will look for something systematized, something simplified, something all on the same plan. And he will not get it; at least he will not get it from me. It is exactly from that simplification and sameness that I pray to be saved, and should be proud if I could save anybody. It is exactly from that order and unity that I call on the name of Liberty to deliver us.

We do not offer perfection; what we offer is proportion. We wish to correct the proportions of the modern state; but proportion is between varied things; and a proportion is hardly ever a pattern. It is as if we were drawing the picture of a living man and they thought we were drawing a diagram of wheels and rods for the construction of a Robot. We do not propose that in a healthy society all land should be held in the same way; or that all property should be owned on the same conditions; or that all citizens should have the same relation to the city. It is our whole point that the central power needs lesser powers to balance and check it, and that these must be of many kinds: some individual, some communal, some official, and so on. Some of them will probably abuse their privilege; but we prefer the risk to that of the State or of the Trust, which abuses its omnipotence.

For instance, I am sometimes blamed for not believing in my own age, or blamed still more for believing in my own religion. I am called medieval; and some have even traced in me a bias in favour of the Catholic Church to which I belong. But suppose we were to take a parallel from these things. If anyone said that medieval kings or modern peasant countries were to blame for tolerating patches of avowed Bolshevism, we should be rather surprised if we found that the remark really referred to their tolerating monasteries. Yet it is quite true in one sense that monasteries are devoted to Communism and that monks are all Communists. Their economic and ethical life is an exception to a general civilization of feudalism or family life. Yet their privileged position was regarded as rather a prop of social order. They give to certain communal ideas their proper and proportionate place in the State; and something of the same thing was true of the Common Land. We should welcome the chance of allowing any guilds or groups of a communal colour their proper and proportionate place in the State; we should be perfectly willing to mark off some part of the land as Common Land. What we say is that merely nationalizing all the land is like merely making monks of all the people; it is giving those ideals more than their proper and proportionate place in the State. The ordinary meaning of Communism is not that some people are Communists, but that all people are Communists. But we should not say, in the same hard and literal sense, that the meaning of Distributism is that all people are Distributists. We certainly should not say that the meaning of a peasant state is that all people are peasants. We should mean that it had the general character of a peasant state; that the land was largely held in that fashion and the law generally directed in that spirit; that any other institutions stood up as recognizable exceptions, as landmarks on that high tableland of equality.

If this is inconsistent, nothing is consistent; if this is unpractical, all human life in unpractical. If a man wants what he calls a flower-garden he plants flowers where he can, and especially where they will determine the general character of the landscape gardening. But they do not completely cover the garden; they only positively colour it. He does not expect roses to grow in the chimney-pots, or daisies to climb up the railings; still less does he expect tulips to grow on the pine, or the monkey tree to blossom like a rhododendron. But he knows perfectly well what he means by a flower-garden; and so does everybody else. If he does not want a flower-garden but a kitchen-garden, he proceeds differently. But he does not expect a kitchen-garden to be exactly like a kitchen. He does not dig out all the potatoes, because it is not a flower-garden and the potato has a flower. He knows the main thing he is trying to achieve; but, not being a born fool, he does not think he can achieve it everywhere in exactly the same degree, or in a manner equally unmixed with things of another sort. The flower-gardener will not banish nasturtiums to the kitchen-garden because some strange people have been known to eat them. Nor will the other class a vegetable as a flower because it is called a cauliflower. So, from our social garden, we should not necessarily exclude every modern machine any more than we should exclude every medieval monastery. And indeed the apologue is appropriate enough; for this is the sort of elementary human reason that men never lost until they lost their gardens: just as that higher reason that is more than human was lost with a garden long ago.

= = = = = = = = = = = = = = = = =

II. Some Aspects Of Big Business

1. The Bluff Of The Big Shops

Twice in my life has an editor told me in so many words that he dared not print what I had written, because it would offend the advertisers in his paper. The presence of such pressure exists everywhere in a more silent and subtle form. But I have a great respect for the honesty of this particular editor; for it was, evidently as near to complete honesty as the editor of an important weekly magazine can possibly go. He told the truth about the falsehood he had to tell.

On both those occasions he denied me liberty of expression because I said that the widely advertised stores and large shops were really worse than little shops. That, it may be interesting to note, is one of the things that a man is now forbidden to say; perhaps the only thing he is really forbidden to say. If it had been an attack on Government, it would have been tolerated. If it had been an attack on God, it would have been respectfully and tactfully applauded. If I had been abusing marriage or patriotism or public decency, I should have been heralded in headlines and allowed to sprawl across Sunday newspapers. But the big newspaper is not likely to attack the big shop; being itself a big shop in its way and more and more a monument of monopoly. But it will be well if I repeat here in a book what I found it impossible to repeat in an article. I think the big shop is a bad shop. I think it bad not only in a moral but a mercantile sense; that is, I think shopping there is not only a bad action but a bad bargain. I think the monster emporium is not only vulgar and insolent, but incompetent and uncomfortable; and I deny that its large organization is efficient. Large organization is loose organization. Nay, it would be almost as true to say that organization is always disorganization. The only thing perfectly organic is an organism; like that grotesque and obscure organism called a man. He alone can be quite certain of doing what he wants; beyond him, every extra man may be an extra mistake. As applied to things like shops, the whole thing is an utter fallacy. Some things like armies have to be organized; and therefore do their very best to be well organized.

You must have a long rigid line stretched out to guard a frontier; and therefore you stretch it tight. But it is not true that you must have a long rigid line of people trimming hats or tying bouquets, in order that they may be trimmed or tied neatly. The work is much more likely to be neat if it is done by a particular craftsman for a particular customer with particular ribbons and flowers. The person told to trim the hat will never do it quite suitably to the person who wants it trimmed; and the hundredth person told to do it will do it badly; as he does. If we collected all the stories from all the housewives and householders about the big shops sending the wrong goods, smashing the right goods, forgetting to send any sort of goods, we should behold a welter of inefficiency. There are far more blunders in a big shop than ever happen in a small shop, where the individual customer can curse the individual shopkeeper. Confronted with modern efficiency the customer is silent; well aware of that organization's talent for sacking the wrong man. In short, organization is a necessary evil — which in this case is not necessary.

I have begun these notes with a note on the big shops because they are things near to us and familiar to us all. I need not dwell on other and still more entertaining claims made for the colossal combination of departments. One of the funniest is the statement that it is convenient to get everything in the same shop. That is to stay, it is convenient to walk the length of the street, so long as you walk indoors, or more frequently underground, instead of walking the same distance in the open air from one little shop to another. The truth is that the monopolists' shops are really very convenient — to the monopolist. They have all the advantage of concentrating business as they concentrate wealth, in fewer and fewer of the citizens. Their wealth sometimes permits them to pay tolerable wages; their wealth also permits them to buy up better businesses and advertise worse goods. But that their own goods are better nobody has ever even begun to show; and most of us know any number of concrete cases where they are definitely worse. Now I expressed this opinion of my own (so shocking to the magazine editor and his advertisers) not only because it is an example of my general thesis that small properties should be revived, but because it is essential to the realization of another and much more curious truth. It concerns the psychology of all these things: of mere size, of mere wealth, of mere advertisement and arrogance. And it gives us the first working model of the way in which things are done to-day and the way in which (please God) they may be undone to-morrow.

There is one obvious and enormous and entirely neglected general fact to be noted before we consider the laws chiefly needed to renew the State. And that is the fact that one considerable revolution could be made without any laws at all. It does not concern any existing law, but rather an existing superstition. And the curious thing is that its upholders boast that it is a superstition. The other day I saw and very thoroughly enjoyed a popular play called It Pays to Advertise; which is all about a young business man who tries to break up the soap monopoly of his father, a more old-fashioned business man, by the wildest application of American theories of the psychology of advertising. One thing that struck me as rather interesting about it was this. It was quite good comedy to give the old man and the young man our sympathy in turn. It was quite good farce to make the old man and the young man each alternately look a fool. But nobody seemed to feel what I felt to be the most outstanding and obvious points of folly. They scoffed at the old man because he was old; because he was old-fashioned; because he himself was healthy enough to scoff at the monkey tricks of their mad advertisements. But nobody really criticized him for having made a corner, for which he might once have stood in a pillory. Nobody seemed to have enough instinct for independence and human dignity to be irritated at the idea that one purse-proud old man could prevent us all from having an ordinary human commodity if he chose. And as with the old man, so it was with the young man. He had been taught by his American friend that advertisement can hypnotize the human brain; that people are dragged by a deadly fascination into the doors of a shop as into the mouth of a snake; that the subconscious is captured and the will paralysed by repetition; that we are all made to move like mechanical dolls when a Yankee advertiser says, "Do It Now." But it never seemed to occur to anybody to resent this. Nobody seemed sufficiently alive to be annoyed. The young man was made game of because he was poor; because he was bankrupt; because he was driven to the shifts of bankruptcy; and so on. But he did not seem to know he was something much worse than a swindler, a sorcerer. He did not know he was by his own boast a mesmerist and a mystagogue; a destroyer of reason and will; an enemy of truth and liberty.

I think such people exaggerate the extent to which it pays to advertise; even if there is only the devil to pay. But in one sense this psychological case for advertising is of great practical importance to any programme of reform. The American advertisers have got hold of the wrong end of the stick; but it is a stick that can be used to beat something else besides their own absurd big drum. It is a stick that can be used also to beat their own absurd business philosophy. They are always telling us that the success of modern commerce depends on creating an atmosphere, on manufacturing a mentality, on assuming a point of view. In short, they insist that their commerce is not merely commercial, or even economic or political, but purely psychological. I hope they will go on saying it; for then some day everybody may suddenly see that it is true.

For the success of big shops and such things really is psychology; not to say psycho-analysis; or, in other words, nightmare. It is not real and, therefore, not reliable. This point concerns merely our immediate attitude, at the moment and on the spot, towards the whole plutocratic occupation of which such publicity is the gaudy banner. The very first thing to do, before we come to any of our proposals that are political and legal, is something that really is (to use their beloved word) entirely psychological. The very first thing to do is to tell these American poker-players that they do not know how to play poker. For they not only bluff, but they boast that they are bluffing. In so far as it really is a question of an instant psychological method, there must be, and there is, an immediate psychological answer. In other words, because they are admittedly bluffing, we can call their bluff.

I said recently that any practical programme for restoring normal property consists of two parts, which current cant would call destructive and constructive; but which might more truly be called defensive and offensive. The first is stopping the mere mad stampede towards monopoly, before the last traditions of property and liberty are lost. It is with that preliminary problem of resisting the world's trend towards being more monopolist, that I am first of all dealing here. Now, when we ask what we can do, here and now, against the actual growth of monopoly, we are always given a very simple answer. We are told that we can do nothing. By a natural and inevitable operation the large things are swallowing the small, as large fish might swallow little fish. The trust can absorb what it likes, like a dragon devouring what it likes, because it is already the largest creature left alive in the land. Some people are so finally resolved to accept this result that they actually condescend to regret it. They are so convinced that it is fate that they will even admit that it is fatality. The fatalists almost become sentimentalists when looking at the little shop that is being bought up by the big company. They are ready to weep, so long as it is admitted that they weep because they weep in vain. They are willing to admit that the loss of a little toy-shop of their childhood, or a little tea-shop of their youth, is even in the true sense a tragedy. For a tragedy means always a man's struggle with that which is stronger than man. And it is the feet of the gods themselves that are here trampling on our traditions; it is death and doom themselves that have broken our little toys like sticks; for against the stars of destiny none shall prevail. It is amazing what a little bluff will do in this world.

For they go on saying that the big fish eats the little fish, without asking whether little fish swim up to big fish and ask to be eaten. They accept the devouring dragon without wondering whether a fashionable crowd of princesses ran after the dragon to be devoured. They have never heard of a fashion; and do not know the difference between fashion and fate. The necessitarians have here carefully chosen the one example of something that is certainly not necessary, whatever else is necessary. They have chosen the one thing that does happen still to be free, as a proof of the unbreakable chains in which all things are bound. Very little is left free in the modern world; but private buying and selling are still supposed to be free; and indeed still are free; if anyone has a will free enough to use his freedom. Children may be driven by force to a particular school. Men may be driven by force away from a public-house. All sorts of people, for all sorts of new and nonsensical reasons, may be driven by force to a prison. But nobody is yet driven by force to a particular shop.

I shall deal later with some practical remedies and reactions against the rush towards rings and corners. But even before we consider these, it is well to have paused a moment on the moral fact which is so elementary and so entirely ignored. Of all things in the world, the rush to the big shops is the thing that could be most easily stopped — by the people who rush there. We do not know what may come later; but they cannot be driven there by bayonets just yet. American business enterprise, which has already used British soldiers for purposes of advertisement, may doubtless in time use British soldiers for purposes of coercion. But we cannot yet be dragooned by guns and sabres into Yankee shops or international stores. The alleged economic attraction, with which I will deal in due course, is quite a different thing: I am merely pointing out that if we came to the conclusion that big shops ought to be boycotted, we could boycott them as easily as we should (I hope) boycott shops selling instruments of torture or poisons for private use in the home. In other words, this first and fundamental question is not a question of necessity but of will. If we chose to make a vow, if we chose to make a league, for dealing only with little local shops and never with large centralized shops, the campaign could be every bit as practical as the Land Campaign in Ireland. It would probably be nearly as successful. It will be said, of course, that people will go to the best shop. I deny it; for Irish boycotters did not take the best offer. I deny that the big shop is the best shop; and I especially deny that people go there because it is the best shop. And if I be asked why, I answer at the end with the unanswerable fact with which I began at the beginning. I know it is not merely a matter of business, for the simple reason that the business men themselves tell me it is merely a matter of bluff. It is they who say that nothing succeeds like a mere appearance of success. It is they who say that publicity influences us without our will or knowledge. It is they who say that "It Pays to Advertise"; that is, to tell people in a bullying way that they must "Do It Now," when they need not do it at all.

=================

2. A Misunderstanding About Method

Before I go any further with this sketch, I find I must pause upon a parenthesis touching the nature of my task, without which the rest of it may be misunderstood. As a matter of fact, without pretending to any official or commercial experience, I am here doing a great deal more than has ever been asked of most of the mere men of letters (if I may call myself for the moment a man of letters) when they confidently conducted social movements or setup social ideals. I will promise that, by the end of these notes, the reader shall know a great deal more about how men might set about making a Distributive State than the readers of Carlyle ever knew about how they should set about finding a Hero King or a Real Superior. I think we can explain how to make a small shop or a small farm a common feature of our society better than Matthew Arnold explained how to make the State the organ of Our Best Self. I think the farm will be marked on some sort of rude map more clearly than the Earthly Paradise on the navigation chart of William Morris; and I think that in comparison with his News from Nowhere this might fairly be called News from Somewhere. Rousseau and Ruskin were often much more vague and visionary than I am; though Rousseau was even more rigid in abstractions, and Ruskin was sometimes very much excited about particular details. I need not say that I am not comparing myself to these great men; I am only pointing out that even from these, whose minds dominated so much wider a field, and whose position as publicists was much more respected and responsible, nothing was as a matter of fact asked beyond the general principles we are accused of giving. I am merely pointing out that the task has fallen to a very minor poet when these very major prophets were not required to carry out and complete the fulfilment of their own prophecies. It would seem that our fathers did not think it quite so futile to have a clear vision of the goal with or without a detailed map of the road; or to be able to describe a scandal without going on to describe a substitute. Anyhow, for whatever reason, it is quite certain that if I really were great enough to deserve the reproaches of the utilitarians, if I really were as merely idealistic or imaginative as they make me out, if I really did confine myself to describing a direction without exactly measuring a road, to pointing towards home or heaven and telling men to use their own good sense in getting there — if this were really all that I could do, it would be all that men immeasurably greater than I am were ever expected to do; from Plato and Isaiah to Emerson and Tolstoy.

But it is not all that I can do; even though those who did not do it did so much more. I can do something else as well; but I can only do it if it be understood what I am doing. At the same time I am well aware that, in explaining the improvement of so elaborate a society, a man may often find it very difficult to explain exactly what he is doing, until it is done. I have considered and rejected half a dozen ways of approaching the problem, by different roads that all lead to the same truth. I had thought of beginning with the simple example of the peasant; and then I knew that a hundred correspondents would leap upon me, accusing me of trying to turn all of them into peasants. I thought of beginning with describing a decent Distributive State in being, with all its balance of different things; just as the Socialists describe their Utopia in being, with its concentration in one thing. Then I knew a hundred correspondents would call me Utopian; and say it was obvious my scheme could not work, because I could only describe it when it was working. But what they would really mean by my being Utopian, would be this: that until that scheme was working, there was no work to be done. I have finally decided to approach the social solution in this fashion: to point out first that the monopolist momentum is not irresistible; that even here and now much could be done to modify it, much by anybody, almost everything by everybody. Then I would maintain that on the removal of that particular plutocratic pressure, the appetite and appreciation of natural property would revive, like any other natural thing. Then, I say, it will be worth while to propound to people thus returning to sanity, however sporadically, a sane society that could balance property and control machinery. With the description of that ultimate society, with its laws and limitations, I would conclude.

Now that may or may not be a good arrangement or order of ideas; but it is an intelligible one; and I submit with all humility that I have a right to arrange my explanations in that order, and no critic has a right to complain that I do not disarrange them in order to answer questions out of their order. I am willing to write him a whole Encyclopaedia of Distributism if he has the patience to read it; but he must have the patience to read it. It is unreasonable for him to complain that I have not dealt adequately with Zoology, State Provision For, under the letter B; or described the honourable social status of the Guild of the Xylographers while I am still dealing alphabetically with the Guild of Architects. I am willing to be as much of a bore as Euclid; but the critic must not complain that the forty-eighth proposition of the second book is not a part of the Pons Asinorum. The ancient Guild of Bridge-Builders will have to build many such bridges.

Now from comments that have come my way, I gather that the suggestions I have already made may not altogether explain their own place and purpose in this scheme. I am merely pointing out that monopoly is not omnipotent even now and here; and that anybody could think, on the spur of the moment, of many ways in which its final triumph can be delayed and perhaps defeated. Suppose a monopolist who is my mortal enemy endeavours to ruin me by preventing me from selling eggs to my neighbours, I can tell him I shall live on my own turnips in my own kitchen-garden. I do not mean to tie myself to turnips; or swear never to touch my own potatoes or beans. I mean the turnips as an example; something to throw at him. Suppose the wicked millionaire in question comes and grins over my garden wall and says, "I perceive by your starved and emaciated appearance that you are in immediate need of a few shillings; but you can't possibly get them," I may possibly be stung into retorting, "Yes, I can. I could sell my first edition of Martin Chuzzlewit." I do not necessarily mean that I see myself already in a pauper's grave unless I can sell Martin Chuzzlewit; I do not mean that I have nothing else to suggest except selling Martin Chuzzlewit; I do not mean to brag like any common politician that I have nailed my colours to the Martin Chuzzlewit policy. I mean to tell the offensive pessimist that I am not at the end of my resources; that I can sell a book or even, if the case grows desperate, write a book. I could do a great many things before I came to definitely anti-social action like robbing a bank or (worse still) working in a bank. I could do a great many things of a great many kinds, and I give an example at the start to suggest that there are many more of them, not that there are no more of them. There are a great many things of a great many kinds in my house, besides the copy of a Martin Chuzzlewit. Not many of them are of great value except to me; but some of them are of some value to anybody. For the whole point of a home is that it is a hotch-potch. And mine, at any rate, rises to that austere domestic ideal. The whole point of one's own house is that it is not only a number of totally different things, which are nevertheless one thing, but it is one in which we still value even the things that we forget. If a man has burnt my house to a heap of ashes, I am none the less justly indignant with him for having burnt everything, because I cannot at first even remember everything he has burnt. And as it is with the household gods, so it is with the whole of that household religion, or what remains of it, to offer resistance to the destructive discipline of industrial capitalism. In a simpler society, I should rush out of the ruins, calling for help on the Commune or the King, and crying out, "Haro! a robber has burnt my house." I might, of course, rush down the street crying in one passionate breath, "Haro! a robber has burnt my front door of seasoned oak with the usual fittings, fourteen window frames, nine curtains, five and a half carpets, 753 books, of which four were editions de luxe, one portrait of my great-grandmother," and so on through all the items; but something would be lost of the fierce and simple feudal cry. And in the same way I could have begun this outline with an inventory of all the alterations I should like to see in the laws, with the object of establishing some economic justice in England. But I doubt whether the reader would have had any better idea of what I was ultimately driving at; and it would not have been the approach by which I propose at present to drive. I shall have occasion later to go into some slight detail about these things; but the cases I give are merely illustrations of my first general thesis: that we are not even at the moment doing everything that could be done to resist the rush of monopoly; and that when people talk as if nothing could now be done, that statement is false at the start; and that all sorts of answers to it will immediately occur to the mind.

Capitalism is breaking up; and in one sense we do not pretend to be sorry it is breaking up. Indeed, we might put our own point pretty correctly by saying that we would help it to break up; but we do not want it merely to break down. But the first fact to realize is precisely that; that it is a choice between its breaking up and its breaking down. It is a choice between its being voluntarily resolved into its real component parts, each taking back its own, and its merely collapsing on our heads in a crash or confusion of all its component parts, which some call communism and some call chaos. The former is the one thing all sensible people should try to procure. The latter is the one thing that all sensible people should try to prevent. That is why they are often classed together.

I have mainly confined myself to answering what I have always found to be the first question, "What are we to do now?" To that I answer, "What we must do now is to stop the other people from doing what they are doing now." The initiative is with the enemy. It is he who is already doing things, and will have done them long before we can begin to do anything, since he has the money, the machinery, the rather mechanical majority, and other things which we have first to gain and then to use. He has nearly completed a monopolist conquest, but not quite; and he can still be hampered and halted. The world has woken up very late; but that is not our fault. That is the fault of all the fools who told us for twenty years that there could never be any Trusts; and are now telling us, equally wisely, that there can never be anything else.

There are other things I ask the reader to bear in mind. The first is that this outline is only an outline, though one that can hardly avoid some curves and loops. I do not profess to dispose of all the obstacles that might arise in this question, because so many of them would seem to many to be quite a different question. I will give one example of what I mean. What would the critical reader have thought, if at the very beginning of this sketch I had gone off into a long disputation about the Law of Libel? Yet, if I were strictly practical, I should find that one of the most practical obstacles. It is the present ridiculous position that monopoly is not resisted as a social force but can still be resented as a legal imputation. If you try to stop a man cornering milk, the first thing that happens will be a smashing libel action for calling it a corner. It is manifestly mere common sense that if the thing is not a sin it is not a slander. As things stand, there is no punishment for the man who does it; but there is a punishment for the man who discovers it. I do not deal here (though I am quite prepared to deal elsewhere) with all these detailed difficulties which a society as now constituted would raise against such a society as we want to constitute. If it were constituted on the principles I suggest, those details would be dealt with on those principles as they arose. For instance, it would put an end to the nonsense whereby men, who are more powerful than emperors, pretend to be private tradesmen suffering from private malice; it will assert that those who are in practice public men must be criticized as potential public evils. It would destroy the absurdity by which an "important case" is tried by a "special jury"; or, in other words, that any serious issue between rich and poor is tried by the rich. But the reader will see that I cannot here rule out all the ten thousand things that might trip us up; I must assume that a people ready to take the larger risks would also take the smaller ones.

Now this outline is an outline; in other words, it is a design, and anybody who thinks we can have practical things without theoretical designs can go and quarrel with the nearest engineer or architect for drawing thin lines on thin paper. But there is another and more special sense in which my suggestion is an outline; in the sense that it is deliberately drawn as a large limitation within which there are many varieties. I have long been acquainted, and not a little amused, with the sort of practical man who will certainly say that I generalize because there is no practical plan. The truth is that I generalize because there are so many practical plans. I myself know four or five schemes that have been drawn up, more or less drastically, for the diffusion of capital. The most cautious, from a capitalist standpoint, is the gradual extension of profit-sharing. A more stringently democratic form of the same thing is the management of every business (if it cannot be a small business) by a guild or group clubbing their contributions and dividing their results. Some Distributists dislike the idea of the workman having shares only where he has work; they think he would be more independent if his little capital were invested elsewhere; but they all agree that he ought to have the capital to invest. Others continue to call themselves Distributists because they would give every citizen a dividend out of much larger national systems of production. I deliberately draw out my general principles so as to cover as many as possible of these alternative business schemes. But I object to being told that I am covering so many because I know there are none. If I tell a man he is too luxurious and extravagant, and that he ought to economize in something, I am not bound to give him a list of his luxuries. The point is that he will be all the better for cutting down any of his luxuries. And my point is that modern society would be all the better for cutting up property by any of these processes. This does not mean that I have not my own favourite form; personally I prefer the second type of division given in the above list of examples. But my main business is to point out that any reversal of the rush to concentrate property will be an improvement on the present state of things. If I tell a man his house is burning down in Putney, he may thank me even if I do not give him a list of all the vehicles which go to Putney, with the numbers of all the taxicabs and the time-table of all the trams. It is enough that I know there are a great many vehicles for him to choose from, before he is reduced to the proverbial adventure of going to Putney on a pig. It is enough that any one of those vehicles is on the whole less uncomfortable than a house on fire or even a heap of ashes. I admit I might be called unpractical if impenetrable forests and destructive floods lay between here and Putney; it might then be as merely idealistic to praise Putney as to praise Paradise. But I do not admit that I am unpractical because I know there are half a dozen practical ways which are more practical than the present state of things. But it does not follow, in fact, that I do not know how to get to Putney. Here, for instance, are half a dozen things which would help the process of Distributism, apart from those on which I shall have occasion to touch as points of principle. Not all Distributists would agree with all of them; but all would agree that they are in the direction of Distributism. (1) The taxation of contracts so as to discourage the sale of small property to big proprietors and encourage the break-up of big property among small proprietors. (2) Something like the Napoleonic testamentary law and the destruction of primogeniture. (3) The establishment of free law for the poor, so that small property could always be defended against great. (4) The deliberate protection of certain experiments in small property, if necessary by tariffs and even local tariffs. (5) Subsidies to foster the starting of such experiments. (6) A league of voluntary dedication, and any number of other things of the same kind. But I have inserted this chapter here in order to explain that this is a sketch of the first principles of Distributism and not of the last details, about which even Distributists might dispute. In such a statement, examples are given as examples, and not as exact and exhaustive lists of all the cases covered by the rule. If this elementary principle of exposition be not understood I must be content to be called an unpractical person by that sort of practical man. And indeed in his sense there is something in his accusation. Whether or no I am a practical man, I am not what is called a practical politician, which means a professional politician. I can claim no part in the glory of having brought our country to its present promising and hopeful condition. Harder heads than mine have established the present prosperity of coal. Men of action, of a more rugged energy, have brought us to the comfortable condition of living on our capital. I have had no part in the great industrial revolution which has increased the beauties of nature and reconciled the classes of society; nor must the too enthusiastic reader think of thanking me for this more enlightened England, in which the employee is living on a dole from the State and the employer on an overdraft at the Bank.

= = = = = = = = = = = = = = = = =

3. A Case In Point

It is as natural to our commercial critics to argue in a circle as to travel on the Inner Circle. It is not mere stupidity, but it is mere habit; and it is not easy either to break into or to escape from that iron ring. When we say things can be done, we commonly mean either that they could be done by the mass of men, or else by the ruler of the State. I gave an example of something that could be done quite easily by the mass; and here I will give an example of something that could be done quite easily by the ruler. But we must be prepared for our critics beginning to argue in a circle and saying that the present populace will never agree or the present ruler act in that way. But this complaint is a confusion. We are answering people who call our ideal impossible in itself. If you do not want it, of course, you will not try to get it; but do not say that because you do not want it, it follows that you could not get it if you did want it. A thing does not become intrinsically impossible merely by a mob not trying to obtain it; nor does a thing cease to be practical politics because no politician is practical enough to do it.

I will start with a small and familiar example. In order to ensure that our huge proletariat should have a holiday, we have a law obliging all employers to shut their shops for half a day once a week. Given the proletarian principle, it is a healthy and necessary thing for a proletarian state; just as the saturnalia is a healthy and necessary thing for a slave state. Given this provision for the proletariat, a practical person will naturally say: "It has other advantages, too; it will be a chance for anybody who chooses to do his own dirty work; for the man who can manage without servants." That degraded being who actually knows how to do things himself, will have a look in at last. That isolated crank, who can really work for his own living, may possibly have a chance to live. A man does not need to be a Distributist to say this; it is the ordinary and obvious thing that anybody would say. The man who has servants must cease to work his servants. Of course, the man who has no servants to work cannot cease to work them. But the law is actually so constructed that it forces this man also to give a holiday to the servants he has not got. He proclaims a saturnalia that never happens to a crowd of phantom slaves that have never been there. Now there is not a rudiment of reason about this arrangement. In every possible sense, from the immediate material to the abstract and mathematical sense, it is quite mad. We live in days of dangerous division of interests between the employer and the employed. Therefore, even when the two are not divided, but actually united in one person, we must divide them again into two parties. We coerce a man into giving himself something he does not want, because somebody else who does not exist might want it. We warn him that he had better receive a deputation from himself, or he might go on strike against himself. Perhaps he might even become a Bolshevist, and throw a bomb at himself; in which case he would have no other course left to his stern sense of law and order but to read the Riot Act and shoot himself. They call us unpractical; but we have not yet produced such an academic fantasy as this. They sometimes suggest that our regret for the disappearance of the yeoman or the apprentice is a mere matter of sentiment. Sentimental! We have not quite sunk to such sentimentalism as to be sorry for apprentices who never existed at all. We have not quite reached that richness of romantic emotion that we are capable of weeping more copiously for an imaginary grocer's assistant than for a real grocer. We are not quite so maudlin yet as to see double when we look into our favourite little shop; or to set the little shopkeeper fighting with his own shadow. Let us leave these hard-headed and practical men of business shedding tears over the sorrows of a non-existent office boy, and

217

proceed upon our own wild and erratic path, that at least happens to pass across the land of the living.

Now if so small a change as that were made to-morrow, it would make a difference: a considerable and increasing difference. And if any rash apologist of Big Business tells me that a little thing like that could make very little difference, let him beware. For he is doing the one thing which such apologists commonly avoid above all things: he is contradicting his masters. Among the thousand things of interest, which are lost in the million things of no interest, in the newspaper reports of Parliament and public affairs, there really was one delightful little comedy dealing with this point. Some man of normal sense and popular instincts, who had strayed into Parliament by some mistake or other, actually pointed out this plain fact: that there was no need to protect the proletariat where there was no proletariat to protect; and that the lonely shopkeeper might, therefore, remain in his lonely shop. And the Minister in charge of the matter actually replied, with a ghastly innocence, that it was impossible; for it would be unfair to the big shops. Tears evidently flow freely in such circles, as they did from the rising politician, Lord Lundy; and in this case it was the mere thought of the possible sufferings of the millionaires that moved him. There rose before his imagination Mr. Selfridge in his agony, and the groans of Mr. Woolworth, of the Woolworth Tower, thrilled through the kind hearts to which the cry of the sorrowing rich will never come in vain. But whatever we may think of the sensibility needed to regard the big store-owners as objects of sympathy, at any rate it disposes at a stroke of all the fashionable fatalism that sees something inevitable in their success. It is absurd to tell us that our attack is bound to fail; and then that there would be something quite unscrupulous in its so immediately succeeding. Apparently Big Business must be accepted because it is invulnerable, and spared because it is vulnerable. This big absurd bubble can never conceivably be burst; and it is simply cruel that a little pin-prick of competition can burst it.

I do not know whether the big shops are quite so weak and wobbly as their champion said. But whatever the immediate effect on the big shops, I am sure there would be an immediate effect on the little shops. I am sure that if they could trade on the general holiday, it would not only mean that there would be more trade for them, but that there would be more of them trading. It might mean at last a large class of little shopkeepers; and that is exactly the sort of thing that makes all the political difference, as it does in the case of a large class of little farmers. It is not in the merely mechanical sense a matter of numbers. It is a matter of the presence and pressure of a particular social type. It is not a question merely of how many noses are counted; but in the more real sense whether the noses count. If there were anything that could be called a class of peasants, or a class of small shopkeepers, they would make their presence felt in legislation, even if it were what is called class legislation. And the very existence of that third class would be the end of what is called the class war; in so far as its theory divides all men into employers and employed. I do not mean, of course, that this little legal alteration is the only one I have to propose; I mention it first because it is the most obvious. But I mention it also because it illustrates very clearly what I mean by the two stages: the nature of the negative and positive reform. If little shops began to gain custom and big shops began to lose it, it would mean two things, both indeed preliminary but both practical. It would mean that the mere centripetal rush was slowed down, if not stopped, and might at last change to a centrifugal movement. And it would mean that there were a number of new citizens in the State to whom all the ordinary Socialist or servile arguments were inapplicable. Now when you have got your considerable sprinkling of small proprietors, of men with the psychology and philosophy of small property, then you can begin to talk to them about something more like a just general settlement upon their own lines; something more like a land fit for Christians to live in. You can make them understand, as you cannot make plutocrats or proletarians understand, why the machine must not exist save as the servant of the man, why the things we produce ourselves are precious like our own children, and why we can pay too dearly for the possession of luxury by the loss of liberty. If bodies of men only begin to be detached from the servile settlements, they will begin to form the body of our public opinion. Now there are a large number of other advantages that could be given to the small man, which can be considered in their place. In all of them I presuppose a deliberate policy of favouring the small man. But in the primary example here given we can hardly even say that there is any question of favour. You make a law that slave-owners shall free their slaves for a day: the man who has no slaves is outside the thing entirely; he does not come under it in law, because he does not come into it in logic. He has been deliberately dragged into it; not in order that all slaves shall be free for a day, but in order that all free men shall be slaves for a lifetime. But while some of the expedients are only common justice to small property, and others are deliberate protection of small property, the point at the moment is that it will be worth while at the beginning to create small property though it were only on a small scale. English citizens and yeomen would once more exist; and wherever they exist they count. There are many other ways, which can be briefly described, by which the break-up of property can be encouraged on the legal and legislative side. I shall deal with some of them later, and especially with the real responsibility which Government might reasonably assume in a financial and economic condition which is becoming quite ludicrous. From the standpoint of any sane person, in any other society, the present problem of capitalist concentration is not only a question of law but of criminal law, not to mention criminal lunacy.

Of that monstrous megalomania of the big shops, with their blatant advertisements and stupid standardization, something is said elsewhere. But it may be well to add, in the matter of the small shops, that when once they exist they generally have an organization of their own which is much more self-respecting and much less vulgar. This voluntary organization, as every one knows, is called a Guild; and it is perfectly capable of doing everything that really needs to be done in the way of holidays and popular festivals. Twenty barbers would be quite capable of arranging with each other not to compete with each other on a particular festival or in a particular fashion, It is amusing to note that the same people who say that a Guild is a dead medieval thing that would never work are generally grumbling against the power of a Guild as a living modern thing where it is actually working. In the case of the Guild of the Doctors, for instance, it is made a matter of reproach in the newspapers, that the confederation in question refuses to "make medical discoveries accessible to the general public." When we consider the wild and unbalanced nonsense that is made accessible to the general public by the public press, perhaps we have some reason to doubt whether our souls and bodies are not at least as safe in the hands of a Guild as they are likely to be in the hands of a Trust. For the moment the main point is that small shops can be governed even if they are not bossed by the Government. Horrible as this may seem to the democratic idealists of the day, they can be governed by themselves.

= = = = = = = = = = = = = = = = =

4. The Tyranny Of Trusts

We have most of us met in literature, and even in life, a certain sort of old gentleman; he is very often represented by an old clergyman. He is the sort of man who has a horror of Socialists without any very definite idea of what they are. He is the man of whom men say that he means well; by which they mean that he means nothing. But this view is a little unjust to this social type. He is really something more than well-meaning; we might even go so far as to say that he would probably be right-thinking, if he ever thought. His principles would probably be sound enough if they were really applied; it is his practical ignorance that prevents him from knowing the world to which they are applicable. He might really be right, only he has no notion of what is wrong. Those who have sat under this old gentleman know that he is in the habit of softening his stern repudiation of the mysterious Socialists by saying that, of course, it is a Christian duty to use our wealth well, to remember that property is a trust committed to us by Providence for the good of others as well as ourselves, and even (unless the old gentleman is old enough to be a Modernist) that it is just possible that we may some day be asked a question or two about the abuse of such a trust. Now all this is perfectly true, so far as it goes, but it happens to illustrate in a rather curious way the queer and even uncanny innocence of the old gentleman. The very phrase that he uses, when he says that property is a trust committed to us by Providence, is a phrase which takes on, when it is uttered to the world around him, the character of an awful and appalling pun. His pathetic little sentence returns in a hundred howling echoes, repeating it again and again like the laughter of a hundred fiends in hell: "Property is a Trust."

Now I could not more conveniently sum up what I meant by this first section than by taking this type of the dear old conservative clergyman, and considering the curious way in which he has been first caught napping, and then as it were knocked on the head. The first thing we have had to explain to him is expressed in that horrible pun about the Trust. While he has been crying out against imaginary robbers, whom he calls Socialists, he has been caught and carried away bodily by real robbers, whom he still could not even imagine. For the gangs of gamblers who make the great combines are really gangs of robbers, in the sense that they have far less feeling than anybody else for that individual responsibility for individual gifts of God which the old gentleman very rightly calls a Christian duty. While he has been weaving words in the air about irrelevant ideals, he has been caught in a net woven out of the very opposite words and notions: impersonal, irresponsible, irreligious. The financial forces that surround him are further away than anything else from the domestic idea of ownership with which, to do him justice, he himself began. So that when he still bleats faintly, "Property is a trust," we shall reply firmly, "A trust is not property."

And now I come to the really extraordinary thing about the old gentleman. I mean that I come to the queerest fact about the conventional or conservative type in modern English society. And that is the fact that the same society, which began by saying there was no such danger to avoid, now says that the danger cannot possibly be avoided. Our whole capitalist community has taken one huge stride from the extreme of optimism to the extreme of pessimism. They began by saying that there could not be Trusts in this country. They have ended by saying that there cannot be anything else except Trusts in this age. And in the course of calling the same thing impossible on Monday and inevitable on Tuesday, they have saved the life of the great gambler or robber twice over; first by calling him a fabulous monster, and second by calling him an almighty fate. Twelve years ago, when I talked of Trusts, people said: "There are no Trusts in England." Now, when I say it, the same people say: "But how do you propose that England should escape from the Trusts?" They talk as if the Trusts had always been a part of the British Constitution, not to mention the Solar System. In short, the pun and parable with which I began this article have exactly and ironically come true. The poor old clergyman is now really driven to talk as if a Trust with a big T were something that had been bestowed on him by Providence. He is driven to abandon all that he originally meant by his own curious sort of Christian individualism, and hastily reconcile himself to something that is more like a sort of plutocratic collectivism. He is beginning, in a rather bewildered way, to understand that he must now say that monopoly and not merely private property is a part of the nature of things. The net had been thrown over him while he slept, because he never thought of such a thing as a net; because he would have denied the very possibility of anybody weaving such a net. But now the poor old gentleman has to begin to talk as if he had been born in the net. Perhaps, as I say, he has had a knock on the head; perhaps, as his enemies say, he was always just a little weak in the head. But, anyhow, now that his head is in the noose, or the net, he will often start preaching to us about the impossibility of escaping from nets and nooses that are woven or spun upon the wheel of the fates. In a word, I wish to point out that the old gentleman was much too heedless about getting into the net and is much too hopeless about getting out of it.

In short, I would sum up my general suggestions so far by saying that the chief danger to be avoided now, and the first danger to be considered now, is the danger of supposing the capitalist conquest more complete than it is. If I may use the terms of the Penny Catechism about the two sins against hope, the peril now is no longer the peril of presumption but rather of despair. It is not mere impudence like that of those who told us, without winking an eyelid, that there were no Trusts in England. It is rather mere impotence like that of those who tell us that England must soon be swallowed up in an earthquake called America. Now this sort of surrender to modern monopoly is not only ignoble, it is also panic-stricken and premature. It is not true that we can do nothing. What I have written so far has been directed to showing the doubtful and the terrified that it is not true that we can do nothing. Even now there is something that can be done, and done at once; though the things so to be done may appear to be of different kinds and even of degrees of effectiveness. Even if we only save a shop in our own street or stop a conspiracy in our own trade, or get a Bill to punish such conspiracies pressed by our own member, we may come in the nick of time and make all the difference.

To vary the metaphor to a military one, what has happened is that the monopolists have attempted an encircling movement. But the encircling movement is not yet complete. Unless we do something it will be complete; but it is not true to say that we can do nothing to prevent it being completed. We are in favour of striking out, of making sorties or sallies, of trying to pierce certain points in the line (far enough apart and chosen for their weakness), of breaking through the gap in the uncompleted circle. Most people around us are for surrender to the surprise; precisely because it was to them so complete a surprise. Yesterday they denied that the enemy could encircle. The day before yesterday they denied that the enemy could exist. They are paralysed as by a prodigy. But just as we never agreed that the thing was impossible, so we do not now agree that it is irresistible. Action ought to have been taken long ago; but action can still be taken now. That is why it is worth while to dwell on the diverse expedients already given as examples. A chain is as strong as its weakest link; a battleline is as strong as its weakest man; an encircling movement is as strong as its weakest point, the point at which the circle may still be broken. Thus, to begin with, if anybody asks me in this matter, "What am I to do now?" I answer, "Do anything, however small, that will prevent the completion of the work of capitalist combination. Do anything that will even delay that completion. Save one shop out of a hundred shops. Save one croft out of a hundred crofts. Keep open one door out of a hundred doors; for so long as one door is open, we are not in prison. Throw up one barricade in their way, and you will soon see whether it is the way the world is going. Put one spoke in their wheel, and you will soon see whether it is the wheel of fate." For it is of the essence of their enormous and unnatural effort that a small failure is as big as a big failure. The modern commercial combine has a great many points in common with a big balloon. It is swollen and yet it is swollen with levity; it climbs and yet it drifts; above all, it is full of gas, and generally of poison gas. But the resemblance most relevant here is that the smallest prick will shrivel the biggest balloon. If this tendency of our time received anything like a reasonably definite check, I believe the whole tendency would soon begin to weaken in its preposterous prestige. Until monopoly is monopolist it is nothing. Until the combine can combine everything, it is nothing. Ahab has not his kingdom so long as Naboth has his vineyard. Haman will not be happy in the palace while Mordecai is sitting in the gate. A hundred tales of human history are there to show that tendencies can be turned back, and that one stumbling-block can be the turning-point. The sands of time are simply dotted with single stakes that have thus marked the turn of the tide. The first step towards ultimately winning is to make sure that the enemy does not win, if it be only that he does not win everywhere. Then, when we have halted his rush, and perhaps fought it to a standstill, we may begin a general counter-attack. The nature of that counter-attack I shall next proceed to consider. In other words, I will try to explain to the old clergyman caught in the net (whose sufferings are ever before my eyes) what it will no doubt comfort him to know: that he was wrong from the first in thinking there could be no net; that he is wrong now in thinking there is no escape from the net; and that he will never know how wrong he was till he finds he has a net of his own, and is once more a fisher of men.

I began by enunciating the paradox that one way of supporting small shops would be to support them. Everybody could do it, but nobody can imagine it being done. In one sense nothing is so simple, and in another nothing is so hard. I went on to point out that without any sweeping change at all, the mere modification of existing laws would probably call thousands of little shops into life and activity. I may have occasion to return to the little shops at greater length; but for the moment I am only running rapidly through certain separate examples, to show that the citadel of plutocracy could even now be attacked from many different sides. It could be met by a concerted effort in the open field of competition. It could be checked by the creation or even correction of a large number of little laws. Thirdly, it could be attacked by the more sweeping operation of larger laws. But when we come to these, even at this stage, we also come into collision with larger questions.

The common sense of Christendom, for ages on end, has assumed that it was as possible to punish cornering as to punish coining. Yet to most readers to-day there seems a sort of vital contradiction, echoed in the verbal contradiction of saying, "Put not your trust in Trusts." Yet to our fathers this would not seem even so much of a paradox as saying, "Put not your trust in princes," but rather like saying, "Put not your trust in pirates." But in applying this to modern conditions, we are checked first by a very modern sophistry.

When we say that a corner should be treated as a conspiracy, we are always told that the conspiracy is too elaborate to be unravelled. In other words, we are told that the conspirators are too conspiratorial to be caught. Now it is exactly at this point that my simple and childlike confidence in the business expert entirely breaks down. My attitude, a moment ago trustful and confiding, becomes disrespectful and frivolous. I am willing to agree that I do not know much about the details of business, but not that nobody could possibly ever come to know anything about them. I am willing to believe that there are people in the world who like to feel that they depend for the bread of life on one particular bounder, who probably began by making large profits on short weight. I am willing to believe that there are people so strangely constituted that they like to see a great nation held up by a small gang, more lawless than brigands but not so brave. In short, I am willing to admit that there may be people who trust in Trusts. I admit it with tears, like those of the benevolent captain in the Bab Ballads who said:

> "It's human nature p'raps; if so,   Oh, isn't human nature low?"

I myself doubt whether it is quite so low as that; but I admit the possibility of this utter lowness; I admit it with weeping and lamentation. But when they tell me it would be impossible to find out whether a man is making a Trust or not — that is quite another thing. My demeanour alters. My spirits revive. When I am told that if cornering were a crime nobody could be convicted of that crime — then I laugh; nay, I jeer.

A murder is usually committed, we may infer, when one gentleman takes a dislike to the appearance of another gentleman in Piccadilly Circus at eleven o'clock in the morning; and steps up to the object of his distaste and dexterously cuts his throat. He then walks across to the kind policeman who is regulating the traffic, and draws his attention to the presence of the corpse on the pavement, consulting him about how to dispose of the encumbrance. That is apparently how these people expect financial crimes to be done, in order to be discovered. Sometimes indeed they are done almost as brazenly, in communities where they can safely be discovered. But the theory of legal impotence looks very extraordinary when we consider the sort of things that the police do discover. Look at the sort of murders they discover. An utterly ordinary and obscure man in some hole-and-corner house or tenement among ten thousand like it, washes his hands in a sink in a back scullery; the operation taking two minutes. The police can discover that, but they could not possibly discover the meeting of men or the sending of messages that turn the whole commercial world upside down. They can track a man that nobody has ever heard of to a place where nobody knew he was going, to do something that he took every possible precaution that nobody should see. But they cannot keep a watch on a man that everybody has heard of, to see whether he communicates with another man that everybody has heard of, in order to do something that nearly everybody knows he is trying all his life to do. They can tell us all about the movements of a man whose own wife or partner or landlady does not profess to know his movements; but they cannot tell when a great combination covering half the earth is on the move. Are the police really so foolish as this; or are they at once so foolish and so wise? Or if the police were as helpless as Sherlock Holmes thought them, what about Sherlock Holmes? What about the ardent amateur detective about whom all of us have read and some of us (alas!) have written. Is there no inspired sleuth to succeed where all the police have failed; and prove conclusively from a greasy spot on the tablecloth that Mr. Rockefeller is interested in oil? Is there no keen-faced man to infer from the late Lord Leverhulme buying up a crowd of soap-businesses that he was interested in soap? I feel inclined to write a new series of detective stories myself, about the discovery of these obscure and cryptic things. They would describe Sherlock Holmes with his monstrous magnifying-glass poring over a paper and making out one of the headlines letter by letter. They would show us Watson standing in amazement at the discovery of the Bank of England. My stories would bear the traditional sort of titles, such as "The Secret of the Skysign" and "The Mystery of the Megaphone" and "The Adventure of the Unnoticed Hoarding."

What these people really mean is that they cannot imagine cornering being treated like coining. They cannot imagine attempted forestalling, or, indeed, any activity of the rich, coming into the realm of the criminal law at all. It would give them a shock to think of such men subjected to such tests. I will give one obvious example. The science of finger-prints is perpetually paraded before us by the criminologists when they merely want to glorify their not very glorious science. Finger-prints would prove as easily whether a millionaire had used a pen as whether a housebreaker had used a jemmy. They might show as clearly that a financier had used a telephone as that a burglar had used a ladder. But if we began to talk about taking the finger-prints of financiers, everybody would think it was a joke. And so it is: a very grim joke. The laughter that leaps up spontaneously at the suggestion is itself a proof that nobody takes seriously, or thinks of taking seriously, the idea of rich men and poor being equal before the law.

That is the reason why we do not treat Trust magnates and monopolists as they would be treated under the old laws of popular justice. And that is the reason why I take their case at this stage, and in this section of my remarks, along with such apparently light and superficial things as transferring custom from one shop to another. It is because in both cases it is a question wholly and solely of moral will; and not in the least, in any sense, a question of economic law. In other words, it is a lie to say that we cannot make a law to imprison monopolists, or pillory monopolists, or hang monopolists if we choose, as our fathers did before us. And in the same sense it is a lie to say that we cannot help buying the best advertised goods or going to the biggest shop or falling in, in our general social habits, with the general social trend. We could help it in a hundred ways; from the very simple one of walking out of a shop to the more ceremonial one of hanging a man on a gallows. If we mean that we do not want to help it, that may be very true, and even in some cases very right. But arresting a forestaller is as easy as falling off a log or walking out of a shop. Putting the log-roller in prison is no more impossible than walking out of the shop is impossible; and it is highly desirable for the health of this discussion that we should realize the fact from the first. Practically about half of the recognized expedients by which a big business is now made have been marked down as a crime in some community of the past; and could be so marked in a community of the future. I can only refer to them here in the most cursory fashion. One of them is the process against which the statesmen of the most respectable party rave day and night so long as they can pretend that it is only done by foreigners. It is called Dumping. There is a policy of deliberately selling at a loss to destroy another man's market. Another is: a process against which the same statesmen of the same party actually have attempted to legislate, so long as it was confined to moneylenders. Unfortunately, however, it is not by any means confined to moneylenders. It is the trick of tying a poorer man up in a tangle of all sorts of obligations that he cannot ultimately discharge, except by selling his shop or business. It is done in one form by giving to the desperate things on the instalment plan or on long credit. All these conspiracies I would have tried as we try a conspiracy to overthrow the State or to shoot the King. We do not expect the man to write the King a post-card, telling him he is to be shot, or to give warning in the newspapers of the Day of Revolution. Such plots have always been judged in the only way in which they can be judged: by the use of common sense as to the existence of a purpose and the apparent existence of a plan. But we shall never have a real civic sense until it is once more felt that the plot of three citizens against one citizen is a crime, as well as the plot of one citizen against three. In other words, private property ought to be protected against private crime, just as public order is protected against private judgment. But private property ought to be protected against much bigger things than burglars and pick-pockets. It needs protection against the plots of a whole plutocracy. It needs defence against the rich, who are now generally the rulers who ought to defend it. It may not be difficult to explain why they do not defend it. But anyhow, in all these cases, the difficulty is in imagining people wanting to do it; not in imagining people doing it. By all means let people say that they do not think the ideal of the Distributive State is worth the risk or even worth the trouble. But do not let them say that no human being in the past has ever taken any risk; or that no children of Adam are capable of taking any trouble. If they chose to take half as much risk to achieve justice as they have already taken to achieve degradation, if they toiled half as laboriously to make anything beautiful as they toiled to make everything ugly, if they had served their God as they have served their Pork King and their Petrol King, the success of our whole Distributive democracy would stare at the world like one of their flaming sky-signs and scrape the sky like one of their crazy towers.

III. Some Aspects Of The Land

1. The Simple Truth

All of us, or at least all those of my generation, heard in our youth an anecdote about George Stephenson, the discoverer of the Locomotive Steam-Engine. It was said that some miserable rustic raised the objection that it would be very awkward if a cow strayed on the railway line, whereupon the inventor replied, "It would be very awkward for the cow." It is supremely characteristic of his age and school that it never seemed to occur to anybody that it might be rather awkward for the rustic who owned the cow.

Long before we heard that anecdote, however, we had probably heard another and more exciting anecdote called "Jack and the Beanstalk." That story begins with the strange and startling words, "There once was a poor woman who had a cow." It would be a wild paradox in modern England to imagine that a poor woman could have a cow; but things seem to have been different in ruder and more superstitious ages. Anyhow, she evidently would not have had a cow long in the sympathetic atmosphere of Stephenson and his steam-engine. The train went forward, the cow was killed in due course; and the state of mind of the old woman was described as the Depression of Agriculture. But everybody was so happy in travelling in trains and making it awkward for cows that nobody noticed that other difficulties remained. When wars or revolutions cut us off from cows, the industrialists discovered that milk does not come originally from cans. On this fact some of us have founded the idea that the cow (and even the miserable rustic) have a use in society, and have been prepared to concede her as much as three acres. But it will be well at this stage to repeat that we do not propose that every acre should be covered with cows; and do not propose to eliminate townspeople as they would eliminate rustics. On many minor points we might have to compromise with conditions, especially at first. But even my ideal, if ever I found it at last, would be what some call a compromise. Only I think it more accurate to call it a balance. For I do not think that the sun compromises with the rain when together they make a garden; or that the rose that grows there is a compromise between green and red. But I mean that even my Utopia would contain different things of different types holding on different tenures: that as in a medieval state there were some peasants, some monasteries, some common land, some private land, some town guilds, and so on, so in my modern state there would be some things nationalized, some machines owned corporately, some guilds sharing common profits, and so on, as well as many absolute individual owners, where such individual owners are most possible. But with these latter it is well to begin, because they are meant to give, and nearly always do give, the standard and tone of the society.

Among the things we have heard a thousand times is the statement that the English are a slow people, a cautious people, a conservative people, and so on. When we have heard a thing as many times as that, we generally either accept it as a truism, or suddenly see that it is quite untrue. And in this case it is quite untrue. The real peculiarity of England is that it is the only country on earth that has not got a conservative class. There are a large number, possibly a majority, of people who call themselves conservative. But the more they are examined, the less conservative they will appear. The commercial class that is in a special sense capitalist is in its nature the very opposite of conservative. By its own profession, it proclaims that it is perpetually using new methods and seeking for new markets. To some of us there seems to be something exceedingly stale about all that novelty. But that is because of the type of mind that is inventing, not because it does not mean to invent. From the biggest financier floating a company to the smallest tout peddling a sewing-machine, the same ideal prevails. It must always be a new company, especially after what has generally happened to the old company. And the sewing-machine must always be a new sort of sewing-machine, even if it is the sort that does not sew. But while this is obvious of the mere capitalist, it is equally true of the pure oligarch. Whatever else an aristocracy is, an aristocracy is never conservative. By its very nature it goes by fashion rather than by tradition. Men living a life of leisure and luxury are always eager for new things; we might fairly say they would be fools if they weren't. And the English aristocrats are by no means fools. They can proudly claim to have played a great part in every stage of the intellectual progress that has brought us to our present ruin.

The first fact about establishing an English peasantry is that it is establishing, for the first time for many centuries, a traditional class. The absence of such a class will be found to be a very terrible fact, if the tug really becomes between Bolshevism and the historic ideal of property. But the converse is equally true and much more comforting. This difference in the quality means that the change will begin to be effective merely by quantity. I mean that we have not been concerned so much with the strength or weakness of a peasantry, as with presence or absence of a peasantry. As the society has suffered from its mere absence, so the society will begin to change by its mere presence. It will be a somewhat different England in which the peasant has to be considered at all. It will begin to alter the look of things, even when politicians think about peasants as often as they do about doctors. They have been known even to think about soldiers.

The primary case for the peasant is of a stark and almost savage simplicity. A man in England might live on the land, if he did not have rent to pay to the landlord and wages to pay to the labourer. He would therefore be better off, even on a small scale, if he were his own landlord and his own labourer. But there are obviously certain further considerations, and to my mind certain common misconceptions, to which the following notes refer roughly in their order. In the first place, of course, it is one thing to say that this is desirable, and another that it is desired. And in the first place, as will be seen, I do not deny that if it is to be desired, it can hardly be as a mere indulgence is desired; there will undoubtedly be required a certain spirit of effort and sacrifice for the sake of an acute national necessity, if we are to ask any landlord to do without rent or any farmer to do without assistance. But at least there really is a crisis and a necessity; to such an extent that the squire would often be only remitting a debt which he has already written off as a bad debt, and the employer only sacrificing the service of men who are already on strike. Still, we shall need the virtues that belong to a crisis; and it will be well to make the fact clear. Next, while there is all the difference between the desirable and the desired, I would point out that even now this normal life is more desired than many suppose. It is perhaps subconsciously desired; but I think it worth while to throw out a few suggestions that may bring it to the surface. Lastly, there is a misconception about what is meant by "living on the land" — and I have added some suggestions about how much more desirable it is than many suppose.

I shall consider these separate aspects of agricultural distributism more or less in the order in which I have just noted them; but here in the preliminary note I am concerned only with the primary fact. If we could create a peasantry we could create a conservative populace; and he would be a bold man who should undertake to tell us how the present industrial deadlock in the great cities is to produce a conservative populace. I am well aware that many would call the conservatism by coarser names; and say that peasants are stupid and stick-in-the-mud and tied to dull and dreary existence. I know it is said that a man must find it monotonous to do the twenty things that are done on a farm, whereas, of course, he always finds it uproariously funny and festive to do one thing hour after hour and day after day in a factory. I know that the same people also make exactly the contrary comment; and say it is selfish and avaricious for the peasant to be so intensely interested in his own farm, instead of showing, like the proletarians of modern industrialism, a selfless and romantic loyalty to somebody else's factory, and an ascetic self-sacrifice in making profits for somebody else. Giving each of these claims of modern capitalism their due weight, it is still permissible to say that in so far as the peasant proprietor is certainly tenacious of the peasant property, is concentrated on the interest or content with the dullness, as the case may be, he does, in fact, constitute a solid block of private property which can be counted on to resist Communism; which is not only more than can be said of the proletariat, but is very much more than any capitalists say of them. I do not believe that the proletariat is honeycombed with Bolshevism (if honey be an apt metaphor for that doctrine), but if there is any truth in the newspaper fears on that subject it would certainly seem that large properties cannot prevent the thing happening, whereas small properties can. But, as a matter of fact, all experience is against the assertion that peasants are dreary and degraded savages, crawling about on all fours and eating grass like the beasts of the field. All over the world, for instance, there are peasant dances; and the dances of peasants are like dances of kings and queens. The popular dance is much more stately and ceremonial and full of human dignity than is the aristocratic dance. In many a modern countryside the countryfolk may still be found on high festivals wearing caps like crowns and using gestures like a religious ritual, while the castle or chateau of the lords and ladies is already full of people waddling about like monkeys to the noises made by negroes. All over Europe peasants have produced the embroideries and the handicrafts which were discovered with delight by artists when they had long been neglected by aristocrats. These people are not conservative merely in a negative sense; though there is great value in that which is negative when it is also defensive. They are also conservative in a positive sense; they conserve customs that do not perish like fashions, and crafts less ephemeral than those artistic movements which so very soon cease to move. The Bolshevists, I believe, have invented something which they call Proletarian Art, upon what principle I cannot imagine; save that they seem to have a mysterious pride in calling themselves a proletariat when they claim to be no longer proletarian. I rather think it is merely the reluctance of the half-educated to relinquish the use of a long word. Anyhow, there never has been in this world any such thing as Proletarian Art. But there has most emphatically been such a thing as Peasant Art.

I suppose that what is really meant is Communist Art; and that phrase alone will reveal much. I suppose a truly communal art would consist in a hundred men hanging on to one huge paint-brush like a battering-ram, and steering it across some vast canvas with the curves and lurches and majestic hesitations that would express, in darkly outlined forms, the composite mind of the community. Peasants have produced art because they were communal but not communist. Custom and a corporate tradition gave unity to their art; but each man was a separate artist. It is that satisfaction of the creative instinct in the individual that makes the peasantry as a whole content and therefore conservative. A multitude of men are standing on their own feet, because they are standing on their own land. But in our country, alas, the landowners have been standing upon nothing, except what they have trampled underfoot.

= = = = = = = = = = = = = = = = =

2. Vows And Volunteers

We have sometimes been asked why we do not admire advertisers quite so much as they admire themselves. One answer is that it is of their very nature to admire themselves. And it is of the very nature of our task that people must be taught to criticize themselves; or rather (preferably) to kick themselves. They talk about Truth in Advertising; but there cannot be any such thing in the sharp sense in which we need truth in politics. It is impossible to put in the cheery terms of "publicity" either the truth about how bad things are, or the truth about how hard it will be to cure them. No advertiser is so truthful as to say, "Do your best with our rotten old typewriter; we can't get anything better just now." But we have really got to say, "Do your best with your rotten old machine of production; don't let it fall to pieces too suddenly." We seldom see a gay and conspicuous hoarding inscribed, "You are in for a rough time if you use our new kitchen-range." But we have really got to say to our friends, "You are in for a rough time if you start new farms on your own; but it is the right thing." We cannot pretend to be offering merely comforts and conveniences. Whatever our ultimate view of labour-saving machinery, we cannot offer our ideal as a labour-saving machine. There is no more question of comfort than there is for a man in a fire, a battle, or a shipwreck. There is no way out of the danger except the dangerous way.

The sort of call that must be made on the modern English is the sort of call that is made before a great war or a great revolution. If the trumpet give an uncertain sound — but it must be unmistakably the sound of a trumpet. The megaphone of mere mercantile self-satisfaction is merely loud and not in the least clear. In its nature it is saying smooth things, even if it is roaring them; it is like one whispering soft nothings, even if its whisper is a horrible yell. How can advertisement bid men prepare themselves for a battle? How can publicity talk in the language of public spirit? It cannot say, "Buy land at Blinkington-on-Sea and prepare yourself for the battle with stones and thistles." It cannot give a certain sound, like the old tocsin that rang for fire and flood, and tell the people of Puddleton that they are in danger of famine. To do men justice, no man did announce the needs of Kitchener's Army like the comforts of the kitchen-range. We did not say to the

236

recruits, "Spend your holiday at Mons." We did not say, "Try our trenches; they are a treat." We made some sort of attempt to appeal to better things. We have to make that appeal again; and in the face of worse things. It is this that is made so difficult by the whole tone of advertisement. For the next thing we have to consider is the need of independent individual action on a large scale. We want to make the need known, as the need for recruits was made known. Education was too commercial in origin, and has allowed itself to be largely swamped by commercial advertisement. It came too much from the town; and now it is nearly driven from the town. Education really meant the teaching of town things to country people who did not want to learn them. I suggest that education should now mean the teaching of country things to town people who do want to learn them. I quite admit it would be much better to begin at least with those who really want it. But I also maintain that there are really a great many people in town and country who do really want it.

Whether we look forward to an Agrarian Law or no, whether our notion of distribution is rigid or rough and ready, whether we believe in compensation or confiscation, whether we look for this law or that law, we ought not to sit down and wait for any law at all. While the grass grows the steed has got to show that he wants grass: the steed has got to explain that he is really a graminivorous quadruped. The fulfilment of parliamentary promises grows rather slower than grass; and if nothing is done before the completion of what is called a constitutional process, we shall be about as near to Distributism as a Labour politician is to Socialism. It seems to me first necessary to revive the medieval or moral method, and call for volunteers.

The English could do what the Irish did. They could make laws by obeying them. If we are, like the original Sinn Feiners, to anticipate legal change by social agreement, we want two sorts of volunteers, in order to make the experiment on the spot. We want to find out how many peasants there are, actual or potential, who would take over the responsibility of small farms, for the sake of self-sufficiency, of real property, and of saving England in a desperate hour. We want to know how many landlords there are who would now give or sell cheaply their land to be cut up into a number of such farms. Honestly, I think the landlord would have the best of the bargain. Or rather I think that the peasant would have the hardest and most heroic part of the bargain. Sometimes it would practically pay the landlord to chuck the land altogether, since he is paying out to something that does not pay him back. But in any case, everybody has got to realize that the situation is, in no cant phrases, one for heroic remedies. It is impossible to disguise that the man who gets the land, even more than the man who gives up the land, will have to be something of a hero. We shall be told that heroes do not grow on every hedgerow, that we cannot find enough to defend all our hedges. We raised three million heroes with the blast of a bugle but a few years ago; and the trumpet we hear to-day is in a more terrible sense the trump of doom.

We want a popular appeal for volunteers to save the land; exactly as volunteers in 1914 were wanted to save the country. But we do not want the appeal weakened by that weak-minded, that wearisome, that dismal and deplorable thing that the newspapers call Optimism. We are not asking babies to look pleasant while their photographs are taken; we are asking grown men to meet a crisis as grave as a great war. We are not asking people to cut a coupon out of a newspaper, but to carve a farm out of a trackless waste; and if it is to be successful, it must be faced in something of the stubborn spirit of the old fulfilment of a vow. St. Francis showed his followers the way to a greater happiness; but he did not tell them that a wandering and homeless life would mean Everything as Nice as Mother Makes It; nor did he advertise it on hoardings as a Home From Home. But we live in a time when it is harder for a free man to make a home than it was for a medieval ascetic to do without one.

The quarrel about the Limehouse slums was a working model of the problem — if we can talk of a working model of something that does not work, and something on which only a madman would model anything. The slum-dwellers actually and definitely say that they prefer their slums to the blocks of flats provided as a refuge from the slums. And they prefer them, it is stated, because the old homes had backyards in which they could pursue "their hobbies of bird-fancying and poultry-rearing." When offered other opportunities on some scheme of allotment, they had the hideous depravity to say that they liked fences round their private yards. So awful and overwhelming is the Red torrent of Communism as it boils through the brains of the working classes.

Now, of course, it might conceivably be necessary, in some wild congestion and convulsion, for people's houses to be piled on top of each other for ever, in the form of a tower of flats. And so it might be necessary for men to climb on other men's shoulders in a flood or to get out of a chasm cloven by an earthquake. And it is logically conceivable, and even mathematically correct, that we might thin the crowds in the London streets, if we could thus arrange men vertically instead of horizontally. If there were only some expedient by which a man might walk about with another man standing above him, and another above that, and so on, it would save a great deal of jostling. Men are arranged like that in acrobatic performances; and a course of such acrobatics might be made compulsory in all the schools. It is a picture that pleases me very much, as a picture. I look forward (in spirit of art for art's sake) to seeing such a living tower moving majestically down the Strand. I like to think of the time of true social organization, when all the clerks of Messrs. Boodle & Bunkham shall no longer come up in their present random and straggling fashion, each from his little suburban villa. They shall not even, as in the immediate and intermediary stage of the Servile State, march in a well-drilled column from the dormitory in one part of London, to the emporium in the other. No, a nobler vision has arisen before me into the very heights of heaven. A toppling pagoda of clerks, one balanced on the top of another, moves down the street, perhaps making acrobatic patterns in the air as it moves, to illustrate the perfect discipline of its social machinery. All that would be very impressive; and it really would, among other things, economize space. But if one of the men near the top of that swaying tower were to say that he hoped some day to be able to revisit the earth, I should sympathize with his sense of exile. If he were to say that it is natural to man to walk on the earth, I should find myself in agreement with his school of philosophy. If he were to say that it was very difficult to look after chickens in that acrobatic attitude and altitude, I should think his difficulty a real one. At first it might be retorted that bird-fancying would be even more appropriate to such an airy perch, but in practice those birds would be very fancy birds. Finally, if he said that keeping chickens that laid eggs was a worthy and valuable social work, much more worthy and valuable than serving Messrs. Boodle & Bunkham with the most perfect discipline and organization, I should agree with that sentiment most of all.

Now the whole of our modern problem is very difficult, and though in one way the agricultural part of it is much the simplest, in another way it is by no means the least difficult. But this Limehouse affair is a vivid example of how we make the difficulty more difficult. We are told again and again that the slum-dwellers of the big towns cannot merely be turned loose on the land, that they do not want to go on the land, that they have no tastes or turn of thought that could make them by any process into a people interested in the land, that they cannot be conceived as having any pleasures except town pleasures, or even any discontents except the Bolshevism of the towns. And then when a whole crowd of them want to keep chickens, we force them to live in flats. When a whole crowd of them want to have fences, we laugh and order them off into communal barracks. When a whole population wishes to insist on palings and enclosures and the traditions of private property, the authorities act as if they were suppressing a Red riot. When these very hopeless slum-dwellers do actually set all their hopes on a rural occupation, which they can still practise even in the slums, we tear them away from that occupation and call it improving their condition. You pick a man up who has his head in a hen-coop, forcibly set him on giant stilts a hundred feet high where he cannot reach the ground, and then say you have saved him from misery. And you add that a man like that can only live on stilts and would never be interested in hens.

Now the very first question that is always asked of those advocating our sort of agricultural reconstruction is this question, which is fundamental because it is psychological. Whatever else we may or may not need for a peasantry, we do certainly need peasants. In the present mixture and muddle of more or less urbanized civilization, have we even the first elements or the first possibilities? Have we peasants, or even potential peasants? Like all questions of this sort, it cannot be answered by statistics. Statistics are artificial even when they are not fictitious, for they always assume the very fact which a moral estimate must always deny; they assume that every man is one man. They are based on a sort of atomic theory that the individual is really individual, in the sense of indivisible. But when we are dealing professedly with the proportion of different loves or hates or hopes or hungers, this is so far from being a fact that can be assumed, it is the very first that must be denied. It is denied by all that deeper consideration which wise men used to call spiritual, but which fools were frightened out of calling spiritual, till they ventured to say it in Greek and call it psychical or psychological. In one sense the highest spirituality insists, of course, that one man is one. But in the sense here involved, the spiritual view has always been that one man was at least two, and the psychological view has shown some taste for turning him into half a dozen. It is no good, therefore, to discuss the number of peasants who are nothing else but peasants. Very probably there are none at all. It is no good asking how many complete and compact yeomen or yokels are waiting all ready in smock-frocks or blouses, their spades and hay-forks clutched in their hand, in the neighbourhood of Brompton or Brixton; waiting for us to give the signal to rush back to the land. If anybody is such a fool as to expect that sort of thing, the fool is not to be found in our small political party. When we are dealing with a matter of this kind, we are dealing with different elements in the same class, or even in the same man. We are dealing with elements which should be encouraged or educated or (if we must bring the word in somewhere) evolved. We have to consider whether there are any materials out of which to make peasants to make a peasantry, if we really choose to try. Nowhere in these notes have I suggested that there is the faintest possibility of it being done, if we do not choose to try.

Now, using words in this sensible sense, I should maintain that there is a very large element still in England that would like to return to this simpler sort of England. Some of them understand it better than others, some of them understand themselves better than others; some would be prepared for it as a revolution; some only cling to it very blindly as a tradition; some have never thought of it as anything but a hobby; some have never heard of it and feel it only as a want. But the number of people who would like to get out of the tangle of mere ramifications and communications in the town, and get back nearer to the roots of things, where things are made directly out of nature, I believe to be very large. It is probably not a majority, but I suspect that even now it is a very large minority. A man does not necessarily want this more than everything else at every moment of his life. No sane person expects any movement to consist entirely of such monomaniacs. But a good many people want it a good deal. I have formed that impression from experience, which is of all things the most difficult to reproduce in controversy. I guess it from the way in which numberless suburbans talk about their gardens. I guess it from the sort of things that they really envy in the rich; one of the most notable of which is merely empty space. I notice it in all the element that desires the country, even if it defaces the country. I notice it in the profound popular interest everywhere, especially in England, in the breeding or training of any kind of animal. And if I wanted a supreme, a symbolic, a triumphant example of all that I mean, I could find it in the case I have quoted of these men living in the most miserable slums of Limehouse, and reluctant to leave them because it would mean leaving behind a rabbit in a rabbit-hutch or a chicken in a hen-coop.

Now if we were really doing what I suggest, or if we really knew what we were doing, we should seize on these slum dwellers as if they were infant prodigies or (even more lucrative) monsters to be exhibited in a fair. We should see that such people have a natural genius for such things. We should encourage them in such things. We should educate them in such things. We should see in them the seed and living principle of a real spontaneous revival of the countryside. I repeat that it would be a matter of proportion and therefore of tact. But we should be on their side, being confident that they are on our side and on the side of the countryside. We should reconstruct our popular education so as to help these hobbies. We should think it worth while to teach people the things they are so eager to teach themselves. We should teach them; we might even, in a burst of Christian humility, occasionally allow them to teach us. What we do is to bundle them out of their houses, where they do these things with difficulty, and drag them shrieking to new and unfamiliar places where they cannot do them at all. This example alone would show how much we are really doing for the rural reconstruction of England.

Though much could be done by volunteers, and by a voluntary bargain between the man who really could do the work and the man who frequently cannot get the rent, there is nothing in our social philosophy that forbids the use of the State power where it can be used. And either by the State subsidy or some large voluntary fund, it seems to me that it would still be possible at least to give the other man something as good as the rent that he does not get. In other words, long before our Communists come to the controversial ethics of confiscation, it seems to me within the resources of civilization to enable Brown to buy from Smith what is now of very little value to Smith and might be of very great value to Brown. I know the current complaint against subsidy, and the general argument that applies equally to subscription; but I do think that a subsidy to restore agriculture would find more repayment in the future than a subsidy to patch up the position of coal; just as I think that in its turn more defensible than half a hundred salaries that we pay to a mob of nobodies for plaguing the poor with sham science and petty tyranny. But there are, as I have already hinted, other ways by which even the State could help in the matter. So long as we have State education, it seems a pity that it can never at any moment be determined by the needs of the State. If the immediate need of the State is to pay some attention to the existence of the earth, there really seems no reason why the eyes of the schoolmasters and schoolboys, staring at the stars, should not be turned in the direction of that planet. At present we have education, not indeed for angels, but rather for aviators. They do not even understand a man's wish to remain tied to the ground. There is in their ideal an insanity that may be truly called unearthly.

Now I suggest such a peasantry of volunteers primarily as a nucleus, but I think it will be a nucleus of attraction. I think it will stand up not only as a rock but as a magnet. In other words, as soon as it is admitted that it can be done, it will become important when a number of other things can no longer be done. When trade is increasingly bad, this will be counted better even by those who count it a second best. When we speak of people leaving the countryside and flocking to the towns, we are not judging the case fairly. Something may be allowed for a social type that would always prefer cinemas and picture post cards even to property and liberty. But there is nothing conclusive in the fact that people prefer to go without property and liberty, with a cinema, to going without property and liberty without a cinema. Some people may like the town so much that they would rather be sweated in the town than free in the country. But nothing is proved by the mere fact that they would rather be sweated in the town than sweated in the country. I believe, therefore, that if we created even a considerable patch of peasantry, the patch would grow. People would fall back on it as they retired from the declining trades. At present the patch is not growing, because there is no patch to grow; people do not even believe in its existence, and can hardly believe in its extension.

So far, I merely propose to suggest that many peasants would now be ready to work alone on the land, though it would be a sacrifice; that many squires would be ready to let them have the land, though it would be a sacrifice; that the State (and for that matter any other patriotic corporation) could be called upon to help either or both in these actions, that it might not be an intolerable or impossible sacrifice. In all this I would remind the reader that I am only dealing with immediately practicable action and not with an ultimate or complete condition; but it seems to me that something of this sort might be set about almost at once. I shall next proceed to consider a misunderstanding about how a group of peasants could live on the land.

=================

3. The Real Life On The Land

We offer one among many proposals for undoing the evil of capitalism, on the ground that ours is the only one that really is a proposal for undoing it. The others are all proposals for overdoing it. The natural thing to do with a wrong operation is to reverse it. The natural action, when property has fallen into fewer hands, is to restore it to more numerous hands. If twenty men are fishing in a river in such a crowd that their fishing-lines all get entangled into one, the normal operation is to disentangle them, and sort them out so that each fisherman has his own fishing-line. No doubt a collectivist philosopher standing on the bank might point out that the interwoven lines were now practically a net; and might be trailed along by a common effort so as to drag the river-bed. But apart from his scheme being doubtful in practice, it insults the intellectual instincts even in principle. It is not putting things right to take a doubtful advantage of their being wrong; and it does not even sound like a sane design to exaggerate an accident. Socialism is but the completion of the capitalist concentration; yet that concentration was itself effected blindly like a blunder. Now this naturalness, in the idea of undoing what was ill done would appeal, I think, to many natural people who feel the long-winded sociological schemes to be quite unnatural. For that reason I suggest in this section that many ordinary men, landlords and labourers, Tories and Radicals, would probably help us in this task, if it were separated from party politics and from the pride and pedantry of the intellectuals.

But there is another aspect in which the task is both more easy and more difficult. It is more easy because it need not be crushed by complexities of cosmopolitan trade. It is harder because it is a hard life to live apart from them. A Distributist for whose work (on a little paper defaced, alas, with my own initials) I have a very lively gratitude, once noted a truth often neglected. He said that living on the land was quite a different thing from living by carting things off it. He proved, far more lucidly than I could, how practical is the difference in economics. But I should like to add here a word about a corresponding distinction in ethics. For the former, it is obvious that most arguments about the inevitable failure of a man growing turnips in Sussex are arguments about his failing to sell them, not about his failing to eat them. Now as I have already explained, I do not propose to reduce all citizens to one type, and certainly not to one turnip-eater. In a greater or less degree, as circumstances dictated, there would doubtless be people selling turnips to other people; perhaps even the most ardent turnip-eater would probably sell some turnips to some people. But my meaning will not be clear if it be supposed that no more social simplification is needed than is implied in selling turnips out of a field instead of top-hats out of a shop. It seems to me that a great many people would be only too glad to live on the land, when they find the only alternative is to starve in the street. And it would surely modify the modern enormity of unemployment, if any large number of people were really living on the land, not merely in the sense of sleeping on the land but of feeding on the land. There will be many who maintain that this would mean a very dull life compared with the excitements of dying in a workhouse in Liverpool; just as there are many who insist that the average woman is made to drudge in the home, without asking whether the average man exults in having to drudge in the office. But passing over the fact that we may soon be faced with a problem at least as prosaic as a famine, I do not admit that such a life is necessarily or entirely prosaic. Rustic populations, largely self-supporting, seem to have amused themselves with a great many mythologies and dances and decorative arts; and I am not convinced that the turnip-eater always has a head like a turnip or that the top-hat always covers the brain of a philosopher. But if we look at the problem from the point of view of the community as a whole, we shall note other and not uninteresting things. A system based entirely on the division of labour is in one sense literally half-witted. That is, each performer of half of an operation does really use only half of his wits. It is not a question in the ordinary sense of intellect, and certainly not in the sense of intellectualism. But it is a question of integrity, in the strict sense of the word. The peasant does live, not merely a simple life, but a complete life. It may be very simple in its completeness, but the community is not complete without that completeness. The community is at present very defective because there is not in the core of it any such simple consciousness; any one man who represents the two parties to a contract. Unless there is, there is nowhere a full understanding of those terms: self-support, self-control, self-government. He is the only unanimous mob and the only universal man. He is the one half of the world which does know how the other half lives.

Many must have quoted the stately tag from Virgil which says, "Happy were he who could know the causes of things," without remembering in what context it comes. Many have probably quoted it because the others have quoted it. Many, if left in ignorance to guess whence it comes, would probably guess wrong. Everybody knows that Virgil, like Homer, ventured to describe boldly enough the most secret councils of the gods. Everybody knows that Virgil, like Dante took his hero into Tartarus and the labyrinth of the last and lowest foundations of the universe. Every one knows that he dealt with the fall of Troy and the rise of Rome, with the laws of an empire fitted to rule all the children of men, with the ideals that should stand like stars before men committed to that awful stewardship. Yet it is in none of these connections, in none of these passages, that he makes the curious remark about human happiness consisting in a knowledge of causes. He says it, I fancy, in a pleasantly didactic poem about the rules for keeping bees. Anyhow, it is part of a series of elegant essays on country pursuits, in one sense, indeed, trivial, but in another sense almost technical. It is in the midst of these quiet and yet busy things that the great poet suddenly breaks out into the great passage, about the happy man whom neither kings nor mobs can cow; who, having beheld the root and reason of all things, can even hear under his feet, unshaken, the roar of the river of hell.

And in saying this, the poet certainly proves once more the two great truths: that a poet is a prophet, and that a prophet is a practical man. Just as his longing for a deliverer of the nations was an unconscious prophecy of Christ, so his criticism of town and country is an unconscious prophecy of the decay that has come on the world through falling away from Christianity. Much may be said about the monstrosity of modern cities; it is easy to see and perhaps a little too easy to say. I have every sympathy with some wild-haired prophet who should lift up his voice in the streets to proclaim the Burden of Brompton in the manner of the Burden of Babylon. I will support (to the extent of sixpence, as Carlyle said) any old man with a beard who will wave his arms and call down fire from heaven upon Bayswater. I quite agree that lions will howl in the high places of Paddington; and I am entirely in favour of jackals and vultures rearing their young in the ruins of the Albert Hall. But in these cases, perhaps, the prophet is less explicit than the poet. He does not tell us exactly what is wrong with the town; but merely leaves it to our own delicate intuitions, to infer from the sudden appearance of wild unicorns trampling down our gardens, or a shower of flaming serpents shooting over our heads through the sky like a flight of arrows, or some such significant detail, that there probably is something wrong. But if we wish in another mood to know intellectually what it is that is wrong with the city, and why it seems to be driving on to dooms quite as unnatural and much more ugly, we shall certainly find it in that profound and piercing irrelevancy of the Latin line.

What is wrong with the man in the modern town is that he does not know the causes of things; and that is why, as the poet says, he can be too much dominated by despots and demagogues. He does not know where things come from; he is the type of the cultivated Cockney who said he liked milk out of a clean shop and not a dirty cow. The more elaborate is the town organization, the more elaborate even is the town education, the less is he the happy man of Virgil who knows the causes of things. The town civilization simply means the number of shops through which the milk does pass from the cow to the man; in other words, it means the number of opportunities of wasting the milk, of watering the milk, of poisoning the milk, and of swindling the man. If ever he protests against being poisoned or swindled, he will certainly be told that it is no good crying over spilt milk; or, in other words, that it is reactionary sentimentalism to attempt to undo what is done or to restore what is perished. But he does not protest very much, because he cannot; and he cannot because he does not know enough about the causes of things — about the primary forms of property and production, or the points where man is nearest to his natural origins.

So far the fundamental fact is clear enough; and by this time this side of the truth is even fairly familiar. A few people are still ignorant enough to talk about the ignorant peasant. But obviously in the essential sense it would be far truer to talk about the ignorant townsman. Even where the townsman is equally well employed, he is not in this sense equally well informed. Indeed, we should see this simple fact clearly enough, if it concerned almost anything except the essentials of our life. If a geologist were tapping with a geological hammer on the bricks of a half-built house, and telling the bricklayers what the clay was and where it came from, we might think him a nuisance; but we should probably think him a learned nuisance. We might prefer the workman's hammer to the geologist's hammer; but we should admit that there were some things in the geologist's head that did not happen to be in the workman's head. Yet the yokel, or young man from the country, really would know something about the origin of our breakfasts, as does the professor about the origin of our bricks. Should we see a grotesque medieval monster called a pig hung topsy-turvy from a butcher's hook, like a huge bat from a branch, it will be the young man from the country who will soothe our fears and still our refined shrieks with some account of the harmless habits of this fabulous animal, and by tracing the strange and secret connection between it and the rashers on the breakfast table. If a thunderbolt or meteoric stone fell in front of us in the street, we might have more sympathy with the policeman who wanted to remove it from the thoroughfare than with the professor who wished to stand in the middle of the thoroughfare, lecturing on the constituent elements of the comet or nebula of which it was a flying fragment. But though the policeman might be justified in exclaiming (in the original Greek) "What are the Pleiades to me?" even he would admit that more information about the soil and strata of the Pleiades can be obtained from a professor than from a policeman. So if some strange and swollen monstrosity called a vegetable marrow surprises us like a thunderbolt, let us not imagine that it is so strange to the man who grows marrows as it is to us, merely because his field and work seem to be as far away as the Pleiades. Let us recognize that he is, after all, a specialist on these mysterious marrows and prehistoric pigs; and treat him like a learned man come from a foreign university. England is now such a long way off from London that its emissaries might at least be received with the respect due to distinguished visitors from China or the Cannibal Islands. But, anyhow, we need no longer talk of them as merely ignorant, in talking of the very thing of which we are ignorant ourselves. One man may think the peasant's knowledge irrelevant, as another may think the professor's irrelevant; but in both cases it is knowledge; for it is knowledge of the causes of things.

Most of us realize in some sense that this is true; but many of us have not yet realized that the converse is also true. And it is that other truth, when we have understood it, that leads to the next necessary point about the full status of the peasant. And the point is this: that the peasant also will have but a partial experience if he grows things in the country solely in order to sell them to the town. Of course, it is only a joke to represent either the ignorance of town or country as being so grotesque as I have suggested for the sake of example. The townsman does not really think that milk is rained from the clouds or that rashers grow on trees, even when he is a little vague about vegetable marrows. He knows something about it; but not enough to make his advice of much value. The rustic does not really think that milk is used as whitewash or marrows as bolsters, even if he never actually sees them used. But if he is a mere producer and not a consumer of them, his position does become as partial as that of any Cockney clerk; nearly as narrow and even more servile. Given the wonderful romance of the vegetable marrow, it is a bad thing that the peasant should only know the beginning of the story, as it is a bad thing that the clerk should only know the end of it.

I insert here this general suggestion for a particular reason. Before we come to the practical expediency of the peasant who consumes what he produces (and the reason for thinking it, as Mr. Heseltine has urged, much more practicable than the method by which he only sells what he produces), I think it well to point out that this course, while it is more expedient, is not a mere surrender to expediency. It seems to me a very good thing, in theory as well as practice, that there should be a body of citizens primarily concerned in producing and consuming and not in exchanging. It seems to me a part of our ideal, and not merely a part of our compromise, that there should be in the community a sort of core not only of simplicity but of completeness. Exchange and variation can then be given their reasonable place; as they were in the old world of fairs and markets. But there would be somewhere in the centre of civilization a type that was truly independent; in the sense of producing and consuming within its own social circle. I do not say that such a complete human life stands for a complete humanity. I do not say that the State needs only the man who needs nothing from the State. But I do say that this man who supplies his own needs is very much needed. I say it largely because of his absence from modern civilization, that modern civilization has lost unity. It is nobody's business to note the whole of a process, to see where things come from and where they go to. Nobody follows the whole winding course of the river of milk as it flows from the cow to the baby. Nobody who is in at the death of the pig is responsible for realizing that the proof of the pig is in the eating. Men throw marrows at other men like cannon balls; but they do not return to them like boomerangs. We need a social circle in which things constantly return to those that threw them; and men who know the end and the beginning and the rounding of our little life.

= = = = = = = = = = = = = = = = =

IV. Some Aspects Of Machinery

1. The Wheel Of Fate

The evil we are seeking to destroy clings about in corners especially in the form of catch-phrases by which even the intelligent can easily be caught. One phrase, which we may hear from anybody at any moment, is the phrase that such and such a modern institution has "come to stay." It is these half-metaphors that tend to make us all half-witted. What is precisely meant by the statement that the steam-engine or the wireless apparatus has come to stay? What is meant, for that matter, even by saying that the Eiffel Tower has come to stay? To begin with, we obviously do not mean what we mean when we use the words naturally; as in the expression, "Uncle Humphrey has come to stay." That last sentence may be uttered in tones of joy, or of resignation, or even of despair; but not of despair in the sense that Uncle Humphrey is really a monument that can never be moved. Uncle Humphrey did come; and Uncle Humphrey will presumably at some time go; it is even possible (however painful it may be to imagine such domestic relations) that in the last resort he should be made to go. The fact that the figure breaks down, even apart from the reality it is supposed to represent, illustrates how loosely these catch-words are used. But when we say, "The Eiffel Tower has come to stay," we are still more inaccurate. For, to begin with, the Eiffel Tower has not come at all. There was never a moment when the Eiffel Tower was seen striding towards Paris on its long iron legs across the plains of France, as the giant in the glorious nightmare of Rabelais came to tower over Paris and carry away the bells of Notre-Dame. The figure of Uncle Humphrey seen coming up the road may possibly strike as much terror as any walking tower or towering giant; and the question that may leap into every mind may be the question of whether he has come to stay. But whether or no he has come to stay he has certainly come. He has willed; he has propelled or precipitated his body in a certain direction; he has agitated his own legs; it is even possible (for we all know what Uncle Humphrey is like) that he has insisted on carrying his own

251

portmanteau, to show the lazy young dogs what he can still do at seventy-three.

Now suppose that what had really happened was something like this; something like a weird story of Hawthorne or Poe. Suppose we ourselves had actually manufactured Uncle Humphrey; had put him together, piece by piece, like a mechanical doll. Suppose we had so ardently felt at the moment the need of an uncle in our home life that we had constructed him out of domestic materials, like a Guy for the fifth of November. Taking, it may be, a turnip from the kitchen-garden to represent his bald and venerable head; permitting the water-butt, as it were, to suggest the lines of his figure; stuffing a pair of trousers and attaching a pair of boots, we could produce a complete and convincing uncle of whom any family might be proud. Under those conditions, it might be graceful enough to say, in the merely social sense and as a sort of polite fiction, "Uncle Humphrey has come to stay." But surely it would be very extraordinary if we afterwards found the dummy relative was nothing but a nuisance, or that his materials were needed for other purposes — surely it would be very extraordinary if we were then forbidden to take him to pieces again; if every effort in that direction were met with the resolute answer, "No, no; Uncle Humphrey has come to stay." Surely we should be tempted to retort that Uncle Humphrey never came at all. Suppose all the turnips were wanted for the self-support of the peasant home. Suppose the water-butts were wanted; let us hope for the purpose of holding beer. Suppose the male members of the family refused any longer to lend their trousers to an entirely imaginary relative. Surely we should then see through the polite fiction that led us to talk as if the uncle had "come," had come with an intention, had remained with a purpose, and all the rest. The thing we made did not come, and certainly did not come to do anything, either to stay or to depart.

Now no doubt most people even in the logical city of Paris would say that the Eiffel Tower has come to stay. And no doubt most people in the same city rather more than a hundred years before would have said that the Bastille had come to stay. But it did not stay; it left the neighbourhood quite abruptly. In plain words, the Bastille was something that man had made and, therefore, man could unmake. The Eiffel Tower is something that man has made and man could unmake; though perhaps we may think it practically probable that some time will elapse before man will have the good taste or good sense or even the common sanity to unmake it. But this one little phrase about the thing "coming" is alone enough to indicate something profoundly wrong about the very working of men's minds on the subject. Obviously a man ought to be saying, "I have made an electric battery. Shall I smash it, or shall I make another?" Instead of that, he seems to be bewitched by a sort of magic and stand staring at the thing as if it were a seven-headed dragon; and he can only say, "The electric battery has come. Has it come to stay?"

Before we begin any talk of the practical problem of machinery, it is necessary to leave off thinking like machines. It is necessary to begin at the beginning and consider the end. Now we do not necessarily wish to destroy every sort of machinery. But we do desire to destroy a certain sort of mentality. And that is precisely the sort of mentality that begins by telling us that nobody can destroy machinery. Those who begin by saying that we cannot abolish the machine, that we must use the machine, are themselves refusing to use the mind.

The aim of human polity is human happiness. For those holding certain beliefs it is conditioned by the hope of a larger happiness, which it must not imperil. But happiness, the making glad of the heart of man, is the secular test and the only realistic test. So far from this test, by the talisman of the heart, being merely sentimental, it is the only test that is in the least practical. There is no law of logic or nature or anything else forcing us to prefer anything else. There is no obligation on us to be richer, or busier, or more efficient, or more productive, or more progressive, or in any way worldlier or wealthier, if it does not make us happier. Mankind has as much right to scrap its machinery and live on the land, if it really likes it better, as any man has to sell his old bicycle and go for a walk, if he likes that better. It is obvious that the walk will be slower; but he has no duty to be fast. And if it can be shown that machinery has come into the world as a curse, there is no reason whatever for our respecting it because it is a marvellous and practical and productive curse. There is no reason why we should not leave all its powers unused, if we have really come to the conclusion that the powers do us harm. The mere fact that we

253

shall be missing a number of interesting things would apply equally to any number of impossible things. Machinery may be a magnificent sight, but not so magnificent as a Great Fire of London; yet we resist that vision and avert our eyes from all that potential splendour. Machinery may not yet be at its best; and perhaps lions and tigers will never be at their best, will never make their most graceful leaps or show all their natural splendours, until we erect an amphitheatre and give them a few live people to eat. Yet that sight also is one which we forbid ourselves, with whatever austere self-denial. We give up so many glorious possibilities, in our stern and strenuous and self-sacrificing preference for having a tolerable time. Happiness, in a sense, is a hard taskmaster. It tells us not to get entangled with many things that are much more superficially attractive than machinery. But, anyhow, it is necessary to clear our minds at the start of any mere vague association or assumption to the effect that we must go by the quickest train or cannot help using the most productive instrument. Granted Mr. Penty's thesis of the evil of machinery, as something like the evil of black magic, and there is nothing in the least unpractical about Mr. Penty's proposal that it should simply stop. A process of invention would cease that might have gone further. But its relative imperfection would be nothing compared with the rudimentary state in which we have left such scientific instruments as the rack and the thumbscrew. Those rude implements of torture are clumsy compared with the finished products that modern knowledge of physiology and mechanics might have given us. Many a talented torturer is left in obscurity by the moral prejudices of modern society. Nay, his budding promise is now nipped even in childhood, when he attempts to develop his natural genius on the flies or the tail of the dog. Our own strong sentimental bias against torture represses his noble rage and freezes the genial current of his soul. But we reconcile ourselves to this; though it be undoubtedly the loss of a whole science for which many ingenious persons might have sought out many inventions. If we really conclude that machinery is hostile to happiness, then it is no more inevitable that all ploughing should be done by machinery than it is inevitable that a shop should do a roaring trade on Ludgate Hill by selling the instruments of Chinese tortures.

Let it be clearly understood that I note this only to make the primary problem clear; I am not now saying, nor perhaps should I ever say, that machinery has been proved to be practically poisonous in this degree. I am only stating, in answer to a hundred confused assumptions, the only ultimate aim and test. If we can make men happier, it does not matter if we make them poorer, it does not matter if we make them less productive, it does not matter if we make them less progressive, in the sense of merely changing their life without increasing their liking for it. We of this school of thought may or may not get what we want; but it is at least necessary that we should know what we are trying to get. And those who are called practical men never know what they are trying to get. If machinery does prevent happiness, then it is as futile to tell a man trying to make men happy that he is neglecting the talents of Arkwright, as to tell a man trying to make men humane that he is neglecting the tastes of Nero.

Now it is exactly those who have the clarity to imagine the instant annihilation of machines who will probably have too much common sense to annihilate them instantly. To go mad and smash machinery is a more or less healthy and human malady, as it was in the Luddites. But it was really owing to the ignorance of the Luddites, in a very different sense from that spoken of scornfully by the stupendous ignorance of the Industrial Economists. It was blind revolt as against some ancient and awful dragon, by men too ignorant to know how artificial and even temporary was that particular instrument, or where was the seat of the real tyrants who wielded it. The real answer to the mechanical problem for the present is of a different sort; and I will proceed to suggest it, having once made clear the only methods of judgment by which it can be judged. And having begun at the right end, which is the ultimate spiritual standard by which a man or a machine is to be valued, I will now begin at the other end; I might say at the wrong end; but it will be more respectful to our practical friends to call it the business end.

If I am asked what I should immediately do with a machine, I have no doubt about the sort of practical programme that could be a preliminary to a possible spiritual revolution of a much wider sort. In so far as the machine cannot be shared, I would have the ownership of it shared; that is, the direction of it shared and the profits of it shared. But when I say "shared" I mean it in the modern mercantile sense of the word "shares." That is, I mean something divided and not merely something pooled. Our business friends bustle forward to tell us that all this is impossible; completely unconscious, apparently, that all this part of the business exists already. You cannot distribute a steam-engine, in the sense of giving one wheel to each shareholder to take home with him, clasped in his arms. But you not only can, but you already do distribute the ownership and profit of the steam-engine; and you distribute it in the form of private property. Only you do not distribute it enough, or to the right people, or to the people who really require it or could really do work for it. Now there are many schemes having this normal and general character; almost any one of which I should prefer to the concentration presented by capitalism or promised by communism. My own preference, on the whole, would be that any such necessary machine should be owned by a small local guild, on principles of profit-sharing, or rather profit-dividing: but of real profit-sharing and real profit-dividing, not to be confounded with capitalist patronage.

Touching the last point, it may be well to say in passing that what I say about the problem of profit-sharing is in that respect parallel to what I say also about the problem of emigration. The real difficulty of starting it in the right way is that it has so often been started in the wrong way; and especially in the wrong spirit. There is a certain amount of prejudice against profit-sharing, just as there is a certain amount of prejudice against emigration, in the industrial democracy of to-day. It is due in both cases to the type and especially the tone of the proposals. I entirely sympathize with the Trade Unionist who dislikes a certain sort of condescending capitalist concession; and the spirit which gives every man a place in the sun which turns out to be a place in Port Sunlight. Similarly, I quite sympathize with Mr. Kirkwood when he resented being lectured about emigration by Sir Alfred Mond, to the extent of saying, "The Scots will leave Scotland when the German Jews leave England." But I think it would be possible to have a more genuinely egalitarian emigration, with a positive policy of self-government for the poor, to which Mr. Kirkwood might be kind; and I think that profit-sharing that began at the popular end, establishing first the property of a guild and not merely the caprice of an employer, would not contradict any true principle of Trades Unions. For the moment, however, I am only saying that something could be done with what lies nearest to us; quite apart from our general ideal about the position of machinery in an ideal social state. I understand what is meant by saying that the ideal in both cases depends upon the wrong ideals. But I do not understand what our critics mean by saying that it is impossible to divide the shares and profits in a machine among definite individuals. Any healthy man in any historical period would have thought it a project far more practicable than a Milk Trust.

= = = = = = = = = = = = = = = = =

2. The Romance Of Machinery

I have repeatedly asked the reader to remember that my general view of our potential future divides itself into two parts. First, there is the policy of reversing, or even merely of resisting, the modern tendency to monopoly or the concentration of capital. Let it be noted that this is a policy because it is a direction, if pursued in any degree. In one sense, indeed, he who is not with us is against us; because if that tendency is not resisted, it will prevail. But in another sense anyone who resists it at all is with us; even if he would not go so far in the reversal as we should. In trying to reverse the concentration at all, he is helping us to do what nobody has done yet. He will be setting himself against the trend of his age, or at least of recent ages. And a man can work in our direction, instead of the existing and contrary direction, even with the existing and perhaps contrary machinery. Even while we remain industrial, we can work towards industrial distribution and away from industrial monopoly. Even while we live in town houses, we can own town houses. Even while we are a nation of shopkeepers, we can try to own our shops. Even while we are the workshop of the world, we can try to own our tools. Even if our town is covered with advertisements, it can be covered with different advertisements. If the mark of our whole society is the trade-mark, it need not be the same trade-mark. In short, there is a perfectly tenable and practicable policy of resisting mercantile monopoly even in a mercantile state. And we say that a great many people ought to support us in that, who might not agree with our ultimate ideal of a state that should not be mercantile — or rather a state that should not be entirely mercantile. We cannot call on England as a nation of peasants, as France or Serbia is a nation of peasants. But we can call on England that has been a nation of shopkeepers to resist being turned into one big Yankee store.

That is why in beginning here the discussion of machinery I pointed out, first, that in the ultimate sense we are free to destroy machinery; and second, that in the immediate sense it is possible to divide the ownership of machinery. And I should say myself that even in a healthy state there would be some ownership of machinery to divide. But when we come to consider that larger test, we must say something about the definition of machinery, and even the ideal of machinery. Now I have a great deal of sympathy with what I may call the sentimental argument for machinery. Of all the critics who have rebuked us, the man I like best is the engineer who says: "But I do like machinery — just as you like mythology. Why should I have my toys taken away any more than you?" And of the various positions that I have to meet, I will begin with his. Now on a previous page I said I agreed with Mr. Penty that it would be a human right to abandon machinery altogether. I will add here that I do not agree with Mr. Penty in thinking machinery like magic — a mere malignant power or origin of evils. It seems to me quite as materialistic to be damned by a machine as saved by a machine. It seems to me quite as idolatrous to blaspheme it as to worship it. But even supposing that somebody, without worshipping it, is yet enjoying it imaginatively and in some sense mystically, the case as we state it still stands.

Nobody would be more really unsuitable to the machine age than a man who really admired machines. The modern system presupposes people who will take mechanism mechanically; not people who will take it mystically. An amusing story might be written about a poet who was really appreciative of the fairy-tales of science, and who found himself more of an obstacle in the scientific civilization than if he had delayed it by telling the fairy-tales of infancy. Suppose whenever he went to the telephone (bowing three times as he approached the shrine of the disembodied oracle and murmuring some appropriate form of words such as vox et praeterea nihil), he were to act as if he really valued the significance of the instrument. Suppose he were to fall into a trembling ecstasy on hearing from a distant exchange the voice of an unknown young woman in a remote town, were to linger upon the very real wonder of that momentary meeting in mid-air with a human spirit whom he would never see on earth, were to speculate on her life and personality, so real and yet so remote from his own, were to pause to ask a few personal questions about her, just sufficient to accentuate her human strangeness, were to ask whether she also had not some sense of this weird psychical tete-a-tete, created and dissolved in an instant, whether she also thought of those unthinkable leagues of valley and forest that lay between the moving mouth and the listening ear — suppose, in short, he were to say all this to the lady at the Exchange who was just about to put him on to 666 Upper Tooting. He would be really and truly expressing the sentiment, "Wonderful thing, the telephone!"; and, unlike the thousands who say it, he would actually mean it. He would be really and truly justifying the great scientific discoveries and doing honour to the great scientific inventors. He would indeed be the worthy son of a scientific age. And yet I fear that in a scientific age he would possibly be misunderstood, and even suffer from lack of sympathy. I fear that he would, in fact, be in practice an opponent of all that he desired to uphold. He would be a worse enemy of machinery than any Luddite smashing machines. He would obstruct the activities of the telephone exchange, by praising the beauties of the telephone, more than if he had sat down, like a more normal and traditional poet, to tell all those bustling business people about the beauties of a wayside flower.

It would of course be the same with any adventure of the same luckless admiration. If a philosopher, when taken for the first time for a ride in a motor-car, were to fall into such an enthusiasm for the marvel that he insisted on understanding the whole of the mechanism on the spot, it is probable that he would have got to his destination rather quicker if he had walked. If he were, in his simple zeal, to insist on the machine being taken to pieces in the road, that he might rejoice in the inmost secrets of its structure, he might even lose his popularity with the garage taxi-driver or chauffeur. Now we have all known children, for instance, who did really in this fashion want to see wheels go round. But though their attitude may bring them nearest to the kingdom of heaven, it does not necessarily bring them nearer to the end of the journey. They are admiring motors; but they are not motoring — that is, they are not necessarily moving. They are not serving that purpose which motoring was meant to serve. Now as a matter of fact this contradiction has ended in a congestion; and a sort of stagnant state of the spirit in which there is rather less real appreciation of the marvels of man's invention than if the poet confined himself to making a penny whistle (on which to pipe in the woods of Arcady) or the child confined himself to making a toy bow or a catapult. The child really is happy with a beautiful happiness every time he lets fly an arrow. It is by no means certain that the business man is happy with a beautiful happiness every time he sends off a telegram. The very name of a telegram is a poem, even more magical than the arrow; for it means a dart, and a dart that writes. Think what the child would feel if he could shoot a pencil-arrow that drew a picture at the other end of the valley or the long street. Yet the business man but seldom dances and claps his hands for joy, at the thought of this, whenever he sends a telegram.

Now this has a considerable relevancy to the real criticism of the modern mechanical civilization. Its supporters are always telling us of its marvellous inventions and proving that they are marvellous improvements. But it is highly doubtful whether they really feel them as improvements. For instance, I have heard it said a hundred times that glass is an excellent illustration of the way in which something becomes a convenience for everybody. "Look at glass in windows," they say; "that has been turned into a mere necessity; yet that also was once a luxury." And I always feel disposed to answer, "Yes, and it would be better for people like you if it were still a luxury; if that would induce you to look at it, and not only to look through it. Do you ever consider how magical a thing is that invisible film standing between you and the birds and the wind? Do you ever think of it as water hung in the air or a flattened diamond too clear to be even valued? Do you ever feel a window as a sudden opening in a wall? And if you do not, what is the good of glass to you?" This may be a little exaggerated, in the heat of the moment, but it is really true that in these things invention outstrips imagination. Humanity has not got the good out of its own inventions; and by making more and more inventions, it is only leaving its own power of happiness further and further behind.

I remarked in an earlier part of this particular meditation that machinery was not necessarily evil, and that there were some who valued it in the right spirit, but that most of those who had to do with it never had a chance of valuing it at all. A poet might enjoy a clock as a child enjoys a musical-box. But the actual clerk who looks at the actual clock, to see that he is just in time to catch the train for the city, is no more enjoying machinery than he is enjoying music. There may be something to be said for mechanical toys; but modern society is a mechanism and not a toy. The child indeed is a good test in these matters; and illustrates both the fact that there is an interest in machinery and the fact that machinery itself generally prevents us from being interested. It is almost a proverb that every little boy wants to be an engine-driver. But machinery has not multiplied the number of engine-drivers, so as to allow all little boys to drive engines. It has not given each little boy a real engine, as his family might give him a toy engine. The effect of railways on a population cannot be to produce a population of engine-drivers. It can only produce a population of passengers; and of passengers a little too like packages. In other words, its only effect on the visionary or potential engine-driver is to put him inside the train, where he cannot see the engine, instead of outside the train where he can. And though he grows up to the greatest and most glorious success in life, and swindles the widow and orphan till he can travel in a first-class carriage specially reserved, with a permanent pass to the International Congress of Cosmopolitan World Peace for Wire-Pullers, he will never perhaps enjoy a railway train again, he will never even see a railway train again, as he saw it when he stood as a ragged urchin and waved wildly from a grassy bank at the passage of the Scotch Express.

We may transfer the parable from engine-drivers to engineers. It may be that the driver of the Scotch Express hurls himself forward in a fury of speed because his heart is in the Highlands, his heart is not here; that he spurns the Border behind him with a gesture and hails the Grampians before him with a cheer. And whether or no it is true that the engine-driver's heart is in the Highlands, it is sometimes true that the little boy's heart is in the engine. But it is by no means true that passengers as a whole, travelling behind engines as a whole, enjoy the speed in a positive sense, though they may approve of it in a negative sense. I mean that they wish to travel swiftly, not because swift travelling is enjoyable, but because it is not enjoyable. They want it rushed through; not because being behind the railway-engine is a rapture, but because being in the railway-carriage is a bore. In the same way, if we consider the joy of engineers, we must remember that there is only one joyful engineer to a thousand bored victims of engineering. The discussion that raged between Mr. Penty and others at one time threatened to resolve itself into a feud between engineers and architects. But when the engineer asks us to forget all the monotony and materialism of a mechanical age because his own science has some of the inspiration of an art, the architect may well be ready with a reply. For this is very much as if architects were never engaged in anything but the building of prisons and lunatic asylums. It is as if they told us proudly with what passionate and poetical enthusiasm they had themselves reared towers high enough for the hanging of Haman or dug dungeons impenetrable enough for the starving of Ugolino.

Now I have already explained that I do not propose anything in what some call the practical way, but should rather be called the immediate way, beyond the better distribution of the ownership of such machines as are really found to be necessary. But when we come to the larger question of machinery in a fundamentally different sort of society, governed by our philosophy and religion, there is a great deal more to be said. The best and shortest way of saying it is that instead of the machine being a giant to which the man is a pygmy, we must at least reverse the proportions until man is a giant to whom the machine is a toy. Granted that idea, and we have no reason to deny that it might be a legitimate and enlivening toy. In that sense it would not matter if every child were an engine-driver or (better still) every engine-driver a child. But those who were always taunting us with unpracticality will at least admit that this is not practical.

I have thus tried to put myself fairly in the position of the enthusiast, as we should always do in judging of enthusiasms. And I think it will be agreed that even after the experiment a real difference between the engineering enthusiasm and older enthusiasms remains as a fact of common sense. Admitting that the man who designs a steam-engine is as original as the man who designs a statue, there is an immediate and immense difference in the effects of what they design. The original statue is a joy to the sculptor; but it is also in some degree (when it is not too original) a joy to the people who see the statue. Or at any rate it is meant to be a joy to other people seeing it, or there would be no point in letting it be seen. But though the engine may be a great joy to the engineer and of great use to the other people, it is not, and it is not meant to be, in the same sense a great joy to the other people. Nor is this because of a deficiency in education, as some of the artists might allege in the case of art. It is involved in the very nature of machinery; which, when once it is established, consists of repetitions and not of variations and surprises. A man can see something in the limbs of a statue which he never saw before; they may seem to toss or sweep as they never did before; but he would not only be astonished but alarmed if the wheels of the steam-engine began to behave as they never did before. We may take it, therefore, as an essential and not an accidental character of machinery that it is an inspiration for the inventor but merely a monotony for the consumer.

This being so, it seems to me that in an ideal state engineering would be the exception, just as the delight in engines is the exception. As it is, engineering and engines are the rule; and are even a grinding and oppressive rule. The lifelessness which the machine imposes on the masses is an infinitely bigger and more obvious fact than the individual interest of the man who makes machines. Having reached this point in the argument, we may well compare it with what may be called the practical aspect of the problem of machinery. Now it seems to me obvious that machinery, as it exists to-day, has gone almost as much beyond its practical sphere as it has beyond its imaginative sphere. The whole of industrial society is founded on the notion that the quickest and cheapest thing is to carry coals to Newcastle; even if it be only with the object of afterwards carrying them from Newcastle. It is founded on the idea that rapid and regular transit and transport, perpetual interchange of goods, and incessant communication between remote places, is of all things the most economical and direct. But it is not true that the quickest and cheapest thing, for a man who has just pulled an apple from an apple tree, is to send it in a consignment of apples on a train that goes like a thunderbolt to a market at the other end of England. The quickest and cheapest thing for a man who has pulled a fruit from a tree is to put it in his mouth. He is the supreme economist who wastes no money on railway journeys. He is the absolute type of efficiency who is far too efficient to go in for organization. And though he is, of course, an extreme and ideal case of simplification, the case for simplification does stand as solid as an apple tree. In so far as men can produce their own goods on the spot, they are saving the community a vast expenditure which is often quite out of proportion to the return. In so far as we can establish a considerable proportion of simple and self-supporting people, we are relieving the pressure of what is often a wasteful as well as a harassing process. And taking this as a general outline of the reform, it does appear true that a simpler life in large areas of the community might leave machinery more or less as an exceptional thing; as it may well be to the exceptional man who really puts his soul into it.

There are difficulties in this view; but for the moment I may well take as an illustration the parallel of the particular sort of modern engineering which moderns are very fond of denouncing. They often forget that most of their praise of scientific instruments applies most vividly to scientific weapons. If we are to have so much pity for the unhappy genius who has just invented a new galvanometer, what about the poor genius who has just invented a new gun? If there is a real imaginative inspiration in the making of a steam-engine, is there not imaginative interest in the making of a submarine? Yet many modern admirers of science would be very anxious to abolish these machines altogether; even in the very act of telling us that we cannot abolish machines at all. As I believe in the right of national self-defence, I would not abolish them altogether. But I think they may give us a hint of how exceptional things may be treated exceptionally. For the moment I will leave the progressive to laugh at my absurd notion of a limitation of machines, and go off to a meeting to demand the limitation of armaments.

================

3. The Holiday Of The Slave

I have sometimes suggested that industrialism of the American type, with its machinery and mechanical hustle, will some day be preserved on a truly American model; I mean in the manner of the Red Indian Reservation. As we leave a patch of forest for savages to hunt and fish in, so a higher civilization might leave a patch of factories for those who are still at such a stage of intellectual infancy as really to want to see the wheels go round. And as the Red Indians could still, I suppose, tell their quaint old legends of a red god who smoked a pipe or a red hero who stole the sun and moon, so the simple folk in the industrial enclosure could go on talking of their own Outline of History and discussing the evolution of ethics, while all around them a more mature civilization was dealing with real history and serious philosophy. I hesitate to repeat this fancy here; for, after all, machinery is their religion, or at any rate superstition, and they do not like it to be treated with levity. But I do think there is something to be said for the notion of which this fancy might stand as a sort of symbol; for the idea that a wiser society would eventually treat machines as it treats weapons, as something special and dangerous and perhaps more directly under a central control. But however this may be, I do think the wildest fancy of a manufacturer kept at bay like a painted barbarian is much more sane than a serious scientific alternative now often put before us. I mean what its friends call the Leisure State, in which everything is to be done by machinery. It is only right to say a word about this suggestion in comparison with our own.

In practice we already know what is meant by a holiday in a world of machinery and mass production. It means that a man, when he has done turning a handle, has a choice of certain pleasures offered to him. He can, if he likes, read a newspaper and discover with interest how the Crown Prince of Fontarabia landed from the magnificent yacht Atlantis amid a cheering crowd; how certain great American millionaires are making great financial consolidations; how the Modern Girl is a delightful creature, in spite of (or because of) having shingled hair or short skirts; and how the true religion, for which we all look to the Churches, consists of sympathy and social progress and marrying, divorcing, or burying everybody without reference to the precise meaning of the ceremony. On the other hand, if he prefers some other amusement, he may go to the Cinema, where he will see a very vivid and animated scene of the crowds cheering the Crown Prince of Fontarabia after the arrival of the yacht Atlantis; where he will see an American film featuring the features of American millionaires, with all those resolute contortions of visage which accompany their making of great financial consolidations; where there will not be lacking a charming and vivacious heroine, recognizable as a Modern Girl by her short hair and short skirts; and possibly a kind and good clergyman (if any) who explains in dumb show, with the aid of a few printed sentences, that true religion is social sympathy and progress and marrying and burying people at random. But supposing the man's tastes to be detached from the drama and from the kindred arts, he may prefer the reading of fiction; and he will have no difficulty in finding a popular novel about the doubts and difficulties of a good and kind clergyman slowly discovering that true religion consists of progress and social sympathy, with the assistance of a Modern Girl whose shingled hair and short skirts proclaim her indifference to all fine distinctions about who should be buried and who divorced; nor, probably, will the story fail to contain an American millionaire making vast financial consolidations, and certainly a yacht and possibly a Crown Prince. But there are yet other tastes that are catered for under the conditions of modern publicity and pleasure-seeking. There is the great institution of wireless or broadcasting; and the holiday-maker, turning away from fiction, journalism, and film drama, may prefer to "listen-in" to a programme that will contain the very latest news of great financial consolidations made by American millionaires; which will most probably contain little lectures on how the Modern Girl can crop her hair or abbreviate her skirts; in which he can hear the very accents of some great popular preacher proclaiming to the world that revelation of true religion which consists of sympathy and social progress rather than of dogma and creed; and in which he will certainly hear the very thunder of cheering which welcomes His Royal Highness the Crown Prince of Fontarabia when he lands from the magnificent yacht Atlantis. There is thus indeed a very elaborate and well-ordered choice placed before him, in the matter of the means of entertainment.

But even the rich variety of method and approach unfolded before us in this alternative seems to some to cover a certain secret and subtle element of monotony. Even here the pleasure-seeker may have that weird psychological sensation of having known the same thing before. There seems to be something recurrent about the type of topic; suggestive of something rigid about the type of mind. Now I think it very doubtful whether it is really a superior mind. If the pleasure-seeker himself were really a pleasure-maker for himself, if he were forced to amuse himself instead of being amused, if he were, in short, obliged to sit down in an old tavern and talk — I am really very doubtful about whether he would confine his conversation entirely to the Crown Prince of Fontarabia, the shingling of hair, the greatness of certain rich Yankees, and so on; and then begin the same round of subjects all over again. His interests might be more local, but they would be more lively; his experience of men more personal but more mixed; his likes and dislikes more capricious but not quite so easily satisfied. To take a parallel, modern children are made to play public-school games, and will doubtless soon be made to listen to the praise of the millionaires on the wireless and in the newspaper. But children left to themselves almost invariably invent games of their own, dramas of their own, often whole imaginary kingdoms and commonwealths of their own. In other words, they produce; until the competition of monopoly kills their production. The boy playing at robbers is not liberated but stunted by learning about American crooks, all of one pattern less picturesque than his own. He is psychologically undercut, undersold, dumped upon, frozen out, flooded, swamped, and ruined; but not emancipated.

Inventions have destroyed invention. The big modern machines are like big guns dominating and terrorizing a whole stretch of country, within the range of which nothing can raise its head. There is far more inventiveness to the square yard of mankind than can ever appear under that monopolist terror. The minds of men are not so much alike as the motor-cars of men, or the morning papers of men, or the mechanical manufacture of the coats and hats of men. In other words, we are not getting the best out of men. We are certainly not getting the most individual or the most interesting qualities out of men. And it is doubtful whether we ever shall, until we shut off this deafening din of megaphones that drowns their voices, this deathly glare of limelight which kills the colours of their complexions, this plangent yell of platitudes which stuns and stops their minds. All this sort of thing is killing thoughts as they grow, as a great white death-ray might kill plants as they grow. When, therefore, people tell me that making a great part of England rustic and self-supporting would mean making it rude and senseless, I do not agree with them; and I do not think they understand the alternative or the problem. Nobody wants all men to be rustics even in normal times; it is very tenable that some of the most intelligent would turn to the towns even in normal times. But I say the towns themselves are the foes of intelligence, in these times; I say the rustics themselves would have more variety and vivacity than is really encouraged by these towns. I say it is only by shutting off this unnatural noise and light that men's minds can begin again to move and to grow. Just as we spread paving-stones over different soils without reference to the different crops that might grow there, so we spread programmes of platitudinous plutocracy over souls that God made various, and simpler societies have made free.

If by machinery saving labour, and therefore producing leisure, be meant the machinery that now achieves what is called mass production, I cannot see any vital value in the leisure; because there is in that leisure nothing of liberty. The man may only work for an hour with his machine-made tools, but he can only run away and play for twenty-three hours with machine-made toys. Everything he handles has to come from a huge machine that he cannot handle. Everything must come from something to which, in the current capitalist phrase, he can only lend "a hand." Now as this would apply to intellectual and artistic toys as well as to merely material toys, it seems to me that the machine would dominate him for a much longer time than his hand had to turn the handle. It is practically admitted that much fewer men are needed to work the machine. The answer of the mechanical collectivists is that though the machine might give work to the few, it could give food to the many. But it could only give food to the many by an operation that had to be presided over by the few. Or even if we suppose that some work, subdivided into small sections, were given to the many, that system of rotation would have to be ruled by a responsible few; and some fixed authority would be needed to distribute the work as much as to distribute the food. In other words, the officials would very decidedly be permanent officials. In a sense all the rest of us might be intermittent or occasional officials. But the general character of the system would remain; and whatever else it is like, nothing can make it like a population pottering about in its own several fields or practising small creative crafts in its own little workshops. The man who has helped to produce a machine-made article may indeed leave off working, in the sense of leaving off turning one particular wheel. He may have an opportunity to do as he likes, in so far as he likes using what the system likes producing. He may have a power of choice — in the sense that he may choose between one thing it produces and another thing it produces. He may choose to pass his leisure hours in sitting in a machine-made chair or lying on a machine-made bed or resting in a machine-made hammock or swinging on a machine-made trapeze. But he will not be in the same position as a man who carves his own hobby-horse out of his own wood or his own hobby out of his own will. For that introduces another principle or purpose; which there is no warrant for supposing will coexist with the principle or purpose of using all the wood so as to save labour or simplifying all the wills so as to save leisure. If our ideal is to produce things as rapidly and easily as possible, we must have a definite number of things that we desire to produce. If we desire to produce them as freely and variously as possible, we must not at the same time try to produce them as quickly as possible. I think it most probable that the result of saving labour by machinery would be then what it is now, only more so: the limitation of the type of thing produced; standardization.

Now it may be that some of the supporters of the Leisure State have in mind some system of distributed machinery, which shall really make each man the master of his machine; and in that case I agree that the problem becomes different and that a great part of the problem is resolved. There would still remain the question of whether a man with a free soul would want to use a machine upon about three-quarters of the things for which machines are now used. In other words, there would remain the whole problem of the craftsman in the sense of the creator. But I should agree that if the small man found his small mechanical plant helpful to the preservation of his small property, its claim would be very considerable. But it is necessary to make it clear, that if the holidays provided for the mechanic are provided as mechanically as at present, and with the merely mechanical alternative offered at present, I think that even the slavery of his labour would be light compared to the grinding slavery of his leisure.

=================

4. The Free Man And The Ford Car

I am not a fanatic; and I think that machines may be of considerable use in destroying machinery. I should generously accord them a considerable value in the work of exterminating all that they represent. But to put the truth in those terms is to talk in terms of the remote conclusion of our slow and reasonable revolution. In the immediate situation the same truth may be stated in a more moderate way. Towards all typical things of our time we should have a rational charity. Machinery is not wrong; it is only absurd. Perhaps we should say it is merely childish, and can even be taken in the right spirit by a child. If, therefore, we find that some machine enables us to escape from an inferno of machinery, we cannot be committing a sin though we may be cutting a silly figure, like a dragoon rejoining his regiment on an old bicycle. What is essential is to realize that there is something ridiculous about the present position, something wilder than any Utopia. For instance, I shall have occasion here to note the proposal of centralized electricity, and we could justify the use of it so long as we see the joke of it. But, in fact, we do not even see the joke of the waterworks and the water company. It is almost too broadly comic that an essential of life like water should be pumped to us from nobody knows where, by nobody knows whom, sometimes nearly a hundred miles away. It is every bit as funny as if air were pumped to us from miles away, and we all walked about like divers at the bottom of the sea. The only reasonable person is the peasant who owns his own well. But we have a long way to go before we begin to think about being reasonable.

There are at present some examples of centralization of which the effects may work for decentralization. An obvious case is that recently discussed in connection with a common plant of electricity. I think it is broadly true that if electricity could be cheapened, the chances of a very large number of small independent shops, especially workshops, would be greatly improved. At the same time, there is no doubt at all that such dependence for essential power on a central plant is a real dependence, and is therefore a defect in any complete scheme of independence. On this point I imagine that many Distributists might differ considerably; but, speaking for myself, I am inclined to follow the more moderate and provisional policy that I have suggested more than once in this place. I think the first necessity is to make sure of any small properties obtaining any success in any decisive or determining degree. Above all, I think it is vital to create the experience of small property, the psychology of small property, the sort of man who is a small proprietor. When once men of that sort exist, they will decide, in a manner very different from any modern mob, how far the central power-house is to dominate their own private house, or whether it need dominate at all. They will perhaps discover the way of breaking up and individualizing that power. They will sacrifice, if there is any need to sacrifice, even the help of science to the hunger for possession. So that I am disposed at the moment to accept any help that science and machinery can give in creating small property, without in the least bowing down to such superstitions where they only destroy it. But we must keep in mind the peasant ideal as the motive and the goal; and most of those who offer us mechanical help seem to be blankly ignorant of what we regard it as helping. A well-known name will illustrate both the thing being done and the man being ignorant of what he is doing.

The other day I found myself in a Ford car, like that in which I remember riding over Palestine, and in which, (I suppose) Mr. Ford would enjoy riding over Palestinians. Anyhow, it reminded me of Mr. Ford, and that reminded me of Mr. Penty and his views upon equality and mechanical civilization. The Ford car (if I may venture on one of those new ideas urged upon us in newspapers) is a typical product of the age. The best thing about it is the thing for which it is despised; that it is small. The worst thing about it is the thing for which it is praised; that it is standardized. Its smallness is, of course, the subject of endless American jokes, about a man catching a Ford like a fly or possibly a flea. But nobody seems to notice how this popularization of motoring (however wrong in motive or in method) really is a complete contradiction to the fatalistic talk about inevitable combination and concentration. The railway is fading before our eyes — birds nesting, as it were, in the railway signals, and wolves howling, so to speak, in the waiting-room. And the railway really was a communal and concentrated mode of travel like that in a Utopia of the Socialists. The free and solitary traveller is returning before our very eyes; not always (it is true) equipped with scrip or scallop, but having recovered to some extent the freedom of the King's highway in the manner of Merry England. Nor is this the only ancient thing such travel has revived. While Mugby Junction neglected its refreshment-rooms, Hugby-in-the-Hole has revived its inns. To that limited extent the Ford motor is already a reversion to the free man. If he has not three acres and a cow, he has the very inadequate substitute of three hundred miles and a car. I do not mean that this development satisfies my theories. But I do say that it destroys other people's theories; all the theories about the collective thing as a thing of the future and the individual thing as a thing of the past. Even in their own special and stinking way of science and machinery, the facts are very largely going against their theories.

Yet I have never seen Mr. Ford and his little car really and intelligently praised for this. I have often, of course, seen him praised for all the conveniences of what is called standardization. The argument seems to be more or less to this effect. When your car breaks down with a loud crash in the middle of Salisbury Plain, though it is not very likely that any fragments of other ruined motor cars will be lying about amid the ruins of Stonehenge, yet if they are, it is a great advantage to think that they will probably be of the same pattern, and you can take them to mend your own car. The same principle applies to persons motoring in Tibet, and exulting in the reflection that if another motorist from the United States did happen to come along, it would be possible to exchange wheels or footbrakes in token of amity. I may not have got the details of the argument quite correct; but the general point of it is that if anything goes wrong with parts of a machine, they can be replaced with identical machinery.   And anyhow the argument could be carried much further; and used to explain a great many other things. I am not sure that it is not the clue to many mysteries of the age. I begin to understand, for instance, why magazine stories are all exactly alike; it is ordered so that when you have left one magazine in a railway carriage in the middle of a story called "Pansy Eyes," you may go on with exactly the same story in another magazine under the title of "Dandelion Locks." It explains why all leading articles on The Future of the Churches are exactly the same; so that we may begin reading the article in the Daily Chronicle and finish it in the Daily Express. It explains why all the public utterances urging us to prefer new things to old never by any chance say anything new; they mean that we should go to a new paper-stall and read it in a new newspaper.   This is why all American caricatures repeat themselves like a mathematical pattern; it means that when we have torn off a part of the picture to wrap up sandwiches, we can tear off a bit of another picture and it will always fit in. And this is also why American millionaires all look exactly alike; so that when the bright, resolute expression of one of them has led us to do serious damage to his face with a heavy blow of the fist, it is always possible to mend it with noses and jaw-bones taken from other millionaires, who are exactly similarly constituted.

Such are the advantages of standardization; but, as may be suspected, I think the advantages are exaggerated; and I agree with Mr. Penty in doubting whether all this repetition really corresponds to human nature. But a very interesting question was raised by Mr. Ford's remarks on the difference between men and men; and his suggestion that most men preferred mechanical action or were only fitted for it. About all those arguments affecting human equality, I myself always have one feeling, which finds expression in a little test of my own. I shall begin to take seriously those classifications of superiority and inferiority, when I find a man classifying himself as inferior. It will be noted that Mr. Ford does not say that he is only fitted to mind machines; he confesses frankly that he is too fine and free and fastidious a being for such tasks. I shall believe the doctrine when I hear somebody say: "I have only got the wits to turn a wheel." That would be real, that would be realistic, that would be scientific. That would be independent testimony that could not easily be disputed. It is exactly the same, of course, with all the other superiorities and denials of human equality that are so specially characteristic of a scientific age. It is so with the men who talk about superior and inferior races; I never heard a man say: "Anthropology shows that I belong to an inferior race." If he did, he might be talking like an anthropologist; as it is, he is talking like a man, and not unfrequently like a fool. I have long hoped that I might some day hear a man explaining on scientific principles his own unfitness for any important post or privilege, say: "The world should belong to the free and fighting races, and not to persons of that servile disposition that you will notice in myself; the intelligent will know how to form opinions, but the weakness of intellect from which I so obviously suffer renders my opinions manifestly absurd on the face of them: there are indeed stately and godlike races — but look at me! Observe my shapeless and fourth-rate features! Gaze, if you can bear it, on my commonplace and repulsive face!" If I heard a man making a scientific demonstration in that style, I might admit that he was really scientific. But as it invariably happens, by a curious coincidence, that the superior race is his own race, the superior type is his own type, and the superior preference for work the sort of work he happens to prefer — I have come to the conclusion that there is a simpler explanation.

Now Mr. Ford is a good man, so far as it is consistent with being a good millionaire. But he himself will very well illustrate where the fallacy of his argument lies. It is probably quite true that, in the making of motors, there are a hundred men who can work a motor and only one man who can design a motor. But of the hundred men who could work a motor, it is very probable that one could design a garden, another design a charade, another design a practical joke or a derisive picture of Mr. Ford. I do not mean, of course, in anything I say here, to deny differences of intelligence, or to suggest that equality (a thing wholly religious) depends on any such impossible denial. But I do mean that men are nearer to a level than anybody will discover by setting them all to make one particular kind of run-about clock. Now Mr. Ford himself is a man of defiant limitations. He is so indifferent to history, for example, that he calmly admitted in the witness-box that he had never heard of Benedict Arnold. An American who has never heard of Benedict Arnold is like a Christian who has never heard of Judas Iscariot. He is rare. I believe that Mr. Ford indicated in a general way that he thought Benedict Arnold was the same as Arnold Bennett. Not only is this not the case, but it is an error to suppose that there is no importance in such an error. If he were to find himself, in the heat of some controversy, accusing Mr. Arnold Bennett of having betrayed the American President and ravaged the South with an Anti-American army, Mr. Bennett might bring an action. If Mr. Ford were to suppose that the lady who recently wrote revelations in the Daily Express was old enough to be the widow of Benedict Arnold, the lady might bring an action. Now it is not impossible that among the workmen whom Mr. Ford perceives (probably quite truly) to be only suited to the mechanical part of the construction of mechanical things, there might be a man who was fond of reading all the history he could lay his hands on; and who had advanced step by step, by painful efforts of self-education, until the difference between Benedict Arnold and Arnold Bennett was quite clear in his mind. If his employer did not care about the difference, of course, he would not consult him about the difference, and the man would remain to all appearance a mere cog in the machine; there would be no reason for finding out that he was a rather cogitating cog. Anybody who knows anything of modern business knows that there are any number of such men who remain in subordinate and obscure positions because their private tastes and talents have no relation to the very stupid business in which they are engaged. If Mr. Ford extends his business over the Solar System, and gives cars to the Martians and the Man in the Moon, he will not be an inch nearer to the mind of the man who is working his machine for him, and thinking about something more sensible. Now all human things are imperfect; but the condition in which such hobbies and secondary talents do to some extent come out is the condition of small independence. The peasant almost always runs two or three sideshows and lives on a variety of crafts and expedients. The village shopkeeper will shave travellers and stuff weasels and grow cabbages and do half a dozen such things, keeping a sort of balance in his life like the balance of sanity in the soul. The method is not perfect; but it is more intelligent than turning him into a machine in order to find out whether he has a soul above machinery.

Upon this point of immediate compromise with machinery, therefore, I am inclined to conclude that it is quite right to use the existing machines in so far as they do create a psychology that can despise machines; but not if they create a psychology that respects them. The Ford car is an excellent illustration of the question; even better than the other illustration I have given of an electrical supply for small workshops. If possessing a Ford car means rejoicing in a Ford car, it is melancholy enough; it does not bring us much farther than Tooting or rejoicing in a Tooting tramcar. But if possessing a Ford car means rejoicing in a field of corn or clover, in a fresh landscape and a free atmosphere, it may be the beginning of many things — and even the end of many things. It may be, for instance, the end of the car and the beginning of the cottage. Thus we might almost say that the final triumph of Mr. Ford is not when the man gets into the car, but when he enthusiastically falls out of the car. It is when he finds somewhere, in remote and rural corners that he could not normally have reached, that perfect poise and combination of hedge and tree and meadow in the presence of which any modern machine seems suddenly to look an absurdity; yes, even an antiquated absurdity. Probably that happy man, having found the place of his true home, will proceed joyfully to break up the car with a large hammer, putting its iron fragments for the first time to some real use, as kitchen utensils or garden tools. That is using a scientific instrument in the proper way; for it is using it as an instrument. The man has used modern machinery to escape from modern society; and the reason and rectitude of such a course commends itself instantly to the mind. It is not so with the weaker brethren who are not content to trust Mr. Ford's car, but also trust Mr. Ford's creed. If accepting the car means accepting the philosophy I have just criticized, the notion that some men are born to make cars, or rather small bits of cars, then it will be far more worthy of a philosopher to say frankly that men never needed to have cars at all. It is only because the man had been sent into exile in a railway-train that he has to be brought back home in a motor-car. It is only because all machinery has been used to put things wrong that some machinery may now rightly be used to put things right. But I conclude upon the whole that it may so be used;

and my reason is that which I considered on a previous page under the heading of "The Chance of Recovery." I pointed out that our ideal is so sane and simple, so much in accord with the ancient and general instincts of men, that when once it is given a chance anywhere it will improve that chance by its own inner vitality because there is some reaction towards health whenever disease is removed. The man who has used his car to find his farm will be more interested in the farm than in the car; certainly more interested than in the shop where he once bought the car. Nor will Mr. Ford always woo him back to that shop, even by telling him tenderly that he is not fitted to be a lord of land, a rider of horses, or a ruler of cattle; since his deficient intellect and degraded anthropological type fit him only for mean and mechanical operations. If anyone will try saying this (tenderly, of course) to any considerable number of large farmers, who have lived for some time on their own farms with their own families, he will discover the defects of the approach.

================

V. A Note On Emigration

1. The Need Of A New Spirit

Before closing these notes, with some words on the colonial aspect of democratic distribution, it will be well to make some acknowledgment of the recent suggestion of so distinguished a man as Mr. John Galsworthy. Mr. Galsworthy is a man for whom I have the very warmest regard; for a human being who really tries to be fair is something very like a monster and miracle in the long history of this merry race of ours. Sometimes, indeed, I get a little exasperated at being so persistently excused. I can imagine few things more annoying, to a free-born and properly constituted Christian, than the thought that if he did choose to wait for Mr. Galsworthy behind a wall, knock him down with a brick, jump on him with heavy boots, and so on, Mr. Galsworthy would still faintly gasp that it was only the fault of the System; that the System made bricks and the System heaved bricks and the System went about wearing heavy boots, and so on. As a human being, I should feel a longing for a little human justice, after all that inhuman mercy.

But these feelings do not interfere with the other feelings I have, of something like enthusiasm, for something that can only be called beautiful in the fair-mindedness of a study like "The White Monkey." It is when this attitude of detachment is applied not to the judgment of individuals but of men in bulk, that the detachment begins to savour of something unnatural. And in Mr. Galsworthy's last political pronouncement the detachment amounts to despair. At any rate, it amounts to despair about this earth, this England, about which I am certainly not going to despair yet. But I think it might be well if I took this opportunity of stating what I, for one, at least feel about the different claims here involved.

It may be debated whether it is a good or a bad thing for England that England has an Empire. It may be debated, at least as a matter of true definition, whether England has an Empire at all. But upon one point all Englishmen ought to stand firm, as a matter of history, of philosophy, and of logic. And that is that it has been, and is, a question of our owning an Empire and not of an Empire owning us.

There is sense in being separated from Americans on the principles of George Washington, and sense in being attached to Americans on the principles of George the Third. But there is no sense in being out-voted and swamped by Americans in the name of the Anglo-Saxon race. The Colonies were by origin English. They owe us that much; if it be only the trivial circumstance, so little valued by modern thought, that without their maker they could never have existed at all. If they choose to remain English, we thank them very sincerely for the compliment. If they choose not to remain English, but to turn into something else, we think they are within their rights. But anyhow England shall remain English. They shall not first turn themselves into something else, and then turn us into themselves. It may have been wrong to be an Empire, but it does not rob us of our right to be a nation.

But there is another sense in which those of our school would use the motto of "England First." It is in the sense that our first step should be to discover how far the best ethical and economic system can be fitted into England, before we treat it as an export and cart it away to the ends of the earth. The scientific or commercial character, who is sure he has found an explosive that will blow up the solar system or a bullet that will kill the man in the moon, always makes a great parade of saying that he offers it first to his own country, and only afterwards to a foreign country. Personally, I cannot conceive how a man can bring himself in any case to offer such a thing to a foreign country. But then I am not a great scientific and commercial genius. Anyhow, such as our little notion of normal ownership is, we certainly do not propose to offer it to any foreign country, or even to any colony, before we offer it to our own country. And we do think it highly urgent and practical to find out first how much of it can really be carried out in our own country. Nobody supposes that the whole English population could live on the English land. But everybody ought to realize that immeasurably more people could live on it than do live on it; and that if such a policy did establish such a peasantry, there would be a recognizable narrowing of the margin of men left over for the town and the colonies. But we would suggest that these ought really to be left over, and dealt with as seems most desirable, after the main experiment has been made where it matters most. And what most of us would complain of in the emigrationists of the ordinary sort is that they seem to think first of the colony and then of what must be left behind in the country; instead of thinking first of the country and then of what must overflow into the colony.

People talk about an optimist being in a hurry; but it seems to me that a pessimist like Mr. Galsworthy is very much in a hurry. He has not tried the obvious reform on England, and, finding it fail, gone into exile to try it elsewhere. He is trying the obvious reform everywhere except where it is most obvious. And in this I think he has a subconscious affinity to people much less reasonable and respectable than himself. The pessimists have a curious way of urging us to counsels of despair as the only solution of a problem they have not troubled to solve. They declare solemnly that some unnatural thing would become necessary if certain conditions existed; and then somehow assume from that that they exist. They never think of attempting to prove that they exist, before they prove what follows from their existence. This is exactly the sort of plunging and premature pessimism, for instance, that people exhibit about Birth Control. Their desire is towards destruction; their hope is for despair; they eagerly anticipate the darkest and most doubtful predictions. They run with eager feet before and beyond the lingering and inconveniently slow statistics; like as the hart pants for the water-brooks they thirst to drink of Styx and Lethe before their hour; even the facts they show fall far short of the faith that they see shining beyond them; for faith is the substance of things hoped for, the evidence of things not seen.

If I do not compare the critic in question with the doctors of this dismal perversion, still less do I compare him with those whose motives are merely self-protective and plutocratic. But it must also be said that many rush to the expedient of emigration, just as many rush to the expedient of Birth Control, for the perfectly simple reason that it is the easiest way in which the capitalists can escape from their own blunder of capitalism. They lured men into the town with the promise of greater pleasures; they ruined them there and left them with only one pleasure; they found the increase it produced at first convenient for labour and then inconvenient for supply; and now they are ready to round off their experiment in a highly appropriate manner, by telling them that they must have no families, or that their families must go to the modern equivalent of Botany Bay. It is not in that spirit that we envisage an element of colonization; and so long as it is treated in that spirit we refuse to consider it. I put first the statement that real colonial settlement must be not only stable but sacred. I say the new home must be not only a home but a shrine. And that is why I say it must be first established in England, in the home of our fathers and the shrine of our saints, to be a light and an ensign to our children.

I have explained that I cannot content myself with leaving my own nationality out of my own normal ideal; or leaving England as the mere tool-house or coal-cellar of other countries like Canada or Australia — or, for that matter, Argentina. I should like England also to have a much more rural type of redistribution; nor do I think it impossible. But when this is allowed for, nobody in his five wits would dream of denying that there is a real scope and even necessity for emigration and colonial settlement. Only, when we come to that, I have to draw a line rather sharply and explain something else, which is by no means inconsistent with my love of England, but I fear is not so likely to make me loved by Englishmen. I do not believe, as the newspapers and national histories always tell me to believe, that we have "the secret" of this sort of successful colonization and need nothing else to achieve this sort of democratic social construction. I ask for nothing better than that a man should be English in England. But I think he will have to be something more than English (or at any rate something more than "British") if he is to create a solid social equality outside England. For something is needed for that solid social creation which our colonial tradition has not given. My reasons for holding this highly unpopular opinion I will attempt to suggest; but the fact that they are rather difficult to suggest is itself an evidence of their unfamiliarity and of that narrowness which is neither national nor international, but only imperial.

I should very much like to be present at a conversation between Mr. Saklatvala and Dean Inge. I have a great deal of respect for the real sincerity of the Dean of St. Paul's, but his subconscious prejudices are of a strange sort. I cannot help having a feeling that he might have a certain sympathy with a Socialist so long as he was not a Christian Socialist. I do not indeed pretend to any respect for the ordinary sort of broad-mindedness which is ready to embrace a Buddhist but draws the line at a Bolshevist. I think its significance is very simple. It means welcoming alien religions when they make us feel comfortable, and persecuting them when they make us feel uncomfortable. But the particular reason I have at the moment for entertaining this association of ideas is one that concerns a larger matter. It concerns, indeed, what is commonly called the British Empire, which we were once taught to reverence largely because it was large. And one of my complaints against that common and rather vulgar sort of imperialism is that it did not really secure even the advantages of largeness. As I have said, I am a nationalist; Eng-land is good enough for me. I would defend England against the whole European continent. With even greater joy would I defend England against the whole British Empire. With a romantic rapture would I defend England against Mr. Ramsay MacDonald when he had become King of Scotland; lighting again the watch fires of Newark and Carlisle and sounding the old tocsins of the Border. With equal energy would I defend England against Mr. Tim Healy as King of Ireland, if ever the gross and growing prosperity of that helpless and decaying Celtic stock became positively offensive. With the greatest ecstasy of all would I defend England against Mr. Lloyd George as King of Wales. It will be seen, therefore, that there is nothing broad-minded about my patriotism; most modern nationality is not narrow enough for me.

But putting aside my own local affections, and looking at the matter in what is called a larger way, I note once more that our Imperialism does not get any of the good that could be got out of being large. And I was reminded of Dean Inge, because he suggested some time ago that the Irish and the French Canadians were increasing in numbers, not because they held the Catholic view of the family, but because they were a backward and apparently almost barbaric stock which naturally (I suppose he meant) increased with the blind luxuriance of a jungle. I have already remarked on the amusing trick of having it both ways which is illustrated in this remark. So long as savages are dying out, we say they are dying out because they are savages. When they are inconveniently increasing, we say they are increasing because they are savages. And from this it is but a simple logical step to say that the countrymen of Sir Wilfred Laurier or Senator Yeats are savages because they are increasing. But what strikes me most about the situation is this: that this spirit will always miss what is really to be learnt by covering any large and varied area. If French Canada is really a part of the British Empire, it would seem that the Empire might at least have served as a sort of interpreter between the British and the French. The Imperial statesman, if he had really been a statesman, ought to have been able to say, "It is always difficult to understand another nation or another religion; but I am more fortunately placed than most people. I know a little more than can be known by self-contained and isolated states like Sweden or Spain. I have more sympathy with the Catholic faith or the French blood because I have French Catholics in my own Empire." Now it seems to me that the Imperial statesman never has said this; never has even been able to say it; never has even tried or pretended to be able to say it. He has been far narrower than a nationalist like myself, engaged in desperately defending Offa's Dyke against a horde of Welsh politicians. I doubt if there was ever a politician who knew a word more of the French language, let alone a word more of the Latin Mass, because he had to govern a whole population that drew its traditions from Rome and Gaul. I will suggest in a moment how this enormous international narrowness affects the question of a peasantry and the extension of the natural ownership of land. But for the moment it is important to make the point clear about the nature of that narrowness. And that is why some light might be thrown on it in that tender, that intimate, that heart-to-heart talk between Mr. Saklatvala and the Dean of St. Paul's. Mr. Saklatvala is a sort of parody or extreme and extravagant exhibition of the point; that we really know nothing at all about the moral and philosophical elements that make up the Empire. It is quite obvious, of course, that he does not represent Battersea. But have we any way of knowing to what extent he represents India? It seems to me not impossible that the more impersonal and indefinite doctrines of Asia do form a soil for Bolshevism. Most of the eastern philosophy differs from the western theology in refusing to draw the line anywhere; and it would be a highly probable perversion of that instinct to refuse to draw the line between meum and tuum. I do not think the Indian gentleman is any judge of whether we in the West want to have a hedge round our fields or a wall round our gardens. And as I happen to hold that the very highest human thought and art consists almost entirely in drawing the line somewhere, though not in drawing it anywhere, I am completely confident that in this the western tendency is right and the eastern tendency is wrong. But, in any case, it seems to me that a rather sharp lesson to us is indicated in these two parallel cases of the Indian who grows into a Bolshevist in our dominions without our being able to influence his growth, and the French Canadian who remains a peasant in our dominions without our getting any sort of advantage out of his stability.

I do not profess to know very much about the French Canadians; but I know enough to know that most of the people who talk at large about the Empire know even less than I do. And the point about them is that they generally do not even try to know any more. The very vague picture that they always call up, of colonists doing wonders in all the corners of the world, never does, in fact, include the sort of thing that French Canadians can do, or might possibly show other people how to do. There is about all this fashionable fancy of colonization a very dangerous sort of hypocrisy. People tried to use the Over-seas Dominion as Eldorado while still using it as Botany Bay. They sent away people that they wanted to get rid of, and then added insult to injury by representing that the ends of the earth would be delighted to have them. And they called up a sort of fancy portrait of a person whose virtues and even vices were entirely suitable for founding an Empire, though apparently quite unsuitable for founding a family. The very language they used was misleading. They talked of such people as settlers; but the very last thing they ever expected them to do was to settle. They expected of them a sort of indistinct individualistic breaking of new ground, for which the world is less and less really concerned to-day. They sent an inconvenient nephew to hunt wild bisons in the streets of Toronto; just as they had sent any number of irrepressible Irish exiles to war with wild Redskins in the streets of New York. They incessantly repeated that what the world wants is pioneers, and had never even heard that what the world wants is peasants. There was a certain amount of sincere and natural sentiment about the wandering exile inheriting our traditions.

There was really no pretence that he was engaged in founding his own traditions. All the ideas that go with a secure social standing were absent from the very discussion; no one thought of the continuity, the customs, the religion, or the folklore of the future colonist. Above all, nobody ever conceived him as having any strong sense of private property. There was in the vague idea of his gaining something for the Empire always, if anything, the idea of his gaining what belonged to somebody else. I am not now discussing how wrong it was or whether it could in some cases be right; I am pointing out that nobody ever entertained the notion of the other sort of right; the special right of every man to his own. I doubt whether a word could be quoted emphasizing it even from the healthiest adventure story or the jolliest Jingo song. I quite appreciate all there is in such songs or stories that is really healthy or jolly. I am only pointing out that we have badly neglected something; and are now suffering from the neglect. And the worst aspect of the neglect was that we learnt nothing whatever from the peoples that were actually inside the Empire which we wished to glorify: nothing whatever from the Irish; nothing whatever from the French Canadian; nothing whatever even from the poor Hindoos. We have now reached a crisis in which we particularly require these neglected talents; and we do not even know how to set about learning them. And the explanation of this blunder, as of most blunders, is in the weakness which is called pride: in other words, it is in the tone taken by people like the Dean of St. Paul's.

Now there will be needed a large element of emigration in the solution of re-creating a peasantry in the modern world. I shall have more to say about the elements of the idea in the next section. But I believe that any scheme of the sort will have to be based on a totally different and indeed diametrically opposite spirit and principle to that which is commonly applied to emigration in England to-day. I think we need a new sort of inspiration, a new sort of appeal, a new sort of ordinary language even, before that solution will even help to solve anything. What we need is the ideal of Property, not merely of Progress — especially progress over other people's property. Utopia needs more frontiers, not less. And it is because we were weak in the ethics of property on the edges of Empire that our own society will not defend property as men defend a right. The Bolshevist is the sequel and punishment of the Buccaneer.

= = = = = = = = = = = = = = = = =

2. The Religion Of Small Property

We hear a great deal nowadays about the disadvantages of decorum, especially from those who are always telling us that women in the last generation were helpless and impotent, and then proceed to prove it by describing the tremendous and towering tyranny of Mrs. Grundy. Rather in the same way, they insist that Victorian women were especially soft and submissive. And it is rather unfortunate for them that, even in order to say so, they have to introduce the name of Queen Victoria. But it is more especially in connection with the indecorous in art and literature that the question arises, and it is now the fashion to argue as if there were no psychological basis for reticence at all. That is where the argument should end; but fortunately these thinkers do not know how to get to the end of an argument. I have heard it argued that there is no more harm in describing the violation of one Commandment than of another; but this is obviously a fallacy. There is at least a case in psychology for saying that certain images move the imagination to the weakening of the character. There is no case for saying that the mere contemplation of a kit of burglar's tools would inflame us all with a desire to break into houses. There is no possibility of pretending that the mere sight of means to murder our maiden aunt with a poker does really make the ill deed done. But what strikes me as most curious about the controversy is this: that while our fiction and journalism is largely breaking down the prohibitions for which there really was a logical case, in the consideration of human nature, they still very largely feel the pressure of prohibitions for which there was never any case at all. And the most curious thing about the criticism we hear directed against the Victorian Age is that it is never directed against the most arbitrary conventions of that age. One of these, which I remember very vividly in my youth, was the convention that there is something embarrassing or unfair about a man mentioning his religion. There was something of the same feeling about his mentioning his money. Now these things cannot possibly be

286

defended by the same psychological argument as the other. Nobody is moved to madness by the mere sight of a church spire, or finds uncontrollable emotions possess him at the thought of an archdeacon's hat. Yet there is still enough of that really irrational Victorian convention lingering in our life and literature to make it necessary to offer a defence, if not an apology, whenever an argument depends upon this fundamental fact in life.

Now when I remark that we want a type of colonization rather represented by the French Canadians, there are probably still a number of sly critics who would point the finger of detection at me and cry, as if they had caught me in something very naughty, "You believe in the French Canadians because they are Catholics"; which is in one sense not only true, but very nearly the whole truth. But in another sense it is not true at all; if it means that I exercise no independent judgment in perceiving that this is really what we do want. Now when this difficulty and misunderstanding arises, there is only one practical way of meeting it in the present state of public information, or lack of information. It is to call what is generally described as an impartial witness; though it is quite probable that he is far less impartial than I am. What is really important about him is that, if he were partial, he would be partial on the other side.

The dear old Daily News, of the days of my youth, on which I wrote happily for many years and had so many good and admirable friends, cannot be accused as yet as being an organ of the Jesuits. It was, and is, as every one knows, the organ of the Nonconformists. Dr. Clifford brandished his teapot there when he was selling it in order to demonstrate, by one symbolical act, that he had long been a teetotaller and was now a Passive Resister. We may be pardoned for smiling at this aspect of the matter; but there are many other aspects which are real and worthy of all possible respect. The tradition of the old Puritan ideal does really descend to this paper; and multitudes of honest and hard-thinking Radicals read it in my youth and read it still.

I therefore think that the following remarks which appeared recently in the Daily News, in an article by Mr. Hugh Martin, writing from Toronto, are rather remarkable. He begins by saying that the Anglo-Saxon has got too proud to bend his back; but the curious thing is that he goes on to suggest, almost in so many words, that the backs of the French Canadians are actually strengthened, not only by being bent over rustic spades, but even by being bent before superstitious altars. I am very anxious not to do my impartial witness an unfair damage in the matter; so I may be excused if I quote his own words at some little length. After saying that the Anglo-Saxons are drawn away to the United States, or at any rate to the industrial cities, he remarks that the French are of course very numerous in Quebec and elsewhere, but that it is not here that the notable development is taking place, and that Montreal, being a large city, is showing signs of the slackening to be seen in other large cities.

"Now look at the other picture. The race that is going ahead is the French race. . . . In Quebec, where there are nearly 2,000,000 Canadians of French origin in a population of 2,350,000, that might have been expected. But as a matter of fact it is not in Quebec that the French are making good most conspicuously . . . nor in Nova Scotia and New Brunswick is the comparative success of the French stock most marked. They are doing splendidly on the land and raising prodigious families. A family of twelve is quite common, and I could name several cases where there have been twenty, who all lived. The day may come when they will equal or outnumber the Scotch, but that is some way ahead. If you want to see what French stock can still achieve, you should go to the northern part of this province of Ontario. It is doing pioneer work. It is bending its back as men did in the old days. It is multiplying and staying on the soil. It is content to be happy without being rich.

"Though I am not a religious man myself, I must confess I think religion has a good deal to do with it. These French Canadians are more Catholic than the Pope. You might call a good many of them desperately ignorant and desperately superstitious. They seem to me to be a century behind the times and a century nearer happiness."

These seem to me, I repeat, to be rather remarkable words; remarkable if they appeared anywhere, arresting and astonishing when they appear in the traditional paper of the Manchester Radicals and the nineteenth-century Nonconformists. The words are splendidly straightforward and unaffected in their literary form; they have a clear ring of sincerity and experience, and they are all the more convincing because they are written by somebody who does not share my own desperate ignorance and desperate superstition. But he proceeds to suggest a reason, and incidentally to make his own independence in the matter quite clear.

"Apart from the fact that their women bear an incredible number of children, you have this other consequence of their submission to the priest, that a social organism is created, which is of incalculable value in the backwoods. The church, the school, the cure, hold each little group together as a unit. Do not think for a moment that I believe a general spread of Catholicism would turn us back into a pioneer people. One might just as reasonably recommend a return to early Scottish Protestantism. I merely record the fact that the simplicity of these people is proving their salvation and is one of the most hopeful things in Canada to-day."

Of course, there are a good many things of an incidental kind that a person with my views might comment on in that passage. I might go off at a gallop on the highly interesting comparison with early Scottish Protestantism. Very early Scottish Protestantism, like very early English Protestantism, consisted chiefly of loot. But if we take it as referring to the perfectly pure and sincere enthusiasm of many Covenanters or early Calvinists, we come upon the contrast that is the point of the whole matter. Early Puritanism was pure Puritanism; but the purer it is the more early it seems. We cannot imagine it as a good thing and also a modern thing. It might have been one of the most honest things in Scotland then. But nobody would be found calling it one of the most hopeful things in Canada to-day. If John Knox appeared to-morrow in the pulpit of St. Giles, he would be a stickit minister. He would be regarded as a raving savage because of his ignorance of German metaphysics. That comparison does not meet the extraordinary case of the thing that is older than Knox and yet also newer than Knox. Or again, I might point out that the common connotation of "submission to the priest" is misleading, even if it is true. It is like talking of the Charge of the Light Brigade as the submission to Lord Raglan. It is still more like talking about the storming of Jerusalem as the submission to the Count of Bouillon. In one sense it is quite true; in another it is very untrue. But I have not the smallest desire here to disturb the impartiality of my witness. I have not the smallest intention of using any of the tortures of the Inquisition to make him admit anything that he did not wish to admit. The admission as it stands seems to me very remarkable; not so much because it is a tribute to Frenchmen as colonists as because it is a tribute to colonists as pious and devout people. But what concerns me most of all in the general discussion of my own theme is the insistence on stability. They are staying on the soil; they are a social organism; they are held together as a unit. That is the new note which I think is needed in all talk of colonization, before it can again be any part of the hope of the world.

A recent description of the Happy Factory, as it exists in America or will exist in Utopia, rose from height to height of ideality until it ended with a sort of hush, as of the ultimate opening of the heavens, and these words about the workman, "He turns out for his homeward journey like a member of the Stock Exchange." Any attempt to imagine humanity in its final perfection always has about it something faintly unreal, as being too good for this world; but the visionary light that breaks from the cloud, in that last phrase, accentuates clearly the contrast which is to be drawn between such a condition and that of the labour of common men. Adam left Eden as a gardener; but he will set out for his homeward journey like a member of the Stock Exchange. St. Joseph was a carpenter; but he will be raised again as a stockbroker. Giotto was a shepherd; for he was not yet worthy to be a stockbroker. Shakespeare was an actor; but he dreamed day and night of being a stockbroker. Burns was a ploughman; but if he sang at the plough, how much more appropriately he would have sung in the Stock Exchange. It is assumed in this kind of argument that all humanity has consciously or unconsciously hoped for this consummation; and that if men were not brokers, it was because they were not able to broke. But this remarkable passage in Sir Ernest Benn's exposition has another application besides the obvious one. A stockbroker in one sense really is a very poetical figure. In one sense he is as poetical as Shakespeare, and his ideal poet, since he does give to airy nothing a local habitation and a name. He does deal to a great extent in what economists (in their poetical way) describe as imaginaries. When he exchanges two thousand Patagonian Pumpkins for one thousand shares in Alaskan Whale Blubber, he does not demand the sensual satisfaction of eating the pumpkin or need to behold the whale with the gross eye of flesh. It is quite possible that there are no pumpkins; and if there is somewhere such a thing as a whale, it is very unlikely to obtrude itself upon the conversation in the Stock Exchange. Now what is the matter with the financial world is that it is a great deal too full of imagination, in the sense of fiction. And when we react against it, we naturally in the first place react into realism. When the stockbroker homeward plods his weary way and leaves the world to darkness and Sir Ernest Benn, we are disposed to insist that it is indeed he who has the darkness and we who have the daylight. He has not only the darkness but the dreams, and all the unreal leviathans and unearthly pumpkins pass before him like a mere scroll of symbols in the dreams of the Old Testament. But when the small proprietor grows pumpkins, they really are pumpkins, and sometimes quite a large pumpkin for quite a small proprietor. If he should ever have occasion to grow whales (which seems improbable) they would either be real whales or they would be of no use to him. We naturally grow a little impatient, under these conditions, when people who call themselves practical scoff at the small proprietor as if he were a minor poet. Nevertheless, there is another side to the case, and there is a sense in which the small proprietor had better be a minor poet, or at least a mystic. Nay, there is even a sort of queer paradoxical sense in which the stockbroker is a man of business.

It is to that other side of small property, as exemplified in the French Canadians, and an article on them in the Daily News, that I devoted my last remarks. The really practical point in that highly interesting statement is, that in this case, being progressive is actually identified with being what is called static. In this case, by a strange paradox, a pioneer is really d settler. In this case, by a still stranger paradox, a settler is a person who really settles. It will be noted that the success of the experiment is actually founded on a certain power of striking root; which we might almost call rapid tradition, as others talk of rapid transit. And indeed the ground under the pioneer's feet can only be made solid by being made sacred. It is only religion that can thus rapidly give a sort of accumulated power of culture and legend to something that is crude or incomplete. It sounds like a joke to say that baptizing a baby makes the baby venerable; it suggests the old joke of the baby with spectacles who died an enfeebled old dotard at five. Yet it is profoundly true that something is added that is not only something to be venerated, but something partly to be venerated for its antiquity — that is, for the unfathomable depth of its humanity. In a sense a new world can be baptized as a new baby is baptized, and become a part of an ancient order not merely on the map but in the mind. Instead of crude people merely extending their crudity, and calling that colonization, it would be possible for people to cultivate the soil as they cultivate the soul. But for this it is necessary to have a respect for the soil as well as for the soul; and even a reverence for it, as having some associations with holy things. But for that purpose we need some sense of carrying holy things with us and taking them home with us; not merely the feeling that holiness may exist as a hope. In the most exalted phrase, we need a real presence. In the most popular phrase, we need something that is always on the spot.

That is, we want something that is always on the spot, and not only beyond the horizon. The pioneer instinct is beginning to fail, as a well-known traveller recently complained, but I doubt whether he could tell us the reason. It is even possible that he will not understand it, in one radiant burst of joyful comprehension, if I tell him that I am all in favour of a wild-goose chase, so long as he really believes that the wild goose is the bird of paradise; but that it is necessary to hunt it with the hounds of heaven. If it be barely possible that this does not seem quite clear to him, I will explain that the traveller must possess something as well as pursue something, or he will not even know what to pursue. It is not enough always to follow the gleam: it is necessary sometimes to rest in the glow; to feel something sacred in the glow of the camp fire as well as the gleam of the polar star. And that same mysterious and to some divided voice, which alone tells that we have here no abiding city, is the only voice which within the limits of this world can build up cities that abide.

As I said at the beginning of this section, it is futile to pretend that such a faith is not a fundamental of the true change. But its practical relation to the reconstruction of property is that, unless we understand this spirit, we cannot now relieve congestion with colonization. People will prefer the mere nomadism of the town to the mere nomadism of the wilderness. They will not tolerate emigration if it merely means being moved on by the politicians as they have been moved on by the policemen. They will prefer bread and circuses to locusts and wild honey, so long as the forerunner does not know for what God he prepares the way.

But even if we put aside for the moment the strictly spiritual ideals involved in the change, we must admit that there are secular ideals involved which must be positive and not merely comparative, like the ideal of progress. We are sometimes taunted with setting against all other Utopias what is in truth the most impossible Utopia; with describing a Merry Peasant who cannot exist except on the stage, with depending on a China Shepherdess who never was seen except on the mantelpiece. If we are indeed presenting impossible portraits of an ideal humanity, we are not alone in that. Not only the Socialists but also the Capitalists parade before us their imaginary and ideal figures, and the Capitalists if possible more than the Socialists. For once that we read of the last Earthly Paradise of Mr. Wells, where men and women move gracefully in simple garments and keep their tempers in a way in which we in this world sometimes find difficult (even when we are the authors of Utopian novels), for once that we see the ideal figure of that vision, we see ten times a day the ideal figure of the commercial advertisers. We are told to "Be Like This Man," or to imitate an aggressive person pointing his finger at us in a very rude manner for one who regards himself as a pattern to the young. Yet it is entirely an ideal portrait; it is very unlikely (we are glad to say) that any of us will develop a chin or a finger of that obtrusive type. But we do not blame either the Capitalists or the Socialists for setting up a type or talismanic figure to fix the imagination. We do not wonder at their presenting the perfect person for our admiration; we only wonder at the person they admire. And it is quite true that, in our movement as much as any other, there must be a certain amount of this romantic picture-making. Men have never done anything in the world without it; but ours is much more of a reality as well as a romance than the dreams of the other romantics. There cannot be a nation of millionaires, and there has never yet been a nation of Utopian comrades; but there have been any number of nations of tolerably contented peasants. In this connection, however, the point is that if we do not directly demand the religion of small property, we must at least demand the poetry of small property. It is a thing about

293

which it is definitely and even urgently practical to be poetical. And it is those who blame us for being poetical who do not really see the practical problem.

For the practical problem is the goal. The pioneer notion has weakened like the progressive notion, and for the same reason. People could go on talking about progress so long as they were not merely thinking about progress. Progressives really had in their minds some notion of a purpose in progress; and even the most practical pioneer had some vague and shadowy idea of what he wanted. The Progressives trusted the tendency of their time, because they did believe, or at least had believed, in a body of democratic doctrines which they supposed to be in process of establishment. And the pioneers and empire-builders were filled with hope and courage because, to do them justice, most of them did at least in some dim way believe that the flag they carried stood for law and liberty, and a higher civilization. They were therefore in search of something and not merely in search of searching. They subconsciously conceived an end of travel and not endless travelling; they were not only breaking through a jungle but building a city. They knew more or less the style of architecture in which it would be built, and they honestly believed it was the best style of architecture in the world. The spirit of adventure has failed because it has been left to adventurers. Adventure for adventure's sake became like art for art's sake. Those who had lost all sense of aim lost all sense of art and even of accident. The time has come in every department, but especially in our department, to make once again vivid and solid the aim of political progress or colonial adventure. Even if we picture the goal of the pilgrimage as a sort of peasant paradise, it will be far more practical than setting out on a pilgrimage which has no goal. But it is yet more practical to insist that we do not want to insist only on what are called the qualities of a pioneer; that we do not want to describe merely the virtues that achieve adventures. We want men to think, not merely of a place which they would be interested to find, but of a place where they would be contented to stay. Those who wish merely to arouse again the social hopes of the nineteenth century must offer not an endless hope, but the hope of an end. Those who wish to continue the building of the old colonial idea must leave off telling us that the Church of Empire is founded entirely on the rolling stone. For it is a sin against the reason to tell men that to travel hopefully is better than to arrive; and when once they believe it, they travel hopefully no longer.

================

VI. A Summary

I once debated with a learned man who had a curious fancy for arranging the correspondence in mathematical patterns; first a thousand words each and then a hundred words each — and then altering them all to another pattern. I accepted as I would always accept a challenge, especially an apparent appeal for fairness, but I was tempted to tell him how utterly unworkable this mechanical method is for a living thing like argument. Obviously a man might need a thousand words to reply to ten words. Suppose I began the philosophic dialogue by saying, "You strangle babies." He would naturally reply, "Nonsense — I never strangled any babies." And even in that obvious ejaculation he has already used twice as many words as I have. It is impossible to have real debate without digression. Every definition will look like a digression. Suppose somebody puts to me some journalistic statement, say, "Spanish Jesuits denounced in Parliament." I cannot deal with it without explaining to the journalist where I differ from him about the atmosphere and implication of each term in turn. I cannot answer quickly if I am just discovering slowly that the man suffers from a series of extraordinary delusions: as (1) that Parliament is a popular representative assembly; (2) that Spain is an effete and decadent country; or (3) that a Spanish Jesuit is a sort of soft-footed court chaplain; whereas it was a Spanish Jesuit who anticipated the whole democratic theory of our day, and actually hurled it as a defiance against the divine right of kings. Each of these explanations would have to be a digression, and each would be necessary. Now in this book I am well aware that there are many digressions that may not at first sight seem to be necessary. For I have had to construct it out of what was originally a sort of controversial causerie; and it has proved impossible to cut down the causerie and only leave the controversy. Moreover, no man can controvert with many foes without going into many subjects, as every one knows who has been heckled. And on this occasion I was, I am happy to say, being heckled by many foes who were also friends. I was discharging the double function of writing essays and of talking over the tea-table, or preferably over the tavern table. To turn this sort of mixture of a gossip and a gospel into anything like a grammar of Distributism has been quite impossible. But I fancy that, even considered as a string of essays, it appears more inconsequent than it really is; and many may read the essays without quite seeing the string. I have decided, therefore, to add this last essay merely in order to sum up the intention of the whole; even if the summary be only a recapitulation. I have had a reason for many of my digressions, which may not appear until the whole is seen in some sort of perspective; and where the digression has no such justification, but was due to a desire to answer a friend or (what is even worse) a disposition towards idle and unseemly mirth, I can only apologize sincerely to the scientific reader and promise to do my best to make this final summary as dull as possible.

If we proceed as at present in a proper orderly fashion, the very idea of property will vanish. It is not revolutionary violence that will destroy it. It is rather the desperate and reckless habit of not having a revolution. The world will be occupied, or rather is already occupied, by two powers which are now one power. I speak, of course, of that part of the world that is covered by our system, and that part of the history of the world which will last very much longer than our time. Sooner or later, no doubt, men would rediscover so natural a pleasure as property. But it might be discovered after ages, like those ages filled with pagan slavery. It might be discovered after a long decline of our whole civilization. Barbarians might rediscover it and imagine it was a new thing.

Anyhow, the prospect is a progress towards the complete combination of two combinations. They are both powers that believe only in combination; and have never understood or even heard that there is any dignity in division. They have never had the imagination to understand the idea of Genesis and the great myths: that Creation itself was division. The beginning of the world was the division of heaven and earth; the beginning of humanity was the division of man and woman. But these flat and platitudinous minds can never see the difference between the creative cleavage of Adam and Eve and the destructive cleavage of Cain and Abel. Anyhow, these powers or minds are now both in the same mood; and it is a mood of disliking all division, and therefore all distribution. They believe in unity, in unanimity, in harmony. One of these powers is State Socialism and the other is Big Business.

They are already one spirit; they will soon be one body. For, disbelieving in division, they cannot remain divided; believing only in combination, they will themselves combine. At present one of them calls it Solidarity and the other calls it Consolidation. It would seem that we have only to wait while both monsters are taught to say Consolidarity. But, whatever it is called, there will be no doubt about the character of the world which they will have made between them. It is becoming more and more fixed and familiar. It will be a world of organization, or syndication, of standardization. People will be able to get hats, houses, holidays, and patent medicines of a recognized and universal pattern; they will be fed, clothed, educated, and examined by a wide and elaborate system; but if you were to ask them at any given moment whether the agency which housed or hatted them was still merely mercantile or had become municipal, they probably would not know, and they possibly would not care.

Many believe that humanity will be happy in this new peace; that classes can be reconciled and souls set at rest. I do not think things will be quite so bad as that. But I admit that there are many things which may make possible such a catastrophe of contentment. Men in large numbers have submitted to slavery; men submit naturally to government, and perhaps even especially to despotic government. But I take it as obvious to any intelligent person that this government will be something more than despotic. It is the very essence of the Trust that it has the power, not only to extinguish military rivalry or mob rebellion as has the State, but also the power to crush any new custom or costume or craft or private enterprise that it does not choose to like. Militarism can only prevent people from fighting; but monopoly can prevent them from buying or selling anything except the article (generally the inferior article) having the trade mark of the monopoly. If anything can be inferred from history and human nature, it is absolutely certain that the despotism will grow more and more despotic, and that the article will grow more and more inferior. There is no conceivable argument from psychology, by which it can be pretended that people preserving such a power, generation after generation, would not abuse it more and more, or neglect everything else more and more. We know what far less rigid rule has become, even when founded by spirited and intelligent rulers.

We can darkly guess the effect of larger powers in the hands of lesser men. And if the name of Caesar came at last to stand for all that we call Byzantine, exactly what degree of dullness are we to anticipate when the name of Harrod shall sound even duller than it does? If China passed into a proverb at last for stiffness and monotony after being nourished for centuries by Confucius, what will be the condition of the brains that have been nourished for centuries by Callisthenes?

I leave out there the particular case of my own country, where we are threatened not with a long decline, but rather with an unpleasantly rapid collapse. But taking monopolist capitalism in a country where it is still in the vulgar sense successful, as in the United States, we only see more clearly, and on a more colossal scale, the long and descending perspectives that point down to Byzantium or Pekin. It is perfectly obvious that the whole business is a machine for manufacturing tenth-rate things, and keeping people ignorant of first-rate things. Most civilized systems have declined from a height; but this starts on a low level and in a flat place; and what it would be like when it had really crushed all its critics and rivals and made its monopoly watertight for two hundred years, the most morbid imagination will find it hard to imagine. But whatever the last stage of the story, no sane man any longer doubts that we are seeing the first stages of it. There is no longer any difference in tone and type between collectivist and ordinary commercial order; commerce has its officialism and communism has its organization. Private things are already public in the worst sense of the word; that is, they are impersonal and dehumanized. Public things are already private in the worst sense of the word; that is, they are mysterious and secretive and largely corrupt. The new sort of Business Government will combine everything that is bad in all the plans for a better world. There will be no eccentricity; no humour; no noble disdain of the world. There will be nothing but a loathsome thing called Social Service; which means slavery without loyalty. This Service will be one of the ideals. I forgot to mention that there will be ideals. All the wealthiest men in the movement have made it quite clear that they are in possession of a number of these little comforts. People always have ideals when they can no longer have ideas.

The philanthropists in question will probably be surprised to learn that some of us regard this prospect very much as we should regard the theory that we are to be evolved back into apes. We therefore consider whether it is even yet conceivable to restore that long-forgotten thing called Self-Government: that is, the power of the citizen in some degree to direct his own life and construct his own environment; to eat what he likes, to wear what he chooses, and to have (what the Trust must of necessity deny him) a range of choice. In these notes upon the notion, I have been concerned to ask whether it is possible to escape from this enormous evil of simplification or centralization, and what I have said is best summed up under two heads or in two parallel statements. They may seem to some to contradict each other, but they really confirm each other.

First, I say that this is a thing that could be done by people. It is not a thing that can be done to people. That is where it differs from nearly all Socialist schemes as it does from plutocratic philanthropy. I do not say that I, regarding this prospect with hatred and contempt, can save them from it. I say that they can save me from it, and themselves from it, if they also regard it with hatred and contempt. But it must be done in the spirit of a religion, of a revolution, and (I will add) of a renunciation. They must want to do it as they want to drive invaders out of a country or to stop the spread of a plague. And in this respect our critics have a curious way of arguing in a circle. They ask why we trouble to denounce what we cannot destroy; and offer an ideal we cannot attain. They say we are merely throwing away dirty water before we can get clean; or rather that we are merely analysing the animalculae in the dirty water, while we do not even venture to throw it away. Why do we make men discontented with conditions with which they must be content? Why revile an intolerable slavery that must be tolerated? But when we in turn ask why our ideal is impossible or why the evil is indestructible, they answer in effect, "Because you cannot persuade people to want it destroyed." Possibly; but, on their own showing, they cannot blame us because we try. They cannot say that people do not hate plutocracy enough to kill it; and then blame us for asking them to look at it enough to hate it. If they will not attack it until they hate it, then we are doing the most practical thing we can do, in showing it to be hateful. A

300

moral movement must begin somewhere; but I do most positively postulate that there must be a moral movement. This is not a financial flutter or a police regulation or a private bill or a detail of book-keeping. It is a mighty effort of the will of man, like the throwing off of any other great evil, or it is nothing. I say that if men will fight for this they may win; I have nowhere suggested that there is any way of winning without fighting.

Under this heading I have considered in their place, for instance, the possibility of an organized boycott of big shops. Undoubtedly it would be some sacrifice to boycott big shops; it would be some trouble to seek out small shops. But it would be about a hundredth part of the sacrifice and trouble that has often been shown by masses of men making some patriotic or religious protest — when they really wanted to protest. Under the same general rule, I have remarked that a real life on the land, men not only dwelling on the land but living off it, would be an adventure involving both stubbornness and abnegation. But it would not be half so ascetic as the sort of adventure which it is a commonplace to attribute to colonists and empire-builders; it is nothing to what has been normally shown by millions of soldiers and monks. Only it is true that monks have a faith, that soldiers have a flag, and that even empire-builders were presumably under the impression that they could assist the Empire. But it does not seem to me quite inconceivable, in the varieties of religious experience, that men might take as much notice of earth as monks do of heaven; that people might really believe in the spades that create as well as in the swords that destroy; and that the English who have colonized everywhere else might begin to colonize England.

Having thus admitted, or rather insisted, that this thing cannot be done unless people do really think it worth doing, I then proceeded to suggest that, even in these different departments, there are more people who think it worth doing than is noticed by the people who do not think it worth noticing. Thus, even in the crowds that throng the big shops, you do in fact hear a vast amount of grumbling at the big shops — not so much because they are big as because they are bad. But these real criticisms are disconnected, while the unreal puffs and praises are connected, like any other conspiracy. When the millionaire owning the stores is criticized, it is by his customers. When he is handsomely complimented, it is by himself. But when he is cursed, it is in the inner chamber; when he is praised (by himself) it is proclaimed from the house-tops. That is what is meant by publicity — a voice loud enough to drown any remarks made by the public.

In the case of the land, as in the case of the shops, I went on to point out that there is, if not a moral agitation, at least the materials of a moral agitation. Just as a discontent with the shops lingers even among those who are shopping, so a desire for the land lingers even in those who are hardly allowed to walk on the ground. I gave the instance of the slum population of Limehouse, who were forcibly lifted into high flats, bitterly lamenting the loss of the funny little farmyards they had constructed for themselves in the corners of their slum. It seems absurd to say of a country that none of its people could be countrymen, when even its cockneys try to be countrymen. I also noted that, in the case of the country, there is now a general discontent, in landlords as well as tenants. Everything seems to point to a simpler life of one man one field, free as far as possible of the complications of rent and labour, especially when the rent is so often unpaid or unprofitable, and the labourers are so often on strike or on the dole. Here again there may often be a million individuals feeling like this; but the million has not become a mob; for a mob is a moral thing. But I will never be so unpatriotic as to suggest that the English could never conduct an agrarian war in England as the Irish did in Ireland. Generally, therefore, under this first principle, the thing would most certainly have to be preached rather like a Crusade; but it is quite untrue and unhistorical to say, as a rule, that when once the Crusade is preached, there are no Crusaders.

And my second general principle, which may seem contradictory but is confirmatory, is this. I think the thing would have to be done step by step and with patience and partial concessions. I think this, not because I have any faith whatever in the silly cult of slowness that is sometimes called evolution, but because of the peculiar circumstances of the case. First, mobs may loot and burn and rob the rich man, very much to his spiritual edification and benefit. They may not unnaturally do it, almost absentmindedly, when they are thinking of something else, such as a dislike of Jews or Huguenots. But it would never do for us to give very violent shocks to the sentiment of property, even where it

302

is very ill-placed or ill-proportioned; for that happens to be the very sentiment we are trying to revive. As a matter of psychology, it would be foolish to insult even an unfeminine feminist in order to awaken a delicate chivalry towards females. It would be unwise to use a sacred image as a club with which to thump an Iconoclast and teach him not to touch the holy images. Where the old-fashioned feeling of property is still honest, I think it should be dealt with by degrees and with some consideration. Where the sense of property does not exist at all, as in millionaires, it might well be regarded rather differently; there it would become a question of whether property procured in certain ways is property at all. As for the case of cornering and making monopolies in restraint of trade, that falls under the first of my two principles. It is simply a question of whether we have the moral courage to punish what is certainly immoral. There is no more doubt about these operations of high finance than there is about piracy on the high seas. It is merely a case of a country being so disorderly and ill-governed that it becomes infested with pirates. I have, therefore, in this book treated of Trusts and Anti-Trust Law as a matter, not merely for the popular protest of a boycott or a strike, but for the direct action of the State against criminals. But when the criminals are stronger than the State, any attempt to punish them will be certainly called a rebellion and may rightly be called a Crusade.

Recurring to the second principle, however, there is another and less abstract reason for recognizing that the goal must be reached by stages. I have here had to consider several things that may bring us a stage nearer to Distributism, even if they are in themselves not very satisfactory to ardent or austere Distributists. I took the examples of a Ford car, which may be made by mass production but is used for individual adventure; for, after all, a private car is more private than a train or a tram. I also took the example of a general supply of electricity, which might lead to many little workshops having a chance for the first time. I do not claim that all Distributists would agree with me in my decision here; but on the whole I am inclined to decide that we should use these things to break up the hopeless block of concentrated capital and management, even if we urge their abandonment when they have done their work. We are concerned to produce a particular sort of men, the sort of men who will not worship machines even if they use machines. But it is essential to insist at every stage that we hold ourselves free not only to cease worshipping machines, but to cease using them. It was in this connection that I criticized certain remarks of Mr. Ford and the whole of that idea of standardization which he may be said to represent. But everywhere I recognize a difference between the methods we may use to produce a saner society and the things which that saner society might itself be sane enough to do. For instance, a people who had really found out what fun it is to make things would never want to make most of them with a machine. Sculptors do not want to turn a statue out with a lathe or painters to print off a picture as a pattern, and a craftsman who was really capable of making pots or pans would be no readier to condescend to what is called manufacturing them. It is odd, by the way, that the very word "manufacture" means the opposite of what it is supposed to mean. It is itself a testimony to a better time when it did not mean the work of a modern factory. In the strict meaning of words, a sculptor does manufacture a statue, and a factory worker does not manufacture a screw.

But, anyhow, a world in which there were many independent men would probably be a world in which there were more individual craftsmen. When we have created anything like such a world, we may trust it to feel more than the modern world does the danger of machinery deadening creation, and the value of what it deadens. And I suggested that such a world might very well make special provision about machines, as we all do about weapons; admitting them for particular purposes, but keeping watch on them in particular ways.

But all that belongs to the later stage of improvement, when the commonwealth of free men already exists; I do not think it inconsistent with using any instruments that are innocent in themselves in order to help such citizens to find a footing. I have also noted that just as I do not think machinery an immoral instrument in itself, so I do not think State action an immoral instrument in itself. The State might do a great deal in the first stages, especially by education in the new and necessary crafts and labours, by subsidy or tariff to protect distributive experiments and by special laws, such as the taxation of contracts. All these are covered by what I call the second principle, that we may use intermediate or imperfect instruments; but it goes along with the first principle, that we must be perfect not only in our patience, but in our passion and our enduring indignation.

Lastly, there are the ordinary and obvious problems like that of population, and in that connection I fully concede that the process may sooner or later involve an element of emigration. But I think the emigration must be undertaken by those who understand the new England, and not by those who want to escape from it or from the necessity of it. Men must realize the new meaning of the old phrase, "the sacredness of private property." There must be a spirit that will make the colonist feel at home and not abroad. And there, I admit, there is a difficulty; for I confess I know only one thing that will thus give to a new soil the sanctity of something already old and full of mystical affections. And that thing is a shrine — the real presence of a sacramental religion.

Thus, unavoidably, I end on the note of another controversy — a controversy that I have no idea of pursuing here. But I should not be honest if I did not mention it, and whatever be the case in that connection it is impossible to deny that there is a doctrine behind the whole of our political position. It is not necessarily the doctrine of the religious authority which I myself receive; but it cannot be denied that it must in a sense be religious. That is to say, it must at least have some reference to an ultimate view of the universe and especially of the nature of man. Those who are thus ready to see property atrophied would ultimately be ready to see arms and legs amputated. They really believe that these could become extinct organs like the appendix. In other words, there is indeed a fundamental difference between my own view and that vision of man as a merely intermediate and changing thing — a Link, if not a Missing Link. The creature, it is claimed, once went on four legs and now goes on two legs. The obvious inference would be that the next stage of evolution will be for a man to stand on one leg. And this will be of very great value to the capitalist or bureaucratic powers that are now to take charge of him. It will mean, for one thing, that only half the number of boots need be supplied to the working classes. It will mean that all wages will be of a one-legged sort. But I would testify at the end, as at the beginning, that I believe in Man standing on two legs and requiring two boots, and that I desire them to be his own boots. You may call it conservative to want this. You may call it revolutionary to

305

attempt to get it. But if that is conservative, I am conservative; if that is revolutionary, I am revolutionary — but too democratic to be evolutionary, anyhow.

The thing behind Bolshevism and many other modern things is a new doubt. It is not merely a doubt about God; it is rather specially a doubt about Man. The old morality, the Christian religion, the Catholic Church, differed from all this new mentality because it really believed in the rights of men. That is, it believed that ordinary men were clothed with powers and privileges and a kind of authority. Thus the ordinary man had a right to deal with dead matter, up to a given point; that is the right of property. Thus the ordinary man had a right to rule the other animals within reason; that is the objection to vegetarianism and many other things. The ordinary man had a right to judge about his own health, and what risks he would take with the ordinary things of his environment; that is the objection to Prohibition and many other things. The ordinary man had a right to judge of his children's health, and generally to bring up children to the best of his ability; that is the objection to many interpretations of modern State education. Now in these primary things in which the old religion trusted a man, the new philosophy utterly distrusts a man. It insists that he must be a very rare sort of man to have any rights in these matters; and when he is the rare sort, he has the right to rule others even more than himself. It is this profound scepticism about the common man that is the common point in the most contradictory elements of modern thought. That is why Mr. Bernard Shaw wants to evolve a new animal that shall live longer and grow wiser than man. That is why Mr. Sidney Webb wants to herd the men that exist like sheep, or animals much more foolish than man. They are not rebelling against an abnormal tyranny; they are rebelling against what they think is a normal tyranny — the tyranny of the normal. They are not in revolt against the King. They are in revolt against the Citizen. The old revolutionist, when he stood on the roof (like the revolutionist in The Dynamiter) and looked over the city, used to say to himself, "Think how the princes and nobles revel in their palaces; think how the captains and cohorts ride the streets and trample on the people." But the new revolutionist is not brooding on that. He is saying, "Think of all those stupid men in vulgar villas or ignorant slums. Think how badly they teach their children; think how they do the wrong thing to the dog and offend the feelings of the parrot." In short, these sages, rightly or wrongly, cannot trust the normal man to rule in the home, and most certainly do not want him to rule in the State. They do not really want to give him any political power. They are willing to give him a vote, because they have long discovered that it need not give him any power. They are not willing to give him a house, or a wife, or a child, or a dog, or a cow, or a piece of land, because these things really do give him power.

Now we wish it to be understood that our policy is to give him power by giving him these things. We wish to insist that this is the real moral division underlying all our disputes, and perhaps the only one really worth disputing. We are far from denying, especially at this time, that there is much to be said on the other side. We alone, perhaps, are likely to insist in the full sense that the average respectable citizen ought to have something to rule. We alone, to the same extent and for the same reason, have the right to call ourselves democratic. A republic used to be called a nation of kings, and in our republic the kings really have kingdoms. All modern governments, Prussian or Russian, all modern movements, Capitalist or Socialist, are taking away that kingdom from the king. Because they dislike the independence of that kingdom, they are against property. Because they dislike the loyalty of that kingdom, they are against marriage.

It is therefore with a somewhat sad amusement that I note the soaring visions that accompany the sinking wages. I observe that the social prophets are still offering the homeless something much higher and purer than a home, and promising a supernormal superiority to people who are not allowed to be normal. I am quite content to dream of the old drudgery of democracy, by which as much as possible of a human life should be given to every human being; while the brilliant author of The First Men in the Moon will doubtless be soon deriding us in a romance called The Last Men on the Earth. And indeed I do believe that when they lose the pride of personal ownership they will lose something that belongs to their erect posture and to their footing and poise upon the planet. Meanwhile I sit amid droves of overdriven clerks and underpaid workmen in a tube or a tram; I read of the great conception of Men Like Gods and I wonder when men will be like men.

Utopia of Usurers and other Essays

A Song Of Swords

"A drove of cattle came into a village called Swords; and was stopped by the rioters." — Daily Paper.

In the place called Swords on the Irish road It is told for a new renown How we held the horns of the cattle, and how We will hold the horns of the devils now Ere the lord of hell with the horn on his brow Is crowned in Dublin town.

Light in the East and light in the West, And light on the cruel lords, On the souls that suddenly all men knew, And the green flag flew and the red flag flew, And many a wheel of the world stopped, too, When the cattle were stopped at Swords.

Be they sinners or less than saints That smite in the street for rage, We know where the shame shines bright; we know You that they smite at, you their foe, Lords of the lawless wage and low, This is your lawful wage.

You pinched a child to a torture price That you dared not name in words; So black a jest was the silver bit That your own speech shook for the shame of it, And the coward was plain as a cow they hit When the cattle have strayed at Swords.

The wheel of the torrent of wives went round To break men's brotherhood; You gave the good Irish blood to grease The clubs of your country's enemies; you saw the brave man beat to the knees: And you saw that it was good.

The rope of the rich is long and long — The longest of hangmen's cords; But the kings and crowds are holding their breath, In a giant shadow o'er all beneath Where God stands holding the scales of Death Between the cattle and Swords.

Haply the lords that hire and lend The lowest of all men's lords, Who sell their kind like kine at a fair, Will find no head of their cattle there; But faces of men where cattle were: Faces of men — and Swords.

Utopia Of Usurers

I. Art and Advertisement

I propose, subject to the patience of the reader, to devote two or three articles to prophecy. Like all healthy-minded prophets, sacred and profane, I can only prophesy when I am in a rage and think things look ugly for everybody. And like all healthy-minded prophets, I prophesy in the hope that my prophecy may not come true. For the prediction made by the true soothsayer is like the warning given by a good doctor. And the doctor has really triumphed when the patient he condemned to death has revived to life. The threat is justified at the very moment when it is falsified. Now I have said again and again (and I shall continue to say again and again on all the most inappropriate occasions) that we must hit Capitalism, and hit it hard, for the plain and definite reason that it is growing stronger. Most of the excuses which serve the capitalists as masks are, of course, the excuses of hypocrites. They lie when they claim philanthropy; they no more feel any particular love of men than Albu felt an affection for Chinamen. They lie when they say they have reached their position through their own organising ability. They generally have to pay men to organise the mine, exactly as they pay men to go down it. They often lie about the present wealth, as they generally lie about their past poverty. But when they say that they are going in for a "constructive social policy," they do not lie. They really are going in for a constructive social policy. And we must go in for an equally destructive social policy; and destroy, while it is still half-constructed, the accursed thing which they construct.

The Example of the Arts

Now I propose to take, one after another, certain aspects and departments of modern life, and describe what I think they will be like in this paradise of plutocrats, this Utopia of gold and brass in which the great story of England seems so likely to end. I propose to say what I think our new masters, the mere millionaires, will do with certain human interests and institutions, such as art, science, jurisprudence, or religion — unless we strike soon enough to prevent them. And for the sake of argument I will take in this article the example of the arts.

Most people have seen a picture called "Bubbles," which is used for the advertisement of a celebrated soap, a small cake of which is introduced into the pictorial design. And anybody with an instinct for design (the caricaturist of the Daily Herald, for instance), will guess that it was not originally a part of the design. He will see that the cake of soap destroys the picture as a picture; as much as if the cake of soap had been used to Scrub off the paint. Small as it is, it breaks and confuses the whole balance of objects in the composition. I offer no judgment here upon Millais's action in the matter; in fact, I do not know what it was. The important point for me at the moment is that the picture was not painted for the soap, but the soap added to the picture. And the spirit of the corrupting change which has separated us from that Victorian epoch can be best seen in this: that the Victorian atmosphere, with all its faults, did not permit such a style of patronage to pass as a matter of course. Michael Angelo may have been proud to have helped an emperor or a pope; though, indeed, I think he was prouder than they were on his own account. I do not believe Sir John Millais was proud of having helped a soap-boiler. I do not say he thought it wrong; but he was not proud of it. And that marks precisely the change from his time to our own. Our merchants have really adopted the style of merchant princes. They have begun openly to dominate the civilisation of the State, as the emperors and popes openly dominated in Italy. In Millais's time, broadly speaking, art was supposed to mean good art; advertisement was supposed to mean inferior art. The head of a black man, painted to advertise somebody's blacking, could be a rough symbol, like an inn sign. The black man had only to be black enough. An artist exhibiting the picture of a negro was expected to know that a black man is not so black as he is painted. He was expected to render a thousand tints of grey and brown and violet: for there is no such thing as a black man just as there is no such thing as a white man. A fairly clear line separated advertisement from art.

The First Effect

I should say the first effect of the triumph of the capitalist (if we allow him to triumph) will be that that line of demarcation will entirely disappear. There will be no art that might not just as well be advertisement. I do not necessarily mean that there will be no good art; much of it might be, much of it already is, very good art. You may put it, if you please, in the form that there has been a vast improvement in advertisements. Certainly there would be nothing surprising if the head of a negro advertising Somebody's Blacking now adays were finished with as careful and subtle colours as one of the old and superstitious painters would have wasted on the negro king who brought gifts to Christ. But the improvement of advertisements is the degradation of artists. It is their degradation for this clear and vital reason: that the artist will work, not only to please the rich, but only to increase their riches; which is a considerable step lower. After all, it was as a human being that a pope took pleasure in a cartoon of Raphael or a prince took pleasure in a statuette of Cellini. The prince paid for the statuette; but he did not expect the statuette to pay him. It is my impression that no cake of soap can be found anywhere in the cartoons which the Pope ordered of Raphael. And no one who knows the small-minded cynicism of our plutocracy, its secrecy, its gambling spirit, its contempt of conscience, can doubt that the artist-advertiser will often be assisting enterprises over which he will have no moral control, and of which he could feel no moral approval. He will be working to spread quack medicines, queer investments; and will work for Marconi instead of Medici. And to this base ingenuity he will have to bend the proudest and purest of the virtues of the intellect, the power to attract his brethren, and the noble duty of praise. For that picture by Millais is a very allegorical picture. It is almost a prophecy of what uses are awaiting the beauty of the child unborn. The praise will be of a kind that may correctly be called soap; and the enterprises of a kind that may truly be described as Bubbles.

II. Letters and the New Laureates

In these articles I only take two or three examples of the first and fundamental fact of our time. I mean the fact that the capitalists of our community are becoming quite openly the kings of it. In my last (and first) article, I took the case of Art and advertisement. I pointed out that Art must be growing worse — merely because advertisement is growing better. In those days

314

Millais condescended to Pears' soap. In these days I really think it would be Pears who condescended to Millais. But here I turn to an art I know more about, that of journalism. Only in my ease the art verges on artlessness.

The great difficulty with the English lies in the absence of something one may call democratic imagination. We find it easy to realise an individual, but very hard to realise that the great masses consist of individuals. Our system has been aristocratic: in the special sense of there being only a few actors on the stage. And the back scene is kept quite dark, though it is really a throng of faces. Home Rule tended to be not so much the Irish as the Grand Old Man. The Boer War tended not to be so much South Africa as simply "Joe." And it is the amusing but distressing fact that every class of political leadership, as it comes to the front in its turn, catches the rays of this isolating lime-light; and becomes a small aristocracy. Certainly no one has the aristocratic complaint so badly as the Labour Party. At the recent Congress, the real difference between Larkin and the English Labour leaders was not so much in anything right or wrong in what he said, as in something elemental and even mystical in the way he suggested a mob. But it must be plain, even to those who agree with the more official policy, that for Mr. Havelock Wilson the principal question was Mr. Havelock Wilson; and that Mr. Sexton was mainly considering the dignity and fine feelings of Mr. Sexton. You may say they were as sensitive as aristocrats, or as sulky as babies; the point is that the feeling was personal. But Larkin, like Danton, not only talks like ten thousand men talking, but he also has some of the carelessness of the colossus of Arcis; "Que mon nom soit fletri, que la France soit libre."

A Dance of Degradation

It is needless to say that this respecting of persons has led all the other parties a dance of degradation. We ruin South Africa because it would be a slight on Lord Gladstone to save South Africa. We have a bad army, because it would be a snub to Lord Haldane to have a good army. And no Tory is allowed to say "Marconi" for fear Mr. George should say "Kynoch." But this curious personal element, with its appalling lack of patriotism, has appeared in a new and curious form in another department of life; the department of literature, especially periodical literature. And the form it takes is the next example I shall give of the way in which the capitalists are now appearing, more and more openly, as the masters and princes of the community.

I will take a Victorian instance to mark the change; as I did in the case of the advertisement of "Bubbles." It was said in my childhood, by the more apoplectic and elderly sort of Tory, that W. E. Gladstone was only a Free Trader because he had a partnership in Gilbey's foreign wines. This was, no doubt, nonsense; but it had a dim symbolic, or mainly prophetic, truth in it. It was true, to some extent even then, and it has been increasingly true since, that the statesman was often an ally of the salesman; and represented not only a nation of shopkeepers, but one particular shop. But in Gladstone's time, even if this was true, it was never the whole truth; and no one would have endured it being the admitted truth. The politician was not solely an eloquent and persuasive bagman travelling for certain business men; he was bound to mix even his corruption with some intelligible ideals and rules of policy. And the proof of it is this: that at least it was the statesman who bulked large in the public eye; and his financial backer was entirely in the background. Old gentlemen might choke over their port, with the moral certainty that the Prime Minister had shares in a wine merchant's. But the old gentleman would have died on the spot if the wine merchant had really been made as important as the Prime Minister. If it had been Sir Walter Gilbey whom Disraeli denounced, or Punch caricatured; if Sir Walter Gilbey's favourite collars (with the design of which I am unacquainted) had grown as large as the wings of an archangel; if Sir Walter Gilbey had been credited with successfully eliminating the British Oak with his little hatchet; if, near the Temple and the Courts of Justice, our sight was struck by a majestic statue of a wine merchant; or if the earnest Conservative lady who threw a gingerbread-nut at the Premier had directed it towards the wine merchant instead, the shock to Victorian England would have been very great indeed.

Haloes for Employers

Now something very like that is happening; the mere wealthy employer is beginning to have not only the power but some of the glory. I have seen in several magazines lately, and magazines of a high class, the appearance of a new kind of article. Literary men are being employed to praise a big business man personally, as men used to praise a king. They not only find political reasons for the commercial schemes — that they have done for some time past — they also find moral defences for the commercial schemers. They describe the capitalist's brain of steel and heart of gold in a way that Englishmen hitherto have been at least in the habit of reserving for romantic figures like Garibaldi or Gordon. In one excellent magazine Mr. T. P. O'Connor, who, when he likes, can write on letters like a man of letters, has some purple pages of praise of Sir Joseph Lyons — the man who runs those teashop places. He incidentally brought in a delightful passage about the beautiful souls possessed by some people called Salmon and Gluckstein. I think I like best the passage where he said that Lyons's charming social acaccomplishments included a talent for "imitating a Jew." The article is accompanied with a large and somewhat leering portrait of that shopkeeper, which makes the parlour-trick in question particularly astonishing. Another literary man, who certainly ought to know better, wrote in another paper a piece of hero-worship about Mr. Selfridge. No doubt the fashion will spread, and the art of words, as polished and pointed by Ruskin or Meredith, will be perfected yet further to explore the labyrinthine heart of Harrod; or compare the simple stoicism of Marshall with the saintly charm of Snelgrove.

Any man can be praised — and rightly praised. If he only stands on two legs he does something a cow cannot do. If a rich man can manage to stand on two legs for a reasonable time, it is called self-control. If he has only one leg, it is called (with some truth) self-sacrifice. I could say something nice (and true) about every man I have ever met. Therefore, I do not doubt I could find something nice about Lyons or Selfridge if I searched for it. But I shall not. The nearest postman or cab-man will provide me with just the same brain of steel and heart of gold as these unlucky lucky men. But I do resent the whole age of patronage being revived under such absurd patrons; and all poets becoming court poets, under kings that have taken no oath, nor led us into any battle.

III. Unbusinesslike Business

The fairy tales we were all taught did not, like the history we were all taught, consist entirely of lies. Parts of the tale of "Puss in Boots" or "Jack and the Beanstalk" may strike the realistic eye as a little unlikely and out of the common way, so to speak; but they contain some very solid and very practical truths. For instance, it may be noted that both in "Puss in Boots" and "Jack and the Beanstalk" if I remember aright, the ogre was not only an ogre but also a magician. And it will generally be found that in all such popular narratives, the king, if he is a wicked king, is generally also a wizard. Now there is a very vital human truth enshrined in this. Bad government, like good government, is a spiritual thing. Even the tyrant never rules by force alone; but mostly by fairy tales. And so it is with the modern tyrant, the great employer. The sight of a millionaire is seldom, in the ordinary sense, an enchanting sight: nevertheless, he is in his way an enchanter. As they say in the gushing articles about him in the magazines, he is a fascinating personality. So is a snake. At least he is fascinating to rabbits; and so is the millionaire to the rabbit-witted sort of people that ladies and gentlemen have allowed themselves to become. He does, in a manner, cast a spell, such as that which imprisoned princes and princesses under the shapes of falcons or stags. He has truly turned men into sheep, as Circe turned them into swine.

Now, the chief of the fairy tales, by which he gains this glory and glamour, is a certain hazy association he has managed to create between the idea of bigness and the idea of practicality. Numbers of the rabbit-witted ladies and gentlemen do really think, in spite of themselves and their experience, that so long as a shop has hundreds of different doors and a great many hot and unhealthy underground departments (they must be hot; this is very important), and more people than would be needed for a man-of-war, or crowded cathedral, to say: "This way, madam," and "The next article, sir," it follows that the goods are good. In short, they hold that the big businesses are businesslike. They are not. Any housekeeper in a truthful mood, that is to say, any housekeeper in a bad temper, will tell you that they are not. But housekeepers, too, are human, and therefore inconsistent and complex; and they do not always stick to truth and bad temper. They are also affected by this queer idolatry of the enormous and elaborate; and cannot help feeling that anything so complicated must go like clockwork. But complexity is no guarantee of accuracy — in clockwork or in anything else. A clock can be as wrong as the human head; and a clock can stop, as suddenly as the human heart.

But this strange poetry of plutocracy prevails over people against their very senses. You write to one of the great London stores or emporia, asking, let us say, for an umbrella. A month or two afterwards you receive a very elaborately constructed parcel, containing a broken parasol. You are very pleased. You are gratified to reflect on what a vast number of assistants and employees had combined to break that parasol. You luxuriate in the memory of all those long rooms and departments and wonder in which of them the parasol that you never ordered was broken. Or you want a toy elephant for your child on Christmas Day; as children, like all nice and healthy people, are very ritualistic. Some week or so after Twelfth Night, let us say, you have the pleasure of removing three layers of pasteboards, five layers of brown paper, and fifteen layers of tissue paper and discovering the fragments of an artificial crocodile. You smile in an expansive spirit. You feel that your soul has been broadened by the vision of incompetence conducted on so large a scale. You admire all the more the colossal and Omnipresent Brain of the Organiser of Industry, who amid all his multitudinous cares did not disdain to remember his duty of smashing even the smallest toy of the smallest child. Or, supposing you have asked him to send you some two rolls of cocoa-nut matting: and supposing (after a due interval for reflection) he duly delivers to you the five rolls of wire netting. You take pleasure in the consideration of a mystery: which coarse minds might have called a mistake. It consoles you to know how big the business is: and what an enormous number of people were needed to make such a mistake.

That is the romance that has been told about the big shops; in the literature and art which they have bought, and which (as I said in my recent articles) will soon be quite indistinguishable from their ordinary advertisements. The literature is commercial; and it is only fair to say that the commerce is often really literary. It is no romance, but only rubbish.

The big commercial concerns of to-day are quite exceptionally incompetent. They will be even more incompetent when they are omnipotent. Indeed, that is, and always has been, the whole point of a monopoly; the old and sound argument against a monopoly. It is only because it is incompetent that it has to be omnipotent. When one large shop occupies the whole of one side of a street (or sometimes both sides), it does so in order that men may be unable to get what they want; and may be forced to buy what they don't want. That the rapidly approaching kingdom of the Capitalists will ruin art and letters, I have already said. I say here that in the only sense that can be called human, it will ruin trade, too.

I will not let Christmas go by, even when writing for a revolutionary paper necessarily appealing to many with none of my religious sympathies, without appealing to those sympathies. I knew a man who sent to a great rich shop for a figure for a group of Bethlehem. It arrived broken. I think that is exactly all that business men have now the sense to do.

IV. The War on Holidays

The general proposition, not always easy to define exhaustively, that the reign of the capitalist will be the reign of the cad — that is, of the unlicked type that is neither the citizen nor the gentleman — can be excellently studied in its attitude towards holidays. The special emblematic Employer of to-day, especially the Model Employer (who is the worst sort) has in his starved and evil heart a sincere hatred of holidays. I do not mean that he necessarily wants all his workmen to work until they drop; that only occurs when he happens to be stupid as well as wicked. I do not mean to say that he is necessarily unwilling to grant what he would call "decent hours of labour." He may treat men like dirt; but if you want to make money, even out of dirt, you must let it lie fallow by some rotation of rest. He may treat men as dogs, but unless he is a lunatic he will for certain periods let sleeping dogs lie.

But humane and reasonable hours for labour have nothing whatever to do with the idea of holidays. It is not even a question

320

of tenhours day and eight-hours day; it is not a question of cutting down leisure to the space necessary for food, sleep and exercise. If the modern employer came to the conclusion, for some reason or other, that he could get most out of his men by working them hard for only two hours a day, his whole mental attitude would still be foreign and hostile to holidays. For his whole mental attitude is that the passive time and the active time are alike useful for him and his business. All is, indeed, grist that comes to his mill, including the millers. His slaves still serve him in unconsciousness, as dogs still hunt in slumber. His grist is ground not only by the sounding wheels of iron, but by the soundless wheel of blood and brain. His sacks are still filling silently when the doors are shut on the streets and the sound of the grinding is low.

The Great Holiday

Now a holiday has no connection with using a man either by beating or feeding him. When you give a man a holiday you give him back his body and soul. It is quite possible you may be doing him an injury (though he seldom thinks so), but that does not affect the question for those to whom a holiday is holy. Immortality is the great holiday; and a holiday, like the immortality in the old theologies, is a double-edged privilege. But wherever it is genuine it is simply the restoration and completion of the man. If people ever looked at the printed word under their eye, the word "recreation" would be like the word "resurrection," the blast of a trumpet.

A man, being merely useful, is necessarily incomplete, especially if he be a modern man and means by being useful being "utilitarian." A man going into a modern club gives up his hat; a man going into a modern factory gives up his head. He then goes in and works loyally for the old firm to build up the great fabric of commerce (which can be done without a head), but when he has done work he goes to the cloak-room, like the man at the club, and gets his head back again; that is the germ of the holiday. It may be urged that the club man who leaves his hat often goes away with another hat; and perhaps it may be the same with the factory hand who has left his head. A hand that has lost its head may affect the fastidious as a mixed metaphor; but, God pardon us all, what an unmixed truth! We could almost prove the whole ease from the habit of calling human beings merely "hands" while they are

321

working; as if the hand were horribly cut off, like the hand that has offended; as if, while the sinner entered heaven maimed, his unhappy hand still laboured laying up riches for the lords of hell. But to return to the man whom we found waiting for his head in the cloak-room. It may be urged, we say, that he might take the wrong head, like the wrong hat; but here the similarity ceases. For it has been observed by benevolent onlookers at life's drama that the hat taken away by mistake is frequently better than the real hat; whereas the head taken away after the hours of toil is certainly worse: stained with the cobwebs and dust of this dustbin of all the centuries.

The Supreme Adventure

All the words dedicated to places of eating and drinking are pure and poetic words. Even the word "hotel" is the word hospital. And St. Julien, whose claret I drank this Christmas, was the patron saint of innkeepers, because (as far as I can make out) he was hospitable to lepers. Now I do not say that the ordinary hotel-keeper in Piccadilly or the Avenue de l'Opera would embrace a leper, slap him on the back, and ask him to order what he liked; but I do say that hospitality is his trade virtue. And I do also say it is well to keep before our eyes the supreme adventure of a virtue. If you are brave, think of the man who was braver than you. If you are kind, think of the man who was kinder than you.

That is what was meant by having a patron saint. That is the link between the poor saint who received bodily lepers and the great hotel proprietor who (as a rule) receives spiritual lepers. But a word yet weaker than "hotel" illustrates the same point — the word "restaurant." There again you have the admission that there is a definite building or statue to "restore"; that ineffaceable image of man that some call the image of God. And that is the holiday; it is the restaurant or restoring thing that, by a blast of magic, turns a man into himself.

This complete and reconstructed man is the nightmare of the modern capitalist. His whole scheme would crack across like a mirror of Shallot, if once a plain man were ready for his two plain duties — ready to live and ready to die. And that horror of holidays which marks the modern capitalist is very largely a horror of the vision of a whole human being: something that is not a "hand" or a "head for figutes." But an awful creature who has met himself in the wilderness. The employers will give time to eat, time to sleep; they are in terror of a time to think.

To anyone who knows any history it is wholly needless to say that holidays have been destroyed. As Mr. Belloc, who knows much more history than you or I, recently pointed out in the "Pall Mall Magazine," Shakespeare's title of "Twelfth Night: or What You Will" simply meant that a winter carnival for everybody went on wildly till the twelfth night after Christmas. Those of my readers who work for modern offices or factories might ask their employers for twelve days' holidays after Christmas. And they might let me know the reply.

V. The Church Of The Servile State

I confess I cannot see why mere blasphemy by itself should be an excuse for tyranny and treason; or how the mere isolated fact of a man not believing in God should be a reason for my believing in Him.

But the rather spinsterish flutter among some of the old Freethinkers has put one tiny ripple of truth in it; and that affects the idea which I wish to emphasise even to monotony in these pages. I mean the idea that the new community which the capitalists are now constructing will be a very complete and absolute community; and one which will tolerate nothing really independent of itself. Now, it is true that any positive creed, true or false, would tend to be independent of itself. It might be Roman Catholicism or Mahomedanism or Materialism; but, if strongly held, it would be a thorn in the side of the Servile State. The Moslem thinks all men immortal: the Materialist thinks all men mortal. But the Moslem does not think the rich Sinbad will live forever; but the poor Sinbad will die on his deathbed. The Materialist does not think that Mr. Haeckel will go to heaven, while all the peasants will go to pot, like their chickens. In every serious doctrine of the destiny of men, there is some trace of the doctrine of the equality of men. But the capitalist really depends on some religion of inequality. The capitalist must somehow distinguish himself from human kind; he must be obviously above it — or he would be obviously below it. Take even the least attractive and popular side of the larger religions to-day; take the mere vetoes imposed by Islam on Atheism or Catholicism. The Moslem veto upon intoxicants cuts across all classes. But it is absolutely necessary for the capitalist (who presides at a Licensing Committee, and also at a large dinner), it is absolutely necessary for him, to make a distinction between gin and champagne. The Atheist veto upon all miracles cuts across all classes. But it is absolutely necessary for the capitalist to make a distinction between his wife (who is an aristocrat and consults crystal gazers and star gazers in the West End), and vulgar miracles claimed by gipsies or travelling showmen. The Catholic veto upon usury, as defined in dogmatic councils, cuts across all classes. But it is absolutely necessary to the capitalist to distinguish more delicately between two kinds of usury; the kind he finds useful and the kind he does not find useful. The religion of the Servile State must have no dogmas or definitions. It cannot afford to have any definitions. For definitions are very dreadful things: they do the two things that most men, especially comfortable men, cannot endure. They fight; and they fight fair.

Every religion, apart from open devil worship, must appeal to a virtue or the pretence of a virtue. But a virtue, generally speaking, does some good to everybody. It is therefore necessary to distinguish among the people it was meant to benefit those whom it does benefit. Modern broad-mindedness benefits the rich; and benefits nobody else. It was meant to benefit the rich; and meant to benefit nobody else. And if you think this unwarranted, I will put before you one plain question. There are some pleasures of the poor that may also mean profits for the rich: there are other pleasures of the poor which cannot mean profits for the rich? Watch this one contrast, and you will watch the whole creation of a careful slavery.

In the last resort the two things called Beer and Soap end only in a froth. They are both below the high notice of a real religion. But there is just this difference: that the soap makes the factory more satisfactory, while the beer only makes the workman more satisfied. Wait and see if the Soap does not increase and the Beer decrease. Wait and see whether the religion of the Servile State is not in every case what I say: the encouragement of small virtues supporting capitalism, the discouragement of the huge virtues that defy it. Many great religions, Pagan and Christian, have insisted on wine. Only one, I think, has insisted on Soap. You will find it in the New Testament attributed to the Pharisees.

VI. Science And The Eugenists

The key fact in the new development of plutocracy is that it will use its own blunder as an excuse for further crimes. Everywhere the very completeness of the impoverishment will be made a reason for the enslavement; though the men who impoverished were the same who enslaved. It is as if a highwayman not only took away a gentleman's horse and all his money, but then handed him over to the police for tramping without visible means of subsistence. And the most monstrous feature in this enormous meanness may be noted in the plutocratic appeal to science, or, rather, to the pseudo-science that they call Eugenics.

The Eugenists get the ear of the humane but rather hazy cliques by saying that the present "conditions" under which people work and breed are bad for the race; but the modern mind will not generally stretch beyond one step of reasoning, and the consequence which appears to follow on the consideration of these "conditions" is by no means what would originally have been expected. If somebody says: "A rickety cradle may mean a rickety baby," the natural deduction, one would think, would be to give the people a good cradle, or give them money enough to buy one. But that means higher wages and greater equalisation of wealth; and the plutocratic scientist, with a slightly troubled expression, turns his eyes and pince-nez in another direction. Reduced to brutal terms of truth, his difficulty is this and simply this: More food, leisure, and money for the workman would mean a better workman, better even from the point of view of anyone for whom he worked. But more food, leisure, and money would also mean a more independent workman. A house with a decent fire and a full pantry would be a better house to make a chair or mend a clock in, even from the customer's point of view, than a hovel with a leaky roof and a cold hearth. But a house with a decent fire and a full pantry would also be a better house in which to refuse to make a chair or mend a clock — a much better house to do nothing in — and doing nothing is sometimes one of the highest of the duties of man. All but the hard-hearted must be torn with pity for this pathetic dilemma of the rich man, who has to keep the poor man just stout enough to do the work and just thin enough to have to do it. As he stood gazing at the leaky roof and the rickety cradle in a pensive manner, there one day came into his mind a new and curious idea — one of the most strange, simple, and horrible ideas that have ever risen from the deep pit of original sin.

The roof could not be mended, or, at least, it could not be mended much, without upsetting the capitalist balance, or, rather, disproportion in society; for a man with a roof is a man with a house, and to that extent his house is his castle. The cradle could not be made to rock easier, or, at least, not much easier, without strengthening the hands of the poor household, for the hand that rocks the cradle rules the world — to that extent. But it occurred to the capitalist that there was one sort of furniture in the house that could be altered. The husband and wife could be altered. Birth costs nothing, except in pain and valour and such old-fashioned things; and the merchant need pay no more for mating a strong miner to a healthy fishwife than he pays when the miner mates himself with a less robust female whom he has the sentimentality to prefer. Thus it might be possible, by keeping on certain broad lines of heredity, to have some physical improvement without any moral, political, or social improvement. It might be possible to keep a supply of strong and healthy slaves without coddling them with decent conditions. As the mill-owners use the wind and the water to drive their mills, they would use this natural force as something even cheaper; and turn their wheels by diverting from its channel the blood of a man in his youth. That is what Eugenics means; and that is all that it means.

Of the moral state of those who think of such things it does not become us to speak. The practical question is rather the intellectual one: of whether their calculations are well founded, and whether the men of science can or will guarantee them any such physical certainties. Fortunately, it becomes clearer every day that they are, scientifically speaking, building on the shifting sand. The theory of breeding slaves breaks down through what a democrat calls the equality of men, but which even an oligarchist will find himself forced to call the similarity of men. That is, that though it is not true that all men are normal, it is overwhelmingly certain that most men are normal. All the common Eugenic arguments are drawn from extreme cases, which, even if human honour and laughter allowed of their being eliminated, would not by their elimination greatly affect the mass. For the rest, there remains the enormous weakness in Eugenics, that if ordinary men's judgment or liberty is to be discounted in relation to heredity, the judgment of the judges must be discounted in relation to their heredity. The Eugenic professor may or may not succeed in choosing a baby's parents; it is quite certain that he cannot succeed in choosing his own parents. All his thoughts, including his Eugenic thoughts, are, by the very principle of those thoughts, flowing from a doubtful or tainted source. In short, we should need a perfectly Wise Man to do the thing at all. And if he were a Wise Man he would not do it.

VII. The Evolution Of The Prison

I have never understood why it is that those who talk most about evolution, and talk it in the very age of fashionable evolutionism, do not see the one way in which evolution really does apply to our modern difficulty. There is, of course, an element of evolutionism in the universe; and I know no religion or philosophy that ever entirely ignored it. Evolution, popularly speaking, is that which happens to unconscious things. They grow unconsciously; or fade unconsciously; or rather, some parts of them grow and some parts of them fade; and at any given moment there is almost always some presence of the fading thing, and some incompleteness in the growing one. Thus, if I went to sleep for a hundred years, like the Sleeping Beauty (I wish I could), I should grow a beard — unlike the Sleeping Beauty. And just as I should grow hair if I were asleep, I should grow grass if I were dead. Those whose religion it was that God was asleep were perpetually impressed and affected by the fact that he had a long beard. And those whose philosophy it is that the universe is dead from the beginning (being the grave of nobody in particular) think that is the way that grass can grow. In any case, these developments only occur with dead or dreaming things. What happens when everyone is asleep is called Evolution. What happens when everyone is awake is called Revolution.

There was once an honest man, whose name I never knew, but whose face I can almost see (it is framed in Victorian whiskers and fixed in a Victorian neck-cloth), who was balancing the achievements of France and England in civilisation and social efficiencies. And when he came to the religious aspect he said that there were more stone and brick churches used in France; but, on the other hand, there are more sects in England. Whether such a lively disintegration is a proof of vitality in any valuable sense I have always doubted. The sun may breed maggots in a dead dog; but it is essential for such a liberation of life that the dog should be unconscious or (to say the least of it) absent-minded. Broadly speaking, you may call the thing corruption, if you happen to like dogs. You may call it evolution, if you happen to like maggots. In either case, it is what happens to things if you leave them alone.

The Evolutionists' Error

Now, the modern Evolutionists have made no real use of the idea of evolution, especially in the matter of social prediction. They always fall into what is (from their logical point of view) the error of supposing that evolution knows what it is doing. They predict the State of the future as a fruit rounded and polished. But the whole point of evolution (the only point there is in it) is that no State will ever be rounded and polished, because it will always contain some organs that outlived their use, and some that have not yet fully found theirs. If we wish to prophesy what will happen, we must imagine things now moderate grown enormous; things now local grown universal; things now promising grown triumphant; primroses bigger than sunflowers, and sparrows stalking about like flamingoes.

In other words, we must ask what modern institution has a future before it? What modern institution may have swollen to six times its present size in the social heat and growth of the future? I do not think the Garden City will grow: but of that I may speak in my next and last article of this series. I do not think even the ordinary Elementary School, with its compulsory education, will grow. Too many unlettered people hate the teacher for teaching; and too many lettered people hate the teacher for not teaching. The Garden City will not bear much blossom; the young idea will not shoot, unless it shoots the teacher. But the one flowering tree on the estate, the one natural expansion which I think will expand, is the institution we call the Prison.

Prisons for All

If the capitalists are allowed to erect their constructive capitalist community, I speak quite seriously when I say that I think Prison will become an almost universal experience. It will not necessarily be a cruel or shameful experience: on these points (I concede certainly for the present purpose of debate) it may be a vastly improved experience. The conditions in the prison, very possibly, will be made more humane. But the prison will be made more humane only in order to contain more of humanity. I think little of the judgment and sense of humour of any man who can have watched recent police trials without realising that it is no longer a question of whether the law has been broken by a crime; but, now, solely a question of whether the situation could be mended by an imprisonment. It was so with Tom Mann; it was so with Larkin; it was so with the poor atheist who was kept in gaol for saying something he had been acquitted of saying: it is so in such cases day by day. We no longer lock a man up for doing something; we lock him up in the hope of his doing nothing. Given this principle, it is evidently possible to make the mere conditions of punishment more moderate, or — (more probably) more secret. There may really be more mercy in the Prison, on condition that there is less justice in the Court. I should not be surprised if, before we are done with all this, a man was allowed to smoke in prison, on condition, of course, that he had been put in prison for smoking.

Now that is the process which, in the absence of democratic protest, will certainly proceed, will increase and multiply and replenish the earth and subdue it. Prison may even lose its disgrace for a little time: it will be difficult to make it disgraceful when men like Larkin can be imprisoned for no reason at all, just as his celebrated ancestor was hanged for no reason at all. But capitalist society, which naturally does not know the meaning of honour, cannot know the meaning of disgrace: and it will still go on imprisoning for no reason at all. Or rather for that rather simple reason that makes a cat spring or a rat run away.

It matters little whether our masters stoop to state the matter in the form that every prison should be a school; or in the more candid form that every school should be a prison. They have already fulfilled their servile principle in the case of the schools. Everyone goes to the Elementary Schools except the few people who tell them to go there. I prophesy that (unless our revolt succeeds) nearly everyone will be going to Prison, with a precisely similar patience.

VIII. The Lash For Labour

If I were to prophesy that two hundred years hence a grocer would have the right and habit of beating the grocer's assistant with a stick, or that shop girls might be flogged, as they already can be fined, many would regard it as rather a rash remark. It would be a rash remark. Prophecy is always unreliable; unless we except the kind which is avowedly irrational, mystical and supernatural prophecy. But relatively to nearly all the other prophecies that are being made around me to-day, I should say my prediction stood an exceptionally good chance. In short, I think the grocer with the stick is a figure we are far more likely to see than the Superman or the Samurai, or the True Model Employer, or the Perfect Fabian Official, or the citizen of the Collectivist State. And it is best for us to see the full ugliness of the transformation which is passing over our Society in some such abrupt and even grotesque image at the end of it. The beginnings of a decline, in every age of history, have always had the appearance of being reforms. Nero not only fiddled while Rome was burning, but he probably really paid more attention to the fiddle than to the fire. The Roi Soleil, like many other soleils, was most splendid to all appearance a little before sunset. And if I ask myself what will be the ultimate and final fruit of all our social reforms, garden cities, model employers, insurances, exchanges, arbitration courts, and so on, then, I say, quite seriously, "I think it will be labour under the lash."

The Sultan and the Sack

Let us arrange in some order a number of converging considerations that all point in this direction. (1) It is broadly true, no doubt, that the weapon of the employer has hitherto been the threat of dismissal, that is, the threat of enforced starvation. He is a Sultan who need not order the bastinado, so long as he can order

330

the sack. But there are not a few signs that this weapon is not quite so convenient and flexible a one as his increasing rapacities require. The fact of the introduction of fines, secretly or openly, in many shops and factories, proves that it is convenient for the capitalists to have some temporary and adjustable form of punishment besides the final punishment of pure ruin. Nor is it difficult to see the commonsense of this from their wholly inhuman point of view. The act of sacking a man is attended with the same disadvantages as the act of shooting a man: one of which is that you can get no more out of him. It is, I am told, distinctly annoying to blow a fellow creature's brains out with a revolver and then suddenly remember that he was the only person who knew where to get the best Russian cigarettes. So our Sultan, who is the orderer of the sack, is also the bearer of the bow-string. A school in which there was no punishment, except expulsion, would be a school in which it would be very difficult to keep proper discipline; and the sort of discipline on which the reformed capitalism will insist will be all of the type which in free nations is imposed only on children. Such a school would probably be in a chronic condition of breaking up for the holidays. And the reasons for the insufficiency of this extreme instrument are also varied and evident. The materialistic Sociologists, who talk about the survival of the fittest and the weakest going to the wall (and whose way of looking at the world is to put on the latest and most powerful scientific spectacles, and then shut their eyes), frequently talk as if a workman were simply efficient or non-efficient, as if a criminal were reclaimable or irreclaimable. The employers have sense enough at least to know better than that. They can see that a servant may be useful in one way and exasperating in another; that he may be bad in one part of his work and good in another; that he may be occasionally drunk and yet generally indispensable. Just as a practical school-master would know that a schoolboy can be at once the plague and the pride of the school. Under these circumstances small and varying penalties are obviously the most convenient things for the person keeping order; an underling can be punished for coming late, and yet do useful work when he comes. It will be possible to give a rap over the knuckles without wholly cutting off the right hand that has offended. Under these circumstances the employers have naturally resorted to fines. But there is a further ground for believing that the process will go beyond fines before it is completed.

(2) The fine is based on the old European idea that everybody possesses private property in some reasonable degree; but not only is this not true to-day, but it is not being made any truer, even by those who honestly believe that they are mending matters. The great employers will often do something towards improving what they call the "conditions" of their workers; but a worker might have his conditions as carefully arranged as a racehorse has, and still have no more personal property than a racehorse. If you take an average poor seamstress or factory girl, you will find that the power of chastising her through her property has very considerable limits; it is almost as hard for the employer of labour to tax her for punishment as it is for the Chancellor of the Exchequer to tax her for revenue. The next most obvious thing to think of, of course, would be imprisonment, and that might be effective enough under simpler conditions. An old-fashioned shopkeeper might have locked up his apprentice in his coal-cellar; but his coal-cellar would be a real, pitch dark coal-cellar, and the rest of his house would be a real human house. Everybody (especially the apprentice) would see a most perceptible difference between the two. But, as I pointed out in the article before this, the whole tendency of the capitalist legislation and experiment is to make imprisonment much more general and automatic, while making it, or professing to make it, more humane. In other words, the hygienic prison and the servile factory will become so uncommonly like each other that the poor man will hardly know or care whether he is at the moment expiating an offence or merely swelling a dividend. In both places there will be the same sort of shiny tiles. In neither place will there be any cell so unwholesome as a coal-cellar or so wholesome as a home. The weapon of the prison, therefore, like the weapon of the fine, will be found to have considerable limitations to its effectiveness when employed against the wretched reduced citizen of our day. Whether it be property or liberty you cannot take from him what he has not got. You cannot imprison a slave, because you cannot enslave a slave.

The Barbarous Revival

(3) Most people, on hearing the suggestion that it may come to corporal punishment at last (as it did in every slave system

I ever heard of, including some that were generally kindly, and even successful), will merely be struck with horror and incredulity, and feel that such a barbarous revival is unthinkable in the modern atmosphere. How far it will be, or need be, a revival of the actual images and methods of ruder times I will discuss in a moment. But first, as another of the converging lines tending to corporal punishment, consider this: that for some reason or other the old full-blooded and masculine humanitarianism in this matter has weakened and fallen silent; it has weakened and fallen silent in a very curious manner, the precise reason for which I do not altogether understand. I knew the average Liberal, the average Nonconformist minister, the average Labour Member, the average middle-class Socialist, were, with all their good qualities, very deficient in what I consider a respect for the human soul. But I did imagine that they had the ordinary modern respect for the human body. The fact, however, is clear and incontrovertible. In spite of the horror of all humane people, in spite of the hesitation even of our corrupt and panic-stricken Parliament, measures can now be triumphantly passed for spreading or increasing the use of physical torture, and for applying it to the newest and vaguest categories of crime. Thirty or forty years ago, nay, twenty years ago, when Mr. F. Hugh O'Donnell and others forced a Liberal Government to drop the cat-o-nine-tails like a scorpion, we could have counted on a mass of honest hatred of such things. We cannot count on it now.

(4) But lastly, it is not necessary that in the factories of the future the institution of physical punishment should actually remind people of the jambok or the knout. It could easily be developed out of the many forms of physical discipline which are already used by employers on the excuses of education or hygiene. Already in some factories girls are obliged to swim whether they like it or not, or do gymnastics whether they like it or not. By a simple extension of hours or complication of exercises a pair of Swedish clubs could easily be so used as to leave their victim as exhausted as one who had come off the rack. I think it extremely likely that they will be.

IX. The Mask Of Socialism

The chief aim of all honest Socialists just now is to prevent the coming of Socialism. I do not say it as a sneer, but, on the contrary, as a compliment; a compliment to their political instinct and public spirit. I admit it may be called an exaggeration; but there really is a sort of sham Socialism that the modern politicians may quite possibly agree to set up; if they do succeed in setting it up, the battle for the poor is lost.

We must note, first of all, a general truth about the curious time we live in. It will not be so difficult as some people may suppose to make the Servile State look rather like Socialism, especially to the more pedantic kind of Socialist. The reason is this. The old lucid and trenchant expounder of Socialism, such as Blatchford or Fred Henderson, always describes the economic power of the plutocrats as consisting in private property. Of course, in a sense, this is quite true; though they too often miss the point that private property, as such, is not the same as property confined to the few. But the truth is that the situation has grown much more subtle; perhaps too subtle, not to say too insane, for straight-thinking theorists like Blatchford. The rich man to-day does not only rule by using private property; he also rules by treating public property as if it were private property. A man like Lord Murray pulled the strings, especially the pursestrings; but the whole point of his position was that all sorts of strings had got entangled. The secret strength of the money he held did not lie merely in the fact that it was his money. It lay precisely in the fact that nobody had any clear idea of whether it was his money, or his successor's money, or his brother's money, or the Marconi Company's money, or the Liberal Party's money, or the English Nation's money. It was buried treasure; but it was not private property. It was the acme of plutocracy because it was not private property. Now, by following this precedent, this unprincipled vagueness about official and unofficial moneys by the cheerful habit of always mixing up the money in the pocket with the money in the till, it would be quite possible to keep the rich as rich as ever in practice, though they might have suffered confiscation in theory. Mr. Lloyd George has four hundred a year as an M. P.; but he not only gets much more as a Minister, but he might at any time get immeasurably more by speculating on State secrets that are necessarily known to him. Some say that he has even attempted something of the kind. Now, it would be quite possible to cut Mr. George down, not to four hundred a year, but to fourpence a day; and still leave him all these other and enormous financial superiorities. It must be remembered that a Socialist State, in any way resembling a modern State, must, however egalitarian it may be, have the handling of huge sums, and the enjoyment of large conveniences; it is not improbable that the same men will handle and enjoy in much the same manner, though in theory they are doing it as instruments, and not as individuals. For instance, the Prime Minister has a private house, which is also (I grieve to inform that eminent Puritan) a public house. It is supposed to be a sort of Government office; though people do not generally give children's parties, or go to bed in a Government office. I do not know where Mr. Herbert Samuel lives; but I have no doubt he does himself well in the matter of decoration and furniture. On the existing official parallel there is no need to move any of these things in order to Socialise them. There is no need to withdraw one diamond-headed nail from the carpet; or one golden teaspoon from the tray. It is only necessary to call it an official residence, like 10 Downing-street. I think it is not at all improbable that this Plutocracy, pretending to be a Bureaucracy, will be attempted or achieved. Our wealthy rulers will be in the position which grumblers in the world of sport sometimes attribute to some of the "gentlemen" players. They assert that some of these are paid like any professional; only their pay is called their expenses. This system might run side by side with a theory of equal wages, as absolute as that once laid down by Mr. Bernard Shaw. By the theory of the State, Mr. Herbert Samuel and Mr. Lloyd George might be humble citizens, drudging for their fourpence a day; and no better off than porters and coal-heavers. If there were presented to our mere senses what appeared to be the form of Mr. Herbert Samuel in an astrakhan coat and a motor-car, we should find the record of the expenditure (if we could find it at all) under the heading of "Speed Limit Extension Enquiry Commission." If it fell to our lot to behold (with the eye of flesh) what seemed to be Mr. Lloyd George lying in a hammock and smoking a costly cigar, we should know that the expenditure would be divided between the "Condition of Rope and Netting

Investigation Department," and the "State of Cuban Tobacco Trade: Imperial Inspector's Report."

Such is the society I think they will build unless we can knock it down as fast as they build it. Everything in it, tolerable or intolerable, will have but one use; and that use what our ancestors used to call usance or usury. Its art may be good or bad, but it will be an advertisement for usurers; its literature may be good or bad, but it will appeal to the patronage of usurers; its scientific selection will select according to the needs of usurers; its religion will be just charitable enough to pardon usurers; its penal system will be just cruel enough to crush all the critics of usurers: the truth of it will be Slavery: and the title of it may quite possibly be Socialism.

The Escape

We watched you building, stone by stone, The well-washed cells and well-washed graves We shall inhabit but not own When Britons ever shall be slaves; The water's waiting in the trough, The tame oats sown are portioned free, There is Enough, and just Enough, And all is ready now but we.

But you have not caught us yet, my lords, You have us still to get. A sorry army you'd have got, Its flags are rags that float and rot, Its drums are empty pan and pot, Its baggage is — an empty cot; But you have not caught us yet.

A little; and we might have slipped When came your rumours and your sales And the foiled rich men, feeble-lipped, Said and unsaid their sorry tales; Great God! It needs a bolder brow To keep ten sheep inside a pen, And we are sheep no longer now; You are but Masters. We are Men.

We give you all good thanks, my lords, We buy at easy price; Thanks for the thousands that you stole, The bribes by wire, the bets on coal, The knowledge of that naked whole That hath delivered our flesh and soul Out of your Paradise.

We had held safe your parks; but when Men taunted you with bribe and fee, We only saw the Lord of Men Grin like an Ape and climb a tree; And humbly had we stood without Your princely barns; did we not see In pointed faces peering out What Rats now own the granary.

It is too late, too late, my lords, We give you back your grace: You cannot with all cajoling Make the wet ditch, or winds that sting, Lost pride, or the pawned wedding rings, Or drink or Death a blacker thing Than a smile upon your face.

The New Raid

The two kinds of social reform, one of which might conceivably free us at last while the other would certainly enslave us forever, are exhibited in an easy working model in the two efforts that have been made for the soldiers' wives — I mean the effort to increase their allowance and the effort to curtail their alleged drinking. In the preliminary consideration, at any rate, we must see the second question as quite detached from our own sympathies on the special subject of fermented liquor. It could be applied to any other pleasure or ornament of life; it will be applied to every other pleasure and ornament of life if the Capitalist campaign can succeed. The argument we know; but it cannot be too often made clear. An employer, let us say, pays a seamstress twopence a day, and she does not seem to thrive on it. So little, perhaps, does she thrive on it that the employer has even some difficulty in thriving upon her. There are only two things that he can do, and the distinction between them cuts the whole social and political world in two. It is a touchstone by which we can — not sometimes, but always — distinguish economic equality from servile social reform. He can give the girl some magnificent sum, such as sixpence a day, to do as she likes with, and trust that her improved health and temper will work for the benefit of his business. Or he may keep her to the original sum of a shilling a week, but earmark each of the pennies to be used or not to be used for a particular purpose. If she must not spend this penny on a bunch of violets, or that penny on a novelette, or the other penny on a toy for some baby, it is possible that she will concentrate her expenditure more upon physical necessities, and so become, from the employer's point of view, a more efficient person. Without the trouble of adding twopence to her wages, he has added twopenny-worth to her food. In short, she has the holy satisfaction of being worth more without being paid more.

This Capitalist is an ingenious person, and has many polished characteristics; but I think the most singular thing about him is his staggering lack of shame. Neither the hour of death nor the day of reckoning, neither the tent of exile nor the house of mourning, neither chivalry nor patriotism, neither womanhood nor widowhood, is safe at this supreme moment from his dirty little expedient of dieting the slave. As similar bullies, when they collect the slum rents, put a foot in the open door, these are always ready to push in a muddy wedge wherever there is a slit in a sundered household or a crack in a broken heart. To a man of any manhood nothing can be conceived more loathsome and sacrilegious than even so much as asking whether a woman who has given up all she loved to death and the fatherland has or has not shown some weakness in her seeking for self-comfort. I know not in which of the two cases I should count myself the baser for inquiring — a case where the charge was false or a case where it was true. But the philanthropic employer of the sort I describe is not a man of any manhood; in a sense he is not a man at all. He shows some consciousness of the fact when he calls his workers "men" as distinct from masters. He cannot comprehend the gallantry of costermongers or the delicacy that is quite common among cabmen. He finds this social reform by half-rations on the whole to his mercantile profit, and it will be hard to get him to think of anything else.

But there are people assisting him, people like the Duchess of Marlborough, who know not their right hand from their left, and to these we may legitimately address our remonstrance and a resume of some of the facts they do not know. The Duchess of Marlborough is, I believe, an American, and this separates her from the problem in a special way, because the drink question in America is entirely different from the drink question in England. But I wish the Duchess of Marlborough would pin up in her private study, side by side with the Declaration of Independence, a document recording the following simple truths: (1) Beer, which is largely drunk in public-houses, is not a spirit or a grog or a cocktail or a drug. It is the common English liquid for quenching the thirst; it is so still among innumerable gentlemen, and, until very lately, was so among innumerable ladies. Most of us remember dames of the last generation whose manners were fit for Versailles, and who drank ale or Stout as a matter of course. Schoolboys drank ale as a matter of course, and their schoolmasters gave it to them as a matter of course. To tell a poor woman that she must not have any until half the day is over is simply cracked, like telling a dog or a child that he must not have water. (2) The public-house is not a secret rendezvous of bad characters. It is the open and obvious place for a certain purpose, which all men used for that purpose until the rich began to be snobs and the poor to become slaves. One might as well warn people against Willesden Junction. (3) Many poor people live in houses where they cannot, without great preparation, offer hospitality. (4) The climate of these picturesque islands does not favour conducting long conversations with one's oldest friends on an iron seat in the park. (5) Halfpast eleven a.m. is not early in the day for a woman who gets up before six. (6) The bodies and minds of these women belong to God and to themselves.

The New Name

Something has come into our community, which is strong enough to save our community; but which has not yet got a name. Let no one fancy I confess any unreality when I confess the namelessness. The morality called Puritanism, the tendency called Liberalism, the reaction called Tory Democracy, had not only long been powerful, but had practically done most of their work, before these actual names were attached to them. Nevertheless, I think it would be a good thing to have some portable and practicable way of referring to those who think as we do in our main concern. Which is, that men in England are ruled, at this minute by the clock, by brutes who refuse them bread, by liars who refuse them news, and by fools who cannot govern, and therefore wish to enslave.

Let me explain first why I am not satisfied with the word commonly used, which I have often used myself; and which, in some contexts, is quite the right word to use. I mean the word "rebel." Passing over the fact that many who understand the justice of our cause (as a great many at the Universities) would still use the word "rebel" in its old and strict sense as meaning only a disturber of just rule. I pass to a much more practical point. The word "rebel" understates our cause. It is much too mild; it lets our enemies off much too easily. There is a tradition in all western life and letters of Prometheus defying the stars, of man at war with the Universe, and dreaming what nature had never dared to dream. All this is valuable in its place and proportion. But it has nothing whatever to do with our ease; or rather it very much weakens it. The plutocrats will be only too pleased if we profess to preach a new morality; for they know jolly well that they have broken the old one. They will be only too pleased to be able to say that we, by our own confession, are merely restless and negative; that we are only what we call rebels and they call cranks. But it is not true; and we must not concede it to them for a moment. The model millionaire is more of a crank than the Socialists; just as Nero was more of a crank than the Christians. And avarice has gone mad in the governing class to-day, just as lust went mad in the circle of Nero. By all the working and orthodox standards of sanity, capitalism is insane. I should not say to Mr. Rockefeller "I am a rebel." I should say "I am a respectable man: and you are not."

Our Lawless Enemies

But the vital point is that the confession of mere rebellion softens the startling lawlessness of our enemies. Suppose a publisher's clerk politely asked his employer for a rise in his salary; and, on being refused, said he must leave the employment? Suppose the employer knocked him down with a ruler, tied him up as a brown paper parcel, addressed him (in a fine business hand) to the Governor of Rio Janeiro and then asked the policeman to promise never to arrest him for what he had done? That is a precise copy, in every legal and moral principle, of the "deportation of the strikers." They were assaulted and kidnapped for not accepting a contract, and for nothing else; and the act was so avowedly criminal that the law had to be altered afterwards to cover the crime. Now suppose some postal official, between here and Rio Janeiro, had noticed a faint kicking inside the brown paper parcel, and had attempted to ascertain the cause. And suppose the clerk could only explain, in a muffled voice through the brown paper, that he was by constitution and temperament a Rebel. Don't you see that he would be rather understating his case? Don't you see he would be bearing his injuries much too meekly? They might take him out of the parcel; but they would very possibly put him into a mad-house instead. Symbolically speaking, that is what they would like to do with us. Symbolically speaking, the dirty misers who rule us will put us in a mad-house — unless we can put them there.

Or suppose a bank cashier were admittedly allowed to take the money out of the till, and put it loose in his pocket, more or less mixed up with his own money; afterwards laying some of both (at different odds) on "Blue Murder" for the Derby. Suppose when some depositor asked mildly what day the accountants came, he smote that astonished inquirer on the nose, crying: "Slanderer! Mud-slinger!" and suppose he then resigned his position. Suppose no books were shown. Suppose when the new cashier came to be initiated into his duties, the old cashier did not tell him about the money, but confided it to the honour and delicacy of his own maiden aunt at Cricklewood. Suppose he then went off in a yacht to visit the whale fisheries of the North Sea. Well, in every moral and legal principle, that is a precise account of the dealings with the Party Funds. But what would the banker say? What would the clients say? One thing, I think, I can venture to promise; the banker would not march up and down the office exclaiming in rapture, "I'm a rebel! That's what I am, a rebel!" And if he said to the first indignant depositor "You are a rebel," I fear the depositor might answer, "You are a robber." We have no need to elaborate arguments for breaking the law. The capitalists have broken the law. We have no need of further moralities. They have broken their own morality. It is as if you were to run down the street shouting, "Communism! Communism! Share! Share!" after a man who had run away with your watch.

We want a term that will tell everybody that there is, by the common standard, frank fraud and cruelty pushed to their fierce extreme; and that we are fighting THEM. We are not in a state of "divine discontent"; we are in an entirely human and entirely reasonable rage. We say we have been swindled and oppressed, and we are quite ready and able to prove it before any tribunal that allows us to call a swindler a swindler. It is the protection of the present system that most of its tribunals do not. I cannot at the moment think of any party name that would particularly distinguish us from our more powerful and prosperous opponents, unless it were the name the old Jacobites gave themselves; the Honest Party.

Captured Our Standards

I think it is plain that for the purpose of facing these new and infamous modern facts, we cannot, with any safety, depend on any of the old nineteenth century names; Socialist, or Communist, or Radical, or Liberal, or Labour. They are all honourable names; they all stand, or stood, for things in which we may still believe; we can still apply them to other problems; but not to this one. We have no longer a monopoly of these names. Let it be understood that I am not speaking here of the philosophical problem of their meaning, but of the practical problem of their use. When I called myself a Radical I knew Mr. Balfour would not call himself a Radical; therefore there was some use in the word. When I called myself a Socialist I knew Lord Penrhyn would not call himself a Socialist; therefore there was some use in the word. But the capitalists, in that aggressive march which is the main fact of our time, have captured our standards, both in the military and philosophic sense of the word. And it is useless for us to march under colours which they can carry as well as we.

Do you believe in Democracy? The devils also believe and tremble. Do you believe in Trades Unionism? The Labour Members also believe; and tremble like a falling teetotum. Do you believe in the State? The Samuels also believe, and grin. Do you believe in the centralisation of Empire? So did Beit. Do you believe in the decentralisation of Empire? So does Albu. Do you believe in the brotherhood of men: and do you, dear brethren, believe that Brother Arthur Henderson does not? Do you cry, "The world for the workers!" and do you imagine Philip Snowden would not? What we need is a name that shall declare, not that the modern treason and tyranny are bad, but that they are quite literally, intolerable: and that we mean to act accordingly. I really think "the Limits" would be as good a name as any. But, anyhow, something is born among us that is as strong as an infant Hercules: and it is part of my prejudices to want it christened. I advertise for godfathers and godmothers.

A Workman's History Of England

A thing which does not exist and which is very much wanted is "A Working-Man's History of England." I do not mean a history written for working men (there are whole dustbins of them), I mean a history, written by working men or from the working men's standpoint. I wish five generations of a fisher's or a miner's family could incarnate themselves in one man and tell the story.

It is impossible to ignore altogether any comment coming from so eminent a literary artist as Mr. Laurence Housman, but I do not deal here so specially with his well known conviction about Votes for Women, as with another idea which is, I think, rather at the back of it, if not with him at least with others; and which concerns this matter of the true story of England. For the true story is so entirely different from the false official story that the official classes tell that by this time the working class itself has largely forgotten its own experience. Either story can be quite logically linked up with Female Suffrage, which, therefore, I leave where it is for the moment; merely confessing that, so long as we get hold of the right story and not the wrong story, it seems to me a matter of secondary importance whether we link it up with Female Suffrage or not.

Now the ordinary version of recent English history that most moderately educated people have absorbed from childhood is something like this. That we emerged slowly from a semi-barbarism in which all the power and wealth were in the hands of Kings and a few nobles; that the King's power was broken first and then in due time that of the nobles, that this piece-meal improvement was brought about by one class after another waking up to a sense of citizenship and demanding a place in the national councils, frequently by riot or violence; and that in consequence of such menacing popular action, the franchise was granted to one class after another and used more and more to improve the social conditions of those classes, until we practically became a democracy, save for such exceptions as that of the women. I do not think anyone will deny that something like that is the general idea of the educated man who reads a newspaper and of the newspaper that he reads. That is the view current at public schools and colleges; it is part of the culture of all the classes that count for much in government; and there is not one word of truth in it from beginning to end.

That Great Reform Bill

Wealth and political power were very much more popularly distributed in the Middle Ages than they are now; but we will pass all that and consider recent history. The franchise has never been largely and liberally granted in England; half the males have no vote and are not likely to get one. It was _never_ granted in reply to pressure from awakened sections of the democracy; in every case there was a perfectly clear motive for granting it solely for the convenience of the aristocrats. The Great Reform Bill was not passed in response to such riots as that which destroyed a Castle; nor did the men who destroyed the Castle get any advantage whatever out of the Great Reform Bill. The Great Reform Bill was passed in order to seal an alliance between the landed aristocrats and the rich manufacturers of the north (an alliance that rules us still); and the chief object of that alliance was to _prevent_ the English populace getting any political power in the general excitement after the French Revolution. No one can read Macaulay's speech on the Chartists, for instance, and not see that this is so. Disraeli's further extension of the suffrage was not effected by the intellectual vivacity and pure republican theory of the mid-Victorian agricultural labourer; it was effected by a politician who saw an opportunity to dish the Whigs, and guessed that certain orthodoxies in the more prosperous artisan might yet give him a balance against the commercial Radicals. And while this very thin game of wire-pulling with the mere abstraction of the vote was being worked entirely by the oligarchs and entirely in their interests, the solid and real thing that was going on was the steady despoiling of the poor of all power or wealth, until they find themselves to-day upon the threshold of slavery. That is The Working Man's History of England.

Now, as I have said, I care comparatively little what is done with the mere voting part of the matter, so long as it is not claimed in such a way as to allow the plutocrat to escape his responsibility for his crimes, by pretending to be much more progressive, or much more susceptible to popular protest, than he ever has been.

346

And there is this danger in many of those who have answered me. One of them, for instance, says that women have been forced into their present industrial situations by the same iron economic laws that have compelled men. I say that men have not been compelled by iron economic laws, but in the main by the coarse and Christless cynicism of other men. But, of course, this way of talking is exactly in accordance with the fashionable and official version of English history. Thus, you will read that the monasteries, places where men of the poorest origin could be powerful, grew corrupt and gradually decayed. Or you will read that the mediaeval guilds of free workmen yielded at last to an inevitable economic law. You will read this; and you will be reading lies. They might as well say that Julius Caesar gradually decayed at the foot of Pompey's statue. You might as well say that Abraham Lincoln yielded at last to an inevitable economic law. The free mediaeval guilds did not decay; they were murdered. Solid men with solid guns and halberds, armed with lawful warrants from living statesmen broke up their corporations and took away their hard cash from them. In the same way the people in Cradley Heath are no more victims of a necessary economic law than the people in Putumayo. They are victims of a very terrible creature, of whose sins much has been said since the beginning of the world; and of whom it was said of old, "Let us fall into the hands of God, for His mercies are great; but let us not fall into the hands of Man."

The Capitalist Is in the Dock

Now it is this offering of a false economic excuse for the sweater that is the danger in perpetually saying that the poor woman will use the vote and that the poor man has not used it. The poor man is prevented from using it; prevented by the rich man, and the poor woman would be prevented in exactly the same gross and stringent style. I do not deny, of course, that there is something in the English temperament, and in the heritage of the last few centuries that makes the English workman more tolerant of wrong than most foreign workmen would be. But this only slightly modifies the main fact of the moral responsibility. To take an imperfect parallel, if we said that negro slaves would have rebelled if negroes had been more intelligent, we should be saying what is reasonable. But if we were to say that it could by any possibility be represented as being the negro's fault that he was at that moment in America and not in Africa, we should be saying what is frankly unreasonable. It is every bit as unreasonable to say the mere supineness of the English workmen has put them in the capitalist slave-yard. The capitalist has put them in the capitalist slaveyard; and very cunning smiths have hammered the chains. It is just this creative criminality in the authors of the system that we must not allow to be slurred over. The capitalist is in the dock to-day; and so far as I at least can prevent him, he shall not get out of it.

The French Revolution And The Irish

It will be long before the poison of the Party System is worked out of the body politic. Some of its most indirect effects are the most dangerous. One that is very dangerous just now is this: that for most Englishmen the Party System falsifies history, and especially the history of revolutions. It falsifies history because it simplifies history. It paints everything either Blue or Buff in the style of its own silly circus politics: while a real revolution has as many colours as the sunrise — or the end of the world. And if we do not get rid of this error we shall make very bad blunders about the real revolution which seems to grow more and more probable, especially among the Irish. And any human familiarity with history will teach a man this first of all: that Party practically does not exist in a real revolution. It is a game for quiet times.

If you take a boy who has been to one of those big private schools which are falsely called the Public Schools, and another boy who has been to one of those large public schools which are falsely called the Board Schools, you will find some differences between the two, chiefly a difference in the management of the voice. But you will find they are both English in a special way, and that their education has been essentially the same. They are ignorant on the same subjects. They have never heard of the same plain facts. They have been taught the wrong answer to the same confusing question. There is one fundamental element in the attitude of the Eton master talking about "playing the game," and the elementary teacher training gutter-snipes to sing, "What is the Meaning of Empire Day?" And the name of that element is "unhistoric." It knows nothing really about England, still less about Ireland or France, and, least of all, of course, about anything like the French Revolution.

Revolution by Snap Division

Now what general notion does the ordinary English boy, thus taught to utter one ignorance in one of two accents, get and keep through life about the French Revolution? It is the notion of the English House of Commons with an enormous Radical majority on one side of the table and a small Tory minority on the other; the majority voting solid for a Republic, the minority voting solid for a Monarchy; two teams tramping through two lobbies with no difference between their methods and ours, except that (owing to some habit peculiar to Gaul) the brief intervals were brightened by a riot or a massacre, instead of by a whisky and soda and a Marconi tip. Novels are much more reliable than histories in such matters. For though an English novel about France does not tell the truth about France, it does tell the truth about England; and more than half the histories never tell the truth about anything. And popular fiction, I think, bears witness to the general English impression. The French Revolution is a snap division with an unusual turnover of votes. On the one side stand a king and queen who are good but weak, surrounded by nobles with rapiers drawn; some of whom are good, many of whom are wicked, all of whom are good-looking. Against these there is a formless mob of human beings, wearing red caps and seemingly insane, who all blindly follow ruffians who are also rhetoricians; some of whom die repentant and others unrepentant towards the end of the fourth act. The leaders of this boiling mass of all men melted into one are called Mirabeau, Robespierre, Danton, Marat, and so on. And it is conceded that their united frenzy may have been forced on them by the evils of the old regime.

That, I think, is the commonest English view of the French Revolution; and it will not survive the reading of two pages of any real speech or letter of the period. These human beings were human; varied, complex and inconsistent. But the rich Englishman, ignorant of revolutions, would hardly believe you if you told him some of the common human subtleties of the case. Tell him that Robespierre threw the red cap in the dirt in disgust, while the king had worn it with a broad grin, so to speak; tell him that Danton, the fierce founder of the Republic of the Terror, said quite sincerely to a noble, "I am more monarchist than you;" tell him that the Terror really seems to have been brought to an end chiefly by the efforts of people who particularly wanted to go on with it — and he will not believe these things. He will not believe them because he has no humility, and therefore no realism. He has never been inside himself; and so could never be inside another man. The truth is that in the French affair everybody occupied an individual position. Every man talked sincerely, if not because he was sincere, then because he was angry. Robespierre talked even more about God than about the Republic because he cared even more about God than about the Republic. Danton talked even more about France than about the Republic because he cared even more about France than about the Republic. Marat talked more about Humanity than either, because that physician (though himself somewhat needing a physician) really cared about it. The nobles were divided, each man from the next. The attitude of the king was quite different from the attitude of the queen; certainly much more different than any differences between our Liberals and Tories for the last twenty years. And it will sadden _some_ of my friends to remember that it was the king who was the Liberal and the queen who was the Tory. There were not two people, I think, in that most practical crisis who stood in precisely the same attitude towards the situation. And that is why, between them, they saved Europe. It is when you really perceive the unity of mankind that you really perceive its variety. It is not a flippancy, it is a very sacred truth, to say that when men really understand that they are brothers they instantly begin to fight.

The Revival of Reality

Now these things are repeating themselves with an enormous reality in the Irish Revolution. You will not be able to make a Party System out of the matter. Everybody is in revolt; therefore everybody is telling the truth. The Nationalists will go on caring most for the nation, as Danton and the defenders of the frontier went on caring most for the nation. The priests will go on caring most for religion, as Robespierre went on caring most for religion. The Socialists will go on caring most for the cure of physical suffering, as Marat went on caring most for it. It is out of these real differences that real things can be made, such as the modern French democracy. For by such tenacity everyone sees at last that there is something in the other person's position. And those drilled in party discipline see nothing either past or present. And where there is nothing there is Satan.

For a long time past in our politics there has not only been no real battle, but no real bargain. No two men have bargained as Gladstone and Parnell bargained — each knowing the other to be a power. But in real revolutions men discover that no one man can really agree with another man until he has disagreed with him.

351

Liberalism: A Sample

There is a certain daily paper in England towards which I feel very much as Tom Pinch felt towards Mr. Pecksniff immediately after he had found him out. The war upon Dickens was part of the general war on all democrats, about the eighties and nineties, which ushered in the brazen plutocracy of to-day. And one of the things that it was fashionable to say of Dickens in drawing-rooms was that he had no subtlety, and could not describe a complex frame of mind. Like most other things that are said in drawing-rooms, it was a lie. Dickens was a very unequal writer, and his successes alternate with his failures; but his successes are subtle quite as often as they are simple. Thus, to take "Martin Chuzzlewit" alone, I should call the joke about the Lord No-zoo a simple joke: but I should call the joke about Mrs. Todgers's vision of a wooden leg a subtle joke. And no frame of mind was ever so selfcontradictory and yet so realistic as that which Dickens describes when he says, in effect, that, though Pinch knew now that there had never been such a person as Pecksniff, in his ideal sense, he could not bring himself to insult the very face and form that had contained the legend. The parallel with Liberal journalism is not perfect; because it was once honest; and Pecksniff presumably never was. And even when I come to feel a final incompatibility of temper, Pecksniff was not so Pecksniffian as he has since become. But the comparison is complete in so far as I share all the reluctance of Mr. Pinch. Some old heathen king was advised by one of the Celtic saints, I think, to burn what he had adored and adore what he had burnt. I am quite ready, if anyone will prove I was wrong, to adore what I have burnt; but I do really feel an unwillingness verging upon weakness to burning what I have adored. I think it is a weakness to be overcome in times as bad as these, when (as Mr. Orage wrote with something like splendid common sense the other day) there is such a lot to do and so few people who will do it. So I will devote this article to considering one case of the astounding baseness to which Liberal journalism has sunk.

Mental Breakdown in Fleet Street

One of the two or three streaks of light on our horizon can be perceived in this: that the moral breakdown of these papers has been accompanied by a mental breakdown also. The contemporary official paper, like the "Daily News" or the "Daily Chronicle" (I mean in so far as it deals with politics), simply cannot argue; and simply does not pretend to argue. It considers the solution which it imagines that wealthy people want, and it signifies the same in the usual manner; which is not by holding up its hand, but by falling on its face. But there is no more curious quality in its degradation than a sort of carelessness, at once of hurry and fatigue, with which it flings down its argument — or rather its refusal to argue. It does not even write sophistry: it writes anything. It does not so much poison the reader's mind as simply assume that the reader hasn't got one. For instance, one of these papers printed an article on Sir Stuart Samuel, who, having broken the great Liberal statute against corruption, will actually, perhaps, be asked to pay his own fine — in spite of the fact that he can well afford to do so. The article says, if I remember aright, that the decision will cause general surprise and some indignation. That any modern Government making a very rich capitalist obey the law will cause general surprise, may be true. Whether it will cause general indignation rather depends on whether our social intercourse is entirely confined to Park Lane, or any such pigsties built of gold. But the journalist proceeds to say, his neck rising higher and higher out of his collar, and his hair rising higher and higher on his head, in short, his resemblance to the Dickens' original increasing every instant, that he does not mean that the law against corruption should be less stringent, but that the burden should be borne by the whole community. This may mean that whenever a rich man breaks the law, all the poor men ought to be made to pay his fine. But I will suppose a slightly less insane meaning. I will suppose it means that the whole power of the commonwealth should be used to prosecute an offender of this kind. That, of course, can only mean that the matter will be decided by that instrument which still pretends to represent the whole power of the commonwealth. In other words, the Government will judge the Government.

Now this is a perfectly plain piece of brute logic. We need not go into the other delicious things in the article, as when it says that "in old times Parliament had to be protected against Royal invasion by the man in the street." Parliament has to be protected now against the man in the street. Parliament is simply the most detested and the most detestable of all our national institutions: all that is evident enough. What is interesting is the blank and staring fallacy of the attempted reply.

When the Journalist Is Ruined

A long while ago, before all the Liberals died, a Liberal introduced a Bill to prevent Parliament being merely packed with the slaves of financial interests. For that purpose he established the excellent democratic principle that the private citizen, as such, might protest against public corruption. He was called the Common Informer. I believe the miserable party papers are really reduced to playing on the degradation of the two words in modern language. Now the word "comnon" in "Common Informer" means exactly what it means in "common sense" or "Book of Common Prayer," or (above all) in "House of Commons." It does not mean anything low or vulgar; any more than they do. The only difference is that the House of Commons really is low and vulgar; and the Common Informer isn't. It is just the same with the word "Informer." It does not mean spy or sneak. It means one who gives information. It means what "journalist" ought to mean. The only difference is that the Common Informer may be paid if he tells the truth. The common journalist will be ruined if he does.

Now the quite plain point before the party journalist is this: If he really means that a corrupt bargain between a Government and a contractor ought to be judged by public opinion, he must (nowadays) mean Parliament; that is, the caucus that controls Parliament. And he must decide between one of two views. Either he means that there can be no such thing as a corrupt Government. Or he means that it is one of the characteristic qualities of a corrupt Government to denounce its own corruption. I laugh; and I leave him his choice.

The Fatigue Of Fleet Street

Why is the modern party political journalism so bad? It is worse even than it intends to be. It praises its preposterous party leaders through thick and thin; but it somehow succeeds in making them look greater fools than they are. This clumsiness clings even to the photographs of public men, as they are snapshotted at public meetings. A sensitive politician (if there is such a thing) would, I should think, want to murder the man who snapshots him at those moments. For our general impression of a man's gesture or play of feature is made up of a series of vanishing instants, at any one of which he may look worse than our general impression records. Mr. Augustine Birrell may have made quite a sensible and amusing speech, in the course of which his audience would hardly have noticed that he resettled his necktie. Snapshot him, and he appears as convulsively clutching his throat in the agonies of strangulation, and with his head twisted on one side as if he had been hanged. Sir Edward Carson might make a perfectly good speech, which no one thought wearisome, but might himself be just tired enough to shift from one leg to the other. Snapshot him, and he appears as holding one leg stiffly in the air and yawning enough to swallow the audience. But it is in the prose narratives of the Press that we find most manifestations of this strange ineptitude; this knack of exhibiting your own favourites in an unlucky light. It is not so much that the party journalists do not tell the truth as that they tell just enough of it to make it clear that they are telling lies. One of their favourite blunders is an amazing sort of bathos. They begin by telling you that some statesman said something brilliant in style or biting in wit, at which his hearers thrilled with terror or thundered with applause. And then they tell you what it was that he said. Silly asses!

Insane Exaggeration

Here is an example from a leading Liberal paper touching the debates on Home Rule. I am a Home Ruler; so my sympathies would be, if anything, on the side of the Liberal paper upon that point. I merely quote it as an example of this ridiculous way of writing, which, by insane exaggeration, actually makes its hero look smaller than he is.

This was strange language to use about the "hypocritical sham," and Mr. Asquith, knowing that the biggest battle of his career was upon him, hit back without mercy. "I should like first to know," said he, with a glance at his supporters, "whether my proposals are accepted?"

That's all. And I really do not see why poor Mr. Asquith should be represented as having violated the Christian virtue of mercy by saying that. I myself could compose a great many paragraphs upon the same model, each containing its stinging and perhaps unscrupulous epigram. As, for example: — "The Archbishop of Canterbury, realising that his choice now lay between denying God and earning the crown of martyrdom by dying in torments, spoke with a frenzy of religious passion that might have seemed fanatical under circumstances less intense. 'The Children's Service,' he said firmly, with his face to the congregation, 'will be held at half-past four this afternoon as usual.'"

Or, we might have: — "Lord Roberts, recognising that he had now to face Armageddon, and that if he lost this last battle against overwhelming odds the independence of England would be extinguished forever, addressed to his soldiers (looking at them and not falling off his horse) a speech which brought their national passions to boiling point, and might well have seemed blood-thirsty in quieter times. It ended with the celebrated declaration that it was a fine day."

Or we might have the much greater excitement of reading something like this: — "The Astronomer Royal, having realised that the earth would certainly be smashed to pieces by a comet unless his requests in connection with wireless telegraphy were seriously considered, gave an address at the Royal Society which, under other circumstances, would have seemed unduly dogmatic and emotional and deficient in scientific agnosticism. This address (which he delivered without any attempt to stand on his head) included a fierce and even ferocious declaration that it is generally easier to see the stars by night than by day."

Now, I cannot see, on my conscience and reason, that any one of my imaginary paragraphs is more ridiculous than the real one. Nobody can believe that Mr. Asquith regards these belated and careful compromises about Home Rule as "the biggest battle of his career." It is only justice to him to say that he has had bigger battles than that. Nobody can believe that any body of men, bodily present, either thundered or thrilled at a man merely saying that he would like to know whether his proposals were accepted. No; it would be far better for Parliament if its doors were shut again, and reporters were excluded. In that case, the outer public did hear genuine rumours of almost gigantic eloquence; such as that which has perpetuated Pitt's reply against the charge of youth, or Fox's bludgeoning of the idea of war as a compromise. It would be much better to follow the old fashion and let in no reporters at all than to follow the new fashion and select the stupidest reporters you can find.

Their Load of Lies

Now, why do people in Fleet-street talk such tosh? People in Fleet-street are not fools. Most of them have realised reality through work; some through starvation; some through damnation, or something damnably like it. I think it is simply and seriously true that they are tired of their job. As the general said in M. Rostand's play, "la fatigue!"

I do really believe that this is one of the ways in which God (don't get flurried, Nature if you like) is unexpectedly avenged on things infamous and unreasonable. And this method is that men's moral and even physical tenacity actually give out under such a load of lies. They go on writing their leading articles and their Parliamentary reports. They go on doing it as a convict goes on picking oakum. But the point is not that we are bored with their articles; the point is that they are. The work is done worse because it is done weakly and without human enthusiasm. And it is done weakly because of the truth we have told so many times in this book: that it is not done for monarchy, for which men will die; or for democracy, for which men will die; or even for aristocracy, for which many men have died. It is done for a thing called Capitalism: which stands out quite clearly in history in many curious ways. But the most curious thing about it is that no man has loved it; and no man died for it.

The Amnesty For Aggression

If there is to rise out of all this red ruin something like a republic of justice, it is essential that our views should be real views; that is, glimpses of lives and landscapes outside ourselves. It is essential that they should not be mere opium visions that begin and end in smoke — and so often in cannon smoke. I make no apology, therefore, for returning to the purely practical and realistic point I urged last week: the fact that we shall lose everything we might have gained if we lose the idea that the responsible person is responsible.

For instance, it is almost specially so with the one or two things in which the British Government, or the British public, really are behaving badly. The first, and worst of them, is the non-extension of the Moratorium, or truce of debtor and creditor, to the very world where there are the poorest debtors and the cruellest creditors. This is infamous: and should be, if possible, more infamous to those who think the war right than to those who think it wrong. Everyone knows that the people who can least pay their debts are the people who are always trying to. Among the poor a payment may be as rash as a speculation. Among the rich a bankruptcy may be as safe as a bank. Considering the class from which private soldiers are taken, there is an atrocious meanness in the idea of buying their blood abroad, while we sell their sticks at home. The English language, by the way, is full of delicate paradoxes. We talk of the private soldiers because they are really public soldiers; and we talk of the public schools because they are really private schools. Anyhow, the wrong is of the sort that ought to be resisted, as much in war as in peace.

Ought to Be Hammered

But as long as we speak of it as a cloudy conclusion, come to by an anonymous club called Parliament, or a masked tribunal called the Cabinet, we shall never get such a wrong righted. Somebody is officially responsible for the unfairness; and that somebody ought to be hammered. The other example, less important but more ludicrous, is the silly boycott of Germans in England, extending even to German music. I do not believe for a moment that the English people feel any such insane fastidiousness. Are the English artists who practise the particularly English art of water-colour to be forbidden to use Prussian blue? Are all old ladies to shoot their Pomeranian dogs? But though England would laugh at this, she will get the credit of it, and will continue: until we ask who the actual persons are who feel sure that we should shudder at a ballad of the Rhine. It is certain that we should find they are capitalists. It is very probable that we should find they are foreigners.

Some days ago the Official Council of the Independent Labour Party, or the Independent Council of the Official Labour Party, or the Independent and Official Council of the Labour Party (I have got quite nervous about these names and distinctions; but they all seem to say the same thing) began their manifesto by saying it would be difficult to assign the degrees of responsibility which each nation had for the outbreak of the war. Afterwards, a writer in the "Christian Commonwealth," lamenting war in the name of Labour, but in the language of my own romantic middle-class, said that all the nations must share the responsibility for this great calamity of war. Now exactly as long as we go on talking like that we shall have war after war, and calamity after calamity, until the crack of doom. It simply amounts to a promise of pardon to any person who will start a quarrel. It is an amnesty for assassins. The moment any man assaults any other man he makes all the other men as bad as himself. He has only to stab, and to vanish in a fog of forgetfulness. The real eagles of iron, the predatory Empires, will be delighted with this doctrine. They will applaud the Labour Concert or Committee, or whatever it is called. They will willingly take all the crime, with only a quarter of the conscience: they will be as ready to share the memory as they are to share the spoil. The Powers will divide responsibility as calmly as they divided Poland.

The Whole Loathsome Load

But I still stubbornly and meekly submit my point: that you cannot end war without asking who began it. If you think somebody else, not Germany, began it, then blame that somebody else: do not blame everybody and nobody. Perhaps you think that a small sovereign people, fresh from two triumphant wars, ought to discrown itself before sunrise; because the nephew of a neighbouring Emperor has been shot by his own subjects. Very well. Then blame Servia; and, to the extent of your influence, you may be preventing small kingdoms being obstinate or even princes being shot. Perhaps you think the whole thing was a huge conspiracy of Russia, with France as a dupe and Servia as a pretext. Very well. Then blame Russia; and, to the extent of your influence, you may be preventing great Empires from making racial excuses for a raid. Perhaps you think France wrong for feeling what you call "revenge," and I should call recovery of stolen goods. Perhaps you blame Belgium for being sentimental about her frontier; or England for being sentimental about her word. If so, blame them; or whichever of them you think is to blame. Or again, it is barely possible that you may think, as I do, that the whole loathsome load has been laid upon us by the monarchy which I have not named; still less wasted time in abusing. But if there be in Europe a military State which has not the religion of Russia, yet has helped Russia to tyrannise over the Poles, that State cares not for religion, but for tyranny. If there be a State in Europe which has not the religion of the Austrians, but has helped Austria to bully the Servians, that State cares not for belief, but for bullying. If there be in Europe any people or principality which respects neither republics nor religions, to which the political ideal of Paris is as much a myth as the mystical ideal of Moscow, then blame that: and do more than blame. In the healthy and highly theological words of Robert Blatchford, drive it back to the Hell from which it came.

Crying Over Spilt Blood

But whatever you do, do not blame everybody for what was certainly done by somebody. It may be it is no good crying over spilt blood, any more than over spilt milk. But we do not find the culprit any more by spilling the milk over everybody; or by daubing everybody with blood. Still less do we improve matters by watering the milk with our tears, nor the blood either. To say that everybody is responsible means that nobody is responsible. If in the future we see Russia annexing Rutland (as part of the old Kingdom of Muscovy), if we see Bavaria taking a sudden fancy to the Bank of England, or the King of the Cannibal Islands suddenly demanding a tribute of edible boys and girls from England and America, we may be quite certain also that the Leader of the Labour Party will rise, with a slight cough, and say: "It would be a difficult task to apportion the blame between the various claims which..."

Revive The Court Jester

I hope the Government will not think just now about appointing a Poet Laureate. I hardly think they can be altogether in the right mood. The business just now before the country makes a very good detective story; but as a national epic it is a little depressing. Jingo literature always weakens a nation; but even healthy patriotic literature has its proper time and occasion. For instance, Mr. Newbolt (who has been suggested for the post) is a very fine poet; but I think his patriotic lyrics would just now rather jar upon a patriot. We are rather too much concerned about our practical seamanship to feel quite confident that Drake will return and "drum them up the Channel as he drummed them long ago." On the contrary, we have an uncomfortable feeling that Drake's ship might suddenly go to the bottom, because the capitalists have made Lloyd George abolish the Plimsoll Line. One could not, without being understood ironically, adjure the two party teams to-day to "play up, play up and play the game," or to "love the game more than the prize." And there is no national hero at this moment in the soldiering line — unless, perhaps, it is Major Archer-Shee — of whom anyone would be likely to say: "Sed miles; sed pro patria." There is, indeed, one beautiful poem of Mr. Newbolt's which may mingle faintly with one's thoughts in such times, but that, alas, is to a very different tune. I mean that one in which he echoes Turner's conception of the old wooden ship vanishing with all the valiant memories of the English:

There's a far bell ringing At the setting of the sun, And a phantom voice is singing Of the great days done. There's a far bell ringing, And a phantom voice is singing Of a fame forever clinging To the great days done. For the sunset breezes shiver, Temeraire, Temeraire, And she's fading down the river....

Well, well, neither you nor I know whether she is fading down the river or not. It is quite enough for us to know, as King Alfred did, that a great many pirates have landed on both banks of the Thames.

Praise and Prophecy Impossible

At this moment that is the only kind of patriotic poem that could satisfy the emotions of a patriotic person. But it certainly is not the sort of poem that is expected from a Poet Laureate, either on the highest or the lowest theory of his office. He is either a great minstrel singing the victories of a great king, or he is a common Court official like the Groom of the Powder Closet. In the first case his praises should be true; in the second case they will nearly always be false; but in either case he must praise. And what there is for him to praise just now it would be precious hard to say. And if there is no great hope of a real poet, there is still less hope of a real prophet. What Newman called, I think, "The Prophetical Office," that is, the institution of an inspired protest even against an inspired religion, certainly would not do in modern England. The Court is not likely to keep a tame prophet in order to encourage him to be wild. It is not likely to pay a man to say that wolves shall howl in Downing-street and vultures build their nests in Buckingham Palace. So vast has been the progress of humanity that these two things are quite impossible. We cannot have a great poet praising kings. We cannot have a great prophet denouncing kings. So I have to fall back on a third suggestion.

The Field for a Fool

Instead of reviving the Court Poet, why not revive the Court Fool? He is the only person who could do any good at this moment either to the Royal or the judicial Courts. The present political situation is utterly unsuitable for the purposes of a great poet. But it is particularly suitable for the purposes of a great buffoon. The old jester was under certain privileges: you could not resent the jokes of a fool, just as you cannot resent the sermons of a curate. Now, what the present Government of England wants is neither serious praise nor serious denunciation; what it wants is satire. What it wants, in other words, is realism given with gusto. When King Louis the Eleventh unexpectedly visited his enemy, the Duke of Burgundy, with a small escort, the Duke's jester said he would give the King his fool's cap, for he was the fool now. And when the Duke replied with dignity, "And suppose I treat him with all proper respect?" the fool answered, "Then I will give it to you." That is the kind of thing that somebody ought to be free to say now. But if you say it now you will be fined a hundred pounds at the least.

Carson's Dilemma

For the things that have been happening lately are not merely things that one could joke about. They are themselves, truly and intrinsically, jokes. I mean that there is a sort of epigram of unreason in the situation itself, as there was in the situation where there was jam yesterday and jam to-morrow but never jam to-day. Take, for instance, the extraordinary case of Sir Edward Carson. The point is not whether we regard his attitude in Belfast as the defiance of a sincere and dogmatic rebel, or as the bluff of a party hack and mountebank. The point is not whether we regard his defence of the Government at the Old Bailey as a chivalrous and reluctant duty done as an advocate or a friend, or as a mere case of a lawyer selling his soul for a fat brief. The point is that whichever of the two actions we approve, and whichever of the four explanations we adopt, Sir Edward's position is still raving nonsense. On any argument, he cannot escape from his dilemma. It may be argued that laws and customs should be obeyed whatever our private feelings; and that it is an established custom to accept a brief in such a case. But then it is a somewhat more established custom to obey an Act of Parliament and to keep the peace. It may be argued that extreme misgovernment justifies men in Ulster or elsewhere in refusing to obey the law. But then it would justify them even more in refusing to appear professionally in a law court. Etiquette cannot be at once so unimportant that Carson may shoot at the King's uniform, and yet so important that he must always be ready to put on his own. The Government cannot be so disreputable that Carson need not lay down his gun, and yet so respectable that he is bound to put on his wig. Carson cannot at once be so fierce that he can kill in what he considers a good cause, and yet so meek that he must argue in what he considers a bad cause. Obedience or disobedience, conventional or unconventional, a solicitor's letter cannot be more sacred than the King's writ; a blue bag cannot be more rational than the British flag. The thing is rubbish read anyway, and the only difficulty is to get a joke good enough to express it. It is a case for the Court Jester. The phantasy of it could only be expressed by some huge ceremonial hoax. Carson ought to be crowned with the shamrocks and emeralds and followed by green-clad minstrels of the Clan-na-Gael, playing "The Wearing of the Green."

Belated Chattiness by Wireless

But all the recent events are like that. They are practical jokes. The jokes do not need to be made: they only need to be pointed out. You and I do not talk and act as the Isaacs brothers talked and acted, by their own most favourable account of themselves; and even their account of themselves was by no means favourable. You and I do not talk of meeting our own born brother "at a family function" as if he were some infinitely distant cousin whom we only met at Christmas. You and I, when we suddenly feel inclined for a chat with the same brother about his dinner and the Coal Strike, do not generally select either wireless telegraphy or the Atlantic Cable as the most obvious and economical channel for that outburst of belated chattiness. You and I do not talk, if it is proposed to start a railway between Catsville and Dogtown, as if the putting up of a station at Dogtown could have no kind of economic effect on the putting up of a station at Catsville. You and I do not think it candid to say that when we are at one end of a telephone we have no sort of connection with the other end. These things have got into the region of farce; and should be dealt with farcically, not even ferociously.

A Fool Who Shall Be Free

In the Roman Republic there was a Tribune of the People, whose person was inviolable like an ambassador's. There was much the same idea in Becket's attempt to remove the Priest, who was then the popular champion, from the ordinary courts. We shall have no Tribune; for we have no republic. We shall have no Priest; for we have no religion. The best we deserve or can expect is a Fool who shall be free; and who shall deliver us with laughter.

The Art Of Missing The Point

Missing the point is a very fine art; and has been carried to something like perfection by politicians and Pressmen to-day. For the point is generally a very sharp point; and is, moreover, sharp at both ends. That is to say that both parties would probably impale themselves in an uncomfortable manner if they did not manage to avoid it altogether. I have just been looking at the election address of the official Liberal candidate for the part of the country in which I live; and though it is, if anything, rather more logical and free from cant than most other documents of the sort it is an excellent example of missing the point. The candidate has to go boring on about Free Trade and Land Reform and Education; and nobody reading it could possibly imagine that in the town of Wycombe, where the poll will be declared, the capital of the Wycombe division of Bucks which the candidate is contesting, centre of the important and vital trade on which it has thriven, a savage struggle about justice has been raging for months past between the poor and rich, as real as the French Revolution. The man offering himself at Wycombe as representative of the Wycombe division simply says nothing about it at all. It is as if a man at the crisis of the French Terror had offered himself as a deputy for the town of Paris, and had said nothing about the Monarchy, nothing about the Republic, nothing about the massacres, nothing about the war; but had explained with great clearness his views on the suppression of the Jansenists, the literary style of Racine, the suitability of Turenae for the post of commander-in-chief, and the religious reflections of Madame de Maintenon. For, at their best, the candidate's topics are not topical. Home Rule is a very good thing, and modern education is a very bad thing; but neither of them are things that anybody is talking about in High Wycombe. This is the first and simplest way of missing the point: deliberately to avoid and ignore it.

The Candid Candidate

It would be an amusing experiment, by the way, to go to the point instead of avoiding it. What fun it would be to stand as a strict Party candidate, but issue a perfectly frank and cynical Election Address. Mr. Mosley's address begins, "Gentlemen, — Sir Alfred Cripps having been chosen for a high judicial position and a seat in the House of Lords, a by-election now becomes necessary, and the electors of South Bucks are charged with the responsible duty of electing, etc., etc." But suppose there were another candidate whose election address opened in a plain, manly style, like this: "Gentlemen, — In the sincere hope of being myself chosen for a high judicial position or a seat in the House of Lords, or considerably increasing my private fortune by some Government appointment, or, at least, inside information about the financial prospects, I have decided that it is worth my while to disburse large sums of money to you on various pretexts, and, with even more reluctance to endure the bad speaking and bad ventilation of the Commons' House of Parliament, so help me God. I have very pronounced convictions on various political questions; but I will not trouble my fellow-citizens with them, since I have quite made up my mind to abandon any or all of them if requested to do so by the upper classes. The electors are therefore charged with the entirely irresponsible duty of electing a Member; or, in other words, I ask my neighbours round about this part, who know I am not a bad chap in many ways, to do me a good turn in my business, just as I might ask them to change a sovereign. My election will have no conceivable kind of effect on anything or anybody except myself; so I ask, as man to man, the Electors of the Southern or Wycombe Division of the County of Buckingham to accept a ride in one of my motor-cars; and poll early to please a pal — God Save the King." I do not know whether you or I would be elected if we presented ourselves with an election address of that kind; but we should have had our fun and (comparatively speaking) saved our souls; and I have a strong suspicion that we should be elected or rejected on a mechanical majority like anybody else; nobody having dreamed of reading an election address any more than an advertisement of a hair restorer.

Tyranny and Head-Dress

But there is another and more subtle way in which we may miss the point; and that is, not by keeping a dead silence about it, but by being just witty enough to state it wrong. Thus, some of the Liberal official papers have almost screwed up their courage to the sticking-point about the bestial coup d'etat in South Africa. They have screwed up their courage to the sticking-point; and it has stuck. It cannot get any further; because it has missed the main point. The modern Liberals make their feeble attempts to attack the introduction of slavery into South Africa by the Dutch and the Jews, by a very typical evasion of the vital fact. The vital fact is simply slavery. Most of these Dutchmen have always felt like slave-owners. Most of these Jews have always felt like slaves. Now that they are on top, they have a particular and curious kind of impudence, which is only known among slaves. But the Liberal journalists will do their best to suggest that the South African wrong consisted in what they call Martial Law. That is, that there is something specially wicked about men doing an act of cruelty in khaki or in vermilion, but not if it is done in dark blue with pewter buttons. The tyrant who wears a busby or a forage cap is abominable; the tyrant who wears a horsehair wig is excusable. To be judged by soldiers is hell; but to be judged by lawyers is paradise.

Now the point must not be missed in this way. What is wrong with the tyranny in Africa is not that it is run by soldiers. It would be quite as bad, or worse, if it were run by policemen. What is wrong is that, for the first time since Pagan times, private men are being forced to work for a private man. Men are being punished by imprisonment or exile for refusing to accept a job. The fact that Botha can ride on a horse, or fire off a gun, makes him better rather than worse than any man like Sidney Webb or Philip Snowden, who attempt the same slavery by much less manly methods. The Liberal Party will try to divert the whole discussion to one about what they call militarism. But the very terms of modern politics contradict it. For when we talk of real rebels against the present system we call them Militants. And there will be none in the Servile State.

The Servile State Again

I read the other day, in a quotation from a German newspaper, the highly characteristic remark that Germany having annexed Belgium would soon re-establish its commerce and prosperity, and that, in particular, arrangements were already being made for introducing into the new province the German laws for the protection of workmen.

I am quite content with that paragraph for the purpose of any controversy about what is called German atrocity. If men I know had not told me they had themselves seen the bayoneting of a baby; if the most respectable refugees did not bring with them stories of burning cottages — yes, and of burning cottagers as well; if doctors did not report what they do report of the condition of girls in the hospitals; if there were no facts; if there were no photographs, that one phrase I have quoted would be quite sufficient to satisfy me that the Prussians are tyrants; tyrants in a peculiar and almost insane sense which makes them pre-eminent among the evil princes of the earth. The first and most striking feature is a stupidity that rises into a sort of ghastly innocence. The protection of workmen! Some workmen, perhaps, might have a fancy for being protected from shrapnel; some might be glad to put up an umbrella that would ward off things dropping from the gentle Zeppelin in heaven upon the place beneath. Some of these discontented proletarians have taken the same view as Vandervelde their leader, and are now energetically engaged in protecting themselves along the line of the Yser; I am glad to say not altogether without success. It is probable that nearly all of the Belgian workers would, on the whole, prefer to be protected against bombs, sabres, burning cities, starvation, torture, and the treason of wicked kings. In short, it is probable — it is at least possible, impious as is the idea — that they would prefer to be protected against Germans and all they represent. But if a Belgian workman is told that he is not to be protected against Germans, but actually to be protected by Germans, I think he may be excused for staring. His first impulse, I imagine, will be to ask, "Against whom? Are there any worse people to come along?"

But apart from the hellish irony of this humanitarian idea, the question it raises is really one of solid importance for people whose politics are more or less like ours. There is a very urgent point in that question, "Against whom would the Belgian workmen be protected by the German laws?" And if we pursue it, we shall be enabled to analyse something of that poison — very largely a Prussian poison — which has long been working in our own commonwealth, to the enslavement of the weak and the secret strengthening of the strong. For the Prussian armies are, pre-eminently, the advance guard of the Servile State. I say this scientifically, and quite apart from passion or even from preference. I have no illusions about either Belgium or England. Both have been stained with the soot of Capitalism and blinded with the smoke of mere Colonial ambition; both have been caught at a disadvantage in such modern dirt and disorder; both have come out much better than I should have expected countries so modern and so industrial to do. But in England and Belgium there is Capitalism mixed up with a great many other things, strong things and things that pursue other aims; Clericalism, for instance, and militant Socialism in Belgium; Trades Unionism and sport and the remains of real aristocracy in England. But Prussia is Capitalism; that is, a gradually solidifying slavery; and that majestic unity with which she moves, dragging all the dumb Germanies after her, is due to the fact that her Servile State is complete, while ours is incomplete. There are not mutinies; there are not even mockeries; the voice of national self-criticism has been extinguished forever. For this people is already permanently cloven into a higher and a lower class: in its industry as much as its army. Its employers are, in the strictest and most sinister sense, captains of industry. Its proletariat is, in the truest and most pitiable sense, an army of labour. In that atmosphere masters bear upon them the signs that they are more than men; and to insult an officer is death.

If anyone ask how this extreme and unmistakable subordination of the employed to the employers is brought about, we all know the answer. It is brought about by hunger and hardness of heart, accelerated by a certain kind of legislation, of which we have had a good deal lately in England, but which was almost invariably borrowed from Prussia. Mr. Herbert Samuel's suggestion that the poor should be able to put their money in little boxes and not be able to get it out again is a sort of standing symbol of all the rest. I have forgotten how the poor were going to benefit eventually by what is for them indistinguishable from dropping sixpence down a drain. Perhaps they were going to get it back some day; perhaps when they could produce a hundred coupons out of the Daily Citizen; perhaps when they got their hair cut; perhaps when they consented to be inoculated, or trepanned, or circumcised, or something. Germany is full of this sort of legislation; and if you asked an innocent German, who honestly believed in it, what it was, he would answer that it was for the protection of workmen.

And if you asked again "Their protection from what?" you would have the whole plan and problem of the Servile State plain in front of you. Whatever notion there is, there is no notion whatever of protecting the employed person _from his employer_. Much less is there any idea of his ever being anywhere except under an employer. Whatever the Capitalist wants he gets. He may have the sense to want washed and well-fed labourers rather than dirty and feeble ones, and the restrictions may happen to exist in the form of laws from the Kaiser or by-laws from the Krupps. But the Kaiser will not offend the Krupps, and the Krupps will not offend the Kaiser. Laws of this kind, then, do not attempt to protect workmen against the injustice of the Capitalist as the English Trade Unions did. They do not attempt to protect workmen against the injustice of the State as the mediaeval guilds did. Obviously they cannot protect workmen against the foreign invader — especially when (as in the comic case of Belgium) they are imposed by the foreign invader. What then are such laws designed to protect workmen against? Tigers, rattlesnakes, hyenas?

Oh, my young friends; oh, my Christian brethren, they are designed to protect this poor person from something which to those of established rank is more horrid than many hyenas. They are designed, my friends, to protect a man from himself — from something that the masters of the earth fear more than famine or war, and which Prussia especially fears as everything fears that which would certainly be its end. They are meant to protect a man against himself — that is, they are meant to protect a man against his manhood.

And if anyone reminds me that there is a Socialist Party in Germany, I reply that there isn't.

The Empire Of The Ignorant

That anarchic future which the more timid Tories professed to fear has already fallen upon us. We are ruled by ignorant people. But the most ignorant people in modern Britain are to be found in the upper class, the middle class, and especially the upper middle class. I do not say it with the smallest petulance or even distaste; these classes are often really beneficent in their breeding or their hospitality, or their humanity to animals.

There is still no better company than the young at the two Universities, or the best of the old in the Army or some of the other services. Also, of course, there are exceptions in the matter of learning; real scholars like Professor Gilbert Murray or Professor Phillimore are not ignorant, though they _are_ gentlemen. But when one looks up at any mass of the wealthier and more powerful classes, at the Grand Stand at Epsom, at the windows of Park-lane, at the people at a full-dress debate or a fashionable wedding, we shall be safe in saying that they are, for the most part, the most ill-taught, or untaught, creatures in these islands.

Literally Illiterate

It is indeed their feeble boast that they are not literally illiterate. They are always saying the ancient barons could not sign their own names — for they know less of history perhaps than of anything else. The modern barons, however, can sign their own names — or someone else's for a change. They can sign their own names; and that is about all they can do. They cannot face a fact, or follow an argument, or feel a tradition; but, least of all, can they, upon any persuasion, read through a plain impartial book, English or foreign, that is not specially written to soothe their panic or to please their pride. Looking up at these seats of the mighty I can only say, with something of despair, what Robert Lowe said of the enfranchised workmen: "We must educate our masters."

I do not mean this as paradoxical, or even as symbolical; it is simply tame and true. The modern English rich know nothing about things, not even about the things to which they appeal. Compared with them, the poor are pretty sure to get some enlightenment, even if they cannot get liberty; they must at least be technical. An old apprentice learnt a trade, even if his master came like any Turk and banged him most severely. The old housewife knew which side her bread was buttered, even if it were so thin as to be almost imperceptible. The old sailor knew the ropes; even if he knew the rope's end. Consequently, when any of these revolted, they were concerned with things they knew, pains, practical impossibilities, or the personal record.

But They Know

The apprentice cried "Clubs?" and cracked his neighbours' heads with the precision and fineness of touch which only manual craftsmanship can give. The housewives who flatly refused to cook the hot dinner knew how much or how little, cold meat there was in the house. The sailor who defied discipline by mutinying at the Nore did not defy discipline in the sense of falling off the rigging or letting the water into the hold. Similarly the modern proletariat, however little it may know, knows what it is talking about.

But the curious thing about the educated class is that exactly what it does not know is what it is talking about. I mean that it is startlingly ignorant of those special things which it is supposed to invoke and keep inviolate. The things that workmen invoke may be uglier, more acrid, more sordid; but they know all about them. They know enough arithmetic to know that prices have risen; the kind Levantine gentleman is always there to make them fully understand the meaning of an interest sum; and the landlord will define Rent as rigidly as Ricardo. The doctors can always tell them the Latin for an empty stomach; and when the poor man is treated for the time with some human respect (by the Coronet) it almost seems a pity he is not alive to hear how legally he died.

Against this bitter shrewdness and bleak realism in the suffering classes it is commonly supposed that the more leisured classes stand for certain legitimate ideas which also have their place in life; such as history, reverence, the love of the land. Well, it might be no bad thing to have something, even if it were something narrow, that testified to the truths of religion or patriotism. But such narrow things in the past have always at least known their own history; the bigot knew his catechism; the patriot knew his way home. The astonishing thing about the modern rich is their real and sincere ignorance — especially of the things they like.

No!

Take the most topical case you can find in any drawing-room: Belfast. Ulster is most assuredly a matter of history; and there is a sense in which Orange resistance is a matter of religion. But go and ask any of the five hundred fluttering ladies at a garden party (who find Carson so splendid and Belfast so thrilling) what it is all about, when it began, where it came from, what it really maintains? What was the history of Ulster? What is the religion of Belfast? Do any of them know where Ulstermen were in Grattan's time; do any of them know what was the "Protestantism" that came from Scotland to that isle; could any of them tell what part of the old Catholic system it really denied?

It was generally something that the fluttering ladies find in their own Anglican churches every Sunday. It were vain to ask them to state the doctrines of the Calvinist creed; they could not state the doctrines of their own creed. It were vain to tell them to read the history of Ireland; they have never read the history of England. It would matter as little that they do not know these things, as that I do not know German; but then German is not the only thing I am supposed to know. History and ritual are the only things aristocrats are supposed to know; and they don't know them.

Smile and Smile

I am not fed on turtle soup and Tokay because of my exquisite intimacy with the style and idiom of Heine and Richter. The English governing class is fed on turtle soup and Tokay to represent the past, of which it is literally ignorant, as I am of German irregular verbs; and to represent the religious traditions of the State, when it does not know three words of theology, as I do not know three words of German.

This is the last insult offered by the proud to the humble. They rule them by the smiling terror of an ancient secret. They smile and smile; but they have forgotten the secret.

The Symbolism Of Krupp

The curious position of the Krupp firm in the awful story developing around us is not quite sufficiently grasped. There is a kind of academic clarity of definition which does not see the proportions of things for which everything falls within a definition, and nothing ever breaks beyond it. To this type of mind (which is valuable when set to its special and narrow work) there is no such thing as an exception that proves the rule. If I vote for confiscating some usurer's millions I am doing, they say, precisely what I should be doing if I took pennies out of a blind man's hat. They are both denials of the principle of private property, and are equally right and equally wrong, according to our view of that principle. I should find a great many distinctions to draw in such a matter. First, I should say that taking a usurer's money by proper authority is not robbery, but recovery of stolen goods. Second, I should say that even if there were no such thing as personal property, there would still be such a thing as personal dignity, and different modes of robbery would diminish it in very different ways. Similarly, there is a truth, but only a half-truth, in the saying that all modern Powers alike rely on the Capitalist and make war on the lines of Capitalism. It is true, and it is disgraceful. But it is _not_ equally true and equally disgraceful. It is not true that Montenegro is as much ruled by financiers as Prussia, just as it is not true that as many men in the Kaiserstrasse, in Berlin, wear long knives in their belts as wear them in the neighbourhood of the Black Mountain. It is not true that every peasant from one of the old Russian communes is the immediate servant of a rich man, as is every employee of Mr. Rockefeller. It is as false as the statement that no poor people in America can read or write. There is an element of Capitalism in all modern countries, as there is an element of illiteracy in all modern countries. There are some who think that the number of our fellow-citizens who can sign their names ought to comfort us for the extreme fewness of those who have anything in the bank to sign it for, but I am not one of these.

In any case, the position of Krupp has certain interesting aspects. When we talk of Army contractors as among the base but active actualities of war, we commonly mean that while the contractor benefits by the war, the war, on the whole, rather suffers by the contractor. We regard this unsoldierly middleman with disgust, or great anger, or contemptuous acquiescence, or commercial dread and silence, according to our personal position and character. But we nowhere think of him as having anything to do with fighting in the final sense. Those worthy and wealthy persons who employ women's labour at a few shillings a week do not do it to obtain the best clothes for the soldiers, but to make a sufficient profit on the worst. The only argument is whether such clothes are just good enough for the soldiers, or are too bad for anybody or anything. We tolerate the contractor, or we do not tolerate him; but no one admires him especially, and certainly no one gives him any credit for any success in the war. Confessedly or unconfessedly we knock his profits, not only off what goes to the taxpayer, but what goes to the soldier. We know the Army will not fight any better, at least, because the clothes they wear were stitched by wretched women who could hardly see; or because their boots were made by harassed helots, who never had time to think. In war-time it is very widely confessed that Capitalism is not a good way of ruling a patriotic or self-respecting people, and all sorts of other things, from strict State organisation to quite casual personal charity, are hastily substituted for it. It is recognised that the "great employer," nine times out of ten, is no more than the schoolboy or the page who pilfers tarts and sweets from the dishes as they go up and down. How angry one is with him depends on temperament, on the stage of the dinner — also on the number of tarts.

Now here comes in the real and sinister significance of Krupps. There are many capitalists in Europe as rich, as vulgar, as selfish, as rootedly opposed to any fellowship of the fortunate and unfortunate. But there is no other capitalist who claims, or can pretend to claim, that he has very appreciably _helped_ the activities of his people in war. I will suppose that Lipton did not deserve the very severe criticisms made on his firm by Mr. Justice Darling; but, however blameless he was, nobody can suppose that British soldiers would charge better with the bayonet because they had some particular kind of groceries inside them. But Krupp can make a plausible claim that the huge infernal machines to which his country owes nearly all of its successes could only have been

377

produced under the equally infernal conditions of the modern factory and the urban and proletarian civilisation. That is why the victory of Germany would be simply the victory of Krupp, and the victory of Krupp would be simply the victory of Capitalism. There, and there alone, Capitalism would be able to point to something done successfully for a whole nation — done (as it would certainly maintain) better than small free States or natural democracies could have done it. I confess I think the modern Germans morally second-rate, and I think that even war, when it is conducted most successfully by machinery, is second-rate war. But this second-rate war will become not only the first but the only brand, if the cannon of Krupp should conquer; and, what is very much worse, it will be the only intelligent answer that any capitalist has yet given against our case that Capitalism is as wasteful and as weak as it is certainly wicked. I do not fear any such finality, for I happen to believe in the kind of men who fight best with bayonets and whose fathers hammered their own pikes for the French Revolution.

The Tower Of Bebel

Among the cloudy and symbolic stories in the beginning of the Bible there is one about a tower built with such vertical energy as to take a hold on heaven, but ruined and resulting only in a confusion of tongues. The story might be interpreted in many ways — religiously, as meaning that spiritual insolence starts all human separations; irreligiously, as meaning that the inhuman heavens grudge man his magnificent dream; or merely satirically as suggesting that all attempts to reach a higher agreement always end in more disagreement than there was before. It might be taken by the partially intelligent Kensitite as a judgment on Latin Christians for talking Latin. It might be taken by the somewhat less intelligent Professor Harnack as a final proof that all prehistoric humanity talked German. But when all was said, the symbol would remain that a plain tower, as straight as a sword, as simple as a lily, did nevertheless produce the deepest divisions that have been known among men. In any case we of the world in revolt — Syndicalists, Socialists, Guild Socialists, or whatever we call ourselves — have no need to worry about the scripture or the allegory. We have the reality. For whatever reason, what is said to have happened to the people of Shinak has precisely and practically happened to us.

None of us who have known Socialists (or rather, to speak more truthfully, none of us who have been Socialists) can entertain the faintest doubt that a fine intellectual sincerity lay behind what was called "L'Internationale." It was really felt that Socialism was universal like arithmetic. It was too true for idiom or turn of phrase. In the formula of Karl Marx men could find that frigid fellowship which they find when they agree that two and two make four. It was almost as broadminded as a religious dogma.

Yet this universal language has not succeeded, at a moment of crisis, in imposing itself on the whole world. Nay, it has not, at the moment of crisis, succeeded in imposing itself on its own principal champions. Herve is not talking Economic Esperanto; he is talking French. Bebel is not talking Economic Esperanto; he is talking German. Blatchford is not talking Economic Esperanto; he is talking English, and jolly good English, too. I do not know whether French or Flemish was Vandervelde's nursery speech, but

I am quite certain he will know more of it after this struggle than he knew before. In short, whether or no there be a new union of hearts, there has really and truly been a new division of tongues.

How are we to explain this singular truth, even if we deplore it? I dismiss with fitting disdain the notion that it is a mere result of military terrorism or snobbish social pressure. The Socialist leaders of modern Europe are among the most sincere men in history; and their Nationalist note in this affair has had the ring of their sincerity. I will not waste time on the speculation that Vandervelde is bullied by Belgian priests; or that Blatchford is frightened of the horse-guards outside Whitehall. These great men support the enthusiasm of their conventional countrymen because they share it; and they share it because there is (though perhaps only at certain great moments) such a thing as pure democracy.

Timour the Tartar, I think, celebrated some victory with a tower built entirely out of human skulls; perhaps he thought _that_ would reach to heaven. But there is no cement in such building; the veins and ligaments that hold humanity together have long fallen away; the skulls will roll impotently at a touch; and ten thousand more such trophies could only make the tower taller and crazier. I think the modern official apparatus of "votes" is very like that tottering monument. I think the Tartar "counted heads," like an electioneering agent. Sometimes when I have seen from the platform of some paltry party meeting the rows and rows of grinning upturned faces, I have felt inclined to say, as the poet does in the "The Vision of Sin" — "Welcome fellow-citizens, Hollow hearts and empty heads."

Not that the people were personally hollow or empty, but they had come on a hollow and empty business: to help the good Mr. Binks to strengthen the Insurance Act against the wicked Mr. Jinks who would only promise to fortify the Insurance Act. That night it did not blow the democratic gale. Yet it can blow on these as on others; and when it does blow men learn many things. I, for one, am not above learning them.

The Marxian dogma which simplifies all conflicts to the Class War is so much nobler a thing than the nose-counting of the parliaments that one must apologise for the comparison. And yet there is a comparison. When we used to say that there were so many thousands of Socialists in Germany, we were counting by skulls. When we said that the majority consisting of Proletarians would be everywhere opposed to the minority, consisting of Capitalists, we were counting by skulls. Why, yes; if all men's heads had been cut off from the rest of them, as they were by the good sense and foresight of Timour the Tartar; if they had no hearts or bellies to be moved; no hand that flies up to ward off a weapon, no foot that can feel a familiar soil — if things were so the Marxian calculation would be not only complete but correct. As we know to-day, the Marxian calculation is complete, but it is not correct.

Now, this is the answer to the questions of some kind critics, whose actual words I have not within reach at the moment, about whether my democracy meant the rule of the majority over the minority. It means the rule of the rule — the rule of the rule over the exception. When a nation finds a soul it clothes it with a body, and does verily act like one living thing. There is nothing to be said about those who are out of it, except that they are out of it. After talking about it in the abstract for decades, this is Democracy, and it is marvellous in our eyes. It is not the difference between ninetynine persons and a hundred persons; it is one person — the people. I do not know or care how many or how few of the Belgians like or dislike the pictures of Wiertz. They could not be either justified or condemned by a mere majority of Belgians. But I am very certain that the defiance to Prussia did not come from a majority of Belgians. It came from Belgium one and indivisible — atheists, priests, princes of the blood, Frenchified shopkeepers, Flemish boors, men, women, and children, and the sooner we understand that this sort of thing can happen the better for us. For it is this spontaneous spiritual fellowship of communities under certain conditions to which the four or five most independent minds of Europe willingly bear witness to-day.

But is there no exception: is there no one faithful among the unfaithful found? Is no great Socialist politician still untouched by the patriotism of the vulgar? Why, yes; the rugged Ramsay MacDonald, scarred with a hundred savage fights against the capitalist parties, still lifts up his horny hand for peace. What further need have we of witnesses? I, for my part, am quite satisfied, and do not doubt that Mr. MacDonald will be as industrious in damping down democracy in this form as in every other.

A Real Danger

Heaven forbid that I should once more wade in those swamps of logomachy and tautology in which the old guard of the Determinists still seem to be floundering. The question of Fate and Free Will can never attain to a conclusion, though it may attain to a conviction. The shortest philosophic summary is that both cause and choice are ultimate ideas within us, and that if one man denies choice because it seems contrary to cause, the other man has quite as much right to deny cause because it seems contrary to choice. The shortest ethical summary is that Determinism either affects conduct or it does not. If it does not, it is morally not worth preaching; if it does, it must affect conduct in the direction of impotence and submission. A writer in the "Clarion" says that the reformer cannot help trying to reform, nor the Conservative help his Conservatism. But suppose the reformer tries to reform the Conservative and turn him into another reformer? Either he can, in which case Determinism has made no difference at all, or he can't, in which case it can only have made reformers more hopeless and Conservatives more obstinate. And the shortest practical and political summary is that working men, most probably, will soon be much too busy using their Free Will to stop to prove that they have got it. Nevertheless, I like to watch the Determinist in the "Clarion" Cockpit every week, as busy as a squirrel — in a cage. But being myself a squirrel (leaping lightly from bough to bough) and preferring the form of activity which occasionally ends in nuts, I should not intervene in the matter even indirectly, except upon a practical point. And the point I have in mind is practical to the extent of deadly peril. It is another of the numerous new ways in which the restless rich, now walking the world with an awful insomnia, may manage to catch us napping.

Must Be a Mystery

There are two letters in the "Clarion" this week which in various ways interest me very much. One is concerned to defend Darwin against the scientific revolt against him that was led by Samuel Butler, and among other things it calls Bernard Shaw a back number. Well, most certainly "The Origin of Species" is a back number, in so far as any honest and interesting book ever can be; but in pure philosophy nothing can be out of date, since the universe must be a mystery even to the believer. There is, however, one condition of things in which I do call it relevant to describe somebody as behind the times. That is when the man in question, thinking of some state of affairs that has passed away, is really helping the very things he would like to hinder. The principles cannot alter, but the problems can. Thus, I should call a man behind the times who, in the year 1872, pleaded for the peaceful German peasants against the triumphant militarism of Napoleon. Or I should call a man out of date who, in the year 1892, wished for a stronger Navy to compete with the Navy of Holland, because it had once swept the sea and sailed up the Thames. And I certainly call a man or a movement out of date that, in the year 1914, when we few are fighting a giant machine, strengthened with all material wealth and worked with all the material sciences, thinks that our chief danger is from an excess of moral and religious responsibility. He reminds me of Mr. Snodgrass, who had the presence of mind to call out "Fire!" when Mr. Pickwick fell through the ice.

The other letter consists of the usual wiredrawn argument for fatalism. Man cannot imagine the universe being created, and therefore is "compelled by his reason" to think the universe without beginning or end, which (I may remark) he cannot imagine either. But the letter ends with something much more ominous than bad metaphysics. Here, in the middle of the "Clarion," in the centre of a clean and combative democratic sheet, I meet again my deplorable old acquaintance, the scientific criminologist. "The so-called evil-doer should not be punished for his acts, but restrained." In forty-eight hours I could probably get a petition to that effect signed by millionaires. A short time ago a Bill was introduced to hold irresponsible and "restrain" a whole new class of people, who were "incapable of managing their affairs with prudence." Read the supporters' names on the back of that Bill, and see what sort of democrats they were.

Now, clearing our heads of what is called popular science (which means going to sleep to a lullaby of long words), let us use our own brains a little, and ask ourselves what is the real difference between punishing a man and restraining him. The material difference may be any or none; for punishment may be very mild, and restraint may be very ruthless. The man, of course, must dislike one as much as the other, or it would not be necessary to restrain him at all. And I assure you he will get no great glow of comfort out of your calling him irresponsible after you have made him impotent. A man does not necessarily feel more free and easy in a straight waistcoat than in a stone cell. The moral difference is that a man can be punished for a crime because he is born a citizen; while he can be constrained because he is born a slave. But one arresting and tremendous difference towers over all these doubtful or arguable differences. There is one respect, vital to all our liberties and all our lives, in which the new restraint would be different from the old punishment. It is of this that the plutocrats will take advantage.

The Plain Difference

The perfectly plain difference is this. All punishment, even the most horrible, proceeds upon the assumption that the extent of the evil is known, and that a certain amount of expiation goes with it. Even if you hang the man, you cannot hang him twice. Even if you burn him, you cannot burn him for a month. And in the case of all ordinary imprisonments, the whole aim of free institutions from the beginning of the world has been to insist that a man shall be convicted of a definite crime and confined for a definite period. But the moment you admit this notion of medical restraint, you must in fairness admit that it may go on as long as the authorities choose to think (or say) that it ought to go on. The man's punishment refers to the past, which is supposed to have been investigated, and which, in some degree at least, has been investigated. But his restraint refers to the future, which his doctors, keepers, and wardens have yet to investigate. The simple result will be that, in the scientific Utopia of the "Clarion," men like Mann or Syme or Larkin will not be put in prison because of what they have done. They will be kept in prison because of what they might do. Indeed, the builders of the new tyranny have already come very near to avowing this scientific and futurist method. When the lawyers tried to stop the "Suffragette" from appearing at all, they practically said: "We do not know your next week's crime, because it isn't committed yet; but we are scientifically certain you have the criminal type. And by the sublime and unalterable laws of heredity, all your poor little papers will inherit it."

This is a purely practical question; and that is why I insist on it, even in such strenuous times. The writers on the "Clarion" have a perfect right to think Christianity is the foe of freedom, or even that the stupidity and tyranny of the present Government is due to the monkish mysticism of Lord Morley and Mr. John M. Robertson. They have a right to think the theory of Determinism as true as Calvin thought it. But I do not like seeing them walk straight into the enormous iron trap set open by the Capitalists, who find it convenient to make our law even more lawless than it is. The rich men want a scientist to write them a _lettre de cachet_ as a doctor writes a prescription. And so they wish to seal up in a public gaol the scandals of a private asylum. Yes; the writers on the "Clarion" are indeed claiming irresponsibility for human beings. But it is the governments that will be irresponsible, not the governed.

But I will tell them one small secret in conclusion. There is nothing whatever wrong in the ancient and universal idea of Punishment — except that we are not punishing the right people.

The Dregs Of Puritanism

One peculiarity of the genuine kind of enemy of the people is that his slightest phrase is clamorous with all his sins. Pride, vain-glory, and hypocrisy seem present in his very grammar; in his very verbs or adverbs or prepositions, as well as in what he says, which is generally bad enough. Thus I see that a Nonconformist pastor in Bromley has been talking about the pathetic little presents of tobacco sent to the common soldiers. This is how he talks about it. He is reported as having said, "By the help of God, they wanted this cigarette business stopped." How one could write a volume on that sentence, a great thick volume called "The Decline of the English Middle Class." In taste, in style, in philosophy, in feeling, in political project, the horrors of it are as unfathomable as hell.

First, to begin with the trifle, note something slipshod and vague in the mere verbiage, typical of those who prefer a catchword to a creed. "This cigarette business" might mean anything. It might mean Messrs. Salmon and Gluckstein's business. But the pastor at Bromley will not interfere with that, for the indignation of his school of thought, even when it is sincere, always instinctively and unconsciously swerves aside from anything that is rich and powerful like the partners in a big business, and strikes instead something that is poor and nameless like the soldiers in a trench. Nor does the expression make clear who "they" are — whether the inhabitants of Britain or the inhabitants of Bromley, or the inhabitants of this one crazy tabernacle in Bromley; nor is it evident how it is going to be stopped or who is being asked to stop it. All these things are trifles compared to the more terrible offences of the phrase; but they are not without their social and historical interest. About the beginning of the nineteenth century the wealthy Puritan class, generally the class of the employers of labour, took a line of argument which was narrow, but not nonsensical. They saw the relation of rich and poor quite coldly as a contract, but they saw that a contract holds both ways. The Puritans of the middle class, in short, did in some sense start talking and thinking for themselves. They are still talking. They have long ago left off thinking. They talk about the loyalty of workmen to their employers, and God knows what rubbish; and the first small certainty about the reverend gentleman whose sentence I have quoted is that his brain stopped working as a clock stops, years and years ago.

Second, consider the quality of the religious literature! These people are always telling us that the English translated Bible is sufficient training for anyone in noble and appropriate diction; and so it is. Why, then, are they not trained? They are always telling us that Bunyan, the rude Midland tinker, is as much worth reading as Chaucer or Spenser; and so he is. Why, then, have they not read him? I cannot believe that anyone who had seen, even in a nightmare of the nursery, Apollyon straddling over the whole breadth of the way could really write like that about a cigarette. By the help of God, they wanted this cigarette business stopped. Therefore, with angels and archangels and the whole company of Heaven, with St. Michael, smiter of Satan and Captain of the Chivalry of God, with all the ardour of the seraphs and the flaming patience of the saints, we will have this cigarette business stopped. Where has all the tradition of the great religious literatures gone to that a man should come on such a bathos with such a bump?

Thirdly, of course, there is the lack of imaginative proportion, which rises into a sort of towering blasphemy. An enormous number of live young men are being hurt by shells, hurt by bullets, hurt by fever and hunger and horror of hope deferred; hurt by lance blades and sword blades and bayonet blades breaking into the bloody house of life. But Mr. Price (I think that's his name) is still anxious that they should not be hurt by cigarettes. That is the sort of maniacal isolation that can be found in the deserts of Bromley. That cigarettes are bad for the health is a very tenable opinion to which the minister is quite entitled. If he happens to think that the youth of Bromley smoke too many cigarettes, and that he has any influence in urging on them the unhealthiness of the habit, I should not blame him if he gave sermons or lectures about it (with magic-lantern slides), so long as it was in Bromley and about Bromley. Cigarettes may be bad for the health: bombs and bayonets and even barbed wire are not good for the health. I never met a doctor who recommended any of them. But the trouble with this sort of man is that he cannot adjust himself to the scale of things. He would do very good service if he would go among the rich aristocratic ladies and tell them not to take drugs in a chronic sense, as people take opium in China. But he would be doing very bad service if he were to go among the doctors and nurses on the field and tell them not to give drugs, as they give morphia in a hospital. But it is the whole hypothesis of war, it is its very nature and first principle, that the man in the trench is almost as much a suffering and abnormal person as the man in the hospital. Hit or unhit, conqueror or conquered, he is, by nature of the case, having less pleasure than is proper and natural to a man.

Fourth (for I need not dwell here on the mere diabolical idiocy that can regard beer or tobacco as in some way evil and unseemly in themselves), there is the most important element in this strange outbreak; at least, the most dangerous and the most important for us. There is that main feature in the degradation of the old middle class: the utter disappearance of its old appetite for liberty. Here there is no question of whether the men are to smoke cigarettes, or the women choose to send cigarettes, or even that the officers or doctors choose to allow cigarettes. The thing is to cease, and we may note one of the most recurrent ideas of the servile State: it is mentioned in the passive mood. It must be stopped, and we must not even ask who has stopped it!

The Tyranny Of Bad Journalism

The amazing decision of the Government to employ methods quite alien to England, and rather belonging to the police of the Continent, probably arises from the appearance of papers which are lucid and fighting, like the papers of the Continent. The business may be put in many ways. But one way of putting it is simply to say that a monopoly of bad journalism is resisting the possibility of good journalism. Journalism is not the same thing as literature; but there is good and bad journalism, as there is good and bad literature, as there is good and bad football. For the last twenty years or so the plutocrats who govern England have allowed the English nothing but bad journalism. Very bad journalism, simply considered as journalism.

It always takes a considerable time to see the simple and central fact about anything. All sorts of things have been said about the modern Press, especially the Yellow Press; that it is Jingo or Philistine or sensational or wrongly inquisitive or vulgar or indecent or trivial; but none of these have anything really to do with the point.

The point about the Press is that it is not what it is called. It is not the "popular Press." It is not the public Press. It is not an organ of public opinion. It is a conspiracy of a very few millionaires, all sufficiently similar in type to agree on the limits of what this great nation (to which we belong) may know about itself and its friends and enemies. The ring is not quite complete; there are old-fashioned and honest papers: but it is sufficiently near to completion to produce on the ordinary purchaser of news the practical effects of a corner and a monopoly. He receives all his political information and all his political marching orders from what is by this time a sort of half-conscious secret society, with very few members, but a great deal of money.

This enormous and essential fact is concealed for us by a number of legends that have passed into common speech. There is the notion that the Press is flashy or trivial _because_ it is popular. In other words, an attempt is made to discredit democracy by representing journalism as the natural literature of democracy. All this is cold rubbish. The democracy has no more to do with the papers than it has with the peerages. The millionaire newspapers are vulgar and silly because the millionaires are vulgar and silly. It is the proprietor, not the editor, not the sub-editor, least of all the reader, who is pleased with this monotonous prairie of printed words. The same slander on democracy can be noticed in the case of advertisements. There is many a tender old Tory imagination that vaguely feels that our streets would be hung with escutcheons and tapestries, if only the profane vulgar had not hung them with advertisements of Sapolio and Sunlight Soap. But advertisement does not come from the unlettered many. It comes from the refined few. Did you ever hear of a mob rising to placard the Town Hall with proclamations in favour of Sapolio? Did you ever see a poor, ragged man laboriously drawing and painting a picture on the wall in favour of Sunlight Soap — simply as a labour of love? It is nonsense; those who hang our public walls with ugly pictures are the same select few who hang their private walls with exquisite and expensive pictures. The vulgarisation of modern life has come from the governing class; from the highly educated class. Most of the people who have posters in Camberwell have peerages at Westminster. But the strongest instance of all is that which has been unbroken until lately, and still largely prevails; the ghastly monotony of the Press.

Then comes that other legend; the notion that men like the masters of the Newspaper Trusts "give the people what they want." Why, it is the whole aim and definition of a Trust that it gives the people what it chooses. In the old days, when Parliaments were free in England, it was discovered that one courtier was allowed to sell all the silk, and another to sell all the sweet wine. A member of the House of Commons humorously asked who was allowed to sell all the bread. I really tremble to think what that sarcastic legislator would have said if he had been put off with the modern nonsense about "gauging the public taste." Suppose the first courtier had said that, by his shrewd, self-made sense, he had detected that people had a vague desire for silk; and even a deep, dim human desire to pay so much a yard for it! Suppose the second courtier said that he had, by his own rugged intellect, discovered a general desire for wine: and that people bought his wine at his price — when they could buy no other! Suppose a third courtier had jumped up and

391

said that people always bought his bread when they could get none anywhere else.

Well, that is a perfect parallel. "After bread, the need of the people is knowledge," said Danton. Knowledge is now a monopoly, and comes through to the citizens in thin and selected streams, exactly as bread might come through to a besieged city. Men must wish to know what is happening, whoever has the privilege of telling them. They must listen to the messenger, even if he is a liar. They must listen to the liar, even if he is a bore. The official journalist for some time past has been both a bore and a liar; but it was impossible until lately to neglect his sheets of news altogether. Lately the capitalist Press really has begun to be neglected; because its bad journalism was overpowering and appalling. Lately we have really begun to find out that capitalism cannot write, just as it cannot fight, or pray, or marry, or make a joke, or do any other stricken human thing. But this discovery has been quite recent. The capitalist newspaper was never actually unread until it was actually unreadable.

If you retain the servile superstition that the Press, as run by the capitalists, is popular (in any sense except that in which dirty water in a desert is popular), consider the case of the solemn articles in praise of the men who own newspapers — men of the type of Cadbury or Harmsworth, men of the type of the small club of millionaires. Did you ever hear a plain man in a tramcar or train talking about Carnegie's bright genial smile or Rothschild's simple, easy hospitality? Did you ever hear an ordinary citizen ask what was the opinion of Sir Joseph Lyons about the hopes and fears of this, our native land? These few small-minded men publish, papers to praise themselves. You could no more get an intelligent poor man to praise a millionaire's soul, except for hire, than you could get him to sell a millionaire's soap, except for hire. And I repeat that, though there are other aspects of the matter of the new plutocratic raid, one of the most important is mere journalistic jealousy. The Yellow Press is bad journalism: and wishes to stop the appearance of good journalism.

There is no average member of the public who would not prefer to have Lloyd George discussed as what he is, a Welshman of genius and ideals, strangely fascinated by bad fashion and bad finance, rather than discussed as what neither he nor anyone else ever was, a perfect democrat or an utterly detestable demagogue. There is no reader of a daily paper who would not feel more concern — and more respect — for Sir Rufus Isaacs as a man who has been a stockbroker, than as a man who happens to be Attorney-General. There is no man in the street who is not more interested in Lloyd George's investments than in his Land Campaign. There is no man in the street who could not understand (and like) Rufus Isaacs as a Jew better than he can possibly like him as a British statesman. There is no sane journalist alive who would say that the official account of Marconis would be better "copy" than the true account that such papers as this have dragged out. We have committed one crime against the newspaper proprietor which he will never forgive. We point out that his papers are dull. And we propose to print some papers that are interesting.

The Poetry Of The Revolution

Everyone but a consistent and contented capitalist, who must be something pretty near to a Satanist, must rejoice at the spirit and success of the Battle of the Buses. But one thing about it which happens to please me particularly was that it was fought, in one aspect at least, on a point such as the plutocratic fool calls unpractical. It was fought about a symbol, a badge, a thing attended with no kind of practical results, like the flags for which men allow themselves to fall down dead, or the shrines for which men will walk some hundreds of miles from their homes. When a man has an eye for business, all that goes on on this earth in that style is simply invisible to him. But let us be charitable to the eye for business; the eye has been pretty well blacked this time.

But I wish to insist here that it is exactly what is called the unpractical part of the thing that is really the practical. The chief difference between men and the animals is that all men are artists; though the overwhelming majority of us are bad artists. As the old fable truly says, lions do not make statues; even the cunning of the fox can go no further than the accomplishment of leaving an exact model of the vulpine paw: and even that is an accomplishment which he wishes he hadn't got. There are Chryselephantine statues, but no purely elephantine ones. And, though we speak in a general way of an elephant trumpeting, it is only by human blandishments that he can be induced to play the drum. But man, savage or civilised, simple or complex always desires to see his own soul outside himself; in some material embodiment. He always wishes to point to a table in a temple, or a cloth on a stick, or a word on a scroll, or a badge on a coat, and say: "This is the best part of me. If need be, it shall be the rest of me that shall perish." This is the method which seems so unbusinesslike to the men with an eye to business. This is also the method by which battles are won.

The Symbolism of the Badge

The badge on a Trade Unionist's coat is a piece of poetry in the genuine, lucid, and logical sense in which Milton defined poetry (and he ought to know) when he said that it was simple, sensuous, and passionate. It is simple, because many understand the word "badge," who might not even understand the word

394

"recognition." It is sensuous, because it is visible and tangible; it is incarnate, as all the good Gods have been; and it is passionate in this perfectly practical sense, which the man with an eye to business may some day learn more thoroughly than he likes, that there are men who will allow you to cross a word out in a theoretical document, but who will not allow you to pull a big button off their bodily clothing, merely because you have more money than they have. Now I think it is this sensuousness, this passion, and, above all, this simplicity that are most wanted in this promising revolt of our time. For this simplicity is perhaps the only thing in which the best type of recent revolutionists have failed. It has been our sorrow lately to salute the sunset of one of the very few clean and incorruptible careers in the most corruptible phase of Christendom. The death of Quelch naturally turns one's thoughts to those extreme Marxian theorists, who, whatever we may hold about their philosophy, have certainly held their honour like iron. And yet, even in this instant of instinctive reverence, I cannot feel that they were poetical enough, that is childish enough, to make a revolution. They had all the audacity needed for speaking to the despot; but not the simplicity needed for speaking to the democracy. They were always accused of being too bitter against the capitalist. But it always seemed to me that they were (quite unconsciously, of course) much too kind to him. They had a fatal habit of using long words, even on occasions when he might with propriety have been described in very short words. They called him a Capitalist when almost anybody in Christendom would have called him a cad. And "cad" is a word from the poetic vocabulary indicating rather a general and powerful reaction of the emotions than a status that could be defined in a work of economics. The capitalist, asleep in the sun, let such long words crawl all over him, like so many long, soft, furry caterpillars. Caterpillars cannot sting like wasps. And, in repeating that the old Marxians have been, perhaps, the best and bravest men of our time, I say also that they would have been better and braver still if they had never used a scientific word, and never read anything but fairy tales.

The Beastly Individualist

Suppose I go on to a ship, and the ship sinks almost immediately; but I (like the people in the Bab Ballads), by reason of my clinging to a mast, upon a desert island am eventually cast.

Or rather, suppose I am not cast on it, but am kept bobbing about in the water, because the only man on the island is what some call an Individualist, and will not throw me a rope; though coils of rope of the most annoying elaboration and neatness are conspicuous beside him as he stands upon the shore. Now, it seems to me, that if, in my efforts to shout at this fellow-creature across the crashing breakers, I call his position the "insularistic position," and my position "the semi-amphibian position," much valuable time may be lost. I am not an amphibian. I am a drowning man. He is not an insularist, or an individualist. He is a beast. Or rather, he is worse than any beast can be. And if, instead of letting me drown, he makes me promise, while I am drowning, that if I come on shore it shall be as his bodily slave, having no human claims henceforward forever, then, by the whole theory and practice of capitalism, he becomes a capitalist, he also becomes a cad.

Now, the language of poetry is simpler than that of prose; as anyone can see who has read what the old-fashioned protestant used to call confidently "his" Bible. And, being simpler, it is also truer; and, being truer, it is also fiercer. And, for most of the infamies of our time, there is really nothing plain enough, except the plain language of poetry. Take, let us say, the ease of the recent railway disaster, and the acquittal of the capitalists' interest. It is not a scientific problem for us to investigate. It is a crime committed before our eyes; committed, perhaps, by blind men or maniacs, or men hypnotised, or men in some other ways unconscious; but committed in broad daylight, so that the corpse is bleeding on our door-step. Good lives were lost, because good lives do not pay; and bad coals do pay. It seems simply impossible to get any other meaning out of the matter except that. And, if in human history there be anything simple and anything horrible, it seems to have been present in this matter. If, even after some study and understanding of the old religious passions which were the resurrection of Europe, we cannot endure the extreme infamy of witches and heretics literally burned alive — well, the people in this affair were quite as literally burned alive. If, when we have really tried to extend our charity beyond the borders of personal sympathy, to all the complexities of class and creed, we still feel something insolent about the triumphant and acquitted man who is in the wrong, here the men who are in the wrong are triumphant and acquitted. It is no subject for science. It is a subject for poetry. But for poetry of a terrible sort.